I

By the same author

The Green Howards
The Kandyan Wars
Men at Arnhem
Suez: The Double War (with Roy Fullick)
The Book of Campden
The Devil's Birthday: The Bridges to Arnhem
The Green Howards: 300 Years of Service
Buller: A Scapegoat?

PLUMER
The Soldiers' General

A BIOGRAPHY OF
FIELD-MARSHAL VISCOUNT PLUMER
OF MESSINES

GEOFFREY POWELL

PEN & SWORD MILITARY CLASSICS

First published in 1990 by Leo Cooper
Published in 2004, in this format, by
PEN & SWORD MILITARY CLASSICS
an imprint of
Pen & Sword Books Limited
47 Church Street
Barnsley
S. Yorkshire
S70 2AS

© Geoffrey Powell, 1990, 2004

ISBN 1 84415 039 9

A CIP record for this book is
available from the British Library

Printed in England by
CPI UK

Contents

Illustrations

Maps

PLUMER FAMILY TREE

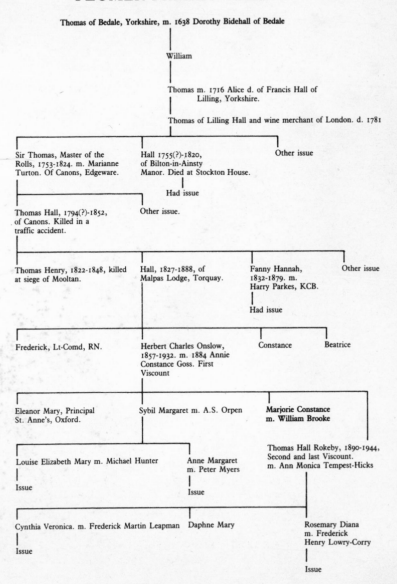

Thomas of Bedale, Yorkshire, m. 1638 Dorothy Bidehall of Bedale

William

Thomas m. 1716 Alice d. of Francis Hall of Lilling, Yorkshire.

Thomas of Lilling Hall and wine merchant of London. d. 1781

Sir Thomas, Master of the Rolls, 1753-1824. m. Marianne Turton. Of Canons, Edgeware.

Hall 1755(?)-1820, of Bilton-in-Ainsty Manor. Died at Stockton House.

Other issue

Had issue

Thomas Hall, 1794(?)-1852, of Canons. Killed in a traffic accident.

Other issue.

Thomas Henry, 1822-1848, killed at siege of Mooltan.

Hall, 1827-1888, of Malpas Lodge, Torquay.

Fanny Hannah, 1832-1879. m. Harry Parkes, KCB.

Other issue

Had issue

Frederick, Lt-Comd, RN.

Herbert Charles Onslow, 1857-1932. m. 1884 Annie Constance Goss. First Viscount

Constance

Beatrice

Eleanor Mary, Principal St. Anne's, Oxford.

Sybil Margaret m. A.S. Orpen

Marjorie Constance m. William Brooke

Louise Elizabeth Mary m. Michael Hunter

Issue

Anne Margaret m. Peter Myers

Issue

Thomas Hall Rokeby, 1890-1944, Second and last Viscount. m. Ann Monica Tempest-Hicks

Cynthia Veronica. m. Frederick Martin Leapman

Issue

Daphne Mary

Rosemary Diana m. Frederick Henry Lowry-Corry

Issue

GLOSSARY

ADC	Aide-de-Camp
ANZAC	Australian and New Zealand Army Corps
BGGS	Brigadier General General Staff
BEF	British Expeditionary Force
BL	British Library
C-in-C	Commander-in-Chief
CEF	Canadian Expeditionary Force
CGS	Chief of the General Staff
CIGS	Chief of the Imperial General Staff
CO	Commanding Officer
CRA	Commander of the Royal Artillery.
DAN	*Détachement d'Armée du Nord*
DMO	Director of Military Operations
DSO	Distinguished Service Order
GAN	Group of Armies of the North
GCB	Knight Grand Cross of the Order of the Bath
GHQ	General Headquarters
GOC	General Officer Commanding
GSO1	General Staff Officer Grade 1
GS02	General Staff Officer Grade 2
IWM	Imperial War Museum
KCB	Knight Commander of the Bath
MC	Military Cross
MGGS	Major-General General Staff
MM	Military Medal
MRF	Matabeleland Relief Force
NAM	National Army Museum
NCO	Non-Commissioned Officer
NLS	National Library of Scotland
OH	Official History
PRO	Public Record Office

psc	Passed Staff College
RA	Royal Artillery
RE	Royal Engineers
RFC	Royal Flying Corps
RUSI	Royal United Services Institute for Defence Studies
VC	Victoria Cross
WO	War Office

Preface

The First World War cast a deep and ineradicable shadow over those of us who grew up in its aftermath. Memories were vivid. My father was twice in action with infantry battalions on the Western Front, first on the Somme in 1916 and then in Flanders 1918. Each time he was wounded within three weeks of arriving. Of his four brothers, the one nearest to him was killed and two others were badly wounded. During long walks over the moors of North Yorkshire, this temporary soldier would enthral his young son with tales of life in the trenches and his views about the war. An avid admirer of writers such as C.E. Montague, Edmund Blunden and Siegfried Sassoon, to whose works he introduced me, he had little respect for the British generals who he blamed for the slaughter among his generation. He admitted only two exceptions. These were Monash, the Australian, and Plumer – 'Old Plum and Apple', as the troops were said to call him.

Some sixty years later, the son set out to discover what was so very special about this General Plumer – Field-Marshal the Viscount Plumer of Messines as he became. From his portraits and photographs he looked rather vacuous. Could he even have been the original for Low's pungent cartoons of Colonel Blimp?

Very soon it became apparent that a man's appearance can seldom have so belied his character. Here was someone both able and loveable, and perhaps too quickly I fell under the spell of his attractive personality, that occupational hazard of biographers. Perhaps I have erred; only my readers can judge. Certainly the only previous biography of Herbert Plumer suffered from this defect in an exaggerated form, that written by General 'Tim' Harington, his close friend and his Chief-of-Staff during his most critical battles.

I quickly discovered why General Sir Charles Harington's book had not been followed by others. There were few sources for Plumer's career readily available. As Miss Rose Coombs, that omniscient authority on the Western Front, discovered, what papers Plumer had kept were destroyed under his instructions before his death by Sergeant Back, his wartime clerk and postwar personal factotum. According to Back, his General had done so to prevent scurrilous stories being written about him and his friends. To match this loss, Harington's own papers have also disappeared, including the copies of the letters from Plumer to his wife which provided much of the framework for his book. Just a few family albums of photographs and other papers have survived; these were compiled by his wife and his eldest daughter, the Hon Eleanor Plumer, and their contents consist largely of newspaper cuttings; all else has gone. Sadly Plumer's widow, like many of her contemporaries, had little sense of history. One of these albums is filled with signatures snipped off the end of letters written by the most distinguished men of that era – statesmen, soldiers, sailors and others. In such a way can the raw material be lost.

So it is that this book is based largely upon the biographies and autobiographies of Plumer's associates, in which references to him can be found, and upon the archives of other men's papers, in some of which are hidden letters from and about him. Because I began work so long after he was dead, I discovered only two men who knew him, both of whom have themselves died since they talked to me about him. If I had started work only ten years earlier, so many more of his acquaintances would still have been alive. His surviving grandchildren, all of whom have given me unstinted help, have no more than childhood memories of a kind and pleasant old gentleman. During my enquiries, I have elicited that others, including the late Cyril Falls, had nurtured ideas of writing about Plumer, but all seem to have been defeated by the problem of unravelling the sources. Because so little has been written about him, Plumer has been almost forgotten and his memory has been neglected. In his own country he is commemorated only by his tomb in Westminster Abbey (a rare honour), by a memorial tablet in a remote Yorkshire church, and a showcase of memorabilia in the Museum of his old Regiment. Perhaps it is ironical that in Ypres, Jerusalem and Malta, streets and squares bear his name, mention of which may produce an immediate spark of recognition.

Tribute must be paid to Tim Harington's *Plumer of Messines* and to his autobiography, *Tim Harington Looks Back*, upon both of which I have depended. Because the writer hero-worshipped his mentor, both books are uncritically eulogistic: *Plumer of Messines*, as its preface accurately declares, 'does not, I hope, contain one unkind word of either the living or the dead. That would certainly have been his wish and is certainly the wish of Lady Plumer'. (For all that, Harington only just succeeds in biting his tongue when he discusses Lloyd George's criticisms of his generals). In writing this, his first book, Harington sought the advice of Brigadier-General Sir James Edmonds, the Official Historian of the Western Front, emphasizing in his letter that he and Lady Plumer were: 'terribly anxious not to have a word against anyone dead or living'. His task, he told Edmonds, 'begins and ends with clearing Plumer from Lloyd George's assertions that he disagreed with Haig over Passchendaele as he certainly did not.'[1] In Harington's eyes the greatest calumny to which Plumer could be subjected was to accuse him of disloyalty to Haig. It says much for both Harington and for Plumer's widow that they both wanted to avoid 'muck-raking' (an expression that would probably have been anathema to both of them), but biographies that avoid all criticism can only be limited in their scope and value. Another difficulty with Harington's biography is that much of it consists of unedited contributions from other admirers of its subject. Nor is it as accurate as it might have been. Harington would seem to have kept no diary; writing more than fifteen years after the events depicted, this by then elderly man's memory was often at fault. The extracts from Plumer's letters to his wife, mentioned earlier, must also be treated with a certain caution; Lady Plumer provided them and Harington does not appear to have seen the originals.[2] Nevertheless, although Harington's book suffers from these limitations, this biography could not have been tackled without the information it contains, and I am deeply in debt to its author.

Any book about the Western Front must lean heavily upon Sir James Edmonds' many-volumed Official History, and upon the diaries, letters and other papers of the first Earl Haig, which have been so brilliantly analysed in turn by the late Alfred Duff Cooper (later Viscount Norwich), by Lord Blake and by Mr John Terraine. Even Haig's diaries should be approached with care. Written with a view to probable publication, although not while the writer lived, a sentence or paragraph was sometimes added when the diaries were typed and bound after the war. And in the end some things that Haig had wanted omitted were after all inserted.[3]

Far more circumspection must be exercised when using the Official History.[4] The very detailed accounts of actions, both great and small, are indispensable to those who study the First World War, especially as so much of Edmonds' source material has been destroyed. However, much of the information he used was provided by the many hundred individuals he consulted in order to supplement the official records, and it is a sad fact that such accounts almost always portray their writers' actions and those of their units in the best possible light. What it more, as Edmonds wrote to a friend in 1950, he did not want to be seen as 'crabbing my contemporaries, who were my friends and splendid fellows in tight places'.[5] Like all professions, the Army closes its ranks to outsiders and, fine historian though Edmonds was, he took great pains to avoid revealing his personal views about his contemporaries to the public at large, some of whom he criticized sharply in private, his strictures sharpened at times by personal malice.

For brevity I have used the term 'British' to describe not only military formations originating from the United Kingdom, but also forces consisting of or containing Australian, New Zealand or Canadian formations. In all cases I am sure that my meaning is clear, and I trust that I have nowhere caused offence to national susceptibilities.

In writing this book I have received generous help from many individuals and organizations. First I must acknowledge the gracious permission of Her Majesty the Queen for allowing me to use material from the Royal Archives; I warmly thank the then Registrar, Miss Elizabeth Cuthbert, for her help while I was working at Windsor.

I am especially grateful to Lord Plumer's grandchildren the Hon Cynthia Leapman, the Hon Rosemary Lowry-Corry, Mrs Michael Hunter, Mrs Peter Myers and her husband, Brigadier Peter Myers, for all the help and encouragement they provided, and for their permission to quote from both published and unpublished family papers, and for permitting me to make use of family photographs. Mrs Lowry-Corry entertained me, and both Mrs Hunter and Mrs Myers allowed me to retain valuable material, the latter for a considerable time.

My thanks are also due to the following for allowing me to quote from manuscript material in their possession: the Trustees of the Liddell Hart Centre for Military Archives for the Hamilton, the Edmonds and the Robertson Papers (together with the family of Field-Marshal Lord Robertson for the last named); the Trustees of the National Library of Scotland; the British Library; the National Army Museum; and the Controller of H.M. Stationery Office for Crown Copyright records in the Public Record Office.

As always seems to be the case, librarians, curators and archivists gave their unstinted help. I must particularly mention Mr D.W. Scott in charge of the York and Lancaster Regiment collection and archives at the Brian O'Malley Library and Arts Centre, Rotherham; Ms Joanne McAusland and Mrs Pat Thompson at the Chipping Campden Branch of the Gloucestershire County Library; Mr George Borg of the Gozo Public Library; De Heer A Debruyne of Het Herinneringmuseum, Ypres, who also devoted a full day to showing me around the Flanders battlefields in his car; Mr R. Suddaby of the Imperial War Museum; Ms Patricia Methven of the Liddell Hart Centre; Mr J.F. Russell of the National Library of Scotland; Mr Richard Tubbs and Mr John Montgomery at the Royal United Services Institute; and Mr M.G. Simms of the Staff College, Camberley. I also received much help from the staffs of the British Library; the Canadian High Commission; the Devon County Library; the Head of Common Services (Records) and the Military Secretary's Department of the Ministry of Defence; the Ministry of Defence (Central) Library; the

Eton College Library; the London Library; the National Library of Malta; the National Archives of Canada; the National Defence Headquarters of Canada; the Middle East Centre of St Antony's College, Oxford; the National Portrait Gallery; the North Yorkshire County Library; the Public Record Office; the Royal Agricultural College; St. Anne's College, Oxford; and the Sheffield City Library.

I am especially grateful to Mr John Terraine for devoting his invaluable time to reading the typescript and commenting in detail upon it. Sir Gawain Bell (who helped me in a variety of other ways as well) and the Hon Cynthia Leapman also read part of the text. Any errors that remain are my responsibility alone. Miss Rose Coombs spent much time in giving me the benefit of her encyclopaedic knowledge of the Western Front. Lady Jean Martin was generous in sharing her research on the background to the Plumer family. The late Major Wellesley Aron of Israel gave me information of inestimable value about Lord Plumer's time in Palestine, while General Ma'aan Abu Nowar of Jordan was also generous in showing me his extensive collection of manuscripts. My old friend De Heer Drs Adrian Groeneweg and his wife Marianne drove me around the Ypres battlefields in conditions nearing those of 1917. Others who helped me in a variety of different ways were Vere Lady Birdwood, Professor Brian Bond, Major John Cooper, Lieutenant Colonel Donald Creighton-Williamson, De Heer Albert Ghekiere of the Messines Museum, Mr David J. Harrison of the Western Front Association (who generously provided me with the 'Spy' cartoon of Lord Plumer), Mr Edward Horne of the Palestine Police Old Comrades Association, Mr Anthony Kirk-Greene, Lord Loch, Dr John Lonsdale, Lieutenant-Colonel Peter Pederson of the Royal Australian Army, the late Brigadier Reggie Rathbone, Mrs Joyce Rawes, Mrs Marjory Taylor of the Friends of St. George's Chapel, Miss Clare Wright and Mr Thomas Woodcock, Somerset Herald.

In the early stages of the book, Ms Charlotte Thompson worked ably for me among various archives. As ever, it was a pleasure to have Tom Hartman as my editor. My wife, Felicity, (as she has done with all my books) read every word at least twice, encouraging and criticizing as need be. Last, I must pay tribute to Toby Buchan. He gave me the idea for the book, and he would have published it but for untoward circumstances. During the thirty months of the book's gestation, he counselled and stimulated me. I am indeed grateful to him.

1 Regimental Officer

The British square had broken. Hacking and stabbing with their long swords and spears, the Fuzzy-Wuzzies[1] were among them. It was the cliché of Victorian military melodrama, the colonial expedition facing extinction.

The square of troops had been advancing towards the enemy, its four sides infantry, in its centre six machine-guns of the Naval Brigade, the ambulances, the ammunition reserves and the staff officers. On the leading face were four kilted companies of the 42nd Highlanders and four of the 65th Regiment of the Line. The Dervish rifle fire thickened, khaki-clad soldiers began to fall. Then, in response to their mounted general's command, the eight leading companies, with a surge of relief and exhilaration, charged the half-naked figures they could just glimpse, crouched among the tangled scrub and rocks of the stark Sudanese landscape. Behind them, the rest of the force hastened, striving to keep their formation over the rough ground. At the sight of the bayonets of the Scots and Yorkshiremen, the Fuzzy-Wuzzies bolted, disappearing into a deep ravine lying just behind their position, so checking the panting British troops who halted at its edge to fire down upon their fleeing enemies.

But it was a trap. A culpable error had been made; the lid had been lifted from the infantry box. Before the rest of the square could catch up with those eight leading companies, an immense horde of Dervishes, several thousand strong, rose from its hiding place in the ravine and curved around the flanks of the now isolated forward line of infantry. The dense smoke from the Martini-Henry rifles hanging in the still air clouded everything. Within minutes the flanks of the isolated line of infantry companies were being crushed inwards. The Dervishes were behind them. On the far right, thirty or forty men of the 65th stood firm, fighting grimly for their lives, but soon nearly all of them were down, dead or wounded. The Gatlings and Gardner guns of the Naval Brigade were overrun, but not before their surviving crews had locked them, so rendering them useless. In a confused mass, for five hundred yards or so, the rest of the shattered British square was driven back, soldiers, sailors, marines, transport drivers and staff officers fighting for survival.

Then the battle of Tamai began to turn. The second brigade square, echeloned to the rear, halted to pour in volleys of rifle fire upon the advancing warriors. On the other flank, two squadrons of cavalry dismounted to do likewise. The six 7-pounder guns of the Royal Artillery added to the hail of metal. As the onward rush of the Sudanese slackened, the units of the broken square began to rally. Soon the 65th had reformed and were driving the Dervishes back.

It was the experience for which the young soldier would crave but often live to regret, if live he did. As the 65th Foot sadly collected their dead, among them they found 'some of our best men – men of good character, smart soldiers, good cricketers; men who, standing at that fatal corner, had not budged an inch'.[2]

Active all the time had been the Adjutant, Captain Herbert Plumer, picking off the Sudanese with his revolver from his position just behind the forward companies. It was his twenty-seventh birthday. Two days later he penned a few hurried lines to his fiancée:

We had an awful battle on Thursday. I hope I may never see a scene like it again. We lost poor, dear old Ford. His body was horribly marked about when we got it, but I trust he was shot dead. Dalgety was badly wounded and I am afraid he will lose his arm. We were very lucky not to have lost more officers, but we lost a lot of men, 32 killed and 22 wounded. Some of our best men. One longed to see active service, but I have seen enough to last me some time.[3]

In the years ahead, the future Field-Marshal was to be known for the care with which he husbanded the lives of his soldiers.

* * *

The Young Herbert Plumer had been adjutant of the 65th Foot for the past five years. A mark of his ability had been his appointment to the post, in effect that of principal staff officer and right-hand man to his colonel.

His was in no way a fashionable regiment, but neither was his own background. The roots of Plumer's family lay deep in the starkly beautiful country of Yorkshire's North Riding, small gentlefolk whose sons might drift away into the professions or trade and then return if they acquired sufficient wealth for a comfortable and dignified retirement. Not until Victoria's time were the often talented sons of country gentlemen barred from entering trade and industry by the snobbery which was to deprive

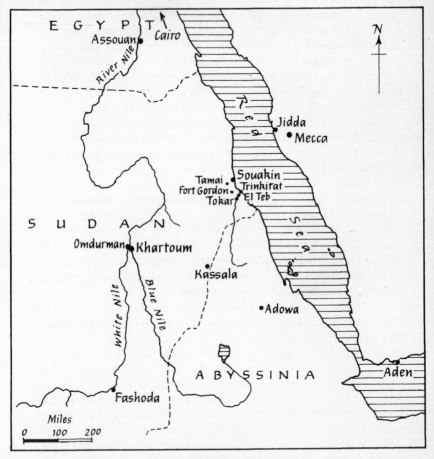

1. Upper Egypt and the Sudan

9

their country of some of its most able people and so make a significant contribution towards its eventual economic decline. The first recorded Plumer was a Thomas of Bedale, who married a local girl in 1638. His grandson, another Thomas, wed in 1716, as his second wife, Alice, the youngest daughter of Francis Hall of Lilling, a hamlet on the southern edge of the North Yorkshire Moors. These Halls were a family of some distinction, and one of Thomas and Alice's sons, yet another Thomas, who died in 1781, became the owner of Lilling Hall. He had been, according to his memorial tablet, a wine merchant of London, who 'because of deteriorating health quit scenes of business to live in his villa'.[4]

The first eminent member of the Plumer family was the wine-merchant's second son, Sir Thomas Plumer, Master of the Rolls, who had made his reputation as defence counsel at Sir Warren Hastings' famous trial for corruption. With the wealth he acquired at the bar, Sir Thomas bought, in 1806, Canon's Park in Edgware, a house built twenty-five years before on the site of the first Duke of Chandos's extravagant palace, which had been raised at a cost of half a million pounds, the profits of the Duke's tenure of the post of Paymaster to the Forces to Queen Anne. When the second and last holder of the title died heavily in debt, the great mansion was demolished and this new and more modest residence erected from the materials of the old.

Although more modest in character and size, still it contained seven reception rooms and seventeen bedrooms. As Sir Thomas wrote to his daughter in Brighton, he was happy to have retired so that he could be better able to assist in the improvement of 'this grand mansion and the gardens which later will be a heavy expense'.[5]

Sir Thomas died in 1824, but his widow, Marianne, lived on in the large house until she died in 1857, the year her great-grandson, Herbert, was born. Herbert's grandfather, Sir Thomas's eldest son, had followed his father into the law and travelled eight miles daily from his charming lodge in the grounds of Canon's Park (one of 'two genteel brick dwelling houses', as auction particulars of 1785 described it) to his work as Registrar of one of the Inns of Court until he was killed in a traffic accident. His widow and her children never quite recovered from the shock which broke up a lovely and loving home, already blighted four years earlier by the death of the eldest son, Thomas Henry, killed as an officer of the East India Company at the siege of Mooltan. Thomas Henry's younger brother was Hall Plumer, Herbert's father, Hall having fallen into use as a given name in the Plumer family. At the end of the 18th century, another Hall Plumer, Sir Thomas's younger brother, had amassed the money to buy Bilton Manor in Ainsty, between York and Harrogate, but within a very few years the estate was to pass out of Plumer hands. As we shall see, confusion between these two Halls was to cause much misunderstanding both locally and among Plumer's descendants.

If the Plumers had managed to retain the 547 acres of Canon's Park, they might have become a wealthy family: London suburbs now cover the land and Canon's Park is a station on the Jubilee Line. But Hall Plumer, to whom the estate passed on the death of his grandmother, straight away sold it, tradition having it that he dissipated his patrimony on drink and horses. Archetypal Victorian ne'er-do-well or not, a little later Hall Plumer had settled in Torquay, not in the splendour which could have been his at Canon's Park, but in a modest yet far from uncomfortable villa, Malpas Lodge; it needed a staff of butler, footman, lady's maid, cook, two housemaids and a kitchenmaid for its upkeep, merely the trappings of a well-off member of the upper reaches of the professional middle classes.[6]

Little is known about young Herbert's childhood except that it was spent at Malpas Lodge in the company of his elder brother, Frederick, and his two sisters, Beatrice and Constance. Eton was a family tradition, and there he was despatched in 1870. Among his contemporaries was Charles à Court, who later assumed the additional surname Repington when he succeeded to the family estates. Until the South African War, the lives of the two ran in parallel. They were together at the Staff College, where Repington was described as the most brilliant student of his year, but an unfortunate liaison with a colleague's wife led to his resignation and a fresh career as an influential military and political journalist.[7] Repington has left us some glimpses of life in the primitive Eton of the seventies, the riot in the High Street on Election Saturday, during which a master was almost chucked into Barnes Pool, the pennies heated on shovels to be flung out of windows to organ-grinders. He complained of the abysmal standard of teaching: mathematics and the classic were imparted, but little or nothing of history, modern languages, literature, science or political economy. Sport was everything.[8]

Throughout his life Eton was to exercise a close hold on Plumer's affection. The little evidence that survives suggests that he was a pleasant, lively, popular but undistinguished boy, remembered for openly and publicly making a book on the Derby and for being caught cutting school to attend Hunt Cup Day at Ascot.[9] Even at cricket, later his passion, he played only for his house, and not very well.[10] Rawlinson and Byng, two fellow Army Commanders in France, were at Eton with him, although both were younger; Byng remembered them both as 'scugs', Etonian slang for persons of no account, but Plumer he described as a 'camouflaged scug', reflecting at the same time that the best men matured late and practically never at school.[11] There is some truth in Byng's comment: Churchill's career followed similar lines. In the philistinism which prevailed among a large part of the British upper and middle classes until the end of the Second World War, intellectual curiosity arrived only with maturity, if at all.

In 1876 Plumer left Eton to be commissioned that September as a sub-lieutenant in the 65th Foot; later that year the rank was re-named second-lieutenant By then his elder brother Frederick was afloat with the Royal Navy. The services were something of a departure for Plumers. Although their Uncle Thomas had been killed thirty years before with the Bengal Native Infantry (another became Chief Justice of Mysore), nothing is known of any other member of the family having made a career in either of the Armed Forces of the Crown.

* * *

It was a time of change for the British Army. The alarm aroused by Prussia's successive invasions of Denmark, Austria-Hungary and France between 1864 and 1870 had alerted the country to the inadequacies of its defences, little having been done to remedy the shortcomings revealed by the Crimean War. The Army was suitable for little more than suppressing colonial risings, and even then it was not always up to the task. It was, then, fear of further German aggression that enabled Edward Cardwell, an especially able and far-sighted Secretary of State for War, to obtain the support he required to push forward a series of much needed reforms, despite the opposition of the Commander-in-Chief, the Duke of Cambridge, the Queen's reactionary first cousin. One of Cardwell's first reforms was to abolish the scandalous system whereby officers purchased their commissions, substituting instead entrance by competitive examination to the Royal Military College at Sandhurst. For the rank and file an engagement of six years with the colours and six with the reserve replaced the old long-term twenty-one-year stint, more often than not a life-sentence, so making it possible at the same time to strengthen units on mobilization and replace casualties as they occurred. An unpopular assault upon conservative prejudices was his linking of single-battalion regiments in pairs, one being stationed abroad and one at home to reinforce the other; these regular units were then harnessed with militia battalions into large regiments which assumed the territorial titles and connections which were to become their future strength and pride. Although Cardwell failed to introduce the sorely needed concept of a General Staff, he did manage to clarify the Army's upper structure and he brought all its branches, including that of the Commander-in-Chief, under his control, exercised through the War Office. At the other end of the scale, his abolition of flogging, allied to other reforms, made the soldier's life that little more bearable.

A very few of the young men who passed this new Sandhurst entrance examination near the top of the list were excused attendance and commissioned direct into their regiments. That Plumer was among this small number suggests that he had not altogether wasted his time at Eton and may provide an explanation for Byng's description of him as a 'camouflaged' scug. Almost straight away he sailed for India to join the 65th Foot at Lucknow at the turn of the year 1876-7, the Regiment still so called because Cardwell's linking was a gradual process. Not until 1881 did the 65th join hands with the 84th to become the 1st and 2nd Battalions of the York and Lancaster Regiment, its title deriving not from the counties themselves but from the old Duchies of York and Lancaster, a large part of the latter having been incorporated at one time into Yorkshire. With its Depot at Sheffield, recruiting was centred upon the towns and countryside nearby, that part of south-west Yorkshire known as Hallamshire, a name which was considered as the title for the new Regiment and one which was later to be used for its Territorial Force battalions.

Successful also in that examination had been Sub-Lieutenant Robert Stephenson Baden-Powell, the future 'B-P' of Boy Scout fame, commissioned into the 13th Hussars, which were stationed alongside Plumer's 65th Foot at Lucknow.

Sickness was the main concern of units stationed in India during the latter part of the 19th century, with cholera and enteric ever-dreaded scourges. Otherwise garrison life followed a pattern that had not changed too much even in the 1930s. The 65th was an efficient unit, one that received regular first-class annual reports; just before Plumer joined, the inspecting general congratulated it on the grounds that he had never seen one of its soldiers drunk, a feat indeed when there was little else but drink and sport to lighten the tedium of the daily routine. The battalion changed station every two or three years, marching from Lucknow to Dinapore, from Dinapore to Morar near Gwalior, one dusty set of lines being very like another. There might be active service on the North-West Frontier, but the 65th did not finds its way there. For the officers, life was rather more agreeable. The axiom of 'half a day's work for half a day's pay' was accepted, even though a subaltern might just be able to live on his pay in India. An adjutant would find plenty to do, and a subaltern who served with Plumer at this time remembered how, even more than his fellow adjutants, Plumer largely ran his battalion, sound experience indeed for the future. As at Eton, he was popular both within and outside his unit, and like most of his fellows he enjoyed to the full the sport and the games so readily available. Slim and not too tall (his later corpulence probably led to his being described as short), he was an able horseman, playing polo for the Regimental team, although upon first acquaintance he wrote home, 'The great game in the Regiment is Polo. Everybody goes in for it. I expect I shall be a great muff at it'.[12] He also gained a reputation as a race-rider. Altogether he was an able and modest young man, not well endowed financially, who developed in those early days that lasting regard for his Yorkshire soldiers which was to remain with him for the rest of his service.

In July 1882, the year Plumer achieved his captaincy, the now 1st Battalion the York and Lancaster Regiment left Morar to embark for Aden, most of its men debilitated by their long service in India, suffering from fever, the ague and various liver complaints. Intensely hot though the barren rocks of that isolated coaling-station at the southern mouth of the Red Sea were, the heat was tempered slightly by sea breezes, and the climate was not too unhealthy. Plumer described it as living in a perpetual dust-storm,[13] but bathing and sea-fishing did a little to temper the boredom. A brother officer remembered the station as the most monotonous in the British Empire. A graver indictment was hardly possible.

Leave was possible for those who could find the passage-money, and from Aden Plumer was able to enjoy some months in England.[14] Then, during his second summer in Aden, he secured a further and shorter leave which he put to good effect by becoming engaged to his second cousin, Annie Constance, the daughter of his father's cousin, George Goss, a comfortably-off London merchant who lived at 5 Devonshire Place, at the northern end of Wimpole Street, one of those graceful Georgian houses, then the dwellings of city men and now divided into the cubicles of medical consultants. Annie Constance was a talented girl, tall and beautiful. Probably the couple had been childhood sweethearts; certainly they had been writing to one another ever since Plumer sailed for India. They were, and so remained to the end of their days, an utterly devoted couple.

Then, and for long afterwards, twenty-six-year-old officers contemplating matrimony were far from popular, and among the letters of congratulation was one from a senior officer of the Regiment, Major George Wolseley; after abusing his young friend for getting married so young, he ended with the words, 'I will forgive the future Mrs Plumer if she makes you go through the Staff College'.[15] The brother of the famous Field-Marshal Lord Wolseley, and later a general himself, George was to continue to keep an eye on the young Plumer.

After returning from leave, Plumer spent a further year in Aden before his battalion at length embarked for home on 24 February, 1884, in HMS

Seraphis, its strength down to fifteen officers and 475 rank and file, many of its best soldiers having succumbed to what one of Plumer's fellow officers described as 'the government bribe of 120 rupees (about £8 sterling) to serve on abroad in whatever regiments they might be required'; it was hardly surprising with prospects for time-expired soldiers bleak. Those who embarked were, however, a fine body of veterans, their health much improved by their time in Aden; the year before, Major-General the Duke of Connaught, the youngest son of Queen Victoria and a career soldier, stopping off at Aden on his way to India, had commended 'the mature age, stature and bearing under arms' of the guard-of-honour which met him when he landed. And in his farewell address the Governor of the Colony had congratulated all concerned on having incurred 'absolutely no crime' during their stay, possibly a unique achievement in that or any other era. It all reflected well on the young adjutant, by then five years in the post.

*   *   *

The Regiment's voyage home was to be unexpectedly interrupted. Two days into the Red Sea, another warship hove in sight to signal 'Required at Trinkitat to take families of 10th Hussars and 89th Regiment off the *Jumna*'. Course was changed and, on 28 February, after being delayed by an explosion in the engine room, HMS *Seraphis* arrived off that small Sudanese port, after threading her way in and out through numerous shoals and coral reefs.

Active service awaited them. It had come about as follows. The Sudan is a vast country, one-third the size of the present U.S.A., largely desert except in the tropical south, its sole highway the narrow valley of the Nile which carved a fertile strip northwards into Egypt. Otherwise a scattering of camel-tracks meandered from water-hole to water-hole, routes along which the slave-traders drove their shackled goods. Except in the south, the people were of mixed race, a cross between Arab and negro which had produced courage, endurance and intelligence.

After a fashion the Sudan had been conquered in the 1820s by Mohammed Ali, that able and energetic officer of Turkish birth, who for a short time implanted an efficient regime into Egypt, then a moribund corner of the Turkish Empire. For the next sixty years the Sudan had smouldered in discontent, exploited for its slaves. Then, in 1881, another Mohammed Ali, the young son of a boat-builder and a member of one of the mystical dervish sects who claimed descent from the Prophet, had proclaimed himself as Mahdi, the Islamic redeemer or messiah, who would establish a kingdom of perfection, a universality of religion, law and common prosperity, in which all opponents, whether Christian, Islamic or pagan, would be slain. As a start, the Mahdi's followers set about slaughtering the largely ineffective Egyptian garrisons scattered around the country, the opening stage of what was to be yet another bloodthirsty tyranny.

As the Sudanese ridded themselves of their Egyptian oppressors, Egypt itself was being transformed. Since 1878 the country's bankrupt finances had been taken over by Britain and France, but in 1882 a patriotic officer, Colonel Arabi Pasha, seized power. Because his revolt was accompanied by the massacre of 150 Europeans in Alexandria, there followed an invasion by a British army commanded by Major-General Sir Garnet Wolseley, George's brother. In a model campaign, Wolseley defeated Arabi Pasha at Tel el Kebir and a British garrison was established in the country. Egypt's over-confident ministers thereupon despatched a virtually untrained force to deal with the Mahdi; in command was a retired Indian Army officer, Colonel Hicks Pasha, who had been appointed Chief-of-Staff to the Egyptian Army. In November, 1882, Hicks and 6000 troops were slaughtered, almost to a man; their weapons, added to what the Mahdiists had already captured, brought their total up to 20,000 rifles and nineteen guns. At the same time, on the other side of the country, Osman Digna, one of the Mahdi's principal lieutenants, had won a series of victories over Egyptian garrisons around Suakin, the Red Sea port. Another Egyptian force under Colonel Valentine Baker Pasha, sent from Cairo to redress matters, was on 4 February, 1884, massacred at El Teb. Over 2000 men were slain, and their weapons, which included four Krupp guns and two Gatlings, together with half a million rounds of ammunition, further augmented the Mahdiist armoury.

Despairing at what he viewed as another example of regrettable imperial expansion, the Liberal Prime Minister, William Gladstone, decided that the Sudan must be evacuated and left to its own devices, and so he despatched to organize the withdrawal Major-General Charles Gordon, that brave, capable but rather too independent a soldier. Previously employed by the Khedive Ismail to crush the slave-trade, Gordon had served for a time as Governor-General of the Sudan, when he had given the country a short taste of sound and honest rule. His instructions for this fresh task were ambiguous, his interpretation selective. In any case he lacked the means to conduct an orderly withdrawal. The consequences were to be his own death on the palace steps in Khartoum and two further wars, one the unsuccessful attempt to rescue him and the second the reconquest of the country in 1898.

Despite Baker's disastrous defeat, the British Government had decided that Suakin must be held and the nearby post at Tokar, besieged by

Osman Digna, relieved. Under the command of Major-General Sir Gerald Graham, 4000 British troops were, therefore, hurriedly concentrated at Trinkitat, most of them from the Cairo garrison, but including three units, one of them the 65th Foot (the old numbers had lingered on and have not even now quite disappeared), diverted on its journey home to join the expedition.

* * *

A letter in the *Sheffield Daily Telegraph*, written by a fellow-passenger in *Seraphis*, commented upon the attitude of Plumer's brother officers towards the forthcoming campaign:

> I found in conversation with the officers that though delighted at the prospect of active service their sympathies were with those they were going to fight against. One of them remarked to me that a man had to live some time in Egypt to be able to appreciate the vile oppression of the Khedive's Government, an oppression which more than justified the revolt of the Mahdi and his Soudanese.[16]

As the men of the 65th leaned chattering over the ship's rails as she steamed into Trinkitat on 28 February, 1884, a harsh view unfolded ashore, but Aden's rocks had accustomed them to such stark, waterless hills, beautiful now as the evening shadows threw into relief their hard red outlines. Half an hour after arriving, the Regiment was landed and met the 10th Hussars and the 89th, the other two units whose voyage home had also been interrupted. Swords had been sharpened on board and greatcoats or blankets were rolled across the men's shoulders, but the orders received through naval channels had mistakenly specified that no kits should be taken ashore, on the assumption that the tasks of these units was only that of baggage guard and that everyone would soon be back on board ship. As it transpired, it was the last some of the soldiers' families ever saw of their men. The women and children of the other two units were brought aboard *Seraphis* and the next day she put out for Plymouth with only eleven unfit men of the 65th on board.

Water-bottles had been filled on the beach, but no one had a change of clothing, nor even a piece of soap, a fork or a plate; most officers were wearing only light boots, quite unsuitable for the jagged terrain ahead. But ill-equipped as it was, the unit then set off for Fort Baker, three miles away, where the rest of the force had concentrated, wading bare-foot through a marsh in which some of the accompanying camels stuck so fast that they had to be abandoned. Only tea and ration biscuits were issued that evening and during the night a savage downpour of rain soaked everybody and everything. Early the next morning, ravenous, wet and wretched, the 65th fell in with the rest of Graham's force, its object to capture the position Osman Digna had taken up at El Teb, five miles or so away, and thus avenge Baker. By that time Tokar had already been relieved.

Graham's force moved in a single square (oblong might better picture it) with guns at each corner and the 65th forming its left-hand face. This diagram shows how it was done.

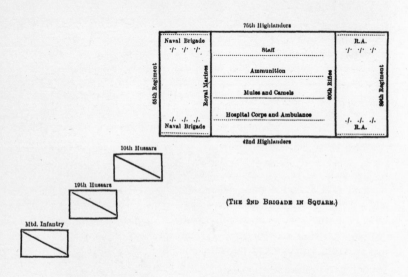

(THE 2ND BRIGADE IN SQUARE.)

After passing the place where the rotting bodies of Baker's Egyptians still stank, the advancing troops caught sight of enemy earthworks, behind which they could pick out the dark faces of the Sudanese. Soon the British came under fire from both rifles and the captured Krupp guns, but the Royal Artillery quickly silenced the latter. The square now changed direction so that the 65th were in the lead. Then, 200 yards short of the earthworks, Plumer's unit, bayonets fixed, charged with a resounding cheer and the Sudanese fled after a short hand-to-hand struggle. The General next formed his force into two lines, with the 65th in the centre of the leading one, in order to follow the fleeing enemy. As the British trudged forward in the sweltering heat of midday, they were charged by small parties of Mahdiists at whom the British cavalry rode with but little effect and at the cost of quite heavy casualties. At 3.30 pm a halt was called; no more Sudanese were to be seen. 187 British soldiers had died; afterwards

825 Sudanese bodies were counted. It had been Herbert Plumer's first taste of war. His letter to his fiancée, written on 2 March, read:

> Just a line to let you know I am all right. We have had a very rough time since we left the ship and a pretty hot fight the day before yesterday, February 29th. I was not touched. The Regiment suffered 7 killed and 32 wounded. Littledale was wounded but I hope is doing well. He behaved splendidly.
>
> I have not attempted to tell you about the fight at El Teb. It was, as you know, my first experience. I could not give you any description because I was rushing about all the time. It seemed to be about half-an-hour, but I believe it really lasted four hours or more. We marched back from Tokar on Tuesday, and did the whole march to Trinkitat that day, some 16 or 17 miles, and the last part we walked on bare feet through a swamp. We stayed at Trinkitat all Wednesday and then came on to Suakin in the *Carysfoot*.[17]

There were tents at Suakin and the filth of the week's campaigning was washed off in the sea. Some officers, of whom the adjutant would have been one, were entertained aboard the Admiral's flagship, an interlude which provided a contrast between the comforts of shipboard life and the squalor of their own. Then, on 11 March, rested and refreshed, the force left Suakin to complete the destruction of Osman Digna's army.

Two days later the battle at Tamai was fought, the story of which has been told. The letter, already quoted, Plumer wrote home afterwards suggests that the full beastliness of war was revealed to him there. On that occasion Graham had moved his force in two separate brigade squares, each capable of supporting the other. If the unwieldy single square of El Teb had been repeated, the outcome might have been very different.[18] The battle had ended in slaughter. Sudanese bodies counted afterwards numbered 2300 and their wounded were estimated at 6000; despite the near disaster in the early stages, total British casualties amounted only to ninety-one killed and 100 wounded, a tribute to British discipline rather than superior weapons, for, as we have seen, the Sudanese were well armed.

After the battle, the survivors of Osman Digna's force retreated into the hills where the lack of water protected them from further British harassment. For the time being the fighting around Red Sea was over, and on 29 March the 65th resumed their interrupted journey home. In all, casualties had been heavy, thirty-nine killed and fifty-five wounded; how many of the wounded survived is not recorded.

The young adjutant had learned much, not least the problems concerned with administering a force under harsh conditions and the need to plan such arrangements in advance. He had also learned that he could surmount the terrors of the battlefield, that self-discovery the outcome of which worries every soldier until he first sees action. His work was to be recognized. Together with five other officers, he was mentioned in despatches and was also awarded the Khedive's Order of Medjidie, 4th Class, together with two campaign medals, one British and one Egyptian.

★   ★   ★

Back in England, on 22 July, 1884, Plumer married by special license his Annie Constance at St Andrew's Church, Wells Street, in Holborn, now no longer there. For the newly-married man the next few months were busy setting up home and cramming for the Staff College examination, which, acting upon George Wolseley's advice, he took the following May. During the examination he managed to break his compasses and he returned to Sheffield, where the 1st battalion had just moved from Dover, certain that he had failed. However, in August, a few weeks after the birth of Eleanor, their first daughter, he discovered that his pessimism had not been justified.[19]

Set up in 1856 in an attempt to remedy the inadequacies of the staff work and the military ignorance of senior officers revealed during the Crimean War, the Staff College at first made little impression. Despite an unprecedented public interest in the Army, funds were short and prejudice against change was intense. The new establishment also lacked prestige, largely because staff appointments continued to be filled as ever by influence rather than from the few available Staff College graduates. Moreover, many regiments were reluctant to release officers to the staff, a problem which still existed even after the First World War. Plumer's regiment was more sensible. The year he joined one officer had passed out from the Staff College and another joined; his contemporary in the Regiment was the notable Colonel G.F.R. Henderson, outstanding instructor of the 1890s and distinguished military historian, whose active career was cut short by ill-health while he was serving as Lord Roberts' Director of Intelligence in the South African War.

Prussia's crushing defeat of France in 1870 provided a fresh impetus towards reform at the College and Cardwell was thus able to effect a number of improvements there. One consequence of this was that a high proportion of Sir Garnet Wolseley's staff officers at Tel el Kebir were 'p.s.c.' ('passed staff college') as they were distinguished in the Army List. Nevertheless, competition for entry among the infantry and cavalry was by no means intense. In Plumer's year only forty-three officers sat for twenty-four places; at the next examination, when the number of vacancies had been increased to thirty-two, only thirteen infantry and cavalry officers qualified and five were admitted even though they had failed the examination.[20]

In Plumer's time at Camberley, the Commandant was Major-General E.H. Clive, a Grenadier Guardsman, a pleasantly genial person, popular among the students but with no pretensions to being a thinking soldier. But there arrived at the same time as Plumer a new Professor of Military Art and History, Colonel J.F. Maurice, possibly one of the best brains in the Army and a brilliant teacher. Repington, who was there with Plumer, described life on the two-year course:

> We had a particularly nice set of young fellows there, and I do not remember any two years of my life which were more profitable or pleasant. We had all served in different parts of the world, and we learnt a lot from each other. We all worked hard, and the Library . . . supplied us with all the literature we required. The Staff College was a valuable institution. The healthy open-air life, the drag and the games, the interesting companionship combined with the two years' freedom from regimental duty in which we had wasted so much of our time without profit, were all a great attraction.[21]

Living in a small house opposite the College gates, their family augmented in February, 1887 by another daughter, Sybil, the Plumers enjoyed it all. During the summer he was said never to have missed a cricket match and during the winter he hunted or rode with the Staff College Drag, showing himself a better horseman than many of his fellow students. (It is a surprising fact that many officers could not ride well and that all infantry officers had to take an equitation course when they arrived.)

Perhaps Plumer allowed his pleasure in the life to interfere with his work; it is recorded that he managed to hunt on four successive days before he took his first year examinations.[22] Certainly he in no way distinguished himself in the final examinations upon which the placings in order of merit depended. Passing out nineteenth of twenty-six officers, his best mark was in mathematics and his position in Military Drawing, Military History and Geography, French, Fortifications, Tactics and Military Law varied between the mediocre and the poor.[23] An anonymous leading article, written in his regimental magazine, *The Tiger and Rose*, after the triumph of his Second Army at the Battle of Messines, included the following:

> The chief qualities for success in war, as it is now being waged on the Western Front . . . are . . . Patience and Resolution. . . . General

Plumer has both these qualities. He has them to a remarkable degree
. . . At the Staff College he was distinguished, not for brilliance –
brilliant men are not always the best soldiers – but for thoroughness
in his work. In the South African War Plumer was the one leader who
never made a mistake.[24]

The writer was almost certainly the academically brilliant Henderson. It
says something about Plumer that his own regimental magazine could
publish such an outspoken assessment of the character of its most senior
and distinguished officer at the moment of his greatest victory.

The acquisition of that 'p.s.c.' was not an immediate passport to the
coveted staff appointment which could more than double an officer's pay
and also provide the settled life so attractive to a young married man, as well
as the professional recognition which could result in brevet, or accelerated,
promotion. It was an age when an officer felt in no way inhibited from
canvassing support or pressing his case: the index to Plumer's personal
War Office file, the contents of which have disappeared, indicates how
he put himself forward for a number of appointments. Although Plumer
was never a member of Wolseley's 'Ring' (that talented group of men he
gathered around him and whose careers advanced in step with his), he had
the ear of that famous soldier's brother, and in 1889 Lord Wolseley, as he
had become, recommended him for a brigade major's appointment.

Meanwhile, after attending the obligatory four-month attachment to
other arms at Aldershot at the end of the course, Plumer soldiered on
with his 1st Battalion at York, the family augmented by Marjorie, yet
another little girl. This was his second tour in Yorkshire, a time during
which he formed his abiding love of the county and its people. Then
the Battalion moved to Ireland where Plumer heard that he had been
appointed D.A.A.G. (the principal staff officer) in Jersey from May,
1890, an inconvenient time as that same month a fourth and last child
was born, a son, christened Thomas Hall Rokeby. Life in Jersey in an
attractive little house with a charming garden was indeed pleasant. Again
cricket and a pack of drag-hounds helped to pass the time, and in 1891
he had published in the Journal of the Royal United Services Institute
an 8000-word article on *The Military Resources of the Island of Jersey*.
Comprehensive, thoughtful and gracefully written, it dealt in a succinct
manner with the island's history, geography, economy, communications
and local forces.[25] It was the first of his only two pieces of published
writing.

Towards the end of Plumer's three-year stay in Jersey, his general
offered him the post of Government Secretary, a tempting opportunity
for a poor man with four small children. Because he had not yet abandoned

his hopes for a successful career in his chosen profession, he declined the offer, but he soon had cause to regret his decision. Quickly his hopes for the further staff appointment for which he had been strongly recommended were dashed, but worse was to follow. He was not, as he had anticipated, posted to his beloved 65th, but to the 2nd Battalion of his Regiment, stationed in Natal. Attempts to effect an exchange between the two Battalions having failed, he sailed for South Africa on 4 November, 1893, leaving at home his wife and children, the expense of moving the family being beyond his means.[26]

Having arranged for the children to be looked after in England, his wife did, however, join him the following August. By then the 2nd Battalion have moved from Pietermaritzburg down to Wynberg in the Cape Colony, seven miles from Cape Town. Wynberg had much of the atmosphere of an English country village, and there the Governor had his country residence, a very English house set in a large garden. The Plumers managed to rent a pleasant little house, overlooking the cricket field and belonging to Cecil Rhodes's secretary. With a couple of ponies and a lot of cricket, much fun was to be had, but it was small compensation for the separation from their four children. To help them enjoy the life was the friendship of the High Commissioner, Sir Henry Loch; this came about because Plumer's Aunt Fanny was the wife of Loch's greatest friend, Sir Henry Parkes, with whom he had been imprisoned by the Chinese in Peking and to whom he owed his life.[27]

For a staff-trained officer approaching forty, South Africa was at the time a professional backwater. Other than a little intelligence work and map-making, with which he had lent a hand in Natal, Plumer was still engaged in the humdrum of commanding a company of less than 100 men, a job which he had been doing for years. Not that the authorities in London had forgotten him completely. During the winter of 1894-5, Plumer was offered a staff appointment in Mauritius, but he rejected this because it would have involved yet another separation. Before he had been told, his wife heard of the offer while she was lunching with his general. Her outspoken reaction perhaps provides an insight into her character. Nothing, she said, would induce her husband to go there, a remark that shocked the general who warned her that she would ruin her husband's career if she were to stand in his way.[28] It may well have been a lesson for her: henceforth she was the best of service wives, furthering her husband's career with charm, grace and shrewdness.

Plumer's fortunes were, however, about to change. Early in 1895 he met for the first time Cecil Rhodes when dining with Lieutenant-General W.H. Goodenough, newly appointed as Army Commander; also present was a certain Dr Leander Starr Jameson, one of Rhodes's close associates.

Rhodes was then at his zenith, Prime Minister of the self-governing Cape Colony, annexer of Bechuanaland and the vast country beyond, which in due course was to bear his name. In 1870 he had arrived in South Africa, a seventeen-year-old parson's son, with the idea of repairing his doubtful health. Diamonds had been discovered in Kimberley and there the youthful Rhodes prospered, consolidating claims to create the monopoly of De Beers Consolidated Mines. From diamonds he moved on to the newly found seams of gold in the Transvaal Rand, where he set up his equally massive trust, Consolidated Goldfields of South Africa. In the intervening years he had returned home, fabulously rich, to resume, at Oxford, his interrupted studies. He accumulated money, not for its own sake, but to acquire the power to fulfil his mission of expanding the British Empire and so civilizing South Africa. With the Europeans scrambling for colonies in every corner of the continent, Rhodes's ambition was for a red bar of British territory on the map running from Cairo to the Cape, linked first by telegraph and then by railway.

Unscrupulous and megalomaniac though he was, Rhodes towered above his contemporaries. Even the German Kaiser, a ruler not unacquainted with the breed, on meeting him was moved to remark, 'There goes a man'.

Shortly after this first meeting with Rhodes, Plumer returned to England with his wife in the spring of 1895 to enjoy six months' leave, a generous allowance as he had been in South Africa for less than eighteen months. Two months were spent in London, followed by a summer on the North Yorkshire moors, where they rented rooms at the secluded little village of Grosmont where they were ideally happy, picnicing and walking, accompanied always by a single fat pony on which the children took turns to ride.[29]

In London, Plumer had seen the Military Secretary at the War Office who, in complimenting him upon the reports he had received from his two generals in Jersey and the work he had carried out for the Intelligence Department in Natal, told him that he could all but promise him a staff appointment in Chester. But it did not come about.[30] Someone else secured the coveted job and, after pressing his claim to appointments in Cork, Colchester, Dublin and even Ashanti,[31] on 9 November, 1895, Plumer sailed once again for the Cape, sadly disappointed, now intent on leaving the Army and finding work in civilian life. His letters to his wife, both during and after the voyage, spoke again and again of his determination to resign. But one of them, written at the end of December, suggests that his wife was far from happy about his sending in his papers.

You must not think that I should be angry with anything you say as regards leaving the service. I still think it would be best to go if I do not get a Staff appointment in 1896. All you say is very true, but I think we must consider that there is a point at which ambition, as we like to call it, becomes selfishness pure and simple. The prospect of a tour in India with its constant partings and separations seems almost unbearable.[32]

Despite her reaction to the prospect of the Mauritius posting, there seems to be small doubt that ambition meant rather more to Plumer's wife than the presence of small children.

But better news awaited Plumer at Cape Town. General Goodenough's Military Secretary had been invalided home for six months, and the general wanted Plumer to act for him while he was away.[33] It was an opportune time. A letter to his wife dated 31 December describes the atmosphere in the Cape:

There seem to be wars and rumours of wars all over the world just now. There is every prospect of trouble in the Transvaal. The Johannesburg people have issued a manifesto this morning practically demanding the franchise, and there are all sorts of wild rumours about to the effect that they have stores of rifles and ammunition and Maxim guns at Johannesburg and are ready to make war on their own account. I fancy there will be trouble at any rate.[34]

Five days later he wrote again:

You can imagine that during the last two days the whole place has been in a state of ferment about Johannesburg. The wildest rumours have been flying about. . . . There is no doubt that Jameson surrendered to the Boers after a lot of hard fighting.[35]

It had happened like this. On 29 December, Dr Jameson, then Administrator of Rhodes's Chartered South Africa Company, had led 600 slouch-hatted policemen and volunteers out of their camp near Mafeking across the Transvaal border in an armed invasion of the Boer Republic. The discovery of gold had attracted to this pastoral country an influx of foreigners of all nationalities, the so-called Uitlanders who threatened soon to outnumber the Boers whose fathers and grandfathers had trekked north to escape British rule. Denied, with good cause, the vote by Paul Kruger, the Transvaal President, who foresaw his people losing control of their country, the Uitlanders had been backed and encouraged by Rhodes and his fellow financier, Alfred Beit. Plumer's 'wild rumours' about the stored weapons in Johannesburg were in no way wild. What is more, both the High Commissioner at the Cape and Joseph Chamberlain, Colonial Secretary in the Conservative Government, had connived at the rebellion plotted by Rhodes and his associates.

The plan was that, when the rising on the Rand took place, Jameson would ride across the border to the aid of the Uitlanders. It was Rhodes's greatest error: the Uitlanders were not the stuff of revolutions. Delays occurred and Jameson became impatient. The result was disastrous, both for 'Dr Jim' and for Rhodes. As the British public broke into jingoistic rejoicing at what they understood was decisive action to assist the 'down-trodden' Uitlanders, Kruger's commandos were rounding up the invaders after a two-day running battle, in which sixty-five members of Jameson's force were either killed or wounded. The rest went to prison, first in Pretoria, the Transvaal's capital, and then to Wormwood Scrubs when the British Government accepted responsibility for their trial. As for Rhodes, he was obliged to resign both from the Premiership and the Board of the Chartered Company. He was to sort out the aftermath of the disastrous business. This fiasco was Plumer's opportunity. On 4 January, 1896, the Governor had left for Pretoria in an attempt to settle the matter and from there he telegraphed Goodenough. On 7 January Plumer wrote home:

The upshot was that he wanted the General to send some officers to Mafeking and Bulawayo to prevent any attempt of avenging the Jameson disaster and to take from the Chartered Company's officers any guns and ammunition they have there. The General is sending Crofton, O'Meara and myself.[36]

Travelling by train up to Mafeking, a further letter recounts what happened when the officers arrived:

The camp was about 30 miles north of Mafeking. . . . We started at 6.30 a.m. It was a lovely morning with a nice breeze and the drive across the veldt was very jolly. It is perfectly flat country, green now that the rains are on but quite brown in winter. Plenty of grass, a few patches of mealies but very few trees and those small.
We reached the camp about 11. It is prettily situated and well laid out. The tents were all standing and everything just as they had left them. The officers lived in mud and brick kraals and they had a corrugated iron hut for a mess. They evidently did themselves pretty well. There was one officer and a few men left behind sick. Our mission was to take over the ammunition they had left, which we did. All the stores were left in an appalling state of confusion and no one seemed responsible. The men left seemed utterly disheartened. One sergeant told us the men did

26

not know where they were going till they were paraded, and that if they had a couple of hours to think it over, at least half would not have gone. It was one of the maddest schemes ever started. Everything points to reckless waste and extravagance. The camp was pitched by a contractor at his own price, he had not been paid. Thousands of pounds' worth of equipment, saddlery, ammunition, etc., was bought (not paid for, I think) and issued anyhow. The men themselves have not been paid, some of them for three months.

The camp was only three miles from the Transvaal border and the Boers, after Jameson's defeat, could have made a raid on it and looted the whole place. They made no attempt to do so, merely patrolling the border and I must say they acted very creditably in this and many other ways.[37]

Having completed their task in Mafeking, Colonel Crofton and Captain O'Meara were ordered back to the Cape, leaving Plumer as Special Commissioner with the local rank of lieutenant-colonel, to carry on to Bulawayo, the rapidly expanding capital of Matabeleland and finish off the job. The journey was 573 miles, the conveyance a coach, 'a regular Buffalo Bill – Wild West – Deadwood affair, hung by huge leather springs on a heavy, strongly built undercarriage, drawn by ten mules,' as Lieutenant-Colonel Robert Baden-Powell was to describe it when he made the same journey shortly afterwards.[38] For Plumer, the journey was

the most horrible thing you could imagine. There was an unfortunate woman with a baby in it. It is a trial if one has to do a railway journey with a baby, but to travel in a coach for six days and five nights with one is beyond description. It was really terrible. You can't sleep and altogether it takes more out of you than anything I have ever experienced before.[39]

It was not just the coach that conjured up the American West. Hard-bitten sunburnt men, six-shooters at their hips and broad-brimmed hats on their heads, herded cattle and drank in the saloons of dusty little tin-roofed towns like Mafeking.

What happened when at last Plumer arrived in Bulawayo can be told in his own words:

What I had to do was to take over all the guns and ammunition belonging to the Chartered Company, and also of course to prevent any armed force starting from here to the Transvaal. As regards the latter there is not the slightest danger. Everything is perfectly quiet here. There was tremendous excitement at the time of Jameson's surrender and if his life had been in danger I believe a number of men would have started off from here in defiance of the Imperial Government or anyone else. The devotion to Jameson is something wonderful; he is simply worshipped by all classes alike. It is the same wherever he has been. He must be a remarkable man . . .

Everything seems prosperous and there are a better class of men up here than I had anticipated. They have started Polo here and I had a game on Wednesday and enjoyed it.

Everybody has been very civil and the company's officers have been most courteous. Of course, the taking over the guns and ammunition is only a formal matter, but still it might have been a rather unpleasant job.[40]

It certainly might. Plumer was all alone, with nothing but the Queen's uniform and his own personality to give him authority. But all went well. Regular officers were not necessarily acceptable in colonial circles and it says something about his tact and diplomacy that the job was done, seemingly without friction. He was also broad-minded enough to appreciate the sense with which the Boers had behaved under such very great provocation.

Plumer was able to observe another facet of life in Bulawayo – the local Rhodesian Horse Volunteers engaged on a field day. With them were the new native police raised from the Matabele to replace Jameson's absent troopers.'What a fine body of men, and how useful they would be in the event of a rising,' Plumer remarked as he rode home at the end of the day. He was mistaken.[41]

On 12 March Plumer returned to the Cape, having handed over to someone more junior who had come up to relieve him. It had been a useful interlude. During his short stay, Plumer had gained a comprehensive knowledge both of the country and its leading citizens, several of whom were both well connected and influential. He had also done a sound job of work with the result that, when he arrived back in Cape Town, Goodenough offered to confirm him in his acting appointment of Military Secretary. It appeared to be just what he needed: a salary on which he could keep his family and responsible work which might well lead to better things. But despite the success he had enjoyed, Plumer refused the offer on the strange grounds that a married man could not satisfactorily carry out the duties. Apparently he was still determined to leave the Army, a catastrophe as his general saw it.[42] But it was not to be.

2 Matabele Rebellion

At the end of March, 1896, just after Plumer had rejected his general's offer to appoint him as his Military Secretary, news reached the Cape that the Matabele had risen and were exterminating the white settlers living in their country. The consternation in Great Britain matched that in South Africa. Immediate help was needed but Bulawayo and the railhead at Mafeking were 500 miles apart. And first the necessary troops had to be raised, equipped and trained, a task that the Government at home insisted should be carried out by British regular officers. After the Jameson fiasco there was no question of putting colonials in charge, even though the Chartered Company was to pay all costs. Plumer's sound work in clearing up after the Jameson Raid, allied to his local knowledge of the country and its leading citizens, marked him as the obvious choice to raise and command such a force.

So it was then that on 2 April, 1896, Plumer again left for the north, his orders to raise a Matabeleland Relief Force of 500 mounted infantrymen (a figure later increased to 750). Its tasks were first to escort arms, ammunition and food to Bulawayo, and second to operate against the insurgents when it arrived. Promoted to the acting rank of lieutenant-colonel, he had to assist him seven other regular officers, one of whom, Major F.E. Kershaw, a fellow York and Lancaster, was Plumer's close friend. All of them received a step in acting rank and a welcome fifteen shillings pay daily.

Setting up camp in Mafeking, Plumer began to recruit; there was no lack of enthusiastic volunteers, many of whom had given up well-paid jobs for the prospect of travel and adventure. Speed was the essence, and on 12 April the first troop left Mafeking for Matabeleland, Plumer having decided that to move in small parties as each troop was raised would provide his junior leaders with the opportunity of learning their job: during the long trek they would have the chance of knocking their troops into shape. A further factor was the need to avoid pressure on the few water holes along the way, many of which could produce only a sparse supply.

On 1 May the last of Plumer's fourteen troops rode out of Mafeking. In just over three weeks, over 750 men had been recruited and equipped as mounted infantrymen. 1150 horses, 602 mules and 45 wagons had been bought from a variety of sources, together with saddlery, medical supplies, signalling equipment, food, weapons, ammunition, individual kits and all the thousand and one articles needed on such a campaign. In addition fodder dumps had to be established along the 570-mile route chosen. Frank Sykes, one of Plumer's troopers, understood what had been involved:

> The heavy work of organising men and material as they came to hand at Mafeking was carried out under the direction of Lieutenant-Colonel Plumer, an officer whose capability and sound experience, though tried to the utmost, were fully equal to the occasion. To arrange, equip, provide for, and despatch into the field such a force of mounted men, all within twenty days, was no small feat, and alone would have sufficed to establish the reputation of the M.R.F. Commander as a military organiser of the highest order. The expedition with which preparations were effected was at the time commented on with surprise by those who were in a position to know what was entailed.[1]

As we shall see, Sykes at times was a far from uncritical commentator.

In general the men were a tough and mature bunch, their average age about twenty-six. Included among them were about 200 men of the British South Africa Police – the Rhodesian force – who had fought with Jameson; sent to England for trial, they had been repatriated and arrived back just when they were most needed. Many of the other recruits had served, at one time or another, in various irregular corps or in the British Army. Some half were British-born, having emigrated to South Africa during the previous three years, but a variety of other races were represented, Cape Dutch, Australians, Americans, Canadians, Germans, Spaniards, Swedes, Russians and Greeks. Many, like Sykes, were educated men.

As well as the mounted Europeans, a body of some 200 so-called 'Cape Boys' had been raised in Johannesburg, largely from among the mine workers, with a Major Robertson, a retired cavalryman, in charge. Insulting though 'Cape Boys' may sound to modern ears, it was not then thought objectionable and was applied to any mixed race inhabitant of the Cape, although its use had gradually been widened to include almost any black man in the Cape or Transvaal working for a white man. Most were, in fact, Zulus or Xhosas. Dressed in European clothes and equipped with a rifle, a bayonet (but no scabbard), a bandolier and a blanket, they marched up on foot to join Plumer's force, to which they provided sterling support.

As the troops in turn marched out of Mafeking, the proceedings were often enlivened by some of the green horses bucking off their sometimes greener riders, but on the whole they looked a capable lot. Their uniforms were cord riding breeches with either boots, leggings or puttees, brown corduroy tunics, felt hats turned up on one side, as well as cavalry cloaks or greatcoats and blue jerseys. They were armed with Martini-Henry rifles, together with nine Maxim guns, seven bought at an exorbitant price from a private arms dealer. Sufficient trained men were found to man these machine guns but there was a shortage of capable signallers.

The high spirits of the horses did not last for long. Carrying a load of some sixteen stones and 14.2 to 15 hands high, their tedious daily treks varied between fifteen and thirty miles or more, for much of the time over sandy flats dotted with clumps of thorn, the file ahead barely visible through the thick clouds of dust they raised. Reveille was at 4 am or earlier, according to the length of the day's march; about 9 am there would be a halt for breakfast and a sleep, heat and the flies permitting. Then at about 4 o'clock it would be 'saddle-up' once again and march for another five hours of so, when the second meal of the day was eaten and a few more hours of sleep enjoyed.

Food was as sparse as the time available for sleep. Officially the ration was a pound of meat and one and a quarter of flour or meal daily, augmented by tea, coffee, sugar, lime juice and a tot of 'dop' (Cape brandy), but the last two items were rarely seen. Sometimes a small amount of rice or tinned vegetables might be forthcoming. Feeding was by messes of four to eight men, one of whom was told off each day to bake the flour on hot embers into small, rock-hard 'cookies'. It was a diet that in due course produced 'veldt-sores' among many of the men. At night each man would roll himself into his blanket, lying on his groundsheet with his night-cap (also an issue) pulled well down over his ears to keep out the night cold.

At many of the outspans water could be found only by scooping out a two-foot hole in the sandy bed of a dry river, far safer to drink than from a stagnant pond that might conceal the body of a dead trek-ox. For all along the route were scattered the stinking carcasses of these animals, killed by the plague of rinderpest that had attacked Southern Africa at the start of the year, all but wiping out the country's stock of draught animals. It was for this reason that Plumer's wagons were drawn by mules instead of oxen, so producing another administrative problem as oxen could live on grass but mules needed fodder, consuming during the march two-fifths of the load they could pull. Hence the dumps that were established along the route.

Throughout the journey the air hardly ever seemed to be free of the pestential stink of rotting oxen. From time to time wagons were encountered, abandoned by their owners when their last oxen had died. It was hardly surprising that the troopers plundered them for liquor, food, clothing or anything else of value. As Trooper Sykes put it, they were a motley body of men, 'many of whom were not in the habit of drawing fine distinctions between *meum* and *tuum*.'[2] A few incorrigibly undisciplined men and some who proved to be below scratch physically were collected and returned to Mafeking for discharge.

* * *

How did this rising come about? The British were not the first to invade what is now Zimbabwe, but which for seventy-five years bore Cecil Rhodes's name. In the middle of the 17th century the Portuguese had forced their way up the Zambesi from the coast, to be repulsed by a combination of disease and unfriendly inhabitants. Then in about 1840 the Matabele, a breakaway section of the warlike Zulus, swept up from the south across the Limpopo, massacring or enslaving all who stood in their way and settling in the fertile land north of the Matopo Hills to raise their cattle.

When the first white gold-prospectors arrived a few years later, accompanied by a handful of hunters, traders and missionaries, there seemed to be room enough for everyone and the Matabele treated them with tolerance. However, in 1888, three emissaries of Cecil Rhodes presented themselves at Gu-Bulawayo, the kraal of Lobengula, the Matabele king, asking for a monopoly of all gold-bearing reefs in the country. After months of intense negotiations, terms were agreed, despite opposition to Rhodes's proposals from a number of quarters, ranging from rival prospectors to some of the King's more far-sighted senior *indunas* (or chiefs), and including the Aborigines Protection Society in London which warned Lobengula of the danger he was facing. For 1000 Martini-Henry rifles, 100,000 rounds of ammunition, a steam-boat on the Zambesi and a payment of £100 monthly, Lobengula agreed to grant an exclusive concession to search for and work all minerals. A year later Rhodes obtained a Royal Charter for his British South Africa Company, which was empowered to take over the concessions he had obtained. In return the Company undertook to act on the advice of the Secretary of State for the Colonies, to maintain an adequate police force to keep law and order, and to treat the natives fairly. *De facto*, if not *de jure*, the British Empire had acquired another vast territory, the continuation of a not uncommon sequence of events with traders absorbed by a Chartered Company which in the end became a colony when it could not cope with its responsibilities.

Rhodes wasted no time in moving in. By April 1890, a so-called 'pioneer

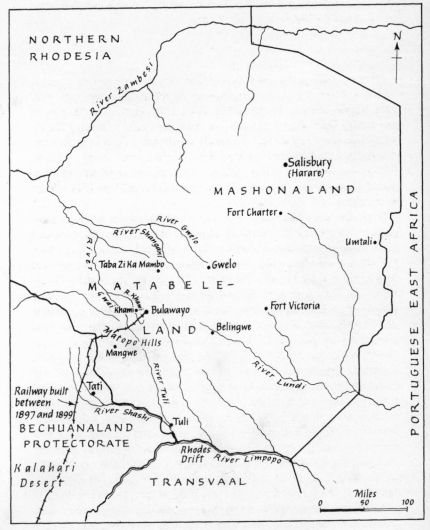

NORTHERN
RHODESIA

N

River Zambesi

•Salisbury
(Harare)

MASHONALAND

Fort Charter•

River Gwelo

River Shangani

Umtali•

River

Taba Zi Ka Mambo

•Gwelo

M A T A B E L E-

R. Gwai *R. Nhamu*

Khami•   •Bulawayo

•Fort Victoria

L A N D

•Belingwe

Matopo Hills

Mangwe•

River Tuli

River Lundi

Tati•

Railway built
between
1897 and 1899

River Shashi

•Tuli

BECHUANALAND
+
PROTECTORATE

*Kalahari
Desert*

Rhodes
Drift   *River Limpopo*

T R A N S V A A L

P O R T U G U E S E   E A S T   A F R I C A

Miles
0   50   100

2. Rhodesia 1896–1900

force' had been raised in the Cape and reached Mafeking; a uniformed body of 180 hand-picked and suitable settlers, it was paid at the generous police rates but attracted also by the promise of a grant of fifteen gold claims and a 3000-acre farm. On the way 200 members of the Company's newly raised British South Africa Police joined them, and the presence of a detachment of blue-jackets to handle the 7-pounders and Maxim guns testified to the Imperial support for the expedition. However, Rhodes was paying all the costs. Because the land was higher and healthier, and also well away from the threat posed by Lobengula's fierce *impis*, the force was directed towards the eastern part of the country, inhabited by the Shonas. In four months it carved a road for its wagons over a distance of 800 miles, passing through the southern edge of the Matabele country and losing horses all the time from the prevalent horse-sickness. Two forts were erected as Mashonaland was entered, one named Charter and one Victoria, and on 11 September the Union Jack was raised at their final destination, christened Fort Salisbury, now the city of Harare.

The pioneer force was then disbanded, its members to peg out their claims, settle on their new farms or drift into the towns that started to spring up around the mines. In from the south poured further seekers after gold, many starved and fever-racked after their arduous trek. Fort Salisbury expanded, first into a mining camp and then into a European-type township. Attempts by both the Portuguese and the Transvaal Republic to interfere with what was happening were quickly checked by diplomatic means.

This occupation of Mashonaland was but the first stage in Rhodes's grand design, his real objective being Matabeleland itself with its rich land and hopes of major gold reefs. In 1893 the opportunity was engineered, the excuse a Matabele raid upon the Shonas who lived in the neighbourhood of Fort Victoria. Not only were the settlers obliged to watch the slaughter and mutilation of their black neighbours by the Matabele but they depended upon these Shonas for labour for their mines and farms. The settlers demanded action and a reluctant Colonial Office was persuaded to allow three columns of hastily raised and trained volunteers, the men encouraged by the promise of claims, farms and looted cattle to invade Matabeleland, supported by a small party of Bechuanaland Border Police who approached from the south-west. In all, the troops numbered no more than 1000, together with a few hundred Shona levies.

Like the Zulus, the Matabele were brave and well-disciplined, their men organized into some forty *impis*, each about 500 strong and distinguished one from another by the colour and pattern of their shields and other insignia. Many carried firearms which ranged from old blunderbusses to modern Martini-Henrys, but their marksmanship was elementary. Nor had their leaders yet learned how to fight a guerrilla campaign and in the early stages of the war they threw their disciplined ranks against their opponents' Maxim guns. By December, after a punishing and bloody little campaign, it was all over. For years Lobengula had tried to avoid open conflict with the white men, knowing that in the long run he could not win. Now he fled northwards to die of dysentery; his *indunas* came into Bulawayo, occupied by their enemies, to ask for peace. The war had cost the Chartered Company £100,000 and a number of lives, but seemingly the Matabele had been crushed. By the New Year the pegging out of mining claims and farms had already begun and another European-type town was starting to spring up four miles away from Lobengula's old kraal. As the future Lord Milner was to write in 1897, 'the blacks have been scandalously treated'.[3]

* * *

Everything seemed to be set fair. British capital and white immigrants poured into the country; in Matabeleland alone the settlers soon numbered 4000. Many of the gold reefs were proving to be profitable; under Rhodes's encouragement, financial and otherwise, a railway was being pushed up from Beira into Mashonaland. The Matabele seemed to be cowed, if not crushed, and few took seriously the rumours of discontent and possible rebellion that began to be heard when Plumer first visited Bulawayo in the early months of 1896. One individual was even threatened with imprisonment by the authorities if he continued to spread alarmist rumours. The authorities were, in fact, fully occupied with other matters, coping not only with the aftermath of the Jameson business but also with the appalling rinderpest scourge, already mentioned, which had spread down from central Africa across the Zambesi, attacking not only the vast herds of game which still covered parts of the country but the domestic cattle as well, a blow to the expanding economy, for the cattle supplied transport as well as food.

For the Matabele the rinderpest was yet another disaster. Their cattle were their wealth, in terms of which the price of a wife, a gun or a blanket was calculated. Already large numbers had either been impounded by the administration after the war or stolen by the new settlers, and to make matters worse the government was exterminating herds in which the rinderpest was found, action seen by the Matabele as the deliberate destruction of what remained of their wealth and an attempt to reduce them to the status of slaves. Compulsory labour on the farms and in the mines reinforced this supposition; in the eyes of the young men hard and continuous labour was the prerogative of their women. Moreover, masters varied: violence, defraudment of wages and rape were not too uncommon. And these Europeans were occupying some of the best of their land. Above all, perhaps the Matabele had suffered a blow to their pride. Only recently had they themselves conquered the country and they were not accustomed to being subordinate to anyone. In only one of the three major engagements of the recent war had they been decisively beaten and some sections of the race had not even been involved in the war. The withdrawal by Jameson of some 300 white police for his foray into the Transvaal and their subsequent capture by the Boers provided the Matabele with both the encouragement and the opportunity they needed.

The plans for the rising were sound but their execution erred. Bulawayo was to have been rushed unexpectedly at night and its inhabitants slaughtered. Then the outlying prospectors, farmers and their families were to be killed. A subtle touch was the leaving open of the road through Mangwe to Bechuanaland down which any whites who tried to do so might escape. Unhappily for the Matabele, their rising began prematurely: before the attack on Bulawayo could be launched, the young warriors began to slaughter isolated whites. Within days 141 men, women and children were dead, mutilated, some tortured and raped. An unnumbered body of black servants and workers suffered the same fate. Despite the warnings, the administration had been taken completely by surprise.

There was panic in Bulawayo when the first news of the massacre reached the town. Men besieged the government store for weapons which were then handed out to individuals, some of whom had little or no idea how to use them. Not everyone in Bulawayo was the archetypical hardbitten frontiersman. Some 600 women and children were collected into the newly built club building, where they huddled fearfully together, several of the women giving birth prematurely. Quickly, however, competent men took charge. A laager of empty wagons was formed around the market square, with machine-guns at each corner and barbed wire outside, while parties of the Rhodesian Horse Volunteers, a part-time force with some 300 members in Bulawayo, rode out to rescue whoever they could from the countryside or to exact what was to be a bitter revenge. Soon every able-bodied man was conscripted into a new body, the Bulawayo Field Force, into which the Volunteers were amalgamated. It was to number about 900 men, divided into fourteen troops, all but 200 being mounted. A high proportion were experienced in warfare of one sort or another, and they possessed about a dozen 7-pounders or machine guns. They were a formidable body. As for the black Matabele police, whose bearing Plumer had so admired and who had made themselves loathed by their fellow tribesmen by their high-handed oppression, half deserted as soon as the trouble began, taking their weapons and newly acquired expertise with them; the rest were disbanded. Other black auxiliaries were, however, available. Some 150 workers, members of a variety of South African races, were recruited into a further unit of 'Cape Boys' (sometimes referred to as 'Colonial Boys') and commanded by Johann Colenbrander, a colourful old pioneer who had been a trumpeter in the Zulu War and acted as Rhodes's agent to Lobengula, before becoming, in 1894, Chief Native Commissioner.

As well as the laager at Bulawayo, three other similar but smaller refuges had been built, at Gwelo, 120 miles towards Salisbury, at Mangwe, and at Belingwe, away to the south-east. The Matabele, rightly wary of the defenders' automatic weapons, avoided attacking such places, but they controlled the rest of the country, despite the regular forays made by the settlers from Bulawayo in attempts, which varied in their success, to bring the *impis* to battle. Throughout April and May a number of such skirmishes and small engagements occurred, most of them inconclusive, but taking a steady toll both of the Rhodesians and their irreplaceable horses. It was near stalemate.

Because of the shortage of transport, which was largely the consequence of the rinderpest, help from Mashonaland had been slow to arrive, although a single convoy with weapons, together with its small escort, had reached Gwelo early in the rising. However, on 27 May a body of 150 men arrived in Bulawayo, having fought its way through for most of the journey. With it was Cecil Rhodes, carrying nothing more lethal than his habitual fly-switch, but always to be seen in the thick of the fighting. To meet him at his destination was Plumer, who had arrived a couple of weeks before.

After crossing into Matabeleland, Plumer had concentrated his individual troops into five squadrons, each commanded by a regular officer, and had marched during daylight so as to lessen the danger of the Matabele ambushing them in the thick bush country. Advanced and flank guards were put out (an unenviable task in such close country) and one troop always acted as close protection for the wagons; each night a small laager was formed with the wagons. Beyond the Mangwe fort, with its square earth breastwork and ditch, the pass through the hills caused the squadrons especial concern. As the men rode through this tortuous defile, where a few determined riflemen could have stopped them with ease, they were grateful for, but perplexed by, the absence of opposition, knowing that the Matabele had held the pass during the previous war. They little realized that it had been left undefended deliberately as a valve through which the white settlers might be encouraged to quit the country.

As the Relief Force neared Bulawayo, a body of white chiefs was gathering to assume charge of what was a very small number of Indians. It was a recipe for friction. First there was Earl Grey, a kind and pleasant man, a close friend of Rhodes and later Governor-General of Canada. A director of the Chartered Company, he had just been appointed as Administrator of the country, a post previously held by Jameson. Reaching Mafeking as Plumer's first troop was leaving for the north, Grey had spent a few days there with him, helping with the organization and equipment, before continuing his journey by coach. Hard on Grey's heels came Colonel Sir Richard Martin, appointed by the Colonial Secretary as Deputy High Commissioner and Commandant-General of Rhodesia; as with Grey, he had left England before the rebellion broke out, his task to take over command of the police and armed forces from the Chartered Company, and so obviate any further Jameson-type provocation of the Boers. As Martin passed through Mangwe in his coach on 14 May, he picked up Plumer and took him on to the capital, where they arrived the same night. There Martin took over control of operations from Grey. Then, on 2 June, came Major-General Sir Frederick Carrington, a grizzled veteran of twenty years of African campaigning, who had been uprooted from his pleasant billet as infantry commander in Gibraltar to run military operations under Martin's political control; his Chief-of-Staff was Lieutenant-Colonel Robert Baden-Powell, Plumer's old companion in Lucknow and the future defender of Mafeking. And, lastly, out of the east had loomed Rhodes, no longer the holder of any official positions, not even a director of the Chartered Company. For all that, Rhodes still towered over those around him, and he was not the man to watch what was happening without interfering. Altogether Plumer had a lot of masters.

On 24 May Plumer's squadrons rode into Bulawayo, a red-earth town of single-storey buildings, mainly corrugated iron. 'The gardens, streets and vacant lots,' as Baden-Powell described the place, 'richly sown with broken bottles, meat tins, rags and paper; scarcely a garden, shrub or tree in the place, the houses generally, if they were not "Bottle stores" (i.e. public-houses), are either dry-goods stores or mining syndicate offices. Everywhere enterprise and rough elements of civilization – not forgetting the liquor branch.'[4]

The welcome received by the troopers, many of whom found old friends in the place, was terrific, but the celebrations were not allowed to last for long. At midnight they departed on what was planned as a three-day expedition against the enemy who had been reported as being out in force

38

just to the north-west of the town. It was the M.R.F.'s first test. Sykes described the preliminaries:

Kits were overhauled, haversacks stocked, and *impedimenta* generally reduced as much as possible, for no wagons were to proceed with the expedition. By nightfall everyone was in a state of suppressed excitement. The weather was magnificent, but the biting cold soon made itself felt, while the full May moon shed an eerie light over the bustling men and patient horses. Orderlies hastened to and fro. Civilians, attached by special permission, kept riding up and down the line seeking some particular squadron. Press correspondents were pestering everyone for information and getting roundly sworn at in consequence, and generally everyone appeared to be endeavouring to do half a dozen things at once. Presently came the order to saddle up, then the order to mount; strict silence was enjoined, and quietly the long line of men and horses filed out of camp.[5]

The operation was to have been a pincer with the Bulawayo Field Force providing the other jaw, but it never snapped. The enemy, some 1000 to 1500 strong, had learned the error of staying to fight it out. Twice they seemed to be making a stand, but twice they disappeared as Plumer's men charged them, firing from the saddle against a hail of what luckily were hopelessly ill-aimed bullets. Even wilder, and perhaps even more dangerous, was the fire of their native allies, who sensibly refused to advance until they were sure that the Matabele had left (after the fight, Plumer recommended that they should be disbanded, and this Grey did). Two only of the force were killed, one of them a Cape Boy from the other arm of the pincer, and six in all were wounded. Estimates suggested that 130 Matabele were killed, but there is no record of a body-count having been made. It had, however, been good training for everyone. The men, Plumer wrote, had displayed great gallantry and dash;[6] they had also learned the importance of the basic military skills of straight shooting and conservation of ammunition.

Plumer's next foray into the Matabele country was, in some ways, a repetition of the first, but on a larger scale and lasting for a longer time. Directed towards the north of the Gwai River, it was planned to last for twenty days. At the same time Carrington launched two other columns, operating parallel to and north of Plumer, to one of which a squadron of his M.R.F. was detached.

In Plumer's column were thirty-two officers, 451 N.C.O.s and men, 474 horses, four Maxims, sixteen wagons and 192 mules. Twenty days' rations were carried for the men, and as much grain for the animals as could be found around Bulawayo. On the wagons were two blankets, a waterproof sheet, and 150 rounds of spare ammunition for each man, another fifty rounds being carried in each of their bandoliers. It was to be wearying work, both for men and animals. The latter, without rugs, suffered from bitterly cold nights which aggravated the hard work and shortage of forage. Horse-sickness was spreading, and ticks were further sapping the health of the animals. One in four of the mules was to die before the expedition ended. The need for the animals to graze for three or four hours in daylight limited the distance that could be covered, and the inevitable mishaps to the wagons in the rough country caused further delays. Among the men, fever and dysentery were on the increase, and the veldt sores, the result of the unhealthy diet, were incapacitating more and more men. Bully beef was the usual meat issue, although sometimes native cattle were captured and small buck, pheasants, partridges or guinea-fowl shot. In general, however, game was far from plentiful in the area, indiscriminate hunting by both the Matabele and the settlers having reduced the once large herds. By the final stages of the march the men's boots and clothing were starting to fall to pieces.

Often traces of Matabele spoor were seen, but when the mounted men tried to follow up the warriors they were usually led into thick bush, all but impenetrable for horsemen. Two or three small skirmishes did occur and from time to time a few stragglers were cut off, but the enemy always seemed to be just ahead of the patrols scouting in front of the main column. There was little to be done but burn the kraals and destroy what food could not be carried away. As Sykes complained,[7] it was small wonder that the enemy were never surprised. From reveille to lights-out, the bugles seemed to sound continuously and hardly a night passed without rockets and star-shells disclosing the position of the laager. Nor, at that stage of the campaign, did he approve of the methods used by the Imperial officers: too much time, he considered, was devoted to inessentials such as the nice alignment of saddles.

One necessary part of this camp discipline was the separation of the drinking, watering and washing areas, but further separated were areas for officers and men. On one occasion the water-guard on duty thought that he recognized a man from his own squadron in what he described as a nude, elderly figure picking his way down to the river-bank. 'Now you old scoundrel, come out o' that; you know its the officers' pool. Go and wash your dirty . . .' The sentence was never finished. The guard had recognized his colonel.[8] 'Elderly' is comparative: Plumer was then thirty-nine and, to judge from a photograph taken during the campaign, he was not carrying surplus weight.

Sykes mentions not only the ferocity of some individuals, but the disgust evoked among the majority by such behaviour. On one occasion when he was out on patrol he saw a prisoner, wrists bound, handed over to another trooper to be escorted back to the laager. The man concerned tied a rope around the native's neck and galloped away; soon the wretched prisoner fell, to be dragged over the rough ground until his body acted as a brake to the horse. In the climate of the atrocities that had been inflicted upon the settlers' families, this sort of thing can always happen, but Sykes was convinced that if Plumer had been able to know what went on in every part of his widely dispersed force, offenders would have been severely punished. Nevertheless, prisoners were always shot, either out-of-hand or later.[9]

The expedition was not a success. It was the age-old problem of catching a lightly equipped enemy operating in his own country. The combination of the failure and the hardships caused dissension among the troopers; one cause of trouble was a shortage of tobacco, a deprivation felt by some even more than the lack of food and its poor quality. Single cigarettes could change hands for 2s.6d, one-third of a man's daily pay, and oddly enough, the exact price they fetched in times of shortage in the Western Desert half a century or so later. The result was that on their return to Bulawayo, one man in six asked for his discharge, to be met with firm refusals. Addressing the unit on parade, Plumer pointed out that they had signed on for as long as their services were required, and that there was much work still to be done; he also told them that he did not underestimate the hardships they had undergone, but that he had been impressed by the readiness and goodwill they had displayed. The newly arrived General 'Freddy' Carrington also spoke to them. A man of few words, he was popular with the old hands, many of whom had served under him previously. An unmilitary figure, he usually dressed on campaign in Boer-type baggy trousers, a whitish jacket and a battered hat with an ill-tied pugaree; the hair on his upper lip, even at a time of large walrus moustaches, was profuse, hanging down over his mouth and almost reaching the tip of his chin. A contemporary described how he had 'raised colonial corps, and commanded them by sheer force of strength and skill of fisticuffs . . . he is a splendid specimen of a man and soldier – tall, strong, active and daring.' The praise, however, was qualified. It was 'in his physical accomplishments that Carrington principally shines and in comparison to them his mental development is very small.'[10] In nearly every respect he was the opposite of his main subordinate.

The first of the other two columns that had set out with Plumer's had fared even worse, largely because of the poor condition of their mules. The third, however, commanded by a Rhodesian, Colonel Spreckley, had done well. This was largely due to Baden-Powell* riding out the night before they started and pin-pointing the position of a large enemy *impi*. Spreckley's troops surprised it and killed some 300, the highest number of casualties inflicted in any engagement.

On their return the troopers learned for the first time of the extension of the rising into Mashonaland. It was disconcerting news. Mistakenly thought to be a peaceful, timid and downtrodden race, firmly under the heel of their traditional Matabele enemies, they had, for all that, seized the opportunity opened up by the absence of so many Europeans in Matabeleland to massacre any settlers they could lay their hands upon. Another 140 men, women and children had died. The result was that British regular units were called in to help. A unit of mounted infantry and some sappers disembarked at the Portuguese port of Beira; from the west the 7th Hussars, together with a further mounted infantry unit, partly found from Plumer's own York and Lancasters, both of which had been standing by in Mafeking, marched across southern Matabeleland to Victoria. At the same time, Carrington despatched a detachment of the Bulawayo Field Force and 100 of Plumer's men were ordered to follow them.

There was little or no rest for the men and animals of the M.R.F. who remained to fight the Matabele. The *impi* defeated by Spreckley had taken refuge among a group of *kopjes* some sixty miles north-east of Bulawayo, the Taba Zi Ka Mambo (inevitably the spelling of the name differed widely). On 29 June, under Plumer's command, the largest force yet put together marched out from Bulawayo to deal it a further blow. As well as 400 of his own mounted men, Plumer had with him two mule-borne mountain guns of the Royal Artillery, together with 100 other Europeans (only twenty-five of them mounted) and 186 men from the two Cape Boy units. There were also two mule-drawn ambulances and two doctors. One can surmise that a further addition was hardly welcome: Rhodes came as well, bringing his own wagon and mess, as was his custom, an entourage unhappily mistaken by a trooper for a hawker's outfit. The famous man had little sense of humour.

Plumer had absorbed the lessons to be learned from the errors he had

---

*Lively and imaginative, 'B-P' was a somewhat unorthodox soldier. He loved what he described as the 'flannel-shirt' life of scouting and shooting in wild country, veldt, mountain or forest. Ability as writer, artist and self-publicist provided him with the money to live in a fashionable cavalry regiment, and also ensured that his early career was minutely charted. His fifth book (he was to write fifty), *The Matabele Campaign*, published in 1897 and illustrated by his charming drawings and not too fuzzy photographs, provides a vivid picture of the campaign. Tim Jeal in *Baden-Powell* (published in 1989, a book that will certainly rank as its subject's definitive biography) has demonstrated that Baden-Powell frequently allowed his imagination far too free a rein when describing his exploits, especially those connected with his intelligence activities.

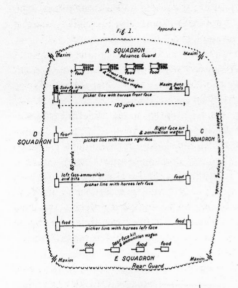

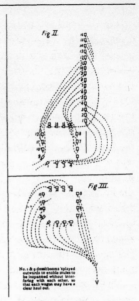

There were sixteen wagons with the column.

Fig. 1 shows the laager as formed for the night.

  ,, 2 ,, the method of coming into laager.

  ,, 3 ,, ,, breaking laager.

The advanced guard formed the front face, the main body the flanks, and the rear guard the rear face of the laager.

Each squadron had a wagon for its kit and ammunition, and this wagon was always placed on the front to be defended by that squadron.

Each squadron had its own picket rope, and these were fixed to front face No. 2, right flank No. 2, left flank No. 3, rear face No. 4.

Only four picket ropes were required; but as each rope had to accommodate about 110 horses, the wagons were necessarily set rather widely apart.

The men slept outside the wagons, behind their saddles; but in cases of alarm certain men were told off to occupy each wagon.

Maxims were posted at the corners of the laager.

The mules were always tethered to the dessilbooms* of the wagons they drew.

* Poles.

seen committed on that first large-scale operation. Among the skills he developed in his troops was that of making and breaking laager quickly, part and parcel of which were such aggravating fads as the correct alignment of saddles; even Sykes was to recognize the importance of such basic military skills. The above diagram shows how it was done:[11]

The arrival of a capable and trained transport officer to join Carrington's staff, combined with the experience already gained, had transformed the administrative arrangements for this next expedition, but the basic supply shortages still existed. To take but one example, the larger part of the stock of Armour bully beef available had, for the past six years, been used to reinforce the parapet of a fort. Of this the troopers were well aware. Only by opening and sniffing the first 200 tins in front of his doubting soldiers could Plumer convince them that it was not all poisonous. It was also about this time that it occurred to those in charge that the shooting of prisoners and the maltreating of women and children only discouraged surrenders, and an order was published on the subject; the consequences were to be far-reaching.[12]

The Taba Zi Ka Mambo Kopjes covered an area some three and a half miles square and consisted of a confused mass of enormous granite boulders, difficult of access, riddled with caves and covered with *wach-een-bitje* (or wait-a-bit) and other needle-sharp thorns. Plumer's plan was to make a twenty-mile approach march in the dark, and then to drive through the *kopjes* at day-break with his infantry, supported by the guns, flushing out the Matabele to the mounted men who would be waiting in the veldt beyond. It was a complicated plan, and it all but worked. The night approach, that difficult operation of war, went well, the men moving so quietly that they passed within 150 yards of the Matabele camp-fires. At 5.30 am the troops stormed the *kopjes* with great dash and courage, the Cape Boys especially distinguishing themselves by the determination with which they clambered up the precipitous rocks. By then the Matabele had learned to shoot much straighter, and at times they stayed to fight to the death, assegai against bayonet. When, in the end, they gave way and fled downhill into the open veldt, the exhausted horses of the mounted men were incapable of effective pursuit, and the surviving Matabele scattered, unharmed. Left behind in the caves were some 500 to 600 women and children, together with 1000 cattle and 2000 goats and an immense quantity of miscellaneous loot, garnered at the outbreak of the rebellion. The number of enemy killed was estimated at between 200 and 500, but this was later ruled as perhaps optimistic. Nevertheless it had been a well-organized and far from unsuccessful operation which had hit the Matabele hard. The spoor suggested that the survivors had made for the shelter of the Matopo hills, to the south-west.

Trying indeed was the return march to Bulawayo. Many horses had broken down and a number of the mounted troopers were obliged to foot-slog back. To the admiration of all, Plumer set an example in fortitude by dismounting and marching with the rest.

*   *   *

Although the Rhodesians had failed to entice the Matabele into a major battle and so destroy their *impis*, the incessant harrying had hit them hard. Their kraals burnt, their crops and food stores destroyed, and their cattle captured, many had been driven to take refuge in the Matopos. These hills, the northern base of which lay fifteen miles north-east of Bulawayo, were larger and far more complex than even the Taba Zi Ka Mambo. Some sixty miles long and twenty deep, they rose from their valleys in tiers of gigantic boulders, in places to a height of 2000 or 3000 feet. Within the hills were hundreds of narrow, fertile and well-watered valleys, most of which could be approached only through defiles, sometimes fortified with stockades or stone breastworks, and passable only by pack animals. The huge blocks of rocks, thrown together in a seemingly careless manner, formed thousands of natural caves. And, of course, there were no proper maps, only Baden-Powell's sketches, of which more later. Too extensive for the type of envelopment Plumer had attempted at Taba Zi Ka Mambo, there seemed to be no alternative to assaulting each defended *kopje* in turn, a daunting task.

Again, Plumer's men were not to have a break. Avoiding as usual what flesh-pots Bulawayo boasted, (although men occasionally obtained leave for a visit, the unit never spent a night there) their commander marched them to a new base at Usher's Farm, six miles south of the hills. They arrived on 13 July. Six nights later they set out on their next operation, having spent the intervening time repairing as best they might the ravages of their previous expedition. With them were seventy-two members of the Matabele Mounted Police, a new force raised to replace the Bulawayo Field Force, disbanded so as to allow its men to return to their civilian occupations. Carrington, who had decided to direct operations personally, now joined the force, and Plumer had to cope, not only with his immediate military superior, but also with Rhodes and Grey who had established their camp near to his own.

In anticipation of the need to ferret the Matabele out of the Matopos, Baden-Powell had, since late June, been engaged in investigating both the hills and their inhabitants. It was extremely dangerous work. Accompanied usually by Jan Grootboom, a courageous black hunter (and a character straight out of Rider Haggard, who had published his *King Solomon's Mines* just ten years earlier), B.P. would ride into the hills under cover of the dark to start studying the Matabele *kraals* and their occupants as soon as the sun rose, sketching and mapping the ground. On one occasion Grootboom removed his European clothes and crept close enough to the enemy to listen to them talking. Then, when Plumer took his force into the Matopos, Carrington attached Baden–Powell to him as second-in-command, intelligence gatherer and general factotum. It seems to have caused no problems that Baden-Powell was a step senior in army rank to Plumer, having been granted the brevet of lieutenant-colonel after the Ashanti campaign which had ended only a few months before. The two men were an effective combination. B.P.s flair and dash complemented

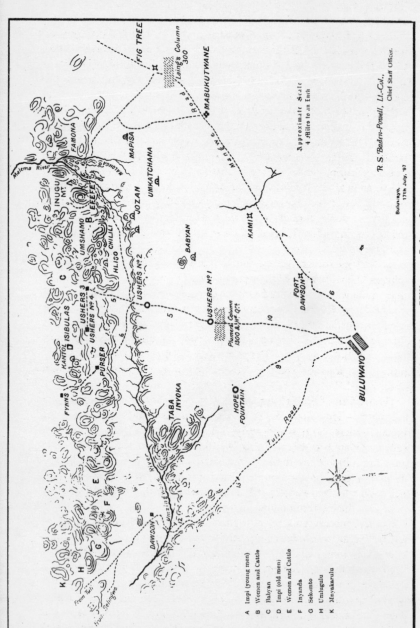

3. Sketch map of the Matopo Hills, 17 July, 1897

R.S. Baden-Powell, Lt.-Col.,
Chief Staff Officer.

Buluwayo,
17th July, '97.

Approximate Scale
4 Miles to an Inch

A   Impi (young men)
B   Women and Cattle
C   Babyan
D   Impi (old men)
E   Women and Cattle
F   Inyanda
G   Sekomto
H   Umlugulu
K   Mvakarulu

Plumer's careful planning and meticulous administration. For the help he gave him, Plumer gave B.P. generous credit.

Plumer's first operation was against an *impi* whose stronghold lay some five miles inside the hills. It was to provide a taste of what was to come. After another well-planned night march, the assault on the *kopjes* again began at dawn. Dislodged from their grass shelters high up on the hill slopes by the fire of the two mountain-guns, the Matabele retreated into the labyrinth of boulders and caves beyond. Commanded by Baden-Powell and supported by a couple of Maxims and a Hotchkiss, the 260 Cape Boys then assaulted the stronghold, clambering over the rocks with their customary dash and courage. The Matabele disappeared after putting up a fierce resistance during which they accounted for fourteen of Plumer's men, four of them killed. Meanwhile, some fifty mounted men had attempted to find a way to the rear of the Matabele stronghold but were thwarted at a narrow defile through which they were obliged to ride in single file and at walking pace. There a white sergeant was killed and an officer wounded.

As everyone recognized, the military skills of the Matabele were developing in line with those of their opponents. The previous war had taught them that it was pointless to charge the *isi-kwa-kwa*, the Maxim gun, and they were now learning to use their numerous rifles, no longer under the misapprehension that the raising of the back-sight increased the impact of the bullet. At Taba Zi Ka Mambo a Rhodesian officer had called out, 'Now then boys, fire low'. From the *kopjes* above was distinctly heard in the native tongue, 'You fire low, too', as an *induna* profited from the advice heard.[13]

The pattern of the fighting in the Matopos was to be repeated again and again – long marches, sharp engagements, and a steady loss of scarce soldiers, both white and black. Sykes was among those who were humiliated to discover that 'we, fully equipped with all the arms and ammunition of modern warfare, should be able to exact only life for life when pitted against a horde of native savages; but he conceded that their local knowledge and speed of movement over the steep and slippery rocks gave them a tremendous advantage.[14]

Plumer's most serious losses occurred during an attack against a stronghold belonging to an *induna* named Sikombo in the south-eastern Matopos. After a very long march around the hills, the assault was launched on 5 August with the engagement following familiar lines. Baden-Powell had previously pin-pointed the enemy position, and the attack was preceded by a bombardment from the guns and intensive fire from the Maxims. Then the Cape Boys, together with three dismounted squadrons of the M.R.F., the latter commanded by Kershaw, Plumer's friend, a quiet and unassuming man, assaulted the *kopjes*, clambering up the steep granite walls. Before they disappeared into the distant hills, the Matabele used their rifles accurately. By the day's end, seven Europeans, among them Kershaw, were dead or dying. A further thirteen men had been wounded, two of them Cape Boys. Numbered among the casualties were eight officers and seven sergeants, hit while leading their men or conspicuously directing the fire of their guns.

* * *

By mid-July it had already become clear to Carrington that to clear the Matopos would take at least another 3000 men, together with a couple of thousand carriers. Others put the figure of soldiers as high as 10,000.[15] What is more, the wet season was approaching which would all but bring the fighting to an end. The war might well drag on indefinitely. Responsible as it was for the payment of all the costs, Rhodes saw that the Chartered Company faced financial ruin and with it the end of his vision of the Empire expanding even further to the north.

Ever since the Matabele had taken refuge in the Matopos, there had been indications that some of the senior *indunas* were weary of it all. Food was becoming scarce and, if the war were to continue during the coming rainy season, no new crops would be planted and starvation would follow. It was, therefore, unfortunate that the acting High Commissioner from the Cape had, on 4 July, issued a proclamation of amnesty for the rebels but had excluded all the important Matabele leaders from its terms, the very men who were capable of persuading their young warriors to lay down their weapons. The *indunas* were, in fact, in no way enthusiastic about accepting an invitation to come in and be hanged.

Rhodes understood the problem. Moreover, he had, during the past few months, come to respect the fighting qualities of the Matabele and to comprehend something of their complaints. Although he lacked any official position, he decided that a direct approach to the *indunas* must somehow be made. The government offer of amnesty he saw as more of a hindrance than a help to his aims. Both Plumer and Carrington, aware as they were of the almost insoluble nature of the military problems facing them, especially after the carnage of 5 August, were to give their reluctant approval to Rhodes's attempts to negotiate, even though Rhodes was to all but ignore their political master, Sir Richard Martin, in so doing.

Rhodes's first attempts to make an approach to the *indunas* failed with some of his emissaries disappearing never to be heard of again. On 9 August, however, Baden-Powell, on one of his scouting expeditions, had brought back a very old African woman who turned out to be a step-mother to Lobengula. Many of her people, she revealed, were tired of the war, so B.P. conceived the plan of carrying her back into the hills on a stretcher and leaving her there with a white flag which would be flown if the *indunas* wanted to talk. Two or three days later observers saw the flag flying and Rhodes arranged for the ever-resourceful Jan Grootboom, together with two African companions, to enter the hills to contact the rebels. This they courageously did and returned with the news that the Matabele were ready for a meeting; they would treat with Rhodes himself, who must be accompanied by no more than three unarmed companions, one of them Colenbrander, who, with Baden-Powell, had been largely responsible for organizing the meeting.

On 21 August Rhodes and his small party rode out of their camp. Few people had expected to see Grootboom return, and many felt the same about Rhodes. One of the four was the *Times* correspondent, De Vere Stant, who afterwards described the scene at the rendevous. In a small basin, rimmed by *kopjes* stood some tree-stumps and the remains of a large ant-heap. There the men dismounted and, almost immediately, the white flag appeared above them. 'At the same time a number of dark forms could be seen gathering around it. Slowly a little procession formed, headed by the flag, and came towards us. The wonderful smile broke out on Rhodes' face as he said, "Yes, yes, there they are. This is one of the moments in life that make it worth living. Here they come!"' Seated a few minutes later on the ant-heap with the *indunas* and their retainers squatting in front of them, Rhodes asked, 'Is it peace?' Came the reply, 'It is peace, my father.'[16]

During the four hours of talks, during which the *indunas* recounted the history of their race and the wrongs they had suffered at the hands of the white men, Rhodes took it upon himself to guarantee the safety of *indunas*, despite the terms of the government proclamation, to disband the hated black police, and to reform the administration. Arrangements were made for a further meeting and the party rode back to camp, elated at their success and glad to be still alive. Stant then rushed off to file his story and wire his agent to buy 'Chartereds'. Rhodes, who only very rarely put pen to paper, sat down to write this note to Plumer:

My dear Plumer,
We had a regular go with the natives to-day, the indaba lasted four hours, they will not fight again unless forced to do so. I am sorry Moncreiffe [one of Plumer's staff officers] was not present, but Colenbrander had a message they only wanted myself and himself. We went through every grievance. There were forty present and all the principal Chiefs.

C.J. Rhodes[17]

At the second *indaba*, held a week later, Plumer, together with two of his officers, was present. Also there were Colenbrander's wife and sister-in-law, seemingly an odd thing for Rhodes to have permitted, but their presence undoubtedly did something to reassure the Matabele that no treachery was intended. Plumer's seven-line description of the meeting is laconic, commenting merely that the young warriors who attended did not appear to be submissive.[18] The account written by J.G.M.C. McDonald, one of Rhodes's young assistants, fills over three exciting pages. As the party arrived at the meeting-place, he wrote, they were surrounded by 500 Matabele, all fully armed. 'What is this?' asked Rhodes. 'How am I to trust you? You asked me to meet you with my friends and wished us to come unarmed, saying that you would carry none either, and what do I find? Five hundred and more fully armed warriors. Until you lay your guns and assegais down, and I order you to do so, all of you, I decline to discuss any matters with you at all.' Addressing the chiefs, who complained that their young men were becoming hard to handle, he told them to reassert their authority and ensure that the weapons were put down. Otherwise he would return to his camp to continue the war.

The continued intransigence of the young men was worrying, but the negotiations went ahead, largely because Rhodes made it clear that he was determined to go as far as he could in righting the wrongs of the Matabele.[19] It was agreed that the talks would continue, and, at the third *indaba* on 16 September, both Martin and Grey were present, the former accompanied by a cavalry escort, a display that initially disturbed the *indunas*. Again Plumer was there. Suspicious of what Rhodes had accomplished, Martin was reluctant to see the war end before the Matabele had been thoroughly trounced, a view also held by most of the settlers who criticized bitterly all that Rhodes was attempting; with some justice they feared that life would be impossible unless the Matabele power was completely broken.

However, Rhodes was to prevail. The war was virtually over and after this third *indaba*, the *indunas* started to come out of the hills to tender their submission and to surrender as few of their weapons as they thought they could get away with. The High Commissioner's original proclamation had, by then, been amended to include the Matabele leaders within its terms, except for those who had perpetrated the murders which had marked the outbreak of the rebellion.

With the fighting ended, the prospect of garrison duty in the grim little isolated forts during the misery of the rainy season held out little attraction for most of the members of the Matabeleland Relief Force, many of whom had left profitable jobs to enlist and were anxious about their chances of finding others. As a result, enthusiasm greeted the news that the unit was to be disbanded in mid-October. Some men took their discharge in Bulawayo, either to find a job, buy a farm or join the police, but ten officers and 289 men marched back to Mafeking to receive their discharges, taking from five to six weeks to complete the long journey. With them went Robertson's Cape Boys. In all Plumer's unit had cost the Chartered Company just a quarter of a million pounds to raise and run for six months.

Congratulations for Plumer and his men poured in from all sides. That from Grey, writing on behalf of the Chartered Company, should be quoted:

Dear Colonel Plumer,

I cannot allow you to break up your camp on the eve of your return march from Mafeking [sic] without conveying to you some expression of the gratitude felt towards you by the inhabitants of Bulawayo for the distinguished services you have rendered to the Government and to the people of Rhodesia. The rapidity with which your column was recruited, horsed, equipped and marched up to the relief of Bulawayo was, in itself, an achievement of which you and every member of your force have abundant reason to be proud. The many conspicuous services your force has rendered in the field, notably the two brilliant engagements on the Khami on the 24th May, only forty-one days after the first detachment leaving Mafeking; your night march to Tabas-i-Mamba, and the capture of the important rebel stronghold; and your several engagements in the Matopos – will be long remembered by the people of Bulawayo. I wish on behalf of the Administration and of the English settlers of Matabeleland to acknowledge with grateful thanks the part played by all your officers, non-commissioned officers, and men who have so gallantly and ably assisted you; and I would venture to hope that many of them like the country in which they have been campaigning for the last six months and its people well enough to induce them to return at an early date, with the object of establishing for themselves a permanent home among us in Rhodesia.

Believe me, my dear Colonel, with all good wishes for your future success,

Always your truly,
Grey[20]

From his own officers, Plumer received this address:

We, the undersigned, as a token of our esteem and in acknowledgement of the kindness and tact you have invariably shown us, beg of you now that the Corps under your Command is about to be disbanded, to accept a pair of Field Glasses which have been ordered for you. The glasses will be forwarded to your address as soon as a certain engraving has been finished, and it is deeply regretted by us that the sudden disbandment of the Force prevents our having the honour and pleasure of making this request in a much more suitable manner. It has been a great pleasure to us to have had the honour to be with you in the Field, and in saying "Good-bye!" we all unite in wishing you a brilliant future in the Service and throughout your life.

(Sixty-five names followed)[21]

But the letter that touched him most was the one he received from the Jesuit priest who had accompanied the unit during most of its battles. He wrote:

It is almost useless to tell you that I join heartily in all the congratulations you receive and will receive. Men more authorised to do so than I am praise your work; still nobody perhaps knows better than I how much you deserve the love your men have for you.
Believe me, my dear Colonel,

Yours sincerely,
M Barthélemy.[22]

In his first independent command and on active service, Plumer had proved himself both to the satisfaction of his superiors and to those who had served under him. As a regular officer of a rather limited and stereotyped background, he had shown a remarkable capacity for commanding irregular troops – independently minded and temperamental individualists by comparison with the rather stolid South Yorkshiremen of his own regiment. By careful planning and meticulous attention to the minutiae of administration, he had raised his corps in a matter of weeks, trained it, marched it over Africa for 500 miles, and kept it sound throughout an extended series of sharp engagements, some less successful than others. All the time he had driven his men hard but kept them in good heart. During this fighting, he had again seen the effect of accurate and disciplined fire; brave as both the Dervishes and Matabele had been, the Maxim gun had proved their master. As a comparatively junior officer, he had coped without friction, so far as is known, with quadripartite control by his military and political masters – Carrington, Martin, Grey and Rhodes, all of them men of character, but the last-named towering above the rest, his natural impatience aggravated by his deteriorating health and testy to boot. Something else Plumer had again experienced was the loss of close friends, not only Kershaw, but another member of his Regiment as well; Captain Shadwell, who arrived with the York and Lancaster Mounted Infantry, died of dysentery after only ten days in the country. Shadwell was, Plumer wrote, 'a great friend of mine, and I feel his death very much.'[23] The loss of such close friends was perhaps something that affected his attitude towards death and suffering in later life.

The coach returned Plumer to Mafeking, and while he was there he started a memorial fund for his corps, Rhodes heading the list of subscribers with £5000. On 18 November, 1896, he arrived at the Cape to embark for England. There he arrived just in time for the happiness of Christmas with his family. Because of the press publicity the campaign had received, he was a household name among a nation avid for tales of military glory. Sent for by General Sir Redvers Buller, his comrade-in-arms in the Sudan and then the Adjutant-General, he was asked where he would like to be sent. His reply was Aldershot, then and until after the Second World War the nerve centre of the British Army and the goal of ambitious officers. There he was sent with the brevet rank of lieutenant-colonel and the appointment of Deputy Assistant Adjutant General, one of four, who in those pre-General-Staff days dealt with all aspects of staff work, not just personnel matters.

On what someone minuted in its War Office file as 'a somewhat cold report!', Carrington had reported upon Plumer raising and commanding his corps with 'conspicuous success' and to his 'having rendered excellent service generally', but he received no decoration, although both Spreckley and another Volunteer officer were both gazetted DSO and Carrington himself added a KCB to his KCMG.[24] This led Grey to protest vigorously to the High Commissioner at Plumer having apparently received no mark of distinction for the work he had done:

The fact that Colonel Plumer was able to raise, horse and equip at Mafeking a force of over 700 men and fight two successful battles against the Matabele, after marching 600 miles within forty-one days of the receipt of the first order given to raise the force, is, if not a unique, at any rate a very remarkable achievement.

And not less remarkable than this achievement was the admirable discipline and bearing of the force thus hurriedly collected throughout the whole of their service in Matabeleland.[25]

For all that, Plumer received no more than his brevet, but it was the step in rank that lifted him out of the ruck.

During January and February, 1897, Plumer spent his leave writing his only book, *An Irregular Corps in Matabeleland*. Published later that year, it brought in a little welcome money and made his name still better known, both inside and outside the service. He must have started it on the voyage home, if not before, but to write 100,000 or so words so rapidly was something of a *tour-de-force*, but not unusual at the time. Sykes, Baden-Powell, Laing and F.C. Selous (the famous African hunter and supposedly the model for Rider Haggard's Allan Quatermain) all produced their books about the campaign within the same time scale. By comparison with the others, Plumer's is pedestrian, a factual record that reads like an official report. Although well written and clear, it says little or nothing about the people with whom he was embroiled, and, but for his sadness at young Shadwell's death, it is devoid of any personal touch. Modesty, perhaps, had triumphed.

3 The Boer War

Plumer's spell of settled family life in Aldershot was not to be prolonged. In the summer of 1899 a fellow staff officer from Aldershot, met at Lord's Cricket Ground, mentioned to Mrs Plumer that he had just received orders to start for the Cape; her husband, he predicted, would be the next to go. He was correct. On 15 July Plumer once again embarked on that familiar journey to South Africa, bound again for Bulawayo.* The War Office was fitting a round peg into a round hole. With war imminent against the two South African republics, the Transvaal and the Orange Free State, Plumer was one of a party of so-called 'special service' officers sent to raise irregular units of mounted infantry for service on the borders of Rhodesia and Bechuanaland, facing the Transvaal. It would only be a short war, or so the War Office surmised, when they minuted the Treasury specifying that enlistments should be for a period of four months only.[1]

The nine special service officers who sailed with Plumer in the RMS *Norman* were surprised by the appearance and habits of their senior, reputedly a successful commander of swash-buckling irregulars. This small, rather delicate and retiring person, short-sighted and apt to disappear with a novel rather than join in the trivial pursuits of shipboard life, was hardly what they had expected.[2] 'Bronzed, dark-eyed and meditative' was how a newspaperman described him a few months later.[3] Both in early and late life, he was known for being sociable and outgoing, characteristics not always obvious at this time. Was this perhaps the effect of yet another separation from the family to which he was so very devoted? Nevertheless, when the party of officers arrived in Bulawayo railway station – for the line from Mafeking had now been completed – Plumer's companions discovered what the Rhodesians thought about him when the platform echoed to

---

*A day or two after Plumer left, Sir Redvers Buller, his commander at Aldershot, wrote a note to Mrs Plumer to reassure her that she could remain in her married quarter and to apologize for failing to see her husband off at Aldershot Station as he was saying farewell to a couple of important guests at the time. Such concerned for his officers was typical of Buller.[4]

cheers and cries of 'good old Plumer' and 'remember the Matopos' from the welcoming crowd.[5]

* * *

In the four years preceding that summer of 1889, relations between Britain and the two Boer republics had been moving steadily towards a climax. Jameson's disastrous foray, which had resulted in Plumer being plucked from obscurity, had brought to a head the ill will simmering between President Paul Kruger's pastoral republic and the expansionist British Empire. Kruger, that shambling, puffy-faced back-veldt Boer, black-coated and top-hatted, a figure of both mockery and hatred to the British public, was an astute statesman who well understood how Britain's latent power could be brought to bear against his country in the event of an all-out war. Intent upon gaining the sympathy of his fellow Boers in the Orange Free State and in the Cape Colony, as well as the Transvaal's many sympathizers in Europe, Kruger curbed the resentment of his people at Jameson's provocation. As a result he ensured that the captured British troops were handed over to their own Government for trial in London, while the leaders of the abortive rebellion in the Transvaal had their death sentences commuted and were released upon payment of heavy fines.

At the same time Kruger put in order his country's defences. Modern rifles were purchased for the 25,000 burgher commandos, reserves of ammunition were accumulated, and the latest equipment was obtained for the very effective regular State Artillery Corps. The two republics between them could field some 50,000 mounted men, to face whom, in the whole of Southern Africa, were less than 10,000 British regulars and about the same number of police and Colonial volunteers.

The follies of Rhodes and Jameson, those of the former exposed at the various trials and enquiries that followed the Raid, had united Kruger's Boers and many others beyond the Transvaal's borders. To the wealth of Transvaal gold-mines had been added a new prestige. If she were to merge with the Orange Free State, the Cape and Natal could well follow suit, despite the latter's English-speaking majority, so creating a powerful South African Republic, independent of the British Crown. It would be the end of the imperialist ambitions of such men as Rhodes and Joseph Chamberlain, the Colonial Secretary.

To restore the situation, Chamberlain chose as High Commissioner Sir Alfred Milner, a self-made man of German parentage, whose academic brilliance, developed as an undergraduate at Balliol, had brought him while still in his thirties to the post of Chairman of the Inland Revenue, the Chancellor's right-hand man. His visions surpassed even those of Chamberlain, and by degrees Milner persuaded him to permit Kruger to be driven into a corner. During the protracted negotiations, Kruger made a succession of concessions, but concessions were not enough. Milner intended to annex the Transvaal, something that could be accomplished only by war. In the end, at a conference held at Bloemfontein on 3 June, 1899, attended also by President Steyn of the Free State, Milner finally broke off all negotiations. It was the culmination of what the Boers described with some justice as 'a century of wrongs'.[6]

Although the newly appointed military commander in Natal estimated that only 2000 reinforcements would be needed, Milner requested what he described as 'an overwhelming force' of 10,000. Despite the successive defeats in the previous war of 1881, culminating in the disaster of Majuba Hill, gross miscalculations were being made locally about the fighting potential and the expertise of the Boers. By 8 September the 10,000 were on their way, drawn from the garrisons of India, Malta, Egypt, Gibraltar and Crete, but until mobilization was ordered and the reserves called up, further troops were not available. On 22 September, however, news broke to the press that mobilization had been ordered and that Buller's 35,000-strong Army Corps was preparing for service in South Africa. Six days later the Transvaal mobilized also, the Free State following suit.

It was clear to the Boer leaders that hopes for success must lie in striking before Buller's troops arrived, so on 9 October Kruger issued an ultimatum, demanding among other things that all British troops who had arrived after 1 June should quit the country, and that those at sea should be turned back. As the Boer leaders well knew, there would be no question of a great imperial power capitulating in such a way. Three days later 21,000 mounted Boers started to move into northern Natal.

* * *

When Plumer arrived at Bulawayo in early August, he barely recognized a town transformed by a new Grand Hotel, running water, electric light and much else. There he once again met Baden-Powell, now a brevet colonel and despatched to South Africa to take command of what were to be Plumer's new Rhodesia Regiment and the Bechuanaland Protectorate Regiment. The task of these two officers was not easy: with war still uncertain, there was a reluctance to volunteer and recruiting was slow. As the Official History put it, 'though there were ne'er-do-wells in plenty, reliable men were only to be found in regular emloyment'.[7] For all that, by the end of September, the two regiments were raised and equipped, the men recruited from the coastal ports rather than up-country, and Plumer's was drilling on the Bulawayo racecourse to the entertainment of

57

4. South Africa
(see also map 2 on p 33)

the local ladies. By then a number of undesirables had been detected and
discharged, and there were to be few disciplinary offences in the future,
the consequence, as Plumer reported, of his force being at all times well
removed from a supply of liquor.[8]

Plumer had, of course, done it all before. As Harvey de Montmorency,
a retired young gunner and apprentice goldminer, who had volunteered on
the outbreak of war, put it, both Baden-Powell and Plumer were 'esteemed
for their tact and ability in dealing with "Scallywags".'[9]

Even though Plumer on this occasion received far less help in such hum-drum matters as collecting supplies, weapons, clothing, oxen, mules and horses, he managed to overcome all difficulties. On the other hand, it says something about the efficiency of the small local headquarters that by 19 August detailed printed orders were ready for distribution; these covered not only full instructions on administrative matters such as ration scales, equipment scales and disciplinary awards, but also the rules for dealing with a multitude of tactical matters, or 'battle drills' as they were one day to be christened.[10]

The orders received by Baden-Powell before he left England were that 'in the even of hostilities with the Transvaal, you should endeavour to demonstrate with the largest possible force at your disposal, in a southerly direction from Tuli, as if making towards Pretoria'.[11] It was one of those broad-brush, optimistic instructions sometimes issued off small-scale maps by commanders or staff officers ignorant of local geography. An earlier internal memo in the War Office had been even more fanciful, suggesting that if 100 men were left at Tuli, guarding the frontier, sixty men with two Maxims could surprise and seize Pietersburg and push on in the direction of Pretoria to 'contain a considerable force of Boers'.[12] That Pietersburg was a large centre of population, separated from the Rhodesian border by 150 miles of almost waterless desert, was ignored. 'It would have been a little reminiscent of Jameson,' as Baden-Powell told the postwar Royal Commission, which reported in 1903 in a million words upon the inadequacies displayed by the British Army during the war.[13] However, Milner encouraged Baden-Powell to ignore his instructions and move his Bechuanaland Regiment towards Mafeking so as to protect it against capture, and in so doing draw Boer forces away from the main battle.[14]

On Milner's instructions, Baden-Powell left Plumer to defend Rhodesia, giving him fresh orders which were a sensible modification of those he had received in London:

1. To defend the border as far as it can be carried out from the neighbourhood of Tuli as a centre.
2. By a display of strength to induce the Boers to detail a strong force to protect their northern district.
3. To create diversions in the north of Transvaal, co-operating with the invasion of the south by your main force, if necessary advancing into Transvaal for the purpose; no portion of your force is to cross the frontier till you receive orders; instructions will be sent to you as to the date for co-operation with the other column.[15]

On 14 October the Boers cut off Baden-Powell in Mafeking, two days after they had invaded Natal. One the same day Plumer's force concentrated at Tuli, twenty miles from the border. It did not amount to much, only five of his own newly raised squadrons, each about eighty men strong, together with 100 British South Africa Police constables and five obsolete or semi-obsolete guns. Six weeks' supplies had already been dumped at Tuli, but thereafter nearly everything needed travelled by sea from Durban to Beira, then by rail and afterwards by ox-wagon over 450 miles of the roughest tracks to Bulawayo, and then on to Tuli. Knowing his qualities so well, Baden-Powell had given him a free hand, ordering him to act on his own responsibility; at the same time Milner withdrew the injunction against crossing the frontier.[16]

The Limpopo River, which marked the 500-mile frontier, was hardly an obstacle. Stretching as far as from London to Aberdeen, it was never dry and was fordable everywhere except during the brief winter floods; woods lined the river banks, and to the north rose rocky hills covered by dense thorn scrub. To defend it with 500 men was asking a lot. Not only might the Boers probe north to cut the new Mafeking-Bulawayo line, but in those early optimistic weeks it was feared that the enemy, fleeing before victorious British armies pressing up from the south, could seek refuge in Rhodesia's empty spaces. The Rhodesian settlers were conscious of another and even more fearful threat: the African tribes, crushed in 1896, might well seize the chance to take their revenge.

The Boers also were worried by the danger of being invaded from across the river, and they had in consequence concentrated their Zoutpansberg commando of 1300 men with three guns thirty miles from Rhodes Drift, the main ford due south of Tuli. To the south-west another 600 strong force, under the very able Assistant-Commandant Grobelaar, was watching the Bechuanaland tribes, traditionally hostile to the Boers, but not fully trusted by the British either. For their supplies the Boers looked to their railhead at Pietersburg, 150 miles away across a barren stretch of country which was to pose administrative problems similar in their way to Plumer's.

The Zoutpansberg commando reached the Limpopo the same day that Plumer arrived at Tuli. Sending forward four of his five squadrons to cover the more vulnerable of the many crossing places, Plumer kept the rest of his force back to defend his base and escort supply convoys. A series of skirmishes then took place along the river bank, in which Plumer at first succeeded in disguising the weakness of his force by aggressive patrolling, so discouraging the Boers from crossing in strength. The wild life added to the danger; very early on a sentry was taken and eaten by a lion.

Many of his men were old hands, skilled in bush fighting, but more of them were raw youngsters who knew nothing of either war or life on the veldt. Among the latter was Trooper Young, a youthful barrister, whose letters describe something of life in Plumer's regiment:

I've had a bit of an exciting time since I last wrote – almost too exciting at one time. Last time I wrote was when we were leaving Tuli for Rhodes Drift. We arrived there all right after much marching, and counter-marching, mostly by night. The second night of it, for the small portion we had for sleep I struck guard; so by the third night I was in a wretched state from wanting to sleep. I was always dropping off to sleep on my horse and suddenly waking up. Moreover I began to see all sorts of strange things. Brooks and trees were transformed into houses and gardens. . . . When we reached Rhodes Drift, our squadron was quartered there alone, and we had a couple of brushes with the enemy to start with. I missed the first, in which we had much the best of it. We only had one man hit, and that only slightly, and in return we bowled over a couple of Dutchmen (others may have been wounded), stampeded their horses, over a hundred in number (we surprised their grazing guard) killed or wounded over twenty of their horses, and jumped seven. The next fight was warm for a bit . . . we had four men wounded, and did an equal amount of damage to them, if not more. We got off very cheap, for their fire was very hot, and very close.[17]

A week before this letter was written, a 400-strong Boer commando had crossed the river, circled around Young's squadron and advanced towards Tuli. Four miles north of the river they overwhelmed a convoy; eight supply wagons were captured, seven men, among them the padre, made prisoner, and the balance of the twenty-six man escort escaped into the bush, four of them wounded.

The Boers then turned their attention to the squadron at Rhodes Drift, which was commanded by Lieutenant-Colonel Spreckley, Plumer's old friend from the Matabele days, later to be killed. Young and another man were despatched to bring in two outlying picquets; as they galloped across the veldt under heavy fire, the second man's horse was shot under him, but Young managed to get through. Further on in Young's letter, we learn what then happened.

They gave us a devil of a time. At first they fired mostly at the horses. They, poor beasts, had no cover, and nearly every one was hit. A few broke loose and bolted. Later they turned their attention to us. Luckily their shell-fire was very wild, or we should have suffered heavily.[18]

Defenceless against the guns and aware that more parties of Boers were nearby, Spreckley decided to slip away. Abandoning wagons, the few surviving horses and men's kits, his squadron reached Tuli after a tortuous seventeen-hour march.

> Altogether, we marched forty miles through awful country, for a long way though brushwood called 'wait-a-bit' thorn, and in the night too; it tore our clothes, hands, arms and faces to bits; then through and over kopjes covered with thick brush. Altogether it was equal to sixty miles of English roads, and we went pretty fast when the way allowed.[19]

It was a serious setback for Plumer. If the commandant of the Zoutpansberg commando had been just that little more aggressive, there was no way of stopping him, but fortunately he advanced no further towards Tuli, contenting himself with digging in a few miles from Rhodes Drift. As was so often the case in these early days of the war, Boer generalship was no better than the British, a combination of muddle, timidity and divided counsel. After crossing the Limpopo, the Boer leaders were uncertain whether their task was to invade Rhodesia or stay on the defensive; what is more, they were rightly concerned about the length and difficulties of their supply line, even though most of what they needed was there for the taking at Tuli, now a well-stocked base with a hospital staffed by nurses.* The arrival of the able Grobelaar with 400 reinforcements did inject fresh spirit into their deliberations, but the Pretoria government then vetoed his proposal to first attack Tuli and then cut the railway, the State Secretary pointing out that the danger to the republic lay, not in the north but in the Cape and Natal where the British forces were collecting.[20]

So the Boers left three detachments, each 400 strong, watching the border, and the rest were withdrawn to Pretoria. For Plumer it was a reprieve. But soon he discovered that even these detachments had been much reduced in strength, and on 1 December he decided to investigate. Leading a force across the river himself, in eighteen hours he covered fifty-four miles of this strange and fever-stricken region of salt-pans and giant baobab trees, but he saw nothing of the Boers. Two weeks later another foray produced similar results. The rains had come and the Limpopo was hardly fordable; it seemed certain that the Boers had, for the time being, withdrawn from the northern Transvaal.

Supporting Plumer, and under his orders, was Colonel J.S. Nicholson, the Commandant-General of the British South Africa Police at Bulawayo.

---

*One nurse remembered the quarter rations to which they were at times reduced and her commander being dubbed 'Starvation Plumer'. He collected nicknames.[21]

Before the outbreak of hostilities, Nicholson had been sufficiently far-sighted to stockpile supplies (merely by overstocking his police stores), and it was largely due to his acumen that Plumer had been able to complete the equipping of his regiment. When Plumer left for Tuli, Nicholson had organized the involved line-of-communication stretching back to Beira, and had placed on a war footing his own police and the Southern Rhodesia Volunteers, who, due to a general shortage of horses, included a body of cyclists. At the same time he persuaded the railway workshop to build three armoured trains; with these and some police and Volunteers, he organized a small column which probed down the railway line to within eighty miles of Mafeking, causing some damage to the Boers as it advanced.

With the Limpopo apparently free of the Boers, Plumer could do one of three things: he could abide by his original instructions and stay where he was; he could follow the Boers towards Pietersburg – logistically all but impossible; or he could move westwards to the railway in an attempt either to take pressure off Baden-Powell in Mafeking or even raise the siege. He chose the last, a bold decision as it left the border undefended against any renewed offensive the Boers might mount against Rhodesia. Starting out on 27 December, he marched his force in small detachments towards the railway line, 175 miles away; before leaving he signalled his intentions to Baden-Powell, but by the time the reply was on its way he had gone.*

Baden-Powell's decision to incarcerate his troops in Mafeking at the outbreak of the war was and still is controversial. It was a place of little or no strategic value, a half-way staging point on the Cape Town-Bulawayo railway, a squalid and dusty frontier town on the edge of the Kalahari Desert. It was, on the other hand, the centre of government of a quarter of a million Africans, most of them warlike. If Boer and Britain had one aim in common during the war, it was to keep the natives quiescent; both also wished to impress them. For the British to have handed Mafeking over to the Boers without a fight would have been an admission of defeat and a gift of vast stores of food, forage, ammunition and railway material. Moreover, for the Boers Mafeking was an emotive place. From nearby Jameson had mounted his raid, and there Rhodes had established his advanced post for the conquest of Rhodesia. Mafeking was also only 160 miles from Pretoria, and the Boers could hardly ignore the presence of a British force so close to their capital. Among the many criticisms made of Baden-Powell was that he failed to use his troops as a roving column to harry the Boers. This

---

*In view of the complexity of the communications, it is extraordinary that they were so dependable. Messages went by runner to Bulawayo, then by telegram to Nicholson's armoured trains, and then again by runner through the enemy lines.

was, as the *Official History* rightly comments, a prospect 'as alluring as it was impractical.'[22] With a regiment of almost raw recruits, lacking spare horses, adequate transport, field artillery or a supply base (once Mafeking had been lost), his end would have been similar to that of Jameson three years before.

Baden-Powell's success in allowing himself to be blockaded in Mafeking was to attract large numbers of Boers to besiege the place. From 13 October, the day he was encircled, until his relief 217 days later, they unwisely committed a powerful force against him – some 8000 for the first five weeks, until Cronje, their commander, moved the larger part southwards to counter the British advance against the Free State, leaving about 2000 to continue the long-drawn-out and often half-hearted siege. Within his twelve-mile perimeter, Baden-Powell mustered less than 1200 men, nearly half of them untrained townsfolk – railwaymen, clerks and store-keepers, armed only with obsolete Martini-Henry single-loaders. Only twice did Baden-Powell attempt an offensive sortie out of his well-designed and constructed defences, and both were repulsed with quite heavy casualties but little loss to the Boers. For weeks at a time only the regular Boer shelling disturbed the peace of the beleaguered garrison, but deadly this could often be; one in six of Baden-Powell's troops and half his officers were either killed or wounded.[23] On the other hand, the scale of the fighting did not match the publicity the siege obtained in the newspapers of Britain and South Africa. Mention has already been made of Baden-Powell's efficient communications with Plumer. In the same way the colourful despatches of the correspondents incarcerated with him sped to Beira and thence to the Cape and London, feeding the public's frenetic interest in the war and their hero-worship of Mafeking's commander. Intent upon maintaining the morale of his garrison, and incidentally furthering his own career, B.P. produced newsworthy copy.

*   *   *

As Plumer's troops rode westwards from Tuli towards the railway line, leaving only a squadron behind to watch the border, the dense and unhealthy lowlands gave way to the breezy, high veldt and brought some relief to the sweltering horses and men. Reaching the railway he entrained his now toughened and battle-wise force and pushed down the line to Gabarones, eighty-seven miles from Mafeking, where he arrived on 13 January, 1900. By then he had taken under his wing the small force which had been operating under Nicholson's orders with the armoured trains, thus increasing his strength to 1000 men, 750 of them combatant troops.

At Crocodile Pools, nine miles south of Gabarones, the station and water supply were in the hands of a party of 400 Boers, recently reinforced from the Mafeking besiegers. Well dug in, they were protected by barbed wire and supported by a 75 mm field gun and three Maxims. Plumer, now in regular touch with Baden-Powell, decided to attack. After making a careful reconnaissance, Major Bird, one of Plumer's regulars who had travelled out with him, on the night of 12 February, led the assault up the steep flanks of the *kopje* on which the Boers were entrenched. It was an utter failure. Control was lost in the dark among the huge boulders and thick bush that covered the *kopje*, and the attackers blundered noisily around. The few who reached the Boer trenches were shot down. Of Bird's 200-strong party, thirty-two were either killed or wounded; the body of one officer, Captain French, was found the next day on the wire, sword in one hand, wire-cutters in the other. For Plumer, as it was to be for many others, this was a radically new form of warfare; an assault on a fortified and wired position, held by determined troops with modern weapons.

De Montmorency had been placed in charge of Plumer's single 12½-pounder gun. He was not an uncritical admirer of Plumer, nor any other senior officer, for that matter. According to his account of this action, he was snubbed when he asked Plumer to elaborate his orders, something, he complained, that happened regularly both to himself and to others.[24] Plumer had taken a dislike to him, de Montmorency speculated, because of an incident when a shell had fallen close to the two of them, causing Plumer to lose his balance and roll down the hillside; as the younger man scrambled down to help his senior, nervous reaction produced from him a roar of laughter, to which Plumer responded with what the writer described as 'an expression of intense hatred'.[25] It could have been that Plumer had other and sounder reasons for disliking de Montmorency who was a small, bumptious, rebellious and conceited individual; nor was he necessarily efficient.[26] Be that as it may, he had little good to say about his commander:

No officers enhanced their reputation during the Boer War so much as Generals French and Plumer. . . . Several of us, who had witnessed Plumer's blunders . . . were surprised at the high position which this officer attained, but doubtless he learned from his mistakes. . . . Plumer suffered from very short eyesight which must be a terrible handicap to a soldier: sometimes for hours he seemed as if he were struck dumb, incapable of issuing an order: he appeared to be awaiting some revelation or inspiration which never came, dreading to make some false move. Although he had neither the geniality, the lovable character, nor the generosity towards his subordinates of General Baden-Powell, he had undoubtedly more of the science and art of war! Plumer had a genius, moreover, for selecting a good man to serve him on his staff and for giving that good man a free hand to work things out to a successful conclusion: but when he lost his man, he was all at sea until he found a fresh one.[27]

That unflattering pen-portrait was tempered by de Montmorency's admiration for Plumer's behaviour under fire, his remarkable coolness and courage.[28] They were to serve together again. After the relief of Mafeking, he was invalided home, but in the summer of 1918 in France, Plumer spotted him at a parade where French decorations were being distributed; putting his arm through that of his old South African comrade, he led him across to the Duke of Connaught to introduce him, a generous action, as the younger man admitted.[29]

Even before that repulse at Crocodile Pools, Plumer had been trying to find a way of circumventing the Boers who were blocking the railway approach to Mafeking. The day before the battle, he had begun to build, with the help of his wagons, a supply base at Kanya, an African village far out to the west, forty miles from the railway and seventy-five from Mafeking. When the Boers discovered what was happening, they started to pull back down the line of the railway, closely followed by Plumer who pushed small columns out to the flanks to attempt to get around them. On 15 March the Boers hit back, forcing Plumer's advanced guard northwards, but this was the signal for him to switch his operations to Kanya, now fully stocked and well defended. Leaving 350 men to hold the railhead at Crocodile Pools, he struck out to Kanya with 560 men and two guns. Four days later he advanced to within 35 miles of Mafeking. Still in close touch with Baden-Powell by means of the native runners who bravely slipped through the Boer lines (since January, Plumer had received ten separate despatches from him), on 23 March he asked permission to move forward into the town, but Baden-Powell's reply, received five days later, assured Plumer that circumstances were in no way critical and did not justify an immediate attack by so small a force. Plumer thereupon decided to take the war right into enemy country and crossed the railway into the Transvaal. In a lightning raid, in which his force covered seventy miles in twenty-six hours without losing a single horse, he did no material damage but drew off further Boer troops from the Mafeking area. It was a ride his men remembered, the burning heat of the day contrasting with the night cold of the high veldt which spread upwards through their bodies from their freezing stirrup irons. Plumer's report of this foray, written in his own legible and authoritative handwriting, lays stress on the health of his troops 'continuing fairly good'.[30]

On his return to his base, Plumer learned that a relief force from the south had reached Vryburg, about 100 miles south of Mafeking. Appreciating that the column would by then be even nearer to its destination, he set off immediately with 350 men to make contact with it and, on the afternoon of 31 March, he once again caught sight of Mafeking's tin roofs. But he had been misled. The information was incorrect. No relief force was in the area. Unmolested by Baden-Powell's garrison, now almost immobile because of losses among the horses, the Boer forces around the town rode out in strength and surrounded him. It was to be a thoroughly unpleasant little action in which Plumer lost forty-nine of his officers and men, killed or wounded, together with seventy-five horses. *The Official History* remarked: 'That it had been extricated without losses still more severe was owing to the masterly handling of the squadrons in successive rearguard positions.'[31] Plumer himself, although wounded in the wrist and arm, put someone else up on his horse and made his way on foot in the blinding heat with the men who had had their horses shot under them. As had happened before in Matabeleland, it was to further increase his standing with his men. For the seriously wounded, it was fortunate that Plumer had established a field hospital with a couple of nursing sisters on the railway line at Gabarones. He was not evacuated there himself, and tended to shoo the doctor off when he made his daily appearance to dress his arm on the grounds that he had something more important to do.[32]

During April Plumer again offered to try to join Baden-Powell in Mafeking, but was rejected for the same reasons as before, and he spent most of the month assisting the non-combatant African population of Mafeking whom Baden-Powell was trying to eject from the town so as to economize on the fast disappearing food stocks. There was still just enough to eat (even a few luxuries had been found to celebrate Christmas) and the Africans helping in the defence of the town could still be fed after a fashion. Some of the non-combatant Africans were, however, close to starvation, and on the night of 4 April one of Plumer's Rhodesian officers, well known to the local tribesmen, crept into the town to help plan the removal of unwanted mouths to Plumer's camp where food for them could be had. Large numbers got through, but some, including women, were intercepted and shot by the Boers. Of one batch of women, nearly all were caught, stripped, flogged and returned to the town.*

---

* Unhappily, inaccurate descriptions have been published of these expulsions of Africans from Mafeking, in which Baden-Powell has been accused of gross inhumanity. Tim Jeal, *Baden-Powell*, 1989, 261-277, puts the record straight.

Plumer also made several attempts to drive herds of cattle through the besieging forces into the town, but the Boers intercepted the cattle and sometimes managed to kill the drovers as well.

At last, on 12 May, after a stultifying six-week wait, used to good effect by Plumer to train his men and weed out the incompetent, a signal arrived with a repetition of the news that a relief column was on its way, confirmed the next day by a native runner who carried a scrap of paper torn from a notebook. On one side was scribbled '11-5-1900. We should be in neighbourhood abt 14th. Look out for us & if you see rockets they will be ours. N. Mahon Col to Lt Col Plumer.' On the other side were the words 'For amount of our supplies read OC IX Lancers. Nos=Naval and Mill x 10. Guns same as boys in Ward family.' The rough-and-ready code, used in the absence of ciphers, would have been incomprehensible to a Boer, or, for that matter, by anyone outside the charmed circle of regular army officers. The commanding officer of the IX Lancers was named 'Little', the Naval and Military Club's address was 94 Piccadilly (94 x 10 — 940). and the Wards had six boys. The last stumped even Plumer, but he made an accurate guess.[33]

Reinforcements had made good Plumer's losses of both men and horses from sickness and battle casualties. From Rhodesia had arrived 200 constables of the British South Africa Police, together with fifty men of the Rhodesia Horse Volunteers. Then, on 14 May, just as he was marching out to meet Colonel Mahon, a 4-gun battery of the Royal Canadian Artillery arrived, accompanied by 100 dismounted men of the 3rd Queensland Mounted Infantry; both units had made the long circuit through Beira and Bulawayo and had been among the first Colonial (as they were then known) units to reach South Africa. So, with 800 effective troops, only 450 of them mounted, Plumer made contact with Mahon early on 15 May eighteen miles west of Mafeking, after marching for twenty-eight miles through the darkness.

The make-up of Mahon's column had been stage-managed with care. Largely composed of South African mounted infantry, many of them Uitlanders from Johannesburg, there was a representative detachment of 100 British infantrymen, drawn equally from English, Irish, Scottish and Welsh regiments, together with the battery of guns. Their march had been arduous – 250 miles in eighteen days, during which they had fought two sharp engagements. Now Mahon, as the senior, took command of Plumer's column, and the next day the two forces started out towards Mafeking, moving parallel with one another. At the same time a 2000-strong commando advanced to intercept them, its commander the formidable Commandant Koos de la Rey, already known as a resourceful leader. Except for a slight British superiority in artillery, the two forces matched one another in numbers, equipment and fighting ability. Mahon, who had anticipated the Boer tactics and kept a strong reserve in hand, thwarted de la Rey's attempt to envelope his flanks. On the left the Boers were in the end to retire, but on the right, to quote the *Times History*, 'Plumer . . . had to fight for every yard of the way towards the town, the enemy in front of him taking up position after position, trying every while to entrap his foremost line.' Casualties were again severe, among them Major Bird, his right-hand man, who had sailed with him from England and was wounded in seven separate places.[34]

Just before dawn on 17 May the exhausted relief force entered the town and the news flashed around the world that Mafeking had been saved. Londoners, depressed by the delay in crushing an enemy who had been so grossly underrated, exploded in a bacchanalia which added the verb 'to maffick' to the English language. Overnight Baden-Powell's status as a national hero was confirmed. The author of the *Times History* had his reservations, suggesting that 'the chorus of approval which greeted the defenders of Mafeking might justly have been diverted in part to the patient worker for its relief'. Plumer's campaign he described as 'certainly the most interesting and instructive of the minor operations carried on during the first year of the war. With a force always at a numerical disadvantage to his opponents, containing no regular troops and very few regular officers, working all the time on the borders of the enemy's country, with miserably inefficient artillery and constant anxiety for supplies, he succeeded by daring, which never exceeded the limits of due precaution, in stopping most effectually any attempt against Rhodesia and in dissipating the energies of the force arrayed against Mafeking.[35] It had been a costly little campaign: of the small party of regular officers who had travelled out in the RMS *Norman*, four were dead, two crippled by wounds and two others had been wounded.

Plumer's qualities had already been noticed. On 10 January the sixty-seven-year-old Field-Marshal Lord Roberts had landed in Cape Town, accompanied by Lord Kitchener as his Chief-of-Staff, to take over charge of the war from the unlucky Buller, who had suffered a succession of serious reverses, Roberts having himself suggested to the Secretary of State for War that the replacement should be made. Only three days after arriving, Roberts had signalled Plumer by way of Beira, 'My warm congratulations to Baden-Powell and yourself on the excellent work you have both been doing. I hope earnestly that he will be able to hold out, and wish we could relieve him, but it is too far to attempt at present.'[36]

At the thanksgiving parade and service held in Mafeking the day after its relief, the ragged appearance of Plumer's travel-worn troops aroused comment. They, in their turn, had something to say. De Montmorency echoed the feelings of a number of his companions when he wrote, 'To me the whole thing was at the time, and has always been, an enigma: what in the world was the use of defending this wretched railway-siding and these tin shanties? To burrow underground on the very first shot being fired in a campaign seemed to me the strangest role ever played by a cavalry leader with a regiment of mounted men.'[37] As we have seen, however, there was another side to the story.

Instead of relieving a starving garrison, Plumer's men had found food enough to last for several weeks on still further reduced scales. Even more aggravating, just two days after they arrived, these battle-weary men were ordered out of the comparative flesh-pots of the town to invade western Transvaal. De Montmorency said it all:

In all my experience of soldiering, I have never known men so sulky, or march with such bad grace as ours that day; after the hard trekking and fighting of the previous few days, the volunteers felt themselves entitled to a rest, more especially as there was a glamour about the relief of Mafeking, which lent colour to the impression that a halting-place had been reached in the even tenor of the operations of war; they resented bitterly being hurried out of the town into the harsher conditions of campaigning on the veld.[38]

★　★　★

Meanwhile, the first, and what might be described as the conventional phase of the war was over. During the long months when Plumer had been all but lost to sight in the wildernesses of Rhodesia and Bechuanaland, the British under Roberts's firm leadership had recovered from their succession of reverses and had advanced into the Boer republics. The long series of defeats which had culminated in Stormberg, Magersfontein and Colenso – the 'Black Week' of December, 1899 – were behind them, although Buller, now relegated to the subordinate command in Natal, had still to meet another major setback at Spion Kop. In each battle the pattern had been similar. For the first time the British infantry had experienced the consequences of attacking determined troops, well-entrenched and armed with modern magazine-rifles. More than once the incredible had occurred: in the face of the withering Boer fire, regular British regiments of the line had broken and run; prisoners-of-war languishing in the Pretoria camps outnumbered the killed by three to one. The largest army Britain had ever sent overseas had suffered a series of reverses at the hands of despised Boer farmers. It had been a national humiliation and one that evoked a wave of rabid anglophobia on the Continent of Europe.

Even by 'Black Week', however, the tide had turned. Since November, in both Natal and the Cape the Boers had been retreating northwards and there had been no indications that they might be moving back to the offensive. On 11 February Roberts began a meticulously prepared advance upon Bloemfontein, the capital of the Free State. Four days later Major-General Sir John French's Cavalry Division raised the siege of Kimberley and Buller relieved Ladysmith in Natal on 24 February. After defeating Cronje at Paardeburg, Roberts's army entered the Free State capital on 13 March; Johannesburg fell on 31 May and Pretoria five days later, after no more than minor fighting which cost the British only 600 casualties. As the Boers started to melt away to their farms, the war seemed to be virtually over.

But the Boers had discovered another form of resistance. During the first week of June, Christaan de Wet, the Commandant General of the Free State forces, cut in three places the Central Railway, the 1000-mile lifeline upon which the British depended; about the same time the Boers captured a large convoy bringing up supplies and made prisoner a body of 500 Yeomanry. These successes put new heart into the Boer leaders, who were about to sue for peace. Here lay their way to continue the struggle. The second phase of the war was about to begin – an implacable guerrilla campaign which was to last for two more years in which parties of Boers varying between twenty and 2000 were to play hide-and-seek with columns of British cavalry and mounted infantry. For almost a couple of years Plumer was to command one of these columns, riding for thousands of miles, striving to corner the elusive enemy.

* * *

Baden-Powell was in command of Plumer's column of resentful Rhodesians and Canadians who rode into the Transvaal after Mafeking's relief, later to be joined by a further force drawn from the town's garrison. For the following three months Plumer quartered the veldt and mountains between the border and the Central Railway, usually reacting to the pin-pricks of the Boers who, under the command of Louis Botha, the Commandant General of the Transvaal, were starting to inflict a succession of minor reverses upon the scattered British forces endeavouring to keep open their supply routes from the south and from Mafeking. Some dozen or so other British columns were busy in this way, some coping with specific Boer threats, some trying to intercept their elusive opponents, and others strengthening the garrisons of threatened towns. It was a foretaste of the future. Fighting against them was a new generation of younger Boer leaders, men who had supplanted their discredited seniors – Botha himself, Christaan de

Wet, Commandant General of the Free State, Koos de la Rey and Jan Smuts.[39]

Baden-Powell, whose reputation among his fellow soldiers did not altogether match his adulation by the British public, relinquished his command on 29 August and left to raise a new police force, Plumer taking his place with the acting rank of brigadier-general. The latter's success in the early months of the war had been recognized with a brevet colonelcy, but he was not among those Baden-Powell recommended for awards after the raising of the siege. It was very strange. Only in November of that year was he appointed Aide de Camp to the Queen and a Companion of the Bath, but the latter award usually arrived with the rations for officers of Plumer's rank – the list contained 207 other names; as for the DSO, the other award which he must have expected, he was missing from the list of 600 or more recipients published on the same date. Nevertheless the civilians at home had again been reminded of his existence. The successive reliefs of the sieges of Ladysmith, Kimberley and Mafeking begot this music-hall jingle:

> The baby's name is Kitchener, Carrington,
> Kekewich, Mafeking, 'Bobs',
> Powell, Majuba,
> Cronje, Plumer,
> Pretoria, Ladysmith Bloggs

This move by Baden-Powell prevented Plumer obtaining a short rest from the rigours of campaigning. In August, Mr Arnold-Foster, a Conservative MP, was sent to South Africa to head a three-man commission which would investigate the possible and eventual settlement of 15,000 discharged soldiers in the country. Roberts had selected Plumer as the third and military member of this commission, a mark of his appreciation of Plumer's understanding of the country, but someone else was to be found to take Plumer's place.[40]

With the move into the Transvaal, Australian and New Zealand units began to replace the Rhodesian and Bechuanaland troopers who had been recruited before the start of the war. Such irregular volunteers of one variety or another, most of them mounted infantry, raised both at home and in the Colonies, were to compose about a quarter of the 250,000-strong British force employed in the latter stages of the war. Most of these men were enlisted on a year's contract, and after a year of discomfort on the veldt they were most reluctant to extend. This produced both instability in units and a shortage of trained and experienced men: by the time an individual had learned his job, he was starting to think about his discharge.

In the aftermath of Empire, it is sometimes hard to comprehend the whole-hearted and enthusiastic support of the young Canadians, New Zealanders and Australians who volunteered to fight in South Africa. For some, of course, it was the attraction of high adventure; for others an escape from boredom. Others could sympathize with the Uitlanders, often men of their own stamp and quite a few themselves Colonials. But for a large number the appeal to aid what was then known as the 'Mother Country' was sufficient, strange though the term may sound to most ears today. It was to happen again, and on a much larger scale, both in 1914 and 1939. There existed a community of spirit among the white races of British stock; at the turn of the century a wandering Englishman would find himself equally at home in any of the white Dominions.

A story current at the time and which then and later evoked much derision was that the War Office asked the Colonies to provide infantry rather than cavalry. It was a misunderstanding which arose from a badly drafted telegram.[41] The intention had been to obtain more mounted infantry, the arm most sorely needed to tackle the Boers on equal terms, the regular cavalry having displayed, as the *Times History* put it, 'the profound conservatism which, as in most regular armies, characterised this arm, debarred it from setting such an example of vigorous originality as was urgently needed for the conduct of the campaign'.[42] Reluctant to reduce the large loads with which they burdened their mounts, they had also, and contrary to expectation, proved to be extremely bad horsemasters under African conditions. Unable to sublimate their traditions of *arme blanche*, they were opposed to fighting dismounted, even though they lacked the skill to shoot from the saddle. Colonial mounted infantry was just what was needed, although other arms were sent as well. Altogether 20,090 Colonials, excluding those recruited from South Africa itself, were to serve in the Boer War, of whom 2328 became casualties.[43]

In his handling of the Australasians and Canadians, Plumer was to display the same sure touch which he had shown before with the Rhodesians. Outwardly there seemed little about this then rather withdrawn and introverted British regular officer to arouse either the respect or the admiration of a bunch of tough and independent young Colonials. Physically he was far from strong and in stature small. In dress he was as pernickety about his appearance on the veldt as he was in barracks or at the races. When he rolled himself up in his blankets at night with his saddle as a pillow, it was said that he donned gloves to help keep his hands in sound order,[44] probably an apocryphal story but an indication of the affectionate regard in which he was held. Nicknames often indicate popularity – usually so –

and, of the many Plumer collected, it was not for nothing that one was 'Dandy Plumer'.*

He was a firm disciplinarian with troops who did not always take kindly to its outward forms and to whom foppish British officers and eyeglasses could be anathema. An Australian Methodist chaplain who served with his column described the troopers 'as rough and unruly a pack as could be got together anywhere in the Empire – all grit perhaps, but so inexperienced and undisciplined as to make it a fine art to manage and get the best out of them'.[45] Plumer avoided unnecessary confrontations. A number of anecdotes illustrate his tactful but firm handling. When a drunken Australian struck him on the chest, Plumer merely instructed those nearby to 'take him away, he doesn't know what he's doing'. Another time, when the column was advancing into the Transvaal, he was riding alongside his Canadian field-battery (later known as 'Plumer's Pets'), when he overtook a Rhodesian bullock-wagon, its load adrift. When he learned that it was grossly overloaded with the kits of 150 men, he ordered half to be dumped. At this an old soldier, an ex-Grenadier, shouted down from above, 'Coloner Plumer, your bloody kit ain't on this bloody wagon'; accepting defeat, Plumer cantered on with the response, 'Do what you damned well like. I only hope you're captured'. Another such tale is of an ex-public schoolboy, up before him on a charge. Plumer, as was his habit, screwed his monocle into his eye and glared at the offender, a corporal. To the dismay of those present, the corporal reached into his pocket and followed suit. 'Sergeant-Major', demanded Plumer, 'does this man always wear an eye-glass.' 'No, sir, not in the dark,' came the reply. 'Go away, get out of it,' ended the episode.[46]

On the other hand, he hit hard when need be, but he delivered his rebukes quietly and never in public to an officer. The tale of his stolen horse bears telling. One morning, his galloper (or ADC) was faced with the unpleasant duty of breaking the news to him that his best pony had disappeared overnight. Plumer immediately made his way to the Australian and New Zealand horse-lines where he quickly detected his erstwhile grey disguised by Condy's fluid into a dirty dun-coloured animal, its tail docked, mane trimmed and identifying hoof-number caked with mud. After reminding the culprit of the fate of horse-thiefs in his own country, he arranged that he would accompany the column for the rest of the day on his flat feet.[47]

---

* Although Plumer was often referred to as small, and appeared so in his photographs, his record of service, compiled in 1896, gives his height as 5'9½". As was the custom, the form was completed in his own handwriting. Was this his true height, or had he added on a bit?

The qualities his troops most admired in him were his outstanding physical courage and the rugged endurance of a man in his mid-forties, old enough to be the father of most of them. There was also his absence of side (what the Americans call 'English') and his sharing of their hardships. The Arabs taught T.E. Lawrence that 'no man could be a leader except he ate the ranks' food, wore their clothes, lived level with them, and yet appeared better in himself'[48], a lesson that Plumer had learned fifteen years earlier. By comparison with most column commanders, his mess was crude: British officers too often in the past took too much comfort from the maxim 'any fool can be uncomfortable'. Above all, perhaps, what his men most liked about him was that meticulous attention to detail and sound judgment that only rarely led to unnecessary loss of life.

During the late August and September of 1900 Plumer's new command operated in the Pretoria area, rounding up the many Boers who had lost the will to fight on, but at the same time taking regular casualties from sniping and occasional shelling from the hard core of 'bitter-enders'. Operating in their own country, often in the neighbourhood of their own farms, food for man and horse was nearby and, when hard pressed, a rifle could be buried and a guerrilla again become a farmer working on his land. The solution adopted by Roberts was to starve them out. Jan Smuts described the consequences: 'Dams everywhere filled with rotting animals. Water undrinkable. Veld covered with slaughtered herds of sheep and goats, cattle and horses. Hungry lambs run bleating around.' [49] As in Matabeleland, Plumer was closely involved in putting this 'scorched earth' policy into effect.[50] Among others, it disgusted de Montmorency, who was at a loss to comprehend why the South African irregulars, who so resembled the Boers, should have carried out the unpleasant task with vindictive hatred.[51] Of Plumer's view we know nothing, but his task could only have revolted him.

The Boer women and children could not be left to starve in such a wilderness, so they were brought together in 'concentration camps' – the official British designation of what were planned as places of refuge, not only from starvation but in some areas from marauding Africans as well. Unfortunately poor administration resulted in disease; in the end some 20,000 people died in these camps, a scandal that shocked liberal opinion everywhere and gave the Boers a propaganda weapon of which they made good use. It was also the case that, until the scale of the deaths became known, the knowledge that their families were safe often encouraged individual Boers to remain in the field so that, in the final stages of the war, Kitchener ordered his column commanders to cease bringing women and children into the camps. Botha echoed the sentiments of many of his countrymen when he said, towards the end of the war, 'One is only too thankful nowadays to know that our wives are under British protection'.[52]

By November Plumer's force was operating east of the Central Railway, around the Delagoa Bay line, the main Boer link with the outer world until blocked in September when their opponents captured Komati Poort on the Portugese border; two weeks earlier, Kruger, a broken man, had passed through to exile in Holland. He died in Switzerland four years later.

As part of a small force in which Plumer commanded the mounted troops, his Australians and New Zealanders took part in what was to be their first pitched battle and the last such engagement of the war, an attack on some Boers entrenched at Rhenoster Kop, about fifteen miles north of the Delagoa Railway. Although both individuals and units came and went, for the rest of the war these Australasians would always be the major element in his command, often a miscellany of small units; in this battle, for instance, his 1200 troopers were drawn from the 1st, and and 3rd Regiments of Australian Bushmen;[53] the New Zealand Mounted Rifles; the Queensland Imperial Bushmen; a Tasmanian unit, the 5th, 29th and 66th Companies of the Imperial Yeomanry (British volunteers raised after 'Black Week'), together with a section of Vickers-Maxim pom-poms.

The attack against the 800 well-entrenched Boers was reminiscent of the earlier British failures, although the scale of the battle was somewhat smaller. In open order, two regular infantry battalions, inadequately covered by artillery fire, assaulted the Boer positions which were concealed among a clutch of bush- and boulder-covered *kopjes*. First the infantry, and then Plumer's mounted troops, were pinned down all day on an open grass plateau under the glaring sun. That night the Boers crept away, their line of withdrawal uncut because three other columns which were to have taken part in the battle failed to arrive in time to close the net. Plumer's losses numbered thirty, of whom six were officers, but the infantry suffered the worst.[54] Plumer had another memory to store away for future use.

It was about this time that a revealing incident occurred. When the term of service of one of Plumer's Australian units was over and the men were, in today's parlance, 'relief-happy', the order came that they should move to assist another column which was in trouble. The protests were loud and mutiny was in the air. A speech to them by a senior general had little effect, but when Plumer paraded them again he merely told them that they would fall in at 7 am and that he would be there and so would they. Nothing more was needed: cheers erupted and that was that.[55]

Rhenoster Kop was fought on 29 November, the date Field-Marshal Roberts returned to England to become Commander-in-Chief in Whitehall. Left in charge to finish off the war was Kitchener, his task seemingly all but complete. But this hard and taciturn man, paradoxically a fine organizer but incapable of delegation or using his staff properly, was quite clear in his own mind that the war was far from over, with large numbers of sturdy guerrillas still to be rounded up. Under Kitchener's command Plumer was to increase his reputation, already established outside Mafeking, as an energetic and capable commander. All the time his name was becoming ever better known at home. Although he never had a war correspondent attached to his column,[56] he was fast becoming a junior member of that band of military leaders to whom, in the absence of professional sportsmen in any number or of pop-stars, the public rendered adulation. His features could now been seen on buttons worn by small boys to depict their current hero; of the twenty-two generals appearing on 'Westward Ho' cigarette cards, Plumer was the most junior. *Vanity Fair* magazine for 29 November, 1900, included a cartoon by Spy entitled 'A Group of Generals' in which the very junior Plumer was shown peeping in from one side as if intruding upon that august gathering.

* * *

The elusive Christiaan de Wet was probably the most able of the Boer commanders remaining in the field, a prototype for guerrilla leaders of the future, although he objected to being described as such. During July and August he had led his Free Staters northwards into the Transvaal and successfully evaded the 29,000 troops deployed to corner him, among them Plumer's column. Returning across the Vaal, he was surprised in his hide-out in November, but escaped and rode south, intending to raid into the Cape Colony. Checked by the flooded and impassable Orange River, he was forced back to his starting point in the north-east of the Free State, still avoiding his pursuers, and there he dispersed his men into small parties to their own home districts.

Five weeks later, on 27 January, 1901, he summoned his burghers for a further attempt on the Cape, his objects to disrupt the British rear areas and rally the Cape Dutch, who, although sympathetic towards their fellow Boers in the two republics, had so far shown a distinct reluctance to join in the fighting. Accompanied by Marthinus Steyn, his President and as irreconcilable as himself, de Wet started south with 2200 men. Kitchener, however, had been forewarned and soon had his columns on de Wet's heels. Making sound use of the railways, a skill of which he was master, Kitchener gathered columns from every part of South Africa to intercept the invaders, among them Plumer's Australians and New Zealanders from the Eastern Transvaal. On 10 February, having eluded his pursuers, de Wet crossed the Orange River, his supplies replenished from a captured train which contained the ammunition, blankets, saddlery, flour and sugar

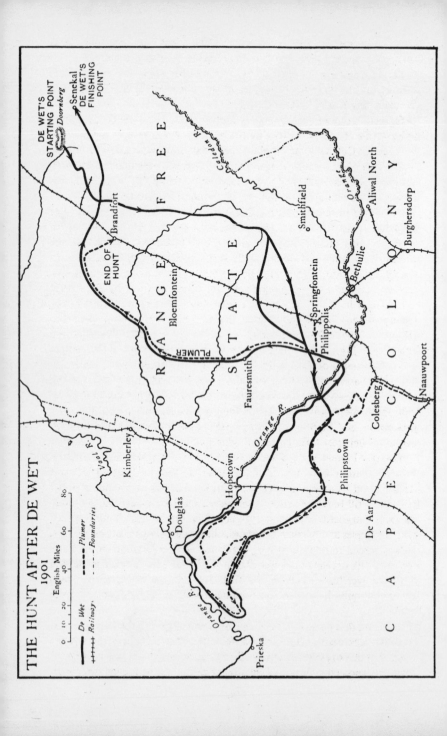

THE HUNT AFTER DE WET
1901

English Miles

De Wet ——— Plumer - - - -
Railway +++++ Boundaries - · - ·

DE WET'S STARTING POINT

Doornberg

Senekal ○ DE WET'S FINISHING POINT

O R A N G E   F R E E   S T A T E

Brandfort

END OF HUNT

Bloemfontein

PLUMER

Fauresmith

Smithfield

Aliwal North

Burghersdorp

Springfontein

Philippolis

Bethulie

Caledon R.

Orange R.

C O L O N Y

Naauwpoort

Colesberg

Kimberley

Vaal R.

Orange R.

Hopetown

Douglas

Philipstown

De Aar

C A P E

Orange R.

Prieska

of which his men were in sore need. The Boer dislike of venturing outside their own republic was such that 800 of his men refused to cross into the Cape, but the chase for the time being slackened when the Orange River rose again, but this time behind them, and the swirling current checked the following British columns.

Plumer's column was among a number poised at Colesberg, twenty miles south of the river, waiting for de Wet. Another was commanded by a certain Colonel Douglas Haig, a cavalry officer who when he left the Staff College had become Brigade Major to French at Aldershot and then accompanied him with the Cavalry Division to South Africa. Now he was adding to his reputation in the role of column commander.

Unleashed in pursuit, Plumer made contact with de Wet the day after the latter crossed the river, and for the subsequent week he clung to the Boers, causing them to abandon their march towards the interior of the Cape Colony and swerve away north-westerly and parallel to the river. In drenching rain the sodden men skirmished across the flooded landscape. In a succession of the delaying actions for which he was famous, de Wet managed to hold off the smaller British force, but on 13 February the capture of 200 broken-down Boer horses indicated that the pace was telling. As the chase continued, the way was marked by derelict and abandoned Boer carts. Nearing the western railway-line on the night of 14 February, de Wet only just managed to get his force across an almost impassable swamp where men, wagons and animals floundered in near hopeless confusion. The following morning forty wagons together with thirty more prisoners fell into Plumer's hands, but the burghers still pressed on, some still astride their spent horses but others now on foot, dragging their feet through the clinging mud.

That day Plumer lost the Boer spoor, but found it again on 16 February. Fifteen columns were now closing in upon de Wet's exhausted and now disheartened band, but Plumer, for a time taking another column under his wing, still bore the brunt of the chase. On 19 February he surprised the Boer rearguard, scattering it in confusion, but he had all but marched both his horses and his men to a standstill. Without either oats or biscuits, he was forced to relinquish the pursuit to another column, but he left a few of his Australians to hang on to de Wet's flank. An advantage de Wet did have over his adversaries was that, arriving first at the farms which lay on his route, he was able to commandeer what animals and feed were available.

Realizing that he now had no hope of penetrating into the Cape, de Wet doubled back eastwards, searching for a passable drift over the swollen river by which to make his escape. By 23 February Plumer was back in the chase and succeeded in overtaking his enemy and capturing his two guns –

dragged so far and with such effort. The troops who pulled off the coup had ridden forty-four miles since dawn. De Wet later wrote, 'It cut me to the heart to give up my guns on that day – the 23rd February – the commemoration day of the Independence of the Orange Free State. . . . My feelings on that day I can never forget!'[57] Two days later Plumer's starving Australians and New Zealanders were again obliged to abandon the chase, and Kitchener, who had assumed personal control of the operation, moved them by rail the 225 miles back to Colesberg, his intention being to place them ahead of de Wet. Shortage of rolling stock delayed the move and the men did not arrive until 27 February, just too late. The following morning, just twenty miles away at Botha's Drift, the burghers managed to cross the river. It was the fifteenth ford they had examined. De Wet described 'the different exclamations of joy, the Psalms and the songs that now rose from the burghers splashing through the water. "Never will we return." "On to the Free State!" "No more of the colony for me." "The Free State." "The Free State for ever!" Then again, "Praise the Lord with cheerful song." "Hurrah!" These were among the expressions which met my ears.'[58]

On 3 March, as de Wet rode for his refuge among the northern hills of his own country, Plumer again took up the hunt, but, although his men covered an average of forty miles each day, he was always a day or so behind his quarry. Eight days later the pursuit was abandoned. Again the Boers had evaporated, dismissed in small parties in the direction of their homes. It was the end of what was to be known as 'The Great de Wet Hunt'. In forty-three days he had ridden 800 miles. Never cornered, he had evaded capture, but he had failed in his object – the raising of the Cape. He had also lost many of his men, all his transport and guns, and, for the time being, much of his prestige.

Plumer's dogged pursuit further enhanced his reputation and won him golden opinions as a bold commander who could not only inspire his troops but drive them as well when need be. As his Australian chaplain recorded, at the time there had been much 'shallow criticism' at his not relieving Mafeking quickly,[59] small though his force was. This is reflected in these sub-Kipling lines:

IN-THE-END PLUMER

You were many days in moving from a spot called Gabarones,
    And some restless little gibes the poets penned,
But the things you had to do, why, you did it, thro' and thro',
    And you got there, little Plumer, in the end;
Yes, you worried thro' and got there, as the bulldog always will,
    And we almost talked about you like a friend,

And as soon as you were sent for to go and smash De Wet,
Why, we knew as it would happen – in the end.

So, Plumer, here's to you, which it is your proper due,
For altho' you seem to potter, why, you always put it thro';
You don't travel by Express,
But you're never in a mess,
Which explains the odes we're singing all along o' little you.

You've a way of keeping quiet so the folks who bide at home
Never buzz about your glory, never send,
To the stationer who sells photographs of all the swells –
Some of whom don't even get there in the end;
But your picture it is hanging in the windows here and there,
Such a smiling, cheeky, boyish face, my friend;
And while such as you are bred, there'll be British Armies led
To victory and glory – in the end.

So, Plumer, here's to you, which it is your proper due,
For, altho' you travel Local, why you always put it thro';
Tho' you seem to puff and fuss,
You do reach the terminus,
Which is why we're gettin' (slowly), little Plumer, fond of you.[60]

During this de Wet chase and afterwards, Plumer was very well served by his Australians and New Zealanders, one unit of which inscribed on the flaps of their turned up 'smasher' hats 'Plumer's Wanderers'. Even though their troopers served in the field for such a short time before obtaining their discharges, the better Colonial units were without doubt a cut above the rest of the Army in South Africa. As even an Australian admitted, best of all were possibly the New Zealanders.[61] Brave and well disciplined when properly led, the ill-nourished products of the British industrial revolution often lacked the initiative needed to fight such a fast-moving war.

Plumer was given no respite. After another but sporadic attempt to find de Wet, his column was moved to Pretoria, where again some of his best units were replaced by newcomers. Then, on 26 March, he rode north with 1300 mounted men along the line of the railway towards Pietersberg, the place that had been so much in his mind when guarding the Rhodesian border eighteen months before. As the *Times History* complained at the time, there was 'a real dearth of aptitude for guerrilla war' among Plumer's fellow column commanders; to make matters worse, their reverses tended to be 'magnified to an excess by public opinion', so producing an even greater reluctance to take risks.[62] Because Plumer was the best man available, he would seem to have been chosen for yet another challenging and arduous assignment.

Pietersburg was the centre of a large and sparsely populated area of the Transvaal, about the size of England, still unpenetrated by British troops. North-west of the Olifants River, which cut the region roughly into two, it was a wilderness of mimosa and dwarf trees, poorly watered and teeming with horse-sickness and malaria. A tangle of wild mountains with fertile and well-watered valleys lay to the east of the river, a healthy country in whose crannies guerrilla bands could shelter, almost safe from detection. Pietersburg itself was the last orthodox base of the Boers, a source of remounts as well as supplies. In the hills some seventy miles to its south-east existed a Boer Government, the driving force for continuing the war and still in touch with European capitals. It was here, during the previous September, that Botha had collected 2000 staunch burghers determined to carry on the struggle to retain their independence.

In a hand-written note on black-edged paper (the old Queen had died in January), Kitchener addressed the Secretary of State for War on 22 March:

> Horse sickness now less and I hope we are getting to the end of it. I propose before long to send an expedition under Plumer to Pietersburg which will cut off Botha's retreat when we push him from Middleburg and Belfast. . . . When can we see the end? It may be another year although I hope the winter will tax them highly.[63]

This was the outline of Kitchener's plan. Then, after Plumer had taken Pietersburg, he was to move his men south to block the drifts across the Olifants, towards which the British columns advancing from the south would drive the Boers as they retreated. That was the intention; its implementation was to be another matter.

Plumer's part was accomplished smoothly and efficiently. Pains had been taken to keep his destination secret and, by 8 April, after a 200-mile march through thick and unhealthy bush, he occupied Pietersburg. Little resistance had been met and only three men had been wounded. A lone sniper, however, a local schoolmaster, was to kill three other Australians, together with five of their horses, just beyond the town, before bravely dying himself. During the journey it had again poured with rain, causing much suffering to the animals in the heavy going, but behind the mounted men moved trains carrying supplies and guarded by three infantry battalions which had augmented Plumer's force, detachments from which were dropped off at intervals to garrison the small Dutch towns along the line.

The night before the Union Jack was raised in the main square 500 Boers left the town for the hills. The forty-nine burghers who remained, together with the women and children, were evacuated down the line to Pretoria, and the flour mills, repair shops and anything else likely to be of value to the Boers in the future were destroyed. As Kitchener was to discover, when later he visited the town, there had also been some looting by the Australasians after their comrades had been killed by the sniper, a matter he considered of sufficient interest to mention to the Secretary of State.[64] The plant of the two local newspapers was also destroyed, but not before some enterprising young officers had produced a final edition, in English, of *De Zoutpansberg Wachter*; it contained a lively account of the rapid capture of the place, and, once again, we find mentioned the 'love and respect' of the troops for their commander.[65]

Leaving some infantry to hold the town, Plumer snatched his mounted men from their comparative comforts on 14 April and rode into the warm, sandy valley of the Olifants River. Here the fords to be blocked proved to be far more numerous than had been supposed and the troops were spread thinly along the seventy-mile stretch Plumer had been given to guard. The day Plumer left Pietersburg, six columns under Lieutenant-General Sir Bindon Blood, a recent arrival from the Indian Army and an expert on the formalised ritual of warfare on the North-Western Frontier, had moved north as planned to drive the Boers on to Plumer. Mustering in all 11,000 rifles, the force was encumbered with too much artillery and too high a proportion of marching infantry. Fighting in the complex labyrinth of hills and valleys they knew so well, the nimble Boers had little difficulty in avoiding their lumbering opponents. As early as 5 April the Boer Government had foreseen the danger and quit its mountain eyrie to escape across the railway to join Botha who had gone ahead. The main body of burghers, after inflicting some delay and losses upon Blood's troops, slipped across the Olifants south of the stretch held by Plumer and followed their Government, even though many of them were by then weary of the struggle and deserting. On 28 April Plumer himself began to withdraw his men, but horse-sickness had already taken such a toll (despite Kitchener's optimism) that when an isolated body of fleeing Boers crossed his path, only 260 mounted men were capable of pursuing them. In all Plumer had managed to intercept and capture only 111 of the enemy.

Almost another year of hard campaigning still lay ahead for Plumer, a year during which he and his Australasians were hardly ever out of the saddle. From the Eastern Transvaal down to the south of the Free

State they roamed, and then back again to the Transvaal, hunting Botha's commando near the Natal border. For much of the time it was merely a question of sweeping up a few prisoners here or a herd of livestock and a few wagons there, losing the odd man from time to time to a sniper or in an ambush. The *Times History* pictured such incidents: 'the cracking of whips and yelling of native drivers; the swarms of nimble Boer horsemen buzzing and stinging, now here, now there; the extended lines of infantry, footsore but undaunted; the flames of a burning farm, perhaps; and overhead the unflecked blue of the sky.'[66] Then afterwards there could be the dead to bury, the carcasses of the oxen and horses left to stink on the veldt, and the wounded to be driven for surgery for agonizing miles in bumping wagons or mule-carts.

In May, 1902, the end came. Harried by overwhelming numbers and with their farms destroyed and flocks destroyed, the Boers had lost the war of attrition, the few thousands still in the field accepting terms of surrender so generous that in the two world wars which were to follow Afrikaner and English-speaking South African units fought alongside other countries of the British Commonwealth. Neither before nor since has the British Army fought a more formidable guerrilla war, one encompassing such vast areas and against so skilled and determined a foe. Although the post-Boer War British Army was to be reorganized upon the lessons it had learned during the early set battles, neither the British nor any other Western army studied the errors committed during the later and guerrilla phase and how such errors might be avoided in the future.

It was perhaps paradoxical that one, and that a false, lesson was learned. Kitchener's system of blockhouses with which he bisected the veldt in an attempt to hamper Boer movements had previously been tried, but without success, by the Spaniards in Cuba in 1898. Many hundred of these oven-like little forts, each manned by a section or so of sweltering and bored soldiers, were built within rifle range of one another and linked by barbed wire fences, sprinkled with mines and alarm guns. Against these lines of fortifications, large bodies of mounted infantry repeatedly attempted to drive their enemy, but although it helped wear the Boers down, few were actually snared and no worthwhile success was ever gained. At the outset of the post-1945 insurrections in Malaya, Kenya and in Cyprus, the British Army used similar methods with different weapons, including air-bombing, but the drives never succeeded. A study of the final two years of the South African War might have obviated much waste of men, material and time.

Plumer's column was broken up in March, 1902, most of his Australians and New Zealanders being due for their discharge. Although by no means rugged, he had survived nearly three years of both physical and mental strain, danger and disease. With his command dissolved and the end of the war in sight, he felt justified in asking for leave. The outcome is described in a letter he wrote home on the sixteenth of the month:

I went to see Lord Kitchener yesterday morning. Before I went in Ian Hamilton [the Chief-of-Staff] told me the Chief was rather doubtful about giving me leave. Lord K. was very nice, as he always is, but you need never flatter yourself that he has any consideration for your feelings or wishes; he simply looks upon you as a pawn in the game and his whole idea is how he is going to make the most use of you. He gravely considered for a very long time, and then said, "Yes, I think on the whole I shall get better value out of you if I let you go now and get you back again, but mind you are to be back the day your three months is up and I shall have a column ready for you." Later he said: "Well, if you see things are going right you may write and ask for an extension of leave, but if they are as they are now you are *not* to ask for it."[69]

Plumer did not return.

4 General Officer

During the voyage home Plumer had much upon which to ponder. Three years earlier he had sailed for Africa as a relatively unknown and youngish officer. He was returning as a household name. The reception he was to receive was quite remarkable. This is one press account:

Colonel Plumer [he must have relinquished his acting rank of brigadier-general when his command broke up] yesterday afternoon reached Southampton on board the transport *City of Vienna*, from South Africa, on three months' leave. The distinguished soldier, who looked remarkably well after three years' absence from England, was met by Mrs. Plumer, and as he left the transport the troops raised three hearty cheers, which were enthusiastically taken up by the crowds on shore. Colonel and Mrs. Plumer travelled home to Farnham by the train reaching there shortly after eight o'clock. The station and its precincts were thronged with people and on the train coming in the crowds cheered loudly. Owing to the wish expressed by Mrs. Plumer, there was no formal reception. On the Colonel entering his carriage, his horses were taken out and he was drawn through the town to his residence amidst great enthusiasm, the streets being lined with people. On reaching his house, Colonel Plumer briefly addressed the crowd, thanking them for this magnificent reception which he said fully compensated him for the hardships he had undergone. The welcome was made more complete by the ringing of the bells in the Parish Church later in the evening.[1]

When he learned that Plumer was in London for a few days, Lord Roberts, now the Commander-in-Chief, invited him and his wife to dinner, writing a brief note in his own hand[2] (in later years a telephone call or letter from an A.D.C. would have sufficed). On 12 May King Edward VII received him, and at an investiture the next day handed him the insignia of Companion of the Bath. Congratulatory letters poured in, including one from his old friend and colleague, Earl Grey, more personal in character than the one written after the Matabele campaign. 'We are all drunk with excitement and Fiz at your success,' he wrote, '& I do congratulate you from the bottom of my heart at the magnificent way you have played the game'.[3] Later, Grey was present at the London offices of the British South Africa Company when Plumer was presented with a splendid sword of honour, subscribed by the Rhodesian people, its hilt of solid Rhodesian gold and its blade and scabbard embellished with the same metal.[4]

Vanity Fair published another and a happy cartoon of him by Spy, in which he looked trim and dapper in civilian clothes and a straw hat. The accompanying eulogy claimed that he was

> a quiet and unassuming fellow . . . one of the very few commanders in the war of whom it may be said that he never made a mistake. His qualities are pluck, judgment, caution and self-reliance, and he deserves all his success, for he has won it wholly off his own bat.[5]

Plumer was well aware how ill-judged this flattery was in part. He had made mistakes in plenty, as every commander does at some time or other. Nothing is more true than Napoleon's reputed adage that the general who makes the fewer mistakes wins the battle. The sadness for a man such as Plumer was the knowledge of the deaths caused by such errors, perhaps of friends with whom he had shared a packet of biscuits the night before. But, as even so harsh a critic as de Montmorency admitted, Plumer, unlike many, learned from his mistakes. Brought home to him by harsh experience had been the consequences of a poorly reconnoitred night-attack over rough ground against a well-entrenched enemy or a daytime assault without enough supporting artillery. Above all, perhaps, he had gained a deep understanding of the vital importance of winning the confidence of his soldiers, of keeping up their morale, of ensuring they knew that he was taking meticulous care to see that their lives were not needlessly thrown away.

* * *

To Kitchener, as long ago as 14 February, 1901, Roberts had written:

> Plumer is a man we must, I think, look after. An ordinary commander would not have hung on as he did outside Mafeking, and since the relief of that place he has done excellent service. Perhaps you would send me a telegram when you receive this to let me know what sort of berth Plumer is best suited. I heard that both Plumer and Byng are coming home, but you have not said anything about it.[6]

And from then on Roberts did proceed to look after him. When writing to his wife from South Africa Plumer had speculated:

> You ask me what I should prefer if I had my choice. Well, it is not much use saying what one would like, but castles in the air don't cost much at any rate, do they, darling? In the first place promotion to major-general would be everything, no matter what anyone says. If I was promoted, a Brigade at Aldershot would be what I should prefer to anything.[7]

A brigade in Aldershot it was to be. While walking in Pall Mall with his wife on 1 June, he read with delight the notice posted outside Marlborough House announcing that peace had been signed.[8] There was now no question of his having to return to South Africa. Soon afterwards he learned that he was to command the 4th Infantry Brigade at Aldershot, and on 1 November, 1902, he was promoted to the rank of major-general.

From being a thirty-nine-year-old major, who had filled but one and that a routine staff job and who had never commanded anything larger than a company, seven years later he was one of the youngest major-generals in the Army. During the last two decades of the century, almost a *sine qua non* for rapid advancement had been membership of one of the two rival 'rings' of influential officers – Wolseley's select band who had worked and fought with him in Africa and Canada, and Roberts's body of able men whom he had gathered about him in Africa. Plumer had belonged to neither, although an entry in the index of his missing War Office Record of Service suggests that on one occasion Wolseley tried, without success, to secure a brigade major's appointment for his brother's friend. Not until the Boer War did Roberts notice Plumer's qualities and start to bring him forward; it could well have been his fellow member of the York and Lancasters, the brilliant Staff College instructor, G.F.R. Henderson, and by then Roberts's Director of Intelligence, who drew his master's attention to this rising young star in his Regiment.

In March, 1903, Plumer travelled from Aldershot to London to give evidence before the Royal Commission of the South African War, otherwise known as the Elgin Committee, after its chairman, Lord Elgin. Among its members was Viscount Esher, that *eminence grise* so aptly described in the *Dictionary of National Biography* as 'possessing all the qualifications for success except the conviction that it was worth while'; among the appointments Esher at one time or another refused were those of Permanent Secretary at both the Colonial and the War Offices, Secretary of State at the latter, Governor of the Cape Colony and Viceroy of India. The Government and the Army were both intent on learning all they could from the myriad errors committed in South

Africa and eradicating the amateurism displayed by both the generals and many of their subordinates in that campaign. As 'Wullie' Robertson, the first cavalry trooper to rise to the rank of Field-Marshal, so shrewdly observed when describing the changes that were to occur in the British Army during the decade prior to the First World War, 'It is perhaps not too much to say that the Empire was saved from destruction by the small community of Boer farmers who, a few years before, had fought against us.'[9]

For a full day Plumer was cross-examined on every aspect of the conduct of the war. His evidence, recorded verbatim, is precise and thoughtful.[10] That same evening, Esher wrote a note to the King, with whom he was on terms of intimate friendship:

> Lord Esher presents his humble duty and begs to inform Your Majesty that General Plumer was examined today, an officer of curious physique but evidently full of intelligence. He commanded a mounted force throughout the war, and although an Infantry soldier, commanding at this moment the 4th Brigade of Infantry at Aldershot, is keenly alive to the necessity of increasing the mobility of your Majesty's army. His experience is most valuable, and his hints upon horsemanship and scouting should prove very useful. He laid special stress upon the importance of having trained regular officers with Colonial and Volunteer troops. Without this assistance, his opinion of such troops is not favourable, which shows once more the importance of increasing the establishment of officers.[11]

In appearance Plumer was hardly the regular officer stereotype. A studio portrait of him in a frock-coat, taken about this time or a little earlier, shows what could have been an up-and-coming partner in a firm of country solicitors, rather than a dashing leader of irregular troops. A greying and voluminous moustache effectively hides the form of his mouth, his air is kindly yet startled; soft yet protuberant eyes look into the distance from under an already receding hairline. For someone who had led a hard and active life, the jaw line is flabby. But this is clearly a man who knows his own mind, not one to be trifled with.

In this letter to the King, possibly in an attempt to strengthen his case for increasing the officer establishment of the Army, Esher had rather overstated Plumer's criticisms of his Colonials. Nevertheless, he had been both surprised and disappointed by the standard of their shooting and horsemastership; he had also found difficulty in persuading them to dig the trenches needed to protect themselves from enemy fire, a common enough British Army failing. It was their independence and self-reliance he most admired, and these qualities were the ones he wanted to see encouraged in the British Regular Army, together with initiative among its officers. The problems of administration and the crying need for a proper General Staff were among the other subjects upon which Plumer had expounded that day.

After less than a year in Aldershot, Plumer received another letter from Roberts telling him that he intended to appoint him to command a district, and asking him whether he preferred Dover or Colchester. As neither he nor his wife liked Dover, he chose Colchester and there they moved just before Christmas, 1903. It was a sad time for them both. His mother, by then widowed, had been living in Tenby with his brother, Frederick, now in the Coastguard Service, and his sister Beatrice; she had died in November, and his wife's mother, with whom they had spent Christmas at 5 Devonshire Place, always their second home, contracted pneumonia and died also in January of 1904.[12]

Barely had they unpacked in Colchester than Plumer heard that they were to move yet again. The news impelled him to write to Roberts on 10 February:

> I feel sure that I owe my nomination to the new Army Council to your kind recommendation and I write to express my gratitude to you.
> The duties are very responsible and I feel very diffident of my ability to perform them properly.
> I can only say that I will do my best to deserve your recommendation.[13]

His supposition had been correct. Two days later there arrived the Commander-in-Chief's reply:

> I felt some compunction in recommending you for the place on the Army Council as I thought it would be inconvenient to make another move so soon after you have settled in Colchester, but it seemed to me desirable you should be known as an Administrator as well as a fighting soldier.
> I trust you will like your work and that I have not incurred Mrs Plumer's displeasure in getting you ordered to London.[14]

Soon after they arrived in London they bought a forty-four-year lease on 22 Ennismore Gardens, a towering seven-storey house at the then rather less fashionable end of Knightsbridge. It was to be their first and their last proper home.

★ ★ ★

Since 1890, British governments had toyed with creating a General Staff on the lines of those of the major European powers, but it needed the Boer War to provide the catalyst. At the end of Elgin's voluminous and critical, but yet rather negative report, published in the summer of 1903, had been a memorandum from Esher recommending that the War Office should be reshaped, with the office of Commander-in-Chief replaced by a Board, similar to that of the Admiralty. Then, Esher, refusing the offer of the Cabinet post of Secretary of State for War, made by Mr A.J. Balfour, the Conservative Prime Minister, instead volunteered to chair another committee, the primary task of which would be to reorganize the War Office. The size decided upon was ideal, Esher and two others, one of whom was Admiral Sir 'Jackie' Fisher, later the driving force in the creation of the new force of 'Dreadnought' battleships. The committee began work in December, 1903; the first of its three reports appeared in January and the last in March, surely a record in the annals of government and a tribute to the committee's modest size. The first of these reports dealt with the machinery of the War Office and the institution of the Committee of Imperial Defence (C.I.D.); the second covered the setting up of a General Staff to plan for war and advise the Government. In an unprecedented way, Esher and his colleagues had been empowered to put their recommendations into effect. Speed was the result, but, as Repington wrote, 'The change was made with scant courtesy and consideration. Lord Roberts, with his chief colleagues, was bundled out of the War Office most unceremoniously.'[15]

Plumer may have thought that Roberts was responsible for his appointment to the new Army Council, and the latter may even have thought that this was so, but the ebullient 'Jackie' Fisher had much to do with it. His letter to Esher, dated 17 January, 1904 read:

Also I still maintain that Smith-Dorrien and Plumer should be the 2nd and 3rd Military Members. . . . Haig, Inspector-General of Cavalry in India, should be brought home as the principal Director. . . . We must have youth and enthusiasm because it is only by the agency of young and enthusiastic believers . . . that our scheme can bear fruit. The first thing of all is that every one of the "old Gang" must be cleared out. The next thing is that everyone of the new men *must be successful men*.

Enclosed with this letter was a note further elaborating upon Plumer's virtues:

3rd Military Member. Supplies & transport: – General Plumer. The only man besides French that *never failed in anything he undertook in*

Africa: They say he has the "luck of the Devil", but the fact is that "the luck of the Devil" is wholly attributable to a minute attention to anything that will ensure the success of his (Satanic Majesty's) designs, and he will leave nothing to chance! Such is Plumer! He is also young, energetic and enthusiastic. "Vote for Plumer and a full belly!" "Every vote against Plumer is a vote given for paper boots and no ammunition!"[16]

To have so impressed Fisher was something of a feat.

The groundwork of the War Office's reorganization had been completed, but as yet there was lacking a proper impetus to get things moving. Balfour was not especially interested in the details of the Army's problems. His Secretary of State Mr. H.O. Arnold-Forster, with whom Plumer had been due to work in South Africa, was preoccupied, to the cost of nearly everything else, with a single subject, of which more later. As for the new Army Council, it suffered from the defects of an ineffective Chief of the General Staff, Lieutenant-General Sir Neville Lyttelton, and the lowly rank of its other three military members, all, like Plumer, mere major-generals and so short on authority. The welcome the new organization received from the press was, in places, muted. *The Spectator* condescended:

> The Military Lords – we trust that the Council, following the analogy of the Admiralty, will collectively be known as "My Lords" . . . form, in all probability, as good a selection as it was in the power of the Government to make. It was important not to take the ablest soldiers away from the field commands, and a class of soldier-administrator has yet to be created. As it stands, all four have done distinguished service in war, and to the public they are known as leaders in the field rather than chiefs of departments.

In touching on the characteristics of the four, the writer was most enthusiastic about Plumer: 'emphatically the soldier's soldier, one of the half-dozen living Generals whom the Army unites in praising. We are convinced that his alert mind and strenuous character will be as valuable at the War Office as on the Veld.'[17]

The Army Council's first meeting took place on 15 February, the tasks it set itself myriad and diffuse, ranging from the organization of a General Staff to such matters as the attachment of Japanese officers and the minimum chest measurement for militia recruits.[18] Plumer himself was perforce to be overly involved in such trifles as the details of uniforms, especially those of the Yeomanry, which produced lengthy exchanges with the Palace;[19] even more than most monarchs, the King's abiding passion was military dress. A more important and controversial matter was the proposal by Kitchener, by then Commander-in-Chief in India, to establish a Staff College there on the lines of Camberley. The Prime Minister, supported by every member of the Army Council, bar one, opposed Kitchener on several grounds, the main one being the danger of fostering rival schools of thought. Among its more vigorous adversaries was Plumer, but it was all to no purpose. With the support of Lord Curzon, the Viceroy, Kitchener won and Quetta was in due course established.[20]

By December criticism was spreading about the little the Army Council was accomplishing. To quote again from *The Spectator*:

> We trusted that the Esher scheme would be so worked and administered that the Army would in future be controlled by a body almost exactly analogous to the Board of the Admiralty. Instead of that, it is to be feared that we have obtained nothing but the old War Office *plus* an Aulic Council of bewildered, if well-meaning, Major-Generals.
>
> These transient and embarrassed phantoms occasionally emit a wail of despair from their water-tight compartments but of a united and coherent control over the Army such as the Board of Admiralty administers there is no sign.[21]

The criticism was, in essence, true, but it was hardly the fault of the major-generals. They lacked direction and rank. A change of government was needed to provide a fresh urgency and in December, 1905, this came about with the Liberals taking office.

Mention has been made of Arnold-Forster's plans for the Army. An enthusiastic proponent of military reform throughout his political career, he was a steadfast critic of the Cardwell system of linked battalions, the one at home finding drafts for the one overseas. While it worked in peacetime, in war it had been found wanting, especially in South Africa. Arnold-Forster's proposals for correcting this were far reaching, the division of the Army into two separate categories. India and the Colonies would be garrisoned by men enlisted on long engagements and these would also provide a small but highly trained force ready to act as a reinforcement; these long-service units would be complemented by a home force of very short engagement men (fifteen months only for the infantry) which would produce a large reserve army if the country were to be drawn into a major war. The scheme managed to arouse antagonism in the Cabinet as well as in the War Office; the arguments were that it would upset the basis of regimental life, and, in any case, troops could never be trained in little more than a year. What made it worse was Arnold-Forster's tendency to attempt to push things through in a tactless and impatient manner. Among the members of the Army Council Plumer alone was persuaded of the merits of the scheme and he gave Arnold-Forster his full support. The two men and their families were close friends, the mutual confidence that existed between them finding expression in a letter Arnold-Forster wrote to Plumer in January, 1905:

> I believe in my heart that my military colleagues are wrong in their view that doing nothing is the best policy for the Army. If they would only look ahead, I am confident they would see that changes and great changes must come.[22]

A further letter written four months later indicates the backing the Secretary of State was receiving from his Quartermaster-General:

> While it is a pleasure for me to find that we are in agreement, it is also a great satisfaction to receive a document written in such perfectly clear and concise terms as your memorandum.[23]

With the change of government, Arnold-Forster's far-reaching concept foundered. R.B. Haldane replaced him at the War Office. The new minister's qualities were by no means overstated in his *Times* obituary:

> one of the most powerful, subtle, and encyclopaedic intellects ever devoted to the public service of this country. He was a lawyer whose profound learning broadened instead of narrowing his sympathies, a philosopher of distinction, an apostle of education, and an administrator of equal courage and efficiency. The work for which as Secretary of State for War he was chiefly responsible is among the most important in the history of the War Office.[24]

He came to his task unburdened with preconceived ideas and with little detailed knowledge of the Army. But he was willing to learn. At his first meeting with the Army Council, on being asked whether he would give a general idea of the reforms he was contemplating, he replied that he was a young and blushing virgin united to a bronzed warrior and that no result of the union could be expected for nine months. There have been a number of variations of the ancedote, which, when repeated to the King, is said to have appealed to his robust sense of humour.

When he assumed office, Haldane made but one change among the

Military Members of the Army Council. He removed Plumer from his post of Quartermaster General, replacing him by Lieutenant-General Sir William Nicholson, described by Haldane as 'one of the cleverest men I ever came across'[25] and earmarked by him to succeed Lyttelton, which he did in 1908. Even the essence of the full story was not known until Harington's biography of Plumer was published in 1935. Harington's informant was Leo Amery, influential journalist and statesman, who was after the Boer War deeply involved in Army Reform and who claimed that Plumer was 'the one senior officer at the War Office who was enlightened enough to appreciate and support Mr Arnold-Forster's scheme for Army reorganization'.[26] It was believed then,[27] and this belief lingered on until after Plumer's death,[28] that he had resigned rather than support a change of policy with which he did not agree. This he never contradicted; neither did he discuss the matter in public, nor, so far as is known, in private either. His dismissal shattered him, as it did his wife, who was prostrated.[29]

Plumer had lost his job because his support for and loyalty to his Secretary of State had isolated him from the other members of the Army Council.[30] As his diary reveals, Arnold-Forster was horrified by what had happened:

I heard today to my infinite sorrow and disgust that Haldane had dismissed Plumer, and dismissed him too in a most wounding fashion, without any apparent reason, without any reward for services rendered, any hopes of early employment, in fact much as he might have discharged a drunken workman. It is too bad.[31]

Arnold-Forster did not let the matter rest. When he visited Haldane the following day, Plumer's treatment was the first subject on the list for discussion. The outgoing Secretary of State recorded:

He told me that it had grieved him to part with Plumer, but that he wanted more brains in the Council. This is all very well, but if he had wanted to get rid of empty heads, there were two on the Council which simply rattled [he was certainly referring to Lyttelton, the CIGS, and Wolfe-Murray, the Master-General of the Ordnance]. As I learned later, the real mischief was that the other Military Members, inspired I have not the slightest doubt by Esher, came separately to Haldane and in turn denounced their gallant and loyal little comrade. Haldane declared he would give him early employment, asked me what I suggested and spoke of a third Division in Aldershot for him.[32]

That Plumer's competence had been attacked is confirmed by the letter that Haldane wrote to his mother (always his confidant in such matters) saying, 'I have been having the disagreeable task of getting rid of incompetent persons of high standing. However, this has been done & I have this afternoon sent a red box to the King telling him of my arrangements'.[33] Who then had been responsible? Esher could have been behind it but no evidence has come to light to confirm that he had, on closer acquaintance with Plumer, changed his mind about his abilities. Perhaps all three military members of the Army Council did 'in turn denounce' him because of his support for Arnold-Forster's policies for army reform, but, of them, the finger certainly points at Sir Charles Douglas, then the Adjutant-General. 'Tim' Harington, Plumer's close friend and Chief-of-Staff on the Western Front, in a letter to Sir James Edmonds, the Official Historian of the First World War, is explicit on the subject: 'I think the only real enemy he had was Douglas who was jealous of him and got him off the Army Council'.[34] Although Douglas was seven years older and that more senior than Plumer, their careers were to run in parallel for a long time. Douglas had been Deputy-Assistant Adjutant and Quartermaster-General of the Suakin Force when Plumer had been adjutant of his battalion; disgraceful as had been the administrative arrangements, adjutant and staff officer could well have clashed on the subject. At Aldershot in 1897 and 1898 they had been fellow staff officers at Aldershot, first on the same level and then with Douglas as Plumer's superior when he was promoted to be Assistant Adjutant-General. There is a suggestion that there could have been some sort of trouble about a married quarter at the time.[35] Both were column commanders in South Africa and both divisional commanders together afterwards in England despite the disparity in age. Then they both moved to the Army Council A sound administrator, but a man of little breadth of vision, Douglas was to work himself to death in October, 1914, as CIGS, an appointment which was beyond his capabilities.

There may, of course, have been others whom Haldane consulted when he first took office. Among them was Colonel Aylmer Haldane, the politician's cousin, who had acted as Nicholson's personal staff officer and was to be a member of the small circle of brilliant younger men from whom Haldane sought advice.[36]

Only two weeks before all this happened, Arnold-Forster had written to Lord Knollys, King Edward's Private Secretary, recommending Plumer in the strongest possible terms for a KCB:

General Plumer is the one member of the newly formed Army Council who has received neither title, promotion nor remuneration . . . General Plumer has asked for nothing, has received nothing, but has deserved much. He has been perfectly loyal, has made no speeches, has discussed the work of the Office inside the Office alone, has laboured steadily and successfully at the work of his Department, and whenever he leaves the Council will be able to look back upon a record of work of which he may be proud and of which the Army will be grateful.

I need not remind you of the service General Plumer rendered during the War; how for months he stuck to his post without support or reinforcements, how he bore hardship and induced others to bear it; how he succeeded where others failed, and how he maintained throughout a modesty of demeanour which has won for him the respect of all soldiers.[37]

The references to speeches and discussions of the work of the War Office were barbed. Arnold-Forster had suffered much from loose talk by his military colleagues on the Army Council, who had, in Amery's words 'freely intrigued' against him.[38]

The reply from the Palace to the Secretary of State's letter was that the King objected to awards and promotions merely because the recipients were members of the Army Council, but that he would certainly not forget Plumer, and that he deserved the award for the work he had done before joining the Army Council.[39]

So it was that Plumer received his KCB when he departed, but this was small compensation for what appeared to be the end of a burgeoning career. With a large house, a son who had just entered Eton, and two daughters at school in Paris, severe financial hardship threatened the couple. Although Lady Plumer had some money of her own, they were largely dependent upon his Army Council salary of £2000 a year. This was now reduced to less than a quarter of that sum, the half pay of a major-general. Long afterwards his wife complained that she had to give her servants a month's notice, but that her husband received less than a week's.[40]

* * *

However, in April, 1906, Plumer was given the 5th Division in Ireland, his headquarters at the Curragh. It was not altogether a military backwater. In due course his formation was to form part of Haldane's planned expeditionary force, and Plumer worked hard to raise it to a high standard of fighting efficiency. Some of his ideas were well ahead of his time, aimed at developing initiative and resource in all ranks. He sent small columns out into the Wicklow mountains, sometimes of infantry alone and sometimes of all arms, to practice guerrilla-type warfare in which they maintained themselves by buying their supplies locally. It was far removed from training as carried out at Aldershot. His close friend, the future General Sir Charles Fergusson and one of his corps commanders in France, recorded these revolutionary training methods; a staff officer at command headquarters at the time, Fergusson remembered being warned to be careful and diplomatic in his dealings with the rather prickly G.O.C. of 5th Division; approaching him with some trepidation, he received from Plumer nothing but extreme courtesy and kindliness.[41]

At the time Ireland was trouble-free and Plumer hunted with the Kildare and rarely missed a race meeting at Leopardstown, the Curragh or Phoenix Park, Dublin. When the Army Commander and his wife were away for the whole of the winter of 1906, the Plumers represented them. Dublin was the centre of a glittering social life, enjoyed by Lady Plumer and probably by her husband as well, who was becoming known as a convivial person. She seems to have been more interested in the social whirl than her children. Long afterwards, Lieutenant Colonel R.E. Key, who had been Plumer's A.D.C. at the time, recounted how the young Thomas Plumer was almost totally ignored by his mother and left to him to entertain during the school holidays.[42] By all accounts, a delightful boy and a keen cricketer, in 1908 Thomas was to move on from Eton to the Royal Agricultural College at Cirencester.

Although Lady Plumer possessed great charm of manner, she was a formidable woman, a power to be reckoned with, utterly devoted to her husband and to furthering his career. The words of the obituary notice in the Parish Magazine of the church where she last worshipped appear to have been chosen with care: 'As a hostess, competent, alert, gracious, shrewd in her estimate of persons and affairs . . .'[43]. In domestic matters, including her children's upbringing, she ruled, but in his professional life Plumer would stand no direct interference. It might have been a sound division of responsibilities if she had been more interested in their children, but all her affection was concentrated upon her husband. Her grandchildren remember meeting her only formally when they were conducted by their mothers to lunch or tea at Ennismore Gardens. Remote and awe-inspiring, she monopolized the conversation, terrifying both the children and their mothers. In contrast, those who remember their grandfather have recollections of the fun and kindness that radiated from him.[44]

Promoted to lieutenant-general in 1908, Plumer's appointment as divisional commander ended the following year. It was London on half-pay once again, but a longer stint this time. For an active man of fifty-two it was a stultifying period, relieved only by the occasional summons to tasks such as commanding one of the opposing sides during the 1910 autumn manoeuvres, in which Robertson was nominated as his Chief-of-Staff, but prevented from so acting through being appointed Commandant at the Staff College.[45] Close involvement with the new Boy Scout movement, founded by his old colleague, Baden-Powell, helped fill the days;[46] as Commissioner for London he threw himself into the work. Then in the summer of 1911, when he was debating whether to accept an appointment offered to him in civilian life, he was asked to take Northern Command at York. His inclination was to retire, but his wife persuaded him to write to Lord Roberts for advice. The perspicacious reply decided him:

18 August 1911.

Dear Plumer,

I find it difficult to answer the question you put to me in your letter of yesterday. The Northern Command is not a very exciting one to the practical soldier, but it is socially a pleasant one, and it keeps you on the active list for seven years longer; if you decided to accept the offer of the Command you would then be not much past sixty-two, and in those seven years no one can foretell what may happen. There is trouble in the air, trouble which seems to be likely to increase rather than lessen, and if war should break out during that time you would bitterly regret having left the Army. I can understand your being disappointed at men younger and junior to you being preferred before you, and the offer of a permanent salary of £500 a year is tempting.

It is, as I have said, difficult to advise, but I feel if I were in the same quandary I would accept the Command and trust to its leading to something better.

I shall be at home all week, if you would like to come and have lunch at 1.30.

With kind regards to Lady Plumer,
Believe me,
Yours very sincerely,
ROBERTS.[47]

He accepted.

For the next three years life was certainly not exciting. Among the more pleasant chores with which he coped was the inspection of the Yeomanry at their annual camps, and on one such visit he received a tribute from an unlikely quarter. Osbert Sitwell, then a Yeomanry subaltern, was enjoying the rural surroundings, the cheerful company and the happy open-air exercise. He possessed, as he admitted, by temperament and through his experience, so far as it went, a profound contempt for the generals of that epoch:

. . . and so, when one day we officers were assembled in a large tent to hear a cavalry commander [he got that point wrong] of the

99

most pronounced and stylised type, with thin legs, an eye-glass and a retrogressive chin, deliver a lecture on modern warfare, I at once went to sleep. . . . However, my inner ear must have been alert and must have decided that I ought to attend to what the General was telling us, for, to my own intense surprise, I suddenly found myself wide awake and listening with absorption to the only military lecture of real interest at which I have ever been privileged to be present. Here, nobody could fail to realise, was an original and resourceful mind at work; this singular little man must be a great soldier.[48]

* * *

For more than a decade the probability of war with Germany had been apparent, not just to the able band of soldiers, Plumer among them, which the Boer War had brought to the front, but to most thinking people in the country. Nonetheless, its outbreak at the height of the 1914 August Bank Holiday revels came as a surprise. Cricket, the problems with Ulster and Home Rule, and the activities of the suffragettes, fighting for women's votes, had been catching the headlines rather than the politics of squabbling Continentals.

The German Reich was the product of three successive wars of conquest, first against Denmark, then the Austro-Hungarian Empire and finally Napoleon III's Third Empire. Delusions of world supremacy were now impelling Germany towards yet another war, and the alliance between Russia and France dictated the strategy by which she intended to fight, a lightning blow against France, combined with a holding operation against Russia; with the former beaten, forces could then be switched eastwards to crush Russia at leisure. Britain, conscious of her isolation, fears exacerbated by the widespread unpopularity evoked by her recent war in South Africa and by Germany's challenge to her naval hegemony, vital to her own and her Empire's security, had sought France's friendship, a move which resulted in the *entente cordiale* but no formal treaty of mutual assistance. Staff talks for the move to France of the six infantry and one cavalry division Expeditionary Force, created by Haldane and Haig, had, however, been held between the General Staffs of the two countries.

The sparks that lit the timber were the shots fired on 28 June, 1914, by the Slav student which killed the Archduke Franz Ferdinand of Austria-Hungary and his wife during their state visit to Sarajevo, the capital of the newly acquired Bosnia. Austrian threats to Serbia, where Slav revolutionaries found refuge and help, precipitated the successive mobilization of the forces first of Austria-Hungary, next of Russia, fearful for her interests in the Balkans, then of Germany, Austria's ally, and then of France. On 28

July Austria declared war on Serbia, and Germany on Russia on 1 August. The next day German troops advanced into Russian Poland and France, and on 3 August Germany and France formally declared war upon one another.

The British Cabinet wavered, but not for long. The plan named after General von Schleiffen for the German assault upon France stipulated a strong right wing and the passage of troops through Belgium. On 2 August the Belgians rejected a German ultimatum and on 4 August the invasion began. It was the action needed to harden British opinion. No British government could accept a hostile presence in the Low Countries. At 11 am that same day Mr Herbert Asquith's Liberal Cabinet declared war.

Britain was far from unprepared. On 18 July King George V had reviewed his fleet at Spithead, the most powerful on the seas, 260 ships, including fifty-nine battleships, drawn up in lines forty miles long. Instead of dispersing after the tactical exercises, Winston Churchill, the young First Lord of the Admiralty, moved the squadrons to their bases in the North Sea, facing Germany. The Army's Expeditionary Force earmarked for France was small in size but fine in quality, the only regular army in Europe. Its soldiers were accurate shots, trained in night operations and concealment, and it was the one army in which most of the senior officers and N.C.O.s possessed first-hand experience of fighting a well-armed, civilized enemy. Its main defect lay in its shortage of trained staff officers, few of whom, or the generals they served, had gained much practice in manoeuvring large bodies of troops. Nevertheless, the two British corps commanders, Sir James Grierson and Sir Douglas Haig, were probably the equal of any of their opponents or allies, the transport and administrative services were soundly organized, and the carefully planned move to France was performed smoothly. Divided into three brigades, each of four battalions, the strength of an infantry division was 18,073, slightly larger than those of the Germans and French; as in both those armies, each of the battalions possessed two machine guns. Despite a grim rearguard action by its more conservative members, the cavalry was well trained in skirmishing and mounted infantry work, unlike its Continental counterparts, from which the obsession with the *arme blanche* had still to be eliminated and which were still equipped with the appurtenances of the Napoleonic Wars, cuirasses and bright clothing included.

Although the first British troops landed in France on 14 August, two of the six divisions were retained temporarily in Britain on the advice of Lord Kitchener, whom Asquith had appointed Secretary of State for War at the outbreak. This was a blow to Sir John French, the Commander-in-Chief, as was Griersons's death of a heart attack just after he had landed. Grierson had previously served as military attaché in Berlin, where he had gained an unrivalled knowledge of the German Army. His death, French noted in his diary, was 'a sad loss for us all'.[49] Immediately he wired to Kitchener, 'I recommend that Lieutenant-General Plumer may be appointed to fill vacancy caused by unfortunate death of General Grierson,'[50] but the telegram crossed with one from Kitchener appointing General Sir Horace Smith-Dorrien, the commander at Aldershot, as the replacement.[51] At the same time, another telegram arrived from French's old friend, General Sir Ian Hamilton, asking to be recommended for the job, but in an affectionate reply French told him that he was too senior and that instead he might take his place in France if anything were to happen to him.[52] (The Gallipoli disaster was to be Hamilton's destiny.) Plumer, with whom he had been associated ever since the Boer War, was the man French wanted: his letter of protest to Kitchener, dated 18 August, was impassioned:

I had already wired asking you to appoint *Plumer* in his place, when your wire reached here and also that of Ian Hamilton forwarded – as I understand – by you.
I very much hope that you will send me Plumer – Hamilton is too senior to command an Army Corps and is already engaged on an important command at home. *Plumer.* Do as I ask you in this matter. I needn't assure you there was no "pressure" of any kind.[53]

Dictatorial and arrogant though he was, it was strange that Kitchener lacked the good sense to consult French before he forced Smith-Dorrien upon him. Despite Smith-Dorrien's great ability, he was, in the circumstances, an unhappy choice. French's dislike of him was common knowledge. In fact, when Kitchener warned Smith-Dorrien on 18 August at the War Office that he was being sent to France, he told him also that Sir Charles Douglas, who had succeeded French in April as CIGS, had just cautioned him that Smith-Dorrien was being put in an impossible position, as French had, for some years shown great jealousy of and personal animus towards him.[54] This jealousy was at the root of French's antipathy. When Smith-Dorrien replaced French at the Aldershot Command in 1907, the latter having left to be Inspector General of the Forces, he instituted a series of reforms which French took as a reflection on his own housekeeping: Smith-Dorrien's insistence that the Aldershot cavalry should learn to fight on foot and to shoot straight, coming from any infantry officer, seems to have caused French especial annoyance.[55]

Kitchener's preference for Smith-Dorrien was soundly based. The latter had served under him both at Omdurman in 1898 and on his staff. He knew him well. A year younger than Plumer, Smith-Dorrien's experience in small colonial wars had been more extensive, and he had commanded a division during the Boer War. Moreover, when Plumer had been side-tracked to comfortable yet not too demanding jobs in Ireland and at York, Smith-Dorrien had been at the centre of things, commanding in Aldershot and on Salisbury Plain.*

Smith-Dorrien was to render French effective service in France, despite being hampered by knowing that he was both disliked and distrusted. A petty-minded man, French had been an unhappy choice for Commander-in-Chief. A note Roberts wrote on him for the Secretary of State is revealing:

> I think he has improved immensely during the past few months, and although he has the greatest defect in a Cavalry Commander of not understanding how to take care of his horses, he is the only man except Birdwood whom I would trust to use a body of Cavalry with dash and intelligence. He is a man of iron nerves who has learned how to cope with Boer tactics.[56]

French was hardly a deep military thinker, nor had he attended the Staff College, but his approach to his duties had, on the whole, been professional. His reforms at Aldershot, then as Inspector General and afterwards as CIGS had been sound, if not especially imaginative. But for command in modern war he was unfit intellectually, psychologically and physically – at sixty-two he had recently suffered a serious heart attack.

So the disappointed Plumer was obliged to brook his impatience at York, but there was work enough to do. With the notable exception of Haig, among the soldiers and politicians only Kitchener and Robertson had foreseen a long war. As a result Kitchener immediately set about improvising a vast mass army. Knowing little and caring less about Haldane's Territorial Force of fourteen infantry divisions and cavalry brigades, he ignored their full potential for expansion through their County Associations. By the end of 1914 more than a million volunteers had responded to 'Your Country Needs You', backed by that legendary poster of Kitchener's piercing eyes and pointed finger. But, unhappily the weapons, uniforms, tents and equipment for a force of this size did not exist, nor the officers and NCOs properly to train it, French having refused to relinquish men from his regular units for the purpose. Of trained staff officers there were none, the Camberley output having proved inadequate even for the regular field formations and the War Office. Fortunately there

---

*Sir Charles Douglas was, of course, CIGS. Kitchener, at the War Office often made decisions without consulting Army Council members, but, so soon after arriving, he could well have taken advice from 'Plumer's only enemy'.

was no lack of enthusiasm or intelligence among the volunteers themselves, but Plumer in Northern Command had to produce order from a sometimes chaotic rabble, as well as superintending the mobilization and training of the local Territorial divisions. He had also to organize the few troops who were available for the defence of the North-East coast; invasion was an unlikely contingency, but the bombardment of Scarborough, Whitby and the Hartlepools by the German fleet in December, 1914, resulting in over 500 civilian casualties, rang the alarm bells.

Meanwhile, in France and Belgium the Regular Army that Plumer knew was nearing destruction. The original four divisions, rising after a few weeks to seven, had by the year's end suffered 89,000 casualties. Although its numbers were derisory by comparison with the eighty or so divisions deployed by the French and the seventy-two by the Germans on the Western Front, this small British Army played a vital role during the opening battles of the war. After first concentrating on the left flank of the French, it was pushed forward to Mons, from where it was obliged to retreat under threat of German encirclement. Casualties during this with-drawal numbered 15,000 but the French during August lost 210,000 men in their offensives in the south, the so-called Battles of the Frontiers. Their doctrine of *offensive à outrance*, their blue-coated and red-trousered *poilus* in their solid ranks clear targets for the German musketry, resulted in defeat and the loss of ten per cent of the ever-courageous French officer corps. By comparison, the well-concealed but outnumbered British professionals (who had taken to heart the lessons learned in the Boer War), fighting their way back from Mons, proved themselves the superior in nearly every respect of their German opponents. Their accurate and rapid rifle fire, mistaken for machine guns, cut swathes in the massed columns in which the Germans, like the French, at that time advanced to the attack, an often forgotten measure of the crudity of their tactical doctrines.

It was providential for the Allies that Moltke, the German Chief of the General Staff, lacked the moral courage to implement the so-called Schlieffen Plan in its entirety. Nervous of his southern left flank, he weakened the northern forces which should have carried out the main hook through Belgium towards Paris. Moreover, during the crisis of the August fighting on the Eastern Front, he permitted two army corps to be diverted from the West and sent to Russia. These fatal errors led to his armies failing to encircle Paris and also to a gap opening between them. Joffre's subsequent counterattack on the Marne brought about the German retreat which was followed by the 'Race for the Sea', each side attempting to outflank the other. Stalemate was the result, with rudimentary lines of trenches stretching from Switzerland to the sea. So vast were the armies deployed that there were no vulnerable flanks, and so weak the offensive weapons yet available that it was all but impossible to breach the improvised defences. This power given to the defence was clearly revealed when for three long weeks during October and November the Germans strove to carve their way through the French and British positions to the east of the Belgium city of Ypres. Afterwards known as the First Battle of Ypres, it was the most bitter fighting experienced by the British Army since Waterloo (or just possibly Inkerman in the Crimea) and Wellington's victory had taken but a single day to bring about. It was a foretaste of what was to come on the Western Front.

5 Second Ypres

Just before Christmas, 1914, a cipher telegram arrived in York from Lord Kitchener ordering Plumer to proceed to France to assume command of V Corps, as part of Smith-Dorrien's Second Army. It ended months of stultifying frustration. At the turn of the year badly needed reinforcements had arrived on the Western Front, among them an Indian Corps, the 1st Canadian Division and two newly formed British divisions collected from garrisons overseas. This increase in the size of the British Expeditionary Force to thirteen infantry and five cavalry divisions brought with it an upheaval in the command structure. Under Sir John French, two armies had been created, one under Haig and the other under Smith-Dorrien. Fresh corps headquarters were needed as well, and this had provided Plumer with his chance. He arrived on 6 January. For Smith-Dorrien, 'His coming was a great joy to me, as he was an old friend of mine, and would be sure to be a delightful person to deal with, and this proved to be the case'.[1]

Plumer's job, that of a corps commander, was in many ways an unsatisfactory one. Corps usually remained static, holding for long periods a stretch of the line into which divisions came and went, some to gain experience, some to rest if times were quiet, and some for a particular operation. There were to be exceptions with the Canadian and the ANZAC Corps, which usually arrived and left as complete formations. The scope of a corps commander could, therefore, be very limited; rarely did he control reserve divisions, these being under either Army Headquarters or GHQ. More often than not his duties would be confined to the day-to-day supervision of events, the control of artillery and engineers, and such like coordinating functions. Because of this a corps commander could be a rather shadowy figure, unknown both to his troops and to the general public, even though he would be commanding 50,000 or so men, and sometimes a force larger than Wellington ever directed in battle.[2]

At first Plumer had charge of only the two newly arrived British divisions, the 27th and 28th, the infantry and artillery of which were regular units, scraped together from India and various scattered colonial stations, among them Plumer's own 1st York and Lancasters. After the losses of 1914, little remained of the old Regular Army other than the battalions and batteries of these two divisions, but strong though the arguments were for using their experienced officers and NCOs for training and commanding the units of Kitchener's New Armies, the strengthening of the Western Front had been given a higher priority. The artillery shortages were pitiful. At first no howitzers or 60-pounders, both essential weapons for this new style trench-warfare, were available to support Plumer's troops, nor did the British possess anything but a few improvised and inadequate trench-mortars with which to oppose the deadly *German Minenzverfer.* When the two divisions relieved the same number of French formations outside Ypres, they mustered only half the French strength in guns, but, for the time being, the lack of weapons hardly mattered. Artillery ammunition was in such short supply that each gun was rationed to just four rounds each day. On one occasion in February, Second Army was allocated one 15-inch gun and one 9.2 inch howitzer in order that they might create a diversion while Haig's First Army attacked: twelve and forty rounds of ammunition respectively were provided for the two weapons.[3] Although the Germans were firing ammunition captured in Belgian and French fortresses, they also were short of shells, but the British shortages were on a different scale altogether.

The formation of Plumer's Corps allowed Sir John French to take over from his allies the southern sector of the Ypres Salient, that half-circle of Flanders Plain, its base the stretch of the Ypres-Yser Canal between St Eloi and Steenstraat, its six-mile radius reaching out towards the German-held ring of ridges looking down upon Ypres, a hub of British communications in Flanders. On their tops these ridges are almost flat, far drier than the valleys carved out of their flanks, down which small streams ran through woods, often unexpectedly lovely and reminiscent of parts of Sussex. From the forward edges of these ridges and their westward branching spurs, artillery observers could gaze into Ypres, through which all traffic for the front flowed, and the low-lying land around the city where the British and French eked out a cold and wet existence.

The trenches Plumer had taken over from the French were in an especially poor state, from the point of view of both drainage and protection. Worse still, during that first winter, the British lacked every type of trench store – duckboards, sandbags, picks, shovels and revetting material – needed for this static warfare that had never been envisaged. Furthermore, the infantry displayed a marked disinclination to dig,[4] although the French whom they had relieved would seem to have been just as reluctant. The result was that conditions were unspeakable, especially

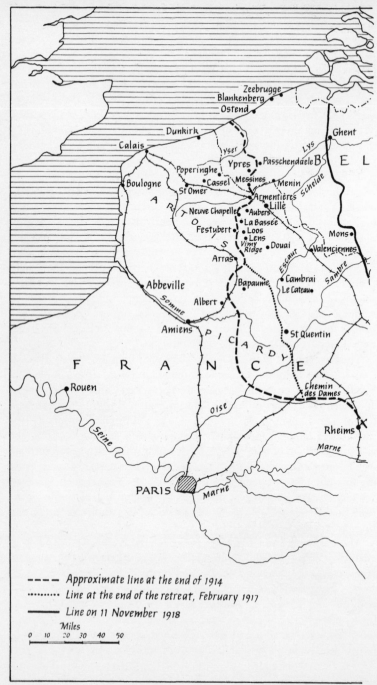

Zeebrugge
Blankenberg
Ostend
Dunkirk
Calais
Ghent
Yser
Poperinghe
Ypres
Passchendaele
B
Boulogne
Cassel
Messines
Menin
St Omer
Armentières
Schelde
Lys
EL
Neuve Chapelle
Lille
Aubers
La Bassée
Loos
Lens
Vimy Ridge
Douai
Mons
Valenciennes
Festubert
A
R
T
O
I
S
Arras
Escaut
Cambrai
Le Cateau
Sambre
Abbeville
Bapaume
Albert
Somme
Amiens
St Quentin
P I C A R D Y
Rouen
F R A N C E
Oise
Chemin des Dames
Rheims
X
Seine
Marne
PARIS
Marne

- - - - Approximate line at the end of 1914
· · · · · · Line at the end of the retreat, February 1917
———— Line on 11 November 1918

Miles
0   10   20   30   40   50

6. The Western Front

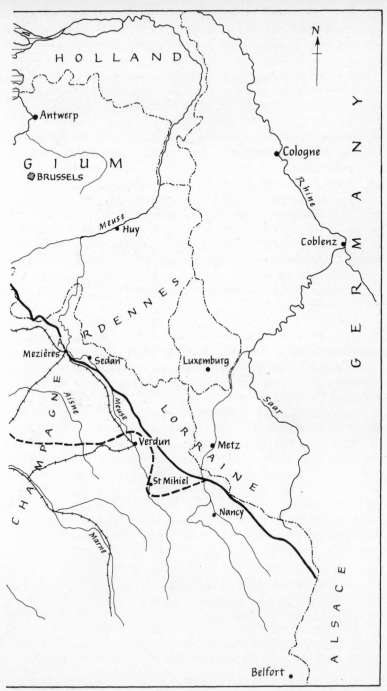

HOLLAND

Antwerp

G I U M

BRUSSELS

Meuse Huy

A R D E N N E S

Mezières Sedan

Aisne

CHAMPAGNE

Meuse

Verdun

St Mihiel

Marne

Luxemburg

L O R R A I N E

Metz

Nancy

Saar

Cologne

Rhine

Coblenz

G E R M A N Y

A L S A C E

Belfort

N

1914–1918

for Plumer's men, their blood thin from long service in stations such as Aden or Suez. The meagre trenches were perpetually water-logged, the men standing knee-deep in freezing slush and needing relief twice daily. 'The men,' Plumer wrote to his wife, 'are having a very bad time! The mud is awful and the state of the trenches indescribable.' His thoughts, he told her, were always for the men in the trenches.[5] Just a few things were happening to make life just that little less unbearable. Warm clothing, including goat-skin jerkins, were making an appearance; baths were being organized at the rear, the underclothing of one batch of men being washed and issued to the next, at the same time as their uniforms were ironed to kill the lice.[6] And a morale-boosting rum ration had started.

It was hardly surprising that the sickness rate was high among men who for several years had not experienced a European winter, so much so that at one point Plumer's 27th Division suffered the indignity of being relieved by men who should have themselves been recovering in reserve.[7] Because the enemy suspected that they were facing troops who were suffering in this way, they gave the forward British troops little peace, the culmination being their capture of St Eloi and the trenches nearby in a surprise attack on 14 March.

Altogether Plumer's V Corps had not made an auspicious start. In some part this was, of course, the consequence of the lack of nearly everything needed to fight under such conditions. Such shortages were to continue, both on the Western Front and elsewhere, throughout the whole of 1915 and much of 1916 as well. They arose from the British reluctance to accept the fact that they might have to fight on land as well as at sea in any coming war, and that the conflict could last longer than a few weeks or months. Soon after the start of hostilities, the War Office did place orders for the *matériel* to wage a large-scale and long-drawn-out conflict, but the absence, first of adequate plant, and later of skilled labour, resulted in continual production delays. Labour shortages were compounded by the Government's reluctance to direct men and women to the factories where they were most needed, and were aggravated by the understandable reluctance of the trade unions to agree to tradesmen being diluted by unskilled men, or, even worse, by women. Even rifles were in short supply until the end of 1915.[8]

* * *

So as to enable him to take over a larger section of the front in order to relieve French divisions for the forthcoming major offensives in Champagne and Artois, Plumer was reinforced by the 1st Canadian Division, among whose units was the very field battery that had served under him outside Mafeking fifteen years before.[9] When the takeover had been completed, he held the larger part of the Ypres Salient, with only two French divisions on his left separating his forces from the Belgians to the north. As before, the defences handed over to him by the French were no more than isolated and flimsy breastworks, insanitary and dangerous, without any proper communication trenches; only the machine-gun posts and the wire entanglements were in any way soundly constructed. French and German bodies from the autumn fighting still lay unburied, their stench fouling the spring air. Overlooked on every side and liable to be attacked from either flank of the Salient, Plumer's three divisions were precariously placed.

On 15 April, the day the relief was finally completed and as Plumer's divisions were striving to improve their newly occupied defences, a liaison officer reported at Second Army Headquarters. He had come from General Putz, the commander of the French XXVI Corps on Plumer's left. His news was that a German prisoner had revealed that an attack had been planned for that very night, and that during it an asphyxiating gas was to be used, discharged from containers spaced along Putz's front. The attack, he told his interrogators, would be postponed if the wind were to set in the wrong direction, and he had in his possession a small sack filled with a kind of gauze which was to be dipped into some solution to counteract the effect of the gas.[10] In passing this information on to the British, Putz added that he did not himself believe the report as the prisoner's account was so suspiciously detailed as to suggest a plant.[10] However, this was not the first such warning the French had received: a Tenth Army bulletin dated 30 March had contained a similar report, but nothing had been done about it, nor had the information been passed on to the British.[11]

Nothing happened that night, nor did an R.F.C. sortie over the German lines the next morning spot any cylinders; subsequent flights failed to discover signs of the troop concentrations that would be expected to herald an attack. But that day yet another warning was received, this time from Belgian sources, indicating that the Germans were manufacturing gas-masks in Ghent.[12]

There was little that could be done. Without knowing the type of gas to be used, protective measures were impossible. In any case, the Germans had not attacked on 15 April, nor were there signs of German reinforcements arriving in the area. The chances were that the intelligence collected was merely a ruse to discourage the French moving their troops south. The result was the Plumer passed on the information to his divisional commanders 'for what it was worth', and he moved a couple of reserve battalions east of Ypres and directed that any units relieved from trench duty should also remain east of the city.[13]

At last, on 22 April, the wind blew favourably for the Germans. It was

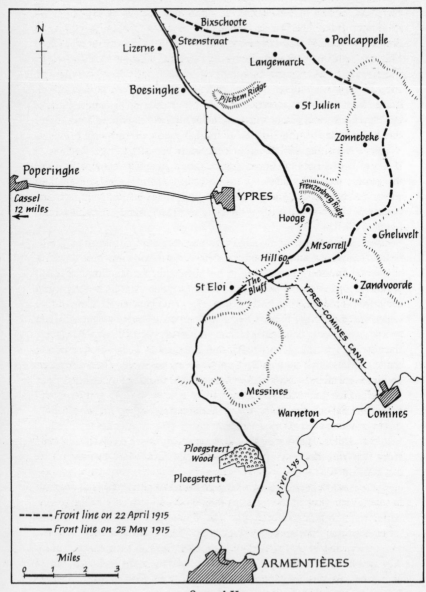

N

Bixschoote

Lizerne •   • Steenstraat   • Poelcappelle

                        Langemarck

Boesinghe •   *Pilckem Ridge*   • St Julien

                                    Zonnebeke

Poperinghe

← Cassel
  12 miles   YPRES

                    Hooge   *Frenzenberg Ridge*

                                    • Gheluvelt

                    △ Mt Sorrell
              Hill 60 △

        St Eloi •   The Bluff   • Zandvoorde

                            YPRES-COMINES CANAL

                                    Comines

                    • Messines

                    Warneton

        Ploegsteert
        Wood

        Ploegsteert •   *River Lys*

- - - Front line on 22 April 1915
——— Front line on 25 May 1915

        Miles
    0   1   2   3   ARMENTIÈRES

7. Second Ypres

a glorious day. Ypres was damaged, but not yet the ruin it was to become; except for the roof of the magnificent Cloth Hall, its mediaeval beauty was still intact. It had been shelled during the morning, but, despite burning timbers, shops and stalls were busy serving khaki-clad customers; Cloth Hall and Cathedral basked in the spring sunshine. Then, at 5 pm, a sudden and furious bombardment by heavy howitzers smashed down upon the city and its nearby villages. At the same time French field-guns could be heard firing somewhat intermittently to the north. What happened next was seen by several senior officers, including two of Plumer's divisional commanders and Smith-Dorrien himself, who was returning on foot to Ypres after visiting Hill 60, the scene of recent and savage fighting in II Corps area. They observed 'two curious greenish-yellow clouds on the ground on either side of Langemarck in front of the German line. These clouds spread laterally, joined up, and, moving before a light wind, became a bluish-white mist, such as is seen over watery meadows on a frosty night.'[14]

Behind this mist the sound of rifle fire suggested that the Germans might be attacking. Soon an odd smell was detected, accompanied by a smarting of the eyes and tingling of the nose and throat. At the same time, French African troops appeared in the rear of the Corps area, some retching and coughing, some pointing to their throats, others continuing their terror-stricken flight. Then, French Territorials from the more northern of the two divisions were observed hurrying rearwards over the Canal bridges. Rapidly the first trickle swelled into a panic-stricken flood of refugees, artillery teams and wagons mingled with the men on foot. The two French divisions had all but vanished, leaving an 8000-yard gap in the Allied front through which the advancing German infantry could pour. Ypres itself, the hub of the Salient, together with its headquarters, guns and store depots was in imminent danger.

It was hardly surprising that these second-line French troops had bolted. More terrifying than anything is the unknown. Not for some time was it realized that to move worsened the choking effects of the chlorine gas; because it was dense, it clung to the ground so that anyone standing up to shoot often escaped the worst, unlike the wounded lying in the trench bottoms. It was providential that the Germans moved warily, edging forward behind the poisonous clouds and its retching French victims. After advancing in this circumspect manner for about a couple of miles they encountered a few resolute platoons of Canadians and a couple of their guns. At this the Germans halted and were seen to start digging. Soon even the rifle fire died away.

Afterwards the Allies learned that the German attack had been launched to divert attention from their forthcoming offensive in the East and to test their new weapon. It had excised nearly a third of the Allied salient, succeeding beyond all expectations, but reserves had not been made ready to exploit the unexpected victory. The British made good use of their reprieve. Acting with speed, the commanders of both the 27th and 28th Divisions moved reserve battalions to the threatened flank, placing them under command of the 1st Canadian Division. At the same time, Smith-Dorrien returned to Plumer's command the 1st Canadian Brigade, which he was holding as an Army reserve four miles to the west of Ypres, two battalions of which he first ordered forward to help plug the gaping gap in the line. That night two other Canadian battalions counter-attacked in support of a similar move planned by the French on their left. Difficult though it was to mount such a hastily improvised operation in the dark over strange ground, the Canadians flung the Germans out of their positions. Because of intense artillery fire, however, they had to be pulled back to their starting line just before dawn, having taken serious losses. Putz's French troops, whom the Canadians were supposed to be supporting, never started. It was a foretaste of much of what would happen during the coming month.

After a night of appalling confusion, some sort of new northward-facing front had been built, made up of ten Canadian and British battalions, strung out covering the gap that had been made between the Canal and the left-hand corner of the original Candian stretch of line. Some troops occupied such crude defences as they found, others lay out in the open, starting to scratch for themselves some sort of cover.

Despite the rudimentary telephone communications in the Salient, cut time and again by the German guns, Plumer had managed to keep in touch with what was happening and the riposte to what could have been an over-whelming defeat had been well managed. Nevertheless, his influence at the start of this Second Battle of Ypres*, as it was to be known, was limited. He had little in the way of a reserve; nor had his Army Commander. It was the men on the spot who had vigorously blocked the German advance, but it says something about their Corps Commander that they had acted boldly, usually without waiting for instructions.

* * *

Joffre's deputy in the north was General Foch who was responsible for the

---

*The naming of battles, carried out after the war by the Battle Nomenclature Committee, was somewhat arbitrary. Fighting never ceased in France and Belgium, waxing and waning from one area to another. The periods of the greater activity received names, such as First, Second and Third Battles of Ypres.

French forces there, and for coordinating the loose and untidy arrangements that existed for mutual help between his own troops and the flanking Belgians and British. As a young officer, Foch had seen something of the Franco-Prussian War, and his being was permeated by the national spirit of *La Revanche*, the determination to right the wrongs of 1870. His Ninth Army had been largely responsible for the German repulse on the Marne the previous September, the battle that had saved Paris. Before that, as Commandant of the *Ecole de Guerre* his influence had done much to direct French strategic thought towards the revival of the Napoleonic doctrine of the all-out offensive, *toujours l'attaque*, regardless of circumstances and losses, the fallibility of which had been exposed in the headlong and costly drive of the French armies across the frontier at the start of the war, that vain attempt to regain the lost provinces of Alsace-Lorraine at a blow, and at the same time crush Prussian militarism.

But, however much Foch might urge Putz to counterattack and recover the lost ground, he obtained little response from his fellow-countryman. The two French divisions had lost, not only most of their artillery, but what little remained of any offensive spirit they may have had. Capable now of no more than collecting their scattered infantry to try to hold the line of the Canal north of Ypres, the pressure to retake the captured French positions fell upon the British, the brunt of it upon Plumer's divisions. What is more, the pressure was intense. This local German attack had developed into a serious threat to the Allied left flank on the Western Front. From the purely military standpoint, there were advantages in abandoning what was left of that dangerous Salient, so shortening the line and reducing the number of troops needed to hold it. But in 1915 ground could not be lightly surrendered. The case against doing so was put by the British Official History. Foch and French

> could not bring themselves to relinquish the Ypres Salient. They had to bear in mind the special political and sentimental values attaching to every acre of the small portion of Belgium remaining unconquered, and the moral effect created among neutrals, if not the belligerent nations themselves, by the German paeans of victory on the gain of the smallest parcel of ground.[15]

Nevertheless, French had his doubts about the value of holding on to what was left of the Salient. Soon after Plumer arrived, French had lunched with him, his two divisional commanders and Smith-Dorrien, and, in discussing the possibility of a retirement behind the Yser Canal, he had told Plumer 'not to waste men in any attempts to regain what the French had lost, but to make his present position perfectly strong against attack'.[16] But the trouble was that French found it difficult to make up his mind, and he also lacked the intellectual gifts to withstand Foch's reasoning and the moral courage to outface his demands to support Putz in his less than half-hearted attempts to recapture his lost ground. Coping with fighting on a scale and of a type for which he was utterly unprepared, French fluctuated between optimism and despair, between support for the importunities of his ally and dejection from the consequences of his actions in so doing, the latter only too clear from the casualty lists which lengthened as the battle progressed and to which he never became indifferent. In the Boer War he had reached what should have 'been his ceiling on the battlefield. Thirteen years later, as a sick and elderly man, he was ill-equipped both by temperament and knowledge for his task. Like most of his seniors, Roberts and Kitchener among them, he had little or no idea of how a staff should be used to lighten his burden; stubborn also, he was too old to adapt himself to the novelty of this siege-type warfare, which he was far from alone in failing to recognize for what it was.

The cost of this indecision in Canadian and British lives was to be great. Early on the second morning of the battle, Plumer had found the time to write a brief note to his wife reassuring her that 'after a very trying night, the French on our left gave way altogether yesterday evening and we were all night in a very awkward position: we still are for that matter, but we are better than we were. I am still all right.'[17] But that day, at French's urging, he was obliged to launch a series of counterattacks that achieved nothing. Utterly inadequate fire support, too hasty mounting and an improvised command structure were a recipe for disaster. By nightfall, along the new northward-facing front, twenty-one Canadian and British battalions, many sadly reduced in number as a result of these abortive counterattacks, faced forty-two German units, and in guns the Allies were outnumbered by five to one. Still, for the time being the line was firm, but every reserve had been committed, including a brigade of the 4th Division that had been moved north from II Corps. More help was on the way. French had placed at Smith-Dorrien's disposal the three infantry brigades of the 50th (Northumbrian) Division, Territorials who had reached France only the week before and who were assembling just to the north of Ypres; the Cavalry Corps, ordered to occupy a rearward line, echeloned back from the Canal behind Putz's troops, were also placed under Second Army. Also on the move north were two more brigades from 4th Division, the Indian Lahore Division and another French division. However, the French had lost seven of the bridges over the Canal, although in their area to the north the Belgians had successfully resisted two attempts by the enemy to cross by rafts and boats. The Germans again used gas during the day, discharged by shells rather than cylinders, a far more effective method against which the British were learning to obtain some sort of protection by binding wet (usually urine-soaked) cloths across their mouths and noses.[18]

One unit that had suffered severely during the day was the 1st York and Lancasters, who lost thirteen officers and 411 of their soldiers. Plumer was obliged to break the news to his wife that their old friend Lieutenant-Colonel Burt had been killed, together with his adjutant and many members of his Regiment. 'You know how I feel about these losses,' he mourned.[19]

* * *

On the the third day of the fighting, 24 April, the Germans struck first, anticipating a message from French that 'vigorous action S. of the Canal will be the best means of checking the enemy's advance from the line Lizerne-Boesinghe'.[20] After an hour-long bombardment concentrated against the Canadians at the north-eastern corner of the abbreviated Salient, at 4 am the Germans again released their container gas. Behind the thick fifteen-foot-high poisonous cloud, twenty-four German battalions assaulted eight now weary and understrength Canadian units. Two Canadian battalions took the full brunt. During the ten minutes of choking terror during which the gas engulfed them, the temptation to tear away the wet rags which impeded their breathing often proved impossible to withstand. But, for the time being, they held their ground; not only were they made of sterner stuff than the unfortunate and elderly French Territorials and the Algerians, but they were prepared for what was to happen. In the end, however, numbers prevailed, more through the crushing effects of the German artillery than the gas. Against the German 5.9-inch howitzers, their fire directed from balloons and aircraft as well as by ground observers, the British had no answer. In the entire V Corps area there were only two medium batteries, both equipped with Boer War vintage weapons.

All this time, Plumer, whom Smith-Dorrien had reported as having been 'very much to the fore' and that he had anticipated nearly every instruction I gave him',[21] had become increasingly doubtful about what was happening. His view was that the British should have held on so as to give the French time to restore the situation, and that if that had proved impossible, V Corps should have evacuated what was left of the Salient, and the British reinforcements should have been used to drive the Germans off any footholds they had secured on the Canal's west bank.[22] In carrying out their orders both to cling to what was left of the Salient and to recover the ground the French had lost, Smith-Dorrien and Plumer faced an impossible task. Their overcrowded defences provided little protection and less concealment from the German guns massed on three sides. On the other hand, to have left the bulk of their infantry west of the Canal would have resulted in it being trapped there if the German guns destroyed the bridges. In the same way, to have moved the British field-guns back out of range of the German mediums and heavies would have prevented them from supporting their infantry.

In making up his mind what to do, Smith-Dorrien was hardly helped by the strangely vague and vacillitating signal he received that day from Robertson, now French's C.G.S. Although signed by him, the wording can only have been French's for this recent Commandant of the Staff College was a master of clarity and brevity:

> He does not wish you to give any ground if it can be helped, but if pressure from the north becomes such that the 28th Division *ought* to fall back from its line, then of course it *must* fall back, for such distance as circumstances necessitate. But we hope that the necessity will not arise. The Germans must be a bit tired by now, and they are numerically inferior to us as far as we can judge. In fact there seems no doubt about it.[23]

This sort of thing could not have helped the Second Army Commander understand his Commander-in-Chief's intentions.

That same day the incessant demand for speed brought about the destruction of another fine formation. The 10th Brigade from 4th Division, full-strength and experienced, had concentrated west of Ypres at 3 pm. Placed under command of the Canadian Division, it was to be the lynch-pin of a force of fifteen battalions earmarked to recover the village of St Julien which had been lost that morning. With zero fixed for 3.30 am the following day, there was not time for the officers to see the ground over which they were to attack. At the rendezvous arranged by the Canadian Divisional Commander, no one met the 10th Brigade Commander, who had been put in charge of the operation, other than the Canadian CRA. In the end only five battalions attacked, fortunately so. In faultless order, the regular battalions of the 10th Brigade shook out in fighting formation. There was little German artillery fire and even less rifle fire, but a few machine guns, firing in enfilade, scythed down the British battalions. The next morning the dead could be seen lying in their straight lines. Within the hour seventy-three officers and 2436 men had been killed or wounded.

Even this loss of the 10th Brigade made little difference. An order to Smith-Dorrien, timed at 4.15 pm that day, directed that 'Every effort must be made *at once* [my italics] to restore and hold line about St Julien or situation of 28th Division will be jeopardised',[24] while a further message informed him, incorrectly, that French reinforcements would leave him clear to employ all his infantry east of the Canal.[25] With Plumer and Smith-Dorrien little more than post-boxes for the onward transmission of French's confused directions, units were thrust into the maelstrom, either to counterattack or hurriedly fill a gap. Many were half trained, quite unfit for complicated manoeuvres. This description is apt:

> Inkerman, the battle of a few hours between man and man, has gone down to history as a soldiers' battle; "Second Ypres" was fought by the brigadiers and regimental officers and the soldiers. But instead of lasting a few hours, it was drawn out over 33 days and nights, and accompanied by the overwhelming employment by the enemy of high explosive shells from heavy artillery, field artillery and *Minenwerfer*, and poison gas.[26]

The pattern was the same on 26 April. The Lahore Division from the south was earmarked by French for another attempt at St Julien, this time in cooperation with the French on their left. It was made unnecessarily complicated. French did not place the Indians under Plumer, but made him responsible for what he called 'pushing on' with the troops on their right. Again no time was allowed for proper preparation. After marching all night, the troops were tired, units were understrength and there was the usual artillery shortage. An unfortunate message of encouragement was sent to the Lahore Division, stating that the enemy could not be very strong or numerous, as they must have lost heavily and be exhausted.[27] The inevitable happened. The French attacked without zest and quickly came to a halt when the Germans released cylinder-gas, a cloud of which drifted across the front of an infantry brigade just as its men were reaching the German wire. Located by enemy aircraft as they moved up for the attack, they had been heavily shelled ever since. Individual 5.9s knocked out complete platoons at a time; the dead lay in heaps. With machine guns adding to the slaughter, it was not surprising that, in the end, they broke. In that 'pushing forward' Plumer had been ordered to carry out on the right of the Indians, a brigade of the Northumbrian Territorials fared just as badly. These far from fully trained troops carried out their instructions with consummate gallantry, advancing across ground covered by the corpses of the 10th Brigade; two-thirds of these Territorials were either killed or wounded, a total of forty-two officers and 1912 soldiers, losses that matched those of the Lahore Division.

The following day Smith-Dorrien wrote a long letter to Robertson, pointing out how small was the number of troops Putz had been able to commit to the attack, and his conviction that no more could be expected in the future, despite protestations to the contrary. If the French were not capable of making what he described as 'a big push', the only position that could be held permanently was the so-called 'G.H.Q. Line', which ran just to the east of the villages of Potijze and Wieltje and which approached to within 2000 yards of Ypres. It was, he made clear, a course of action that would involve surrendering a great deal of territory; at the same time he emphasized that, although he was preparing for the worst, the time for such a withdrawal had not yet come. In any case, it could not be carried out in one fell swoop because of 'the enormous amount of guns and paraphernalia' which would have to be brought back first. If the worst were to happen, he added, and the French failed to do something really vigorous, it might become impossible to hold any line east of Ypres at all.[28]

For someone of French's stubborn temperament, this was not a welcome letter. At 2.15 that day Robertson telephoned Smith-Dorrien with his master's reactions. The careful note he kept of what he said read:

> Chief does not regard situation so unfavourable as your letter represents. He thinks you have abundance of troops and especially notes the large reserves you have. He wishes you to act vigorously with the full means available in co-operating with and assisting the French attack having regard to his previous instructions that the combined attack should be simultaneous.[29]

Two hours later, this unciphered signal was despatched to Smith-Dorrien:

> Chief directs you to hand over forthwith to General Plumer the command of all troops engaged in the present operations about Ypres. You should lend General Plumer your Brigadier-General General Staff and such other officers of the various branches of the staff as he may require. General Plumer should send all reports direct to G.H.Q. from which he will receive his orders. Acknowledge. Addressed Second Army repeated V. Corps.[30]

This unciphered signal could be read by all the operators, clerks and staff officers through whose hands it passed. It could even have been a deliberate discourtesy. Although Smith-Dorrien had done all he could to avoid a clash with his Commander-in-Chief since he arrived in France, his masterly handling of his troops at Le Cateau during the retreat from Mons, an action that had been fought against French's express wishes, had further increased his superior's dislike for him. On the other hand, it could have been more than personal antipathy that caused French to act as he did. So far as he was concerned, Second Army had conspicuously failed to recover the lost ground, unreasonable though the orders to do so may have been. Smith-Dorrien's letter to Robertson, woolly in parts, could well have been written by a man whose powers were flagging.

Simultaneous with this unciphered signal, a letter was despatched to Plumer ordering him to consolidate the line he was holding so as to render it more secure against attack, and to prepare a rearward line in case withdrawal should become necessary.[31] This was just what Smith-Dorrien had recommended, and for which he had been so cuttingly reproved.

Plumer's reply to these fresh instructions, which he sent on 28 April, was firm and unequivocal, a clear sign that he was in charge and intended to fight the battle in future as he thought best. He had, he pointed out to GHQ, already instructed his divisions to consolidate and strengthen their lines. He continued:

I have given instructions that the subsidiary French attack is to be supported by the Artillery and Infantry fire of the troops under the command of G.O.C Lahore, Canadian and 28th Divisions. All the units which have been engaged have suffered heavy losses and have repeated and continuous calls upon them, and in my opinion the support I have indicated is *all that they should be called upon to give* [my italics] until the French have made appreciable progress and gained some material ground. Further local attacks which were necessary in the first instance to keep back the enemy and to retain as much ground as possible will now only cause further heavy losses without effecting any material improvement in the general situation.

The present ground, Plumer went on to assert, could not be held permanently, and the retirement, if it were to be carried out, would be that more difficult and costly the longer it were to be delayed. To complete the withdrawal, he declared, would require four nights.[32]

Plumer's personal reaction to French's behaviour to Smith-Dorrien was typical of the man. In his letter to his wife of 30 April, in which he broke the news to her about Burt's death, he also wrote:

Things have not been made better by Sir John French slighting Sir Horace, and taking practically all my force away from him and leaving me independent of him. It is the last thing I wanted. It is not fair because Smith-Dorrien and I were in absolute agreement as to what should be done, and I am only doing now what I should have been doing if I had remained under Smith-Dorrien. He, Smith-Dorrien, feels it very much of course; he came to see me yesterday and had a long talk.[33]

* * *

For the moment French's views matched those of Plumer, for at 10 am on that morning of 28 April, the latter heard from Robertson that the Commander-in-Chief thought that it would 'in all probability be necessary to-night to commence measures for the withdrawal from the Salient to a more westerly line' and directing him to 'take such preliminary measures for commencing retirement to-night, if in the C-in-C's opinion it proves necessary'.[34] But changes were to come. Later that morning French visited Foch, who objected strongly to the proposed withdrawal and confirmed his protests afterwards in a note that specified six different reasons against French's proposed shortening of the line, ranging from tactical considerations to his belief that a withdrawal would be 'a confession of impotence' which would lead to 'the moral ascendancy' passing to the Germans.[35]

Foch's protests caused French to postpone Plumer's withdrawal in order to await the outcome of an attack planned by Foch for 29 April, but which was to be delayed for twenty-four hours. It was an unhappy business, French vacillating between Foch's pressure for further offensives and his own knowledge of the true state of affairs in the Salient, made clear to him both by Smith-Dorrien and by Plumer. As the Official History baldly put it, he passed from optimism to pessimism so that 'It was naturally most difficult for his subordinates to follow his moods, particularly when his mind was on the border between one phase of thought and the next, and when, at the entreaty of General Foch, he waived his own views and more than once agreed to wait a little longer before withdrawing his men and to order one more counterattack.'[36]

Another of those fruitless counterattacks had taken place on 27 April, the day of Smith-Dorrien's rebuff. That morning, all that was left of the Lahore Division, still directly under Smith-Dorrien, had been flung against the German line in a fruitless attempt to assist a French attack on their left. Pinned to the ground in their assembly position by the enemy artillery, the French failed to move.* Just before dark, another and more or less combined attack by some Indian units and French colonials cost more lives and ended in the panic-stricken rout of the Algerians when they were drenched with gas-shells. Further north, the French had made some progress around Steenstraat and Lizerne, but only at the cost of 4000 killed and wounded.

What happened between 28 April and 1 May came close to black comedy, if such words can be used about the horrors that were occurring. Both the French and the British would seem to have treated circumspectly

---

*Against the description of the incident in the copy of the Official History used by the author has been pencilled 'dirty bastards'. The verdict of an embittered participant? To fight with allies is never easy.

Foch's demands for further attacks. To quote once again the Official Historian, 'The orders that the British were only to attack if our Allies actually left their trenches were perhaps natural, but they could hardly lead to decisive results as the French possibly had their eyes on the British front with similar thoughts in mind.' A footnote reminds us of those lines.

> Lord Chatham with his sword undrawn
> Kept waiting for Sir Richard Strachan:
> Sir Richard, longing to be at 'em,
> Kept waiting too, – for whom? Lord Chatham.[37]

Knowing that nothing was to be gained by Foch's demands and only too aware of the indecision of French, it is clear that during this period Plumer temporised to save further unnecessary loss of life.

Three times French postponed the inevitable withdrawal, but on 1 May, the day of a final vain and half-hearted attempt to launch a coordinated Allied counterattack, Foch informed French that Joffre had overridden him, the major French operations in the south having been given priority over the needs of the troops around Ypres, who were now to act on the defensive. Two days before, Plumer's staff had issued the preliminary orders for the withdrawal from the tip of the Salient to positions just east of the 'GHQ Line'. The plan involved also a large reduction in the number of units crammed into the area: to be moved back across the Canal were the Lahore and the 50th Divisions, together with the 2nd Cavalry Division, whose dismounted regiments (the equivalent of about a brigade of infantry) had been drawn into the battle under Plumer's command on 26 April. This would leave Plumer's three original divisions to hold the much reduced Salient, one of them the 1st Canadian, but hardly Canadian any longer, all three of its weary infantry brigades having been pulled back across the Canal and replaced by units from II Corps. The Canadians had lost 5000 men.

At last, at 12 am on 1 May, Plumer received the long-awaited authority. That night, and without incident, he brought back the Lahore Division and the bulk of the Canadian artillery across the Canal bridges. At the same time his own headquarters at Poperinghe, under continual fire from a single German 15-inch gun, was shifted to a village nine miles SSW of Ypres and his advanced headquarters just to the west of the city was closed down, French having formed the opinion that it was dangerously far forward. The instructions to move were not to Plumer's liking.[38]

The following night the cavalry, two brigades of the 50th Division and much of the still remaining artillery was evacuated by the light of the fires raging in and around Ypres. It was a remarkable achievement as a major

German attack, supported by gas, had been beaten off during the day. Then, on the night of 3 May, the final stages of the withdrawal were completed, although yet another enemy attack was not finally halted until 9 pm. A few wounded had to be left behind under the care of medical staff, but most were brought away by the retreating troops. When the rolls were called next morning, only a single man could not be accounted for, and even he eventually turned up, having fallen asleep in an empty trench. Not until morning did the Germans discover that the trenches in front of them were empty. Among those who edged forward across the abandoned wasteland was Rudolph Binding, a German officer, who described it:

> The battlefield is fearful. One is overcome by a peculiar sour, heavy and penetrating smell of corpses. Men that were killed last October lie half in a swamp and half in yellow-sprouting beet-fields. The legs of an Englishman, still encased in puttees, stick out into a trench, the corpse being built into the parapet; a soldier hangs his rifle on them. . . . Cattle and pigs lie about, half rotten; broken trees, drives razed to the ground; crater upon crater in the roads and in the fields. Such is a six-months'-old battlefield.[39]

With complete success Plumer had withdrawn from close contact with the enemy – that most difficult operation of war. It was a tribute, not just to the discipline, courage and strong nerve of the troops, British, Canadian and Indian, all exhausted after a week's hard fighting, but to the excellent staff work of his own headquarters, many members of which were inexperienced and half-trained, dealing with formations unknown to them until after the battle had begun.

Most of the surplus troops were dispersed elsewhere as they were pulled out of the Salient, so reducing Plumer's Force (as it had, by then, been designated officially) to its original two British divisions and the 4th Division which had, bit by bit, completely replaced the Canadians. Nevertheless, despite its reduced size, Plumer's Force was not returned to the command of Smith-Dorrien's Second Army, but remained directly under GHQ.

Feeling intensely the way he had been slighted, Smith-Dorrien wrote to French on 6 May suggesting that this evident lack of faith in him constituted a weak link in the command chain and that, for the good of the cause, it would be better if he were to serve elsewhere. It was the opportunity for which French had been waiting. That same evening Smith-Dorrien received written instructions to hand over command of the Second Army to Plumer and to return home. No explanation was vouchsafed, but Smith-Dorrien already knew his fate before the letter arrived. During the day, he had run into Robertson who had served under him and liked him, and who was disquieted by the dismissal. Drawing his senior to one side, Robertson whispered into his ear, "Orace, you're for 'ome'.[40] Whether Wullie still dropped his aspirates naturally or did so for effect has never been established.

Some thought that French had dismissed the most able senior officer in the British Army, but it had been an unfortunate partnership and one better ended. If a sounder relationship had existed between the two men, Smith-Dorrien, as Army Commander, would have been better placed to take a firm line with French and so avoid much of the chaos and resultant losses of that last April week. Though he failed to assert himself, Plumer did not.

Sir Edmund Allenby, who had been commanding the Cavalry Corps, took over V Corps from Plumer, while another cavalryman, Major-General Julian Byng, Plumer's old school-fellow, replaced Allenby. In his first instruction to Second Army, issued from the new headquarters he had opened at Oxelaer, on the south side of the base of Cassel Hill to the west of Poperinghe, and dated 8 May, Plumer emphasised the importance of avoiding asking First Army for reinforcements, whatever happened in the north. The reason was that Haig was attacking Aubers Ridge in conjunction with a French offensive further south. Called off after twenty-four hours because there was insufficient artillery ammunition to ensure its success, the failure was but a prelude to another and worse setback at Festubert later in May; this defeat matched in results if not in scale the major French offensive launched between Lys and Arras which cost them 100,000 casualties and convinced the enemy for the time being of the effectiveness of their defences on the Western Front. But the fighting outside Ypres continued while all this was happening.

Between 5 and 7 May, as intense efforts were being made to strengthen the new British line, small German attacks with strictly limited objectives, each one supported by heavy shelling, were launched. In one of these Hill 60 was lost, largely because the Germans released their gas along the line of the British defences, rather than across them, so that the fumes clung to every trench instead of rolling away. This 'rubbish heap of shell and mine-torn earth, timber and dead bodies'[41] churned and pulverised into a desolation of shapeless cavities, had cost 3000 casualties to defend. It was to remain in German hands until June, 1917. Then during the next five days, the enemy launched a series of attacks against the Frezenberg Ridge, little more than a fold in the water-logged ground, but a bastion of Plumer's new defences. As Foch had predicted, the British withdrawal had encouraged them to do so. By the weight of their artillery, they pulverized the meagre British ramparts and trenches, killing, wounding or burying the defenders, most of them fresh drafts from the United Kingdom, half-trained and only partially disciplined. Not altogether untypical were the losses suffered by the other regular battalion of Plumer's York and Lancasters, reduced in a single counterattack from 900 to eighty-seven rifles commanded by a sergeant.[42] On 9 May alone eleven battalion commanders were killed or wounded. However, the Germans were also running short of ammunition, supplies of which had been diverted to the fighting further south, as had some of their infantry as well.[43] By 13 May mutual exhaustion brought the fighting to a halt. Plumer's old V Corps had lost yet another 9000 men. In all, the 28th Division during the course of Second Ypres had suffered 15,000 casualties, almost its original strength, and its few surviving infantry had been replaced by dismounted regiments of the Cavalry Corps.

The respite was only brief. During the next nine days every available sapper unit together with large working parties from all arms toiled feverishly to construct rearward defence lines. At the same time the French finally cleared the German pocket that had been established on the west bank of the Canal, north of Ypres. It even seemed that the enemy's efforts to capture Ypres had finally ceased, when, on 24 May, they summoned up their resources for a final bid. At first light along a five-mile stretch of the line, running north from the Bellewaarde Ridge, the Germans released a cloud of gas more dense than anything before seen. So close were the German positions that the British could hear the gas hissing from the cylinders, and so thick were the poison clouds that they rose at times forty feet in the air, blotting houses from view. The British machine-gunners were wearing the first proper gas-masks, flannel bags with eye-pieces, but the gas combined with the crushing bombardment told. By the day's end the Bellewaarde Ridge and the village of Hooge were in German hands; they had gained another strip of mud a few hundred yards deep.

From the entries in French's diary, one senses that he was far removed from reality. On 25 May he wrote:

The final report received from 2nd Army to-night shows that the enemy's very violent gas attack has resulted in a . . . retirement of the centre of our line to the East of Ypres. This is, of course, unfortunate but on the whole it may be said that the situation might have been much worse. All the troops occupying the trenches which were thus affected had recently received large drafts composed of men who had never been in action before. It is also to be feared that Regimental and Company Commanders have been very slack in insisting on the proper use of the precautions against gas. In fact the whole incident is largely due to this. The result is that these young soldiers have become to a certain extent demoralized – nor is this to be wondered at.[44]

The next day he directed his Adjutant General to send a strongly worded memo to Plumer, expressing his disapproval of the slackness displayed by these unfortunate regimental officers,[45] themselves often inexperienced, dealing with raw troops and without proper protective equipment. French returns to the subject in his diary entry for 27 May. 'The 2nd Army has never been properly handled,' he complained. 'There is evidence of restlessness and want of confidence amongst them. I feel sure, however, that if Plumer is properly backed up he will put all this right.'[46] It is just a little hard to decide from these entries whether French was having a final fling against Smith-Dorrien or whether he was starting to seek another scapegoat for these successive failures.

Nevertheless Ypres had been held. After that attack on 25 May the Germans finally brought the operations to an end. The two sides had fought one another to a standstill, although neither fully realised what had happened 'on the other side of the hill'. The Germans were short of ammunition, but British supplies were completely spent, French reporting to the War Office on 27 May that he was obliged to close down the fighting at Festubert until his reserves could be replenished. Against Plumer two fresh German divisions might have produced a decisive result, but it had been necessary for them to switch the larger part of their reserves east to the Russian front.

In the twenty-three days of this northern fighting, British casualties at 60,000 were double those of the Germans, and that figure does not include the French and Belgian losses. How could that be with the machine-gun and magazine-loading rifle apparently giving the defender the advantage? The German predominance in artillery, their use of gas and the British shortage of shells had, of course, much to do with it. But there was a further explanation for the long British casualty lists. Some of the more junior of the French officers serving on the Western Front at that time were to describe the sacrifice of British troops in unprepared counter- attacks as 'magnificent but not war'; their grandfathers had said much the same in the Crimea.[47] It is perhaps ironic that those same French officers did not realize that those counterattacks had been insisted upon by their own higher command, but had been carried out by their Allies in too conscientious a manner. Commenting upon Second Ypres, Liddell Hart wrote, 'But the real indictment of leadership arises when attacks that are inherently vain are ordered merely because if they could succeed they would be useful'.[48] Perhaps that contentious thinker overstated the case against Foch and French, but there is a high degree of truth in his harsh condemnation. The failure of the Allied generals at this stage of the war lay, however, in their lack of understanding of the true nature of this trench-warfare. It has often been claimed that it was merely siege-warfare under a new name, but the analogy is not altogether accurate: after all, besieged forces are completely surrounded and so are denied the flexibility of being able to give ground under pressure and hold major counterattack forces well back out of harm's way. Nevertheless clear similarities did exist. Artillery and engineers were the predominant arms, and ground could be gained only by massively supported step-by-step operations, each with a limited objective to be consolidated before the next could be attempted. It was a lesson that the Germans were just starting to learn, but the Allies not as yet. Only some revolutionary new weapon might have speeded up this process of breaching the other side's defences and so breaking the *impasse* that was being experienced at Gallipoli as well as on the Western Front. Gas could have been the answer if the Germans had not made use of it before they had accumulated sufficient supplies of it, so allowing the Allies time to develop protective measures. The tank, already being tested in England, might have been another.

How much, then, could Plumer be blamed for the misfortunes? As was the case with his divisional commanders, during April he could do little more to influence that 'soldiers' battle' than scrape together what reserves could be found to block gaps and mount French's successive and hasty counterattacks. He was at the time learning a new trade, the skills of which had been practised beforehand by neither the British nor any other army; even though trench warfare had played a large part in both the American Civil War and the recent Russo-Japanese War, the need for such skills had not even been envisaged. Neither the British nor the French had given thought to developing defensive tactics until Robertson tackled the problem during his time as Commandant of the Staff College. As for Douglas, when filling the position of Inspector General of the Forces before becoming CIGS, he had not even allowed withdrawals to be practised.[49] Fighting his first major battle, Plumer was serving alongside and under officers who had at least learned something about trench warfare in the hard school of experience during the previous six months; in the initial turmoil of the sudden German offensive, it would have been difficult indeed for him to have criticized the orders he was receiving, or to have argued against their validity. Smith-Dorrien, as Army Commander and with his longer experience of conditions on the Western Front, might have done so if his relations with French had been on a sounder footing.

Everything changed as soon as Plumer took charge and obtained approval to withdraw from the tip of the Salient, and as soon as French ceased to interfere with the daily conduct of operations. Given freedom of action, Plumer set about removing the unneeded troops from the crowded battle area. That done, he sorted out the organizational muddle that had come about through the hasty cramming of troops into the Salient. However, once the fighting broke out again, it was much the same sort of 'soldiers' battle' as it had been before. This Plumer could do little to influence. The preliminaries were what mattered, and it was in this defensive fighting, as it had been in his soundly conducted withdrawal, that the careful planning counted: the provision of water, food and stores to enable units to fight at their best; the coordination of the artillery fire-plans; the preparation of the defensive positions; the operational plans to cope with emergencies as they might occur; the training of the troops when opportunity offered. In these fields, so much of which concerned logistics (a useful although anachronistic term), Plumer was revealing himself as a master, as he had done on the South African veldt.

His reaction to the chaotic slaughter of the last week of April is not known. Either he never discussed the matter with others, or, if he did do so, nothing has come to light. But we do know what he thought about the death or injury of those for whom he was responsible. Effective, careful planning could do something to alleviate this.

6 Army Commander

There is now a need to look further than that small patch of ground around Ypres and discover how, during 1915, the war was progressing elsewhere. For the Allies it was to be a sadly disappointing year, one of successive failures. On the Western Front alone the British suffered 285,000 casualties during 1915, all but a small number either killed or wounded.[1] It is hard to visualize such figures in terms of human life: the population of a large London borough, or say of Newcastle-upon-Tyne, numbers a quarter of a million men, women and children; an attacking infantry company wiped out in minutes by a couple of machine guns represents the young men of fighting age of a large village or small town.

Let us turn to Haig's First Army. In a succession of abortive offensives, planned primarily to help the French, it bore the brunt of the fighting that summer and autumn. Both materially and psychologically the German occupation of vast stretches of France, including the country's major manufacturing area around Lille, had hardened French determination to drive out the invaders, whatever the cost might be. The curve on the map of that huge German salient between Rheims and Amiens, jutting forward to within fifty miles of Paris, suggested how victory might be won, and throughout the year Joffre's strategy was based upon successive attempts to sever the base of this bulge by attacks launched from its flanks in Artois and Champagne. Each one was to fail, as had their predecessors during the autumn and winter of 1914.

In March, at Neuve Chapelle, Haig launched the first of a series of attempts to draw the German reserves away from the French front. It had been well planned and rehearsed, and on the first day the First Army infantry broke into the German lines. The lack of both reserves and ammunition then cost it its impetus, a pattern of events that was regularly to be repeated in the future months and years. Casualties totalled 13,000 with the Germans losing a like number, but the able manner in which it had been launched persuaded both the Germans and the French to revise their previously held view that British were fit for no more than holding a stretch of the line and that they were not capable of mounting an effective attack. At Aubers Ridge and Festubert, during May, two further offensives by First Army, carried out to relieve pressure against the renewed French drive in Artois, both failed in much the same way, largely because of the utter inadequacy of the British artillery support and the adept manner in which the Germans had learned to conceal and protect their machine guns. It was altogether a sorry story, but at Festubert what amounted to a new philosophy of warfare for the Western Front was expounded. In a letter to Haig dated 14 May French directed that the attacks should be prosecuted in such a way that the Germans were to be given no rest by either day or night, so that they would be 'relentlessly worn down by exhaustion and loss' until their defences collapsed. At the same time French warned Haig that progress would probably be slow.[2] It had been called 'attrition' during the American Civil War, the relentless crushing of the enemy by superior numbers, but as yet the British lacked the resources to trade life for life in this way. Before Verdun, in 1916, the Germans were to develop fully this desperate philosophy.

On 25 September Kitchener's New Army divisions first fought in a major battle and bitter the experience was. This Battle of Loos, which lasted until early October, was launched to support yet another French attempt to cut the base of the German salient, this time from the Champagne side. These enthusiastic civilian volunteers of the New Army had arrived in France only a few weeks before, ill prepared because regular officers and NCOs had not been made available to train them and lead them into battle. Once again the artillery support was inadequate, but Haig's divisions managed to break through the first line of trenches. Unfortunately French made the error of holding the three reserve divisions too far back and retaining them under his own control. As a result, Haig's initial success could not be exploited. To compound this mistake, the staff work, especially in these new formations, was bad, largely because of the absence of even a core of adequately trained staff officers: the pre-war complement had been just two for each regular division and a single one for each territorial division and already nearly one-third of the Camberley output had been killed.[3] As Lord Roberts had warned the Royal Commission on the War in South Africa, 'staff officers could not be improvised'.[4]

The cost to the British Army of the Battle of Loos was 50,000 dead and wounded, losses that shocked the country as the long casualty lists appeared daily in the press. If this was attrition, the balance lay on the debit side. For the French, it had been even worse: to advance a mere 3000 metres in Champagne had cost them 200,000 men. Such 'awful slaughter and the pitiably small results'[5] as the Official Historian described the 1915 fighting on the Western Front, confirmed the view of many of the country's leaders that the barrier of machine-guns, wire and now concrete that stretched from the sea to the Swiss border was impenetrable. If, then, stalemate had been reached, a solution must be sought away from the Western Front, possibly by making use of the traditional flexibility of British sea-power to land expeditionary forces elsewhere; in such a way, and with Allied support, the principal props that appeared to be supporting the main enemy, Germany, might be knocked away. The supporters of such a policy became known as 'Easterners' as opposed to the 'Westerners' who argued that the war could be won only by destroying the armies of that main enemy on the Western Front, costly though such a victory might be. The Easterners hoped that by defeating Turkey, the Austro-Hungarian Empire and Bulgaria, and by intensifying the blockade of her ports, German resistance could be steadily eroded. The result was the worldwide 'side-shows', as they were termed, which proliferated to draw in 3 1/2 million men of the British Empire, as opposed to the 5 1/2 million engaged on the Western Front.

The best known of these side-shows was Gallipoli, to which 410,000 British and 79,000 French troops were diverted; half became casualties, a high proportion from disease. Turkish loses were on the same scale. Forced in the end to withdraw, the Allies had suffered another crushing defeat, but it had been a real effort to help the hard-pressed Russians; success at Gallipoli might have prevented, or at least staved off the Russian Revolution. Then, after Gallipoli had been evacuated, a fresh Anglo-French expedition to Salonika to help the Serbs resist the Austrians and their Bulgarian allies resulted in another disease-ridden stalemate. Even in Mesopotamia, the British and Indian force pushed on too far and too fast up the Tigris towards Baghdad, only to be besieged at Kut-al-Amara, where 10,000 men surrendered igonminously the following April. To equip such expeditionary forces, especially the Gallipoli expedition, the Western Front was starved of both guns and ammunition, shortages that were to be felt until the summer of 1916.

* * *

After repulsing the German assaults on Ypres during April and May, Plumer directed the attention of his Second Army to assimilating the new techniques of trench-warfare and improving, as best its units could, their defences with the limited supplies of such stores as were available of barbed wire, sand-bags, concrete, tools, pumps and the rest of the thousand and one items needed to construct positions in a near-swamp. After lengthening his front northwards in early June so as to include Boesinghe, Plumer's eight divisions, now organized into three corps, held the whole of the Ypres Salient, much reduced after the May withdrawal, and the line running south to beyond Armentières, a total of twenty miles of front. With fresh British divisions arriving regularly in France, three during May and a further thirteen during July, August and September,[6] barely trained through they were, there was much force in Joffre's demand that the British should take over even more of the 475 miles of front line. As it was, the length of the British front doubled between April and September from thirty-six to seventy miles.

Compared with areas such as Ypres, much of this long French front was 'quiet', as the jargon of the day put it, but their losses had been intolerably high as a result of their successive attempts to breach the German line. Joffre went so far as to propose that the British should evacuate what was left of the Ypres Salient so as to shorten the line and thereby save six divisions that could then be used to reinforce the French in the south. This suggestion Sir John French rejected on two grounds. First, such a withdrawal would have a seriously adverse effect on the morale of the forces concerned; secondly, if the British shortened their line in this way, so could the Germans and thus release divisions for offensive operations on his front.[7] Both of the Allies had conducted a *volte-face*, the British who in the spring had wished to abandon the Salient completely and the French who had insisted upon its retention. The redoubtable Joffre could, in contradiction of the physical solidity of his appearance, display a startling flexibility of mind and approach when the occasion demanded it. Nor was he especially concerned about retaining Belgian territory for psychological reasons.

Time and again during the summer Plumer was charged with mounting comparatively small-scale attacks on his front so as to discourage the Germans from moving their reserves southwards to the main battlefields. More often than not the focus of these operations was the Bellewaarde Ridge, above the bitterly contested château and village of Hooge, a slip of high ground that jutted to within two miles of Ypres and overlooked the greater part of the country to the east of the city.

Plumer entrusted the first of these attacks to Allenby's V Corps. Planned for 16 June, to coincide with French and British operations in the south, the preparations for this attack, made under Plumer's supervision, were meticulous in their detail, setting an altogether new standard for the future. So as to overcome the recurrent problem of passing information back from the leading troops, telephone and telegraph lines were laid in triplicate and along different routes; these were supplemented by visual signalling and a carrier-pigeon service.* Eight lines of jumping-off trenches were dug

---

*Pigeons had been used previously, but only for intelligence purposes. By 1918, over 20,000 birds, controlled by 380 handlers, were doing their bit.

133

behind the forward positions and the newly available high-explosive shells were used to cut the wire, and they did so effectively. A complete squadron of the Royal Flying Corps was attached to Allenby for artillery registration and observation, and the little heavy artillery Plumer possessed was placed in support of the attack. The trouble was that there were only 115 guns in all with 19,000 rounds of ammunition (a pitifully small quantity) available to Allenby, but the first assault wave of infantry, a brigade in strength, swept forward in fine fashion to capture the German front line, at some points only fifty yards away from the British forward jumping-off trenches. As planned, the guns then lifted their fire to tackle the next objective, but when the men of the second brigade rose to their feet to pass through the leading brigade, an Irish battalion in reserve further back rushed forward to join in the fight, carrying another unit with it on the crest of its unrestrainable and ill-disciplined enthusiasm. The result was chaos, with the infantry overtaking its protective barrage and the crowded mass of disorganized men a prime target for the German guns, with which the few British 'heavies', short as they were of ammunition, had failed to cope. The assaulting division lost 3500 men; 157 German prisoners were taken and the enemy suffered some 300 other casualties.[8] It was an example of how poor training and worse discipline could nullify sound planning and reckless courage.

Four weeks later another and more successful attempt was made upon Hooge. A mine was detonated under the German defences of the village, leaving a crater 120 feet across and 20 deep in which was buried the defending enemy company. By dispensing with any preliminary bombardment, complete surprise was gained, and the trenches beyond the crater were captured and consolidated. It was a small job, neatly done.[9] But on 29 July the Germans introduced another new and even more frightful weapon. Just before dawn the troops manning the trenches on the far side of this Hooge crater glimpsed figures hunched under some heavy weight advancing from the direction of the German trenches. Suddenly a rushing noise was heard like the escape of air from a blast-furnace. From those hunched figures, long tongues of flame flickered out and a bright glare engulfed the entire crater area. In the British trenches men exploded into living torches, their clothes blazing; in seconds they were cinders. Even the best of troops could not stand firm against this new weapon – the *Flammenwerfer*. The panic-stricken British battalion fled.[10]

To recapture the heap of rubble that had been Hooge took a complete division. Again Plumer insisted upon meticulous preparation, perhaps even more so than before. To mislead the Germans about the place of attack, three flanking divisions simulated preparations on their fronts, and its timing was disguised by shelling the German trenches each morning at irregular intervals. For once even the heavy artillery and the ammunition seemed to be adequate. When the bombardment proper began just before dawn on 9 August, the German defenders took refuge in their dug-outs and were overrun. The disputed ground had again changed hands, but at a cost of another 2000 casualties, with the enemy probably losing the same number of men.[11] This attack was marked by two innovations on the British side, neither at the time fully successful. An attempt was made to use wireless to communicate between divisional and brigade headquarters and for the first time some of the British troops wore the new steel helmets; strange as they were to the troops, in the dim early morning light their wearers were too often mistaken for Germans.[12]

The day the attack went in, French paid one of his regular visits to Second Army Headquarters in order to discuss the battle with Plumer and his three corps commanders. He afterwards noted in his diary: 'All seems to be going well in the 2nd Army. The whole atmosphere and tone in the command seems to be greatly improved.'[13] Any doubts he may have entertained about the capacity of Second Army three months earlier would seem to have disappeared.

During the September Loos fighting, Plumer's role was again to deceive the enemy about the real direction of the British attack, but he was also required to plan to join in a general offensive should the Germans retire on his front, or to send south troops to follow up any success that Haig might achieve. Hooge was again the main battleground, and again mines, four in all, were sprung, but again the small patch of ground won in the early stages of the operation was later lost. Much the same happened in a similar attack launched by another of Plumer's corps south of Armentières. It was the story as before: little ammunition or artillery could be spared for such subsidiary operations. The attacks which Plumer had been ordered to carry out drew off no more than local German reserves, and, like the main offensive at Loos, nothing was accomplished. Once again it had been demonstrated that to launch such attacks without adequate artillery support was to throw away men's lives. This sort of thing, combined with the regular wastage of routine trench-warfare, was, by the year's end, to cost Second Army a total of 125,000 casualties.

* * *

Confined during the second half of 1915 and the whole of 1916 to such a secondary role in which he could do little more than teach his formations to plan soundly and thereby minimize losses, Plumer had often to accept divisions from the First and Third Armies (the latter established in July, 1915) which had been seriously damaged in the much heavier fighting that took place further south; these would be exchanged for his own experienced and, by degrees, better trained formations. A case in point were two New Army divisions that had suffered heavily at Loos. Warning Plumer what was about to happen, Robertson suggested that he should ask French to speak to these two divisions on his next visit, who, he wrote, 'when they arrive have no confidence in themselves nor in each other, and the 21st and 24th are now inclined to think I suppose that they have been rather failures. The sooner they are told that they have done their duty as well as they could by him the better'.[14]

Such tactful handling was frequently needed to bolster the pride and confidence of badly smashed formations which had within days, if not hours, lost the greater part of their few experienced infantry leaders and a high proportion of the rank and file. Looking quite a long way ahead, a case in point was recounted by Major-General Tom Bridges, one of Plumer's fellow passengers on his voyage to South Africa in 1899 and who had afterwards watched with admiration his progress in that war. In March, 1917, Bridges's 19th Division was moved north to join Second Army:

Not long after our arrival in his area, General Plumer came to see me and had tea in the mess. This was a habit of his which made contact much easier. He said that he had had a letter from General Gough stating that he did not consider that the Division was in a good state. This was to us like impunging the chastity of Caesar's wife. I recounted to the Army Commander what the Division had done, our heavy casualties, our tardy reinforcements and my own difficulties with Gough. Army Commanders should not expect from New Army divisions the same consistent performances that were registered by Guards, Canadians and Australians, who were kept up to strength and had pools of their own reinforcements to draw from. . . . General Plumer was satisfied.[15]

With such sympathetic handling and proper training, this division was to perform brilliantly later that year.

Another, and more junior, officer also remembered how well Plumer handled such problems. Anthony Eden, future Prime Mininster, had, at the age of eighteen, been commissioned direct from Eton into the Yeoman Rifles, a part of the New Army 41st Division, his unit raised from the sons of North Yorkshire farmers and the like. Eden thought that much of their final three months' training at Aldershot before they left for France had been a waste of time, the emphasis having been on open warfare, whereas all they picked up from any wounded officer returning from the

Front was the need to learn about trench warfare. Only once did they spend forty-eight hours in practice trenches on Laffan's Plain.[16] Their introduction to the techniques of trench warfare in Plumer's Army was to be gentle and took place in April, 1916, south of Messines at Ploegsteert Wood – 'Plugstreet', of course, to everyone. The western approaches were still sylvan, barely scarred by shellfire, and the trenches were well built. Even the birds sang at times, Eden remembered. It was all in complete contrast to conditions just a short distance further north; what was more, the country was almost flat and, unlike the Salient, the Yeoman Rifles were not overlooked from ridges from which fire could be directed on everything that moved.[17]

A few months later, after the Yeoman Rifles had twice been smashed in the Somme battles, they returned to Plumer's command. By then Eden had become adjutant and was the one officer who had served continuously with the unit since it left England. He described a visit paid to them by Plumer. 'At a superficial glance, Plumer with his eye-glass, medium height, somewhat portly figure and run-away chin might not be impressive, but watch his methods for a while or hear him speak and you would soon know that here was a skilled and painstaking commander who was a master of every detail of his job. A man to be trusted.'[18] There were no special parades for the visit, the day being treated as a rest day. Accompanied by a single staff officer and his Major-General Royal Engineers, Plumer questioned those he met about:

the arrangements we made for the stationing and care of the men's weapons and equipment in their huts, their food, their baths,* their clean clothing; then the inspection began of every hut and building in the camp. Plumer found much of what he did not approve and clear, firm orders were given to his staff on the action to be taken to mend matters. . . . For the riflemen, especially for the few survivors of the battalion he had known [It had been raised in Northern Command when he was at York], Plumer had kindly words. He would ask them about present conditions or sometimes recall the small north country towns or villages which were their homes, while the later recruits watched and marvelled at this general who seemed so much at ease

---

*The comparison may be unfair, but other VIPs could have a different touch. The future Field-Marshal Lord Ironside, conducting Lord Curzon around France, found conversation difficult and pointed out, when they reached a bathhouse, how happy and healthy the young soldiers looked with their clear skins. To this Curzon replied, 'Yes, once before I have seen the lower classes in their baths. I used to think that they had dark skins all covered with hair, but I see they have not.'[19]

and interested in them and their cookhouses. The next day things began to happen, with a luxurious clatter of duckboards in the lead.[20]

This simplicity and sincerity were among the qualities Archbishop Cosmo Lang, a friend from their days in York together, remembered about Plumer.[21] Although he could be an amusing and inspiring public speaker,[22] unlike French and other generals, he did not make a habit of addressing troops on parade,[23] but preferred to multiply his informal contacts with them. This was not easy. At one point Second Army numbered three-quarters of a million men and women, few of whom could have heard his voice or even seen him, although most daylight hours were spent in a continuous series of visits to headquarters, rearward installations and fighting units resting or training. Those who did encounter him walking around their billets or places of work, or sitting his horse or standing by the roadside as they marched in to or out of the line, became aware that they were serving in 'Old Plum and Apple's Army', something unusual in the mass warfare of the 20th century in which few soldiers knew the names of even their brigade or divisional commanders.

Of course, neither his appearance nor manner could appeal to everyone, understandably so as the war dragged on and disillusionment spread even more widely. In South Africa de Montmorency had not taken to him. It was the same with Thomas Hughes, a rather superior product of Eton and Trinity College, Cambridge, and a pupil of Edwin Lutyens. Because the company of the officers' mess of the Artists' Rifles did not appeal, he transferred to the Royal Flying Corps. Acerbic by nature, both generals and their staff officers he found equally distasteful, the latter possibly more so. For Plumer he developed a special contempt, although he was almost as rude about Kitchener and that hero of the Royal Flying Corps, the then Brigadier General Hugh Trenchard, both of whom he also met. The first time Plumer visited his squadron, Hughes noted in his diary that 'the general showed quite a childish pleasure and ignorance in everything and asked questions with the privileged imbecility of a judge'.[24] On the next visit:

Old Plumer tottered up within a quarter of an hour of the time, but the dear old thing had quite forgotten the medals (I am told it was the ribbons as our George [the King, of course] likes pinning medals on breasts) so all he did was to ask each victim to step forward while Colonel Salmond [his Station Copmmander, who also had a distinguished career waiting for him] in a grim, angry voice read out his case from the charge sheet.[25]

138

On another visit, when a pilot was putting a Nieuport through its paces for Plumer's benefit, Hughes noticed that 'The old man watched with the vacant expression of a snail climbing up the glass in an aquarium'.[26] The technicalities of these newly invented flying machines could have been as strange to a general touching sixty years of age as computers were to a similar generation of the 1970s; in actual fact, Plumer was an enthusiastic proponent of this new air arm, of which he made excellent use. But even Hughes had to make the grudging admission that he had heard two other generals talking quite warmly about Plumer, and his staff as well.[27]

Another officer to record his views on Plumer was Brigadier General Jack. The 'dear old gentleman holds the confidence of his troops whether times be good or bad. The operations of his Second Army had been notably soundly planned and successful'.[28] Nevertheless, Jack was not wholly uncritical. When Plumer asked Jack what his brigade needed, the request for a 'typewriting machine' evoked a rather uncomprehending laugh; however, when Jack told him that his borrowed machine 'makes a noise like a travelling tank and mutilates the paper copies', his Army Commander laughed in a more natural manner and said that he would do his best.[29] On a subsequent visit to this brigade, Plumer asked, 'Well Jack, how are your men?' and seemed astonished to be told that they were pretty tired but would be fit to attack again with a few days's rest. 'After all,' Jack commented, 'when he put the question, the Brigade had been out of line for little over 24 hours, following eight days of more or less severe fighting, outposts, marching, hard work in bad weather, without shelter, without sufficient rest, and sometimes short of food. "Plum" is most human, but it is the old story, those who live right away from the troops engaged cannot possibly understand the strain and weariness affecting troops at the Front.'[30] There could indeed be this gap in comprehension, but with an army commander, as with any other leader, there was this need to drive as well as encourage.

* * *

After the successive and fruitless British offensives of 1915, culminating in the ill-managed Loos, French's departure was inevitable. Sixty-two years old, he had suffered a heart attack in November, 1914, and throughout the following year he was frequently in bed with bouts of fever and what may have been recurrences of the heart trouble, complaints accentuated by the stress of responsibilities with which he was inadequately equipped to cope. His lack of decision and failure to control his temper became increasingly apparent to those around him; in indiscreet letters he wrote to his mistress he revealed his anxiety about the outcome of coming battles, his sadness at the thought of the severe losses his troops would suffer, his consequent hatred of war and his knowledge that he would be removed if he were to fail.[31]

Nothing has come to light to indicate Plumer's views about his Commander-in-Chief, but it was probably much the same as that of Haig, his fellow Army Commander, who had little good to say for him. During the Boer War and before that at Aldershot, Haig had been French's senior staff officer, and the two men were close friends, so close that the affluent Haig (his money came from the whisky) had loaned his senior the large sum of £2000, so rescuing him from insolvency and most probably saving his career.[32] By today's standards, such a transaction might seem dubious, but a century or so ago less suspicion would have been aroused by such an arrangement between friends and gentlemen. By the outbreak of the war, Haig was recording his doubts about French's strategic insights and his misgivings at French's opposition to his suggestion that a high proportion of officers and NCOs should be left behind at home to train the large army that Haig, like Kitchener, was sure would be needed to fight a lengthy war.[33] On 11 August, before embarking for France, he even went so far as to tell King George V, with whom he was on intimate terms, about his doubts of the selection of French for the command.[34] Nothing that happened in France caused Haig to revise his opinion about his senior.

Matters came to a head when Robertson visited Haig in October, 1915, after a week spent in London. Haig recorded his conversation with French's principal staff officer:

Robertson told me that, when he was in London, Lord Stamfordham [the King's Private Secretary] called him up on the telephone from Sandringham and asked him by the King's orders whether he did not consider the time had come to replace Sir J. French. Robertson did not answer. He saw the King afterwards in London, and now he had come to discuss the point with me. I told him at once that up to date I had been most loyal to French and did my best to stop all criticisms of him or his methods. Now at last, in view of what had happened in the recent battle over the reserves, and in view of the seriousness of the general military situation, I had come to the conclusion that it was not fair to the Empire to retain French in command on this main battle front. Moreover, none of my officers commanding Corps had a high opinion of Sir J's military ability or military views; in fact, *they had no confidence in him*. Robertson quite agreed, and left me saying "He knew now how to act, and would report to Stamfordham". He also told me that the members of the Cabinet who had up to the present been opposed to removing French had come round to the other option.[35]

Because Plumer retained no papers, we do not know whether Robertson visited him as well.

Despite Haig's protestation of loyalty to Robertson, he had, in fact, already discussed French with his warm admirer, Haldane, who, on the outbreak of the war, had been obliged to leave the Government as a result of an infamous and ungrounded public outcry that he was pro-German in sympathy. Asquith had, however, sent him to France in early October to discover the reasons for the Loos failure, and there he learned from Haig how unsatisfactory the command arrangements had been during the battle, and how many of his colleagues considered that, if such conditions continued, it would be difficult to win the war.[36]

There could only be one outcome. With some difficulty the Government persuaded French to resign and, on 19 December, Haig replaced him as Commander-in-Chief. He was the obvious successor, although Bridges noted that 'Popular opinion pointed to Haig as the *pretendant,* though Plumer would probably have had the army's vote. But happily the choice of Commander-in-Chief was not part of our duty'.[37] As commander of I Corps and afterwards First Army, Haig's experience of modern warfare surpassed that of any other senior British general. Neither in peace nor in war could Plumer match his record, and Haig was the senior, having been promoted over Plumer's head in November, 1914, in recognition of his work with I Corps. His reputation as a thinking soldier had, however, been established well before the war. Recalled by Haldane from India in August, 1906, to serve, first as Director of Military Training at the War Office, and then as Director of Staff Duties, in these posts Haig was to be largely responsible for giving shape to Haldane's plans for the reform of the Army, in particular the organisation of the six-division Expeditionary Force, small but more efficient than any other Army, and the creation of the volunteer Territorial Force.

Chosen over the heads of his seniors, including Plumer, for the key appointment of Aldershot Command, he had prepared the two divisions that were to form I Corps that he was to take into battle. By the end of 1915 his reputation stood high indeed, despite the reverses his Army had suffered during the year.

When the full facts of French's sacking became known in 1952 with the publication of the relevant extracts from Haig's diaries, their writer was much criticized for intriguing to supplant his old friend. There is some force in this. Haig was both ambitious and politically adept, shrewdly capable of looking after his own interests. But fundamentally he was honest and straightforward, and there can be small doubt that he helped to get rid of French because he was convinced that his senior was endangering his country's safety, and that, in any case, he was better equipped to take charge. He was not the first, nor will he be the last, to act in such a way.

Haig, like nearly all his fellow soldiers, was a convinced Westerner, firm in his belief that the war could only be won by defeating the German armies in battle on the Western Front. Both during and after the war Haig was to be condemned for the terrible loss of life suffered by his troops, losses on a scale never before experienced by his country. Either ignored or forgotten by his critics was the fact that such casualties were the inevitable concomitant of large-scale land warfare fought by mass armies that could be brought to the battlefield and supplied when they arrived there by the network of railways that intersected Western Europe. Even the American Civil War, fought half a century earlier, had involved 2 1/2 million men, of whom 620,000 died. In the First World War Great Britain, her Dominions and Colonies lost a million dead, small in relation to the worldwide total of thirteen million. Figures such as these are meaningless in the context of the tragedy of each individual death, but are quoted as a reminder of the means of destruction available to the industrialized world.

Such losses, so unexpected and so immense, had to be blamed on someone, and as the man who commanded on the Western Front for three years, Haig was to suffer denigration as an insensitive and incompetent butcher, even though he was lauded at the moment of victory. His main critic, both during and after the war, was Lloyd George, relations between whom and the Commander-in-Chief were to be soured by mutual incompatability; Churchill was another, as were the prominent post-war military writers, Liddell Hart and J.F.C. Fuller, their strictures being regurgitated subsequently by a horde of lesser men. Clearly though he could express himself on paper, Haig combined taciturnity with an inability to cope with lucid talk and argument, handicaps which gave an altogether wrong impression of his intelligence and powers of comprehension. The brilliant Haldane, master of so many different disciplines, when writing in 1917 to congratulate Haig upon his promotion to Field-Marshal, stressed that 'The necessity of a highly trained mind, and of the intellectual equipment which it carries, is at last recognized among our people'.[38] Haig made his mistakes in plenty. What man carrying such responsibilities does not, in any walk of life? But among those who led the Allied armies to eventual victory, it is not easy to name his superior. During the past forty years historians of the calibre of Duff Cooper, John Terraine and Lord Blake have done much to restore his reputation as a thinking and educated soldier, a man of insight and imagination, and compassionate as well.

* * *

Not only around Ypres, but along almost the whole of the British front, the Germans held the higher and drier ground. With the French determined to recover their lost territory and the Belgians reluctant to lose the small strip of their country not in German occupation, there were two reasons, the first tactical and the second political, why the Allies were continually impelled towards the offensive. The consequence of this was that, by comparison with the Germans, the improvement of their defences took a lower priority with the Allies. The enemy, intending during 1916 to attack only at Verdun, never ceased working on their lines. As the Official History described it, 'German wire was a real obstacle, the French and British wire was often little better than a conventional sign. Deep-mined dugouts, of which the enemy, at it was to be discovered on the Somme had sufficient to shelter most of the garrisons of the front defences, were practically unknown on the Allied side.'[39] This did not mean that the Germans stayed rigidly on the defensive. In a number of areas they carried out small, local attacks, two of which, during the winter of 1915-16, were beaten off on Plumer's front, the first in December, when phosgene gas was used for the first time, and the second on 12 February. Two days after this the Germans attacked, this time against an artificial mound known as The Bluff, alongside the narrow valley through which ran the now smashed and stagnant Ypres-Comines Canal, two miles to the south of the city, and previously a pleasant picnic-spot for its citizens. The British positions were captured, after three small mines had been exploded under them, and a series of poorly organized counterattacks all failed. One of the best artillery observations posts the British possessed around Ypres had been lost with 1300 casualties. It took another and carefully planned counterattack two weeks later to recover the place at a cost of a further 1300 men.[40]

After Haig took over command, he started a series of regular weekly conferences with his Army Commanders, held in turn at each of their headquarters, at which information was exchanged and each other's problems discussed. But four days after the loss of The Bluff, the visit Haig paid to Plumer was for a special purpose. After talking to him, together with the Second Army Corps Commanders, Haig delivered the following warning:

I then spoke to General Plumer alone; he admitted that the defences were bad but said that he had been short of men, and weather had been bad, etc. that he had withdrawn troops to train by my orders. I pointed out that before the Loos battle we had made 16 miles of trenches in open ground and under close view of the enemy. He then said he was quite ready to go if I thought it desirable. He was only too anxious to do what was best. Altogether he behaved in such a straightforward way and is such a thorough gentleman that I said I would think over the matter and let him know tomorrow. I added that it is a matter of small importance to get rid of any Army Commander. At the same time this is no time to have any doubts about anyone's capacity to discharge his duty. I got back to St Omer in time for lunch. After thinking over the matter, I wrote to Sir H. Plumer that I wished him to continue in his Command, and to do his utmost to strengthen his defences with as little delay as possible. If, however, after a reasonable time I found but little improvement in the general arrangements and conditions of the 2nd Army, I should feel it my duty in view of the great task which lies before this Army, to ask him to resign his Command. Meantime, I would give him every assistance in my power, and with the prospect of fair weather and drier ground his work would be much easier, and I felt sure that the defences would soon be quite satisfactory.

Privately I feel sure that Plumer is too kind to some of his subordinate Commanders, e.g. General Pilcher 17th Division, Fanshawe 5th Corps, Haldane 3rd Division, who are, I fear, not fit for their appointments. In the morning I received a reply from Plumer thanking me for my letter and saying that he would do as I wished and also act on my advice to press his Corps Commanders to necessary action.[41]

Plumer's apparent readiness to resign suggests that he had been forewarned of what might be happening. Haig had, in fact, visited Plumer already intent upon sacking him. He had warned his wife the previous day that he would be in London on the Saturday but he had not told her that the purpose of the trip was to discuss Plumer's replacement. His decision to cancel his visit, when she learned about it, understandably disappointed and apparently aggravated her also.[42] Robertson, now elevated to CIGS, had also been warned of Haig's intentions, and had been asked to 'try and give Plumer some other job so as to let him down lightly'; on 18 February Haig wrote to him again to say that he had changed his mind and was giving Plumer another chance, adding that he had told him 'to take hold of his Corps Commanders more, and to make them in their turn grip their Generals of Division and so on down the line'.[43] In his reply Robertson agreed that Plumer had never been quite hard enough with his Corps Commanders, who, in his opinion, were 'not too good'.[44]

There is little doubt that Haig had decided to get rid of Plumer some weeks before, possibly even before he took over command. During the first week of January he had written to the King to say that he had paid a second visit to Plumer who now struck him 'as knowing much more about his Command than he did on my first visit', an indication that he had even before that been in touch with King George on the subject of his Army Commander.[45]

It is probable that Haig lacked confidence in someone who looked even older than his fifty-eight years, and who had been shelved in mid-career, to be brought forward again largely under French's influence. Although Haig was no more than four years younger than Plumer, he often referred to him in his dairy as 'old' Plumer. It is not uncommon in any walk of life for an individual to dislike having an immediate subordinate older than himself, especially if he had previously been his senior. In any case, Haig had a rooted objection to employing older men. In a long report upon his attachment to the French cavalry in 1884, he had commented unfavourably upon the age of their officers;[46] as Inspector General of Cavalry to Kitchener in India after the Boer War, he made a similar criticism about the Indian Cavalry.[47] And even before he succeeded French, he had discussed with Asquith, the Prime Minister, the need to get rid of old generals so as to promote younger officers.[48]

There is small doubt that Plumer was at this time nervous about his new superior. This applied to all Haig's immediate subordinates and to his staff, who tended to avoid questioning him or making suggestions. This aloof man even avoided lunching with his Army Commanders after those weekly conferences for fear that they would degenerate into 'luncheon parties', as he told his wife.[49] And Haig rather enjoyed being heavy-handed. After he had been in the chair for about a month, he recorded in his diary with apparent satisfaction that he had seen Plumer before a conference to learn what his Army Commander intended to say on some particular subject; the latter had listened to his criticisms and had thereupon agreed to amend his statement accordingly.[50]

Personal relations between Haig and Plumer never seem to have been really sound. With both Gough and Rawlinson, Haig was on outwardly friendly terms, the latter even going so far as to address him by letter as 'My dear Douglas'. Plumer, like nearly everyone else, was invariably formal in his approach. If Haig did dislike Plumer, and there is no explicit evidence one way or another, the reason can possibly be traced to Haig's time as a Staff College student. With him there was Brigadier General Edmonds, the Official Historian of the Great War. In recounting in later years how, so far as possible, Haig always avoided going near Plumer, Edmonds wrote:

This attitude went a long way back and . . . dated from the time when Haig was a student at the Staff College and Plumer, as an outside examiner, gave Haig a low place, which was the sort of thing Haig never forgot.[51]

But meticulous though Edmonds was in compiling his multi-volumed *magnum opus*, in later life he could distort and exaggerate both in conversation and his correspondence.

★　★　★

Throughout the whole of 1916, during the course of which some of the bloodies battles of the war were being fought further south, Plumer was involved in no more than smallish engagements, all secondary in their nature, but still expensive in men's lives. After that setback at The Bluff, he decided upon retaliatory measures against the enemy, probably as a result of Haig's rebuke. The 600-yard-deep salient, a mile south of The Bluff, was chosen as the objective. The site of yet another observation post from which the Germans could survey the British lines, it had been the scene of much heavy fighting in the past: a carved-up wasteland of sticky mud, the two sides between them had already exploded thirty-three mines beneath it.

The detonation of a further six mines at first light on 27 March heralded the assault by two battalions of Major-General Sir Aylmer Haldane's 3rd Division, two brigades of which had been heavily engaged in the fighting at The Bluff. Haldane was, of course, cousin to the politician and one of the subjects of Haig's censure. To get surprise, there was no preliminary bombardment, and a larger part of the salient was captured without too much difficulty, despite the inevitable mistakes that arose because the fresh craters transformed the appearance of the landscape. Foul weather hampered consolidation, rain flooding what trenches still remained, the drainage of which had been destroyed by the explosions. Twice Haldane toured his front-line positions, wading up to his waist in water, and not until 3 April was the whole salient secured, a task that in the end sucked in the whole of the 3rd Division, as one brigade after another relieved its utterly exhausted fellows.

On the night of 3/4 April a brigade of the 2nd Canadian Division took the place of the now quite spent British troops. Its commander, the experienced Major-General Turner, who had won both the VC and DSO in the Boer War and who had been through the 1915 Ypres fighting, like Haldane waded through the liquid mud to learn for himself the full extent of the miseries awaiting his troops. Not often was a handover carried out in quite such foul conditions. Parapets had been destroyed; what trenches still existed had collapsed; there was no wire and the craters formed impassable barriers to carrying parties. Despite intense efforts by working parties from Turner's two reserve brigades to try to improve the defences, the morass and an intense bombardment defeated their efforts. Before dawn on 6

April, a German counterattack broke through the Canadian positions, such as they were. The struggle continued for two further weeks, but in the end both sides were glad to bring it to an end.[52] For Plumer this further failure was profoundly depressing.[53]

This had been the first major action of the 2nd Canadian Division, which had moved from its training areas in England to France the previous September to form part of the new Canadian Corps. Undoubtedly Turner, experienced though he was, had not handled his Division as he should have done. The sequel was described by Haig in his diary:

> General Plumer commanding 2nd Army wishes to remove General Turner commanding 2nd Canadian Division and Brig. Gen. Ketchen, commanding the 2nd Canadian Brigade. Another letter mentions "some feeling against the English" exists among some of the Canadians. So the question is a difficult one. No doubt these two Officers are not very efficient, but as regards the G.O.C. Div I doubt if we can find a Canadian officer with the training and knowledge to replace Turner. But the main point is whether the danger of a serious feud between the Canadians and the British is greater than the retention of a couple of incompetent commanders? After careful thought I have decided not to concur with Plumer as regards Turner but to keep him on. My reasons are that the conditions were abnormally difficult, but that all did their best and made a gallant fight.[54]

It was somewhat ironic that, after suffering Haig's censure for not being tough enough with his generals, Plumer's request to remove two whom he judged to be incompetent should have been rejected. But Haig, who possessed an acute political sense, and whose responsibilities were far more wide-ranging than those of an army commander, was undoubtedly correct. The principle was already established that the Canadians should fight as an integral corps under their own officers, even though Byng was, for the time being, commanding it. As in the next war, the problem was to find enough capable generals and staff officers from their very small regular cadre and their part-time militia, some members of which owed their positions more to political and social influence than to military ability. The Canadians were not alone in this; much the same applied both to the Australians and to the British Territorials. And there was a further difficulty. In Haig's words, 'The main difficulty in training Colonial staff officers is that they will not leave their units.'[55]

Like Turner, Haldane, the commander of the 3rd Division, almost became a victim of St Eloi. His performance during the battle had confirmed the poor esteem in which Haig held him, and only the intervention of his Corps Commander saved him from the sack.[56] A harsh critic of Plumer, who, he complained, failed to defend him against Haig, he accused both men of 'deliberately shutting their eyes to facts that we at the front have to face'.[57] Not that the rancorous Haldane approved of many of those senior to him.[58] Regarding Plumer, could it have been that his conscience was uneasy about advice he had tendered to his cousin at the time of Plumer's removal from the War Office? But even Haldane appears to have liked Plumer personally.[59]

During June the Canadians saw more hard fighting in Plumer's area, this time their entire Canadian Corps, fighting as such. They were driven off Mount Sorrel, between Hooge and Hill 60 after a bombardment described by a German participant: 'The whole enemy position was a cloud of dust and dirt, into which timber, tree trunks, weapons and equipment was continuously hurled up, and occasionally human bodies.'[60] But, as the commander of the German attacking division had warned his superiors, Mount Sorrel would be difficult to retain and could become another Bluff.[61] After a hastily organized Canadian counterattack had failed with heavy casualties, ten days later they regained the lost ground after a carefully planned attack. The two sides were left almost exactly where they had been at the start, but the Canadians had lost 8400 men, as against about 5600 Germans. Again the bitter balance of attrition had been cast in favour of the enemy.

*   *   *

With a total of thirty-eight British infantry divisions in France and Belgium by the end of 1915, the pressure from the French to use them was strong, even though most, especially the New Army divisions, still had much to learn and lacked experienced leaders and staff officers. Even before Haig took over as Commander-in-Chief, the Allies had laid plans for simultaneous offensives to be launched during 1916 on the French, the British and the Russian fronts, with the Italians, who had entered the war on the Allied side in May, 1915, attacking the Austro-Hungarians on their eastern frontier. In the event the Germans forestalled the Allies by opening the Battle of Verdun in February, its object to wear down their enemy in a series of methodical attacks, each with a limited objective against a focal point in the French line; these the defenders would be impelled to retain, regardless of their losses in so doing. It is still argued whether General von Falkenhayn, who had replaced Moltke as Chief of the German General Staff after the failure of the Schlieffen Plan, was trying merely to destroy by attrition France's will to resist (her dead already totalled a million), or whether his main object was to break through into the Allied rear areas.

The German tactics at Verdun were based upon the surprise effect of short but overwhelming bombardments in which some 1400 guns, howitzers and mortars would be used; after this a thin line of skirmishers would advance to pin-point the resistance, bombers and flame-throwers supporting them as they edged forward. The ground won would then be consolidated by infantry that had been held well back in the early stages, and the weight of artillery would be used to crush any French counterattacks. Such was the theory and it worked in places, but the French fought with grim determination. General Pétain's often successful counterattacks were to a great extent modelled upon German methods – strictly limited objectives, painstakingly exact planning and overwhelming supporting fire. They foreshadowed the methods by which Plumer was to win his great victories in Flanders the following year. For ten months this fighting in front of Verdun continued, between them the two antagonists lost 3/4 of a million men, and at the end of it all the front line was much as it had been in February. But the French army had been bled almost to death, and it would never be the same again.

The German offensive at Verdun hastened the planned takeover of the French-held stretch of the line around Arras, and, by early March, 1916, the British occupied a continuous line from the Somme to the Ypres Salient. Fresh reinforcements continued to arrive, nineteen more infantry divisions during the first six months of the year, nine of them from Egypt, the consequences of the evacuation of Gallipoli, and including five Australian and a New Zealand division. To cope with these extra forces, two more British Armies came into existence, the Fourth and the Reserve, the latter later renamed the Fifth.

At the time he took over command Haig had instructed Plumer to consider a scheme for an offensive in the direction of Lille,[62] plans for which Plumer had first begun to work upon under French's instructions in July, 1915. In April, Haig examined Plumer's fresh proposals and gave orders that the necessary preparations should be put in hand.[63] It was a strategic concept on a grand scale. After the German line had been breached, their railway communications into Belgium would be severed and their forces there pushed back into the sea; a turning movement southwards would then roll up the German line.

The area of the River Somme had, however, already been agreed with the French as the place for the major Franco-British offensive for 1916, not for any special strategic reason but because the forces of the two Allies met there, and in such a joint attack Joffre could be sure that the British were playing a full part. Another factor in favour of the Somme was the drier going – chalk wolds as opposed to the mud of Flanders. But Haig never lost sight of the advantages that could accrue from an offensive in the north, and as the Verdun fighting intensified and it became doubtful whether the French would be able to spare the troops for the Somme, he ordered Plumer on 28 May to accelerate his preparatory measures. A week later he warned Rawlinson, who was in charge of the Somme offensive, that the attack there might be halted if strong resistance were to be met. 'Plumer's Ypres operation would then begin, to assist which the HQ reserve would be switched north from the Somme area to the Second Army.[64]

The story of the Somme is only too well known. Rawlinson did meet strong resistance there, strong indeed; the Allies persevered and the switch to the north never happened. For the British Army the Somme was to be the battleground for 1916 and the graveyard for much of it. On 1 July, the opening day, the eleven British assault divisions lost 57,000 men, 20,000 of them killed. For 154 days the battles or series of battles continued until winter and mutual exhaustion ended it all. The lessons of the American Civil War, the Boer War and the methods by which the Germans attacked at Verdun might have been better studied. The words of the German report on the first day's fighting are apt:

The British Army . . . had not yet reached a sufficiently high tactical standard. The training of the infantry was clearly behind that of the German; the superficially trained British were particularly clumsy in the movement of large masses. On the other hand, small bodies, such as machine-gun crews, bombers, and trench-blockers and special patrols, thanks to their native independence of character, fought very well. The strong, usually young, and well-armed British soldier followed his officers blindly, and the officers, active and personally brave, went ahead of their men with great courage. But, owing to insufficient training, they were not skilful in action, often irregular lines and with small columns followed close behind them.[65]

The British profited from their bitter experience on that first day and started to learn their trade. On their right the five French divisions suffered far less, partly because they were led by the survivors of men who had been through the long series of abortive offensives of 1914 and 1915.

The controversy over casualty figures for the Somme fighting lasted over half a century. The British lost 415,000 men, the French 195,000. Exact German losses were never known, partly because they were deliberately concealed. Eventually the German Official History put the figure at about 500,000,[66] but this excluded the less seriously wounded, so there was not much in it. Towards the end of 1916, however, Ludendorff was to admit that 'The German Army had been fought to a standstill and was utterly worn out'.[67] What the Germans had set out to do at Verdun, the British accomplished on the Somme, but at a fearful cost, not only in the huge number of their most vigorous young men slain, but in their country's loss of confidence in its military leaders, the repercussions of which were felt throughout the rest of the war and into the next.

* * *

Plumer's preparations for a possible offensive on his front, planned against the Messines ridge, had the secondary object of distracting enemy attention from the Somme area. Gun emplacements and assembly trenches were dug, some real and some dummy, and the artillery dug passages through the belts of the German wire. Communications and rest billets were harassed. The German trenches were continually raided, seventeen times during the days immediately prior to the start of the Somme. Prominent in these raids were the newly arrived Australians and New Zealanders, who, by 8 July, made up nearly one-third of Plumer's then 338,000 strong army.

I ANZAC Corps, commanded by the British General Birdwood and comprising the 1st and 2nd Australian and the New Zealand Divisions, had arrived from Gallipoli in the spring of the year, and II ANZAC, commanded by Lieutenant-General A.J. Godley (who had served on Plumer's staff after Mafeking) and consisting of the 4th and 5th Australian Divisions, followed them. Perhaps it was an act of special foresight to place these ANZACs under Plumer, or perhaps they had merely been sent into the quiet part of the line around Armentières in order to ease them gently into the Western Front. Plumer had, however, a better understanding of the peculiar characteristics of these fine troops than any other senior British general, an insight he had obtained from his years with them in Africa. Godley, an aloof, ambitious man, who cared nothing for popularity, after reorganizing the New Zealand Military Forces before the war, had commanded them at Gallipoli; soon after arriving in Europe, he had written to the King's Assistant Private Secretary, expressing his troops' pleasure at 'having gone to Plumer's Army, as he had so much to do with the Australians and New Zealanders in South Africa, and knows and likes them and they know and like him'.[68] The Australian Official Historian said much the same, describing Plumer as 'the old army-commander, who had had experience of dominion troops in the Boer War, and whom the Australians on their side came to regard with much respect and affection'.[69] Numerous anecdotes confirm this. There was the soldier calling out to an Australian battalion marching down the road on a quiet night, 'Where are you off to, Aussie?'. Back bounced the reply, 'We don't know, but thank God we're going to Daddy Plumer's Army.'[70] After the Somme, they were reputed to have been in the habit of singing 'Take me back to Daddy Plumer's Army' when senior officers visited them.

After what they had been through in Gallipoli, these ANZACs had decided that the Western Front could offer them no worse than their experiences in that ill-managed campaign. Many were also doubting the competence of some senior British officers. When the 2nd Australians' commander reported his arrival to Plumer in March, he made it clear that they were quite sure that things would not be half so bad in Europe, hopes that Plumer's temporary ADC, enjoying a short respite from his gunner regiment at the front, judged to be mistaken except for the fact that they might be better supplied.[72] Repington, when he visited Plumer on 10 July, heard from his old friend that 'The Canadians and Australians were both very cock-o-hoop when they first came to this front, but all of them now have had their lesson. Even the Anzacs have learnt that they do not know everything, but they are excellent at raiding.'[73]

Plumer also told Repington that the ANZACs would be 'trekking south soon', and so they did. On the Somme they proved their excellence in more serious matters than raiding. What they experienced at Pozières, in Gough's Fifth Army, did little to raise their opinion of senior British commanders.

During his visit Repington learned that Plumer was confident that he could hold on in the north, even though he was being 'skinned', as he put it, of his best troops, although he would need reinforcements as well as heavy artillery if the Germans were to attack. And such was Plumer's role during the long months of the Somme, the despatch south of fit and trained divisions and the receipt, in return, of the shattered remnants of formations which needed resting, rebuilding and training, before, as could happen, they were thrust back into the maelstrom once again. Bridges summed it up:

General Plumer was the Cinderella of the Army Commanders and the Ypres Salient was his unsavoury kitchen. Nothing of the good things in warlike equipment came his way, and the trenches were generally manned by the tired troops of divisions that had been bled white elsewhere. . . . But I doubt if he ever complained, and for my part I would sooner have had him behind me than any other Army Commander I had been with, for he was intrinsically sound and as loyal to subordinates as he was to those above him.[74]

7 Messines - The Preparations

Nevertheless, after that long wait on the side-lines, 1917 was to be Plumer's year. During the summer and autumn months, he fought the Battle of Messines, winning the most comprehensive British victory so far achieved in the war and was then to be deeply involved in what was to go down in history as the Battle of Passchendaele, that bitter struggle from which he emerged with his reputation even further enhanced.

It has been a matter for speculation and argument as to just how much Plumer's successes were due to his Major-General General Staff, 'Tim' Harington, whom Haig had posted to Second Army in June, 1916. A spare, highly strung man with a great sense of humour and charm of manner, Harington, who had been christened Charles but was never known as such, was commissioned into the King's Liverpool Regiment in 1892. After attending the Staff College, he had worked in the War Office and been mobilized as a GSO 2 at the outbreak of war. Promoted in April, 1915, to be GSO 1 of the 49th (West Riding) Division, he was for a long time its sole regular staff officer. There he caught the eye of Plumer, whom he had never before met and who, Harington remembered, visited his divisional headquarters almost every day. Plumer picked him for command of a brigade, but instead he was posted as BGGS to the newly formed Canadian Corps, a satisfying experience and one that taught him something of politics, exemplified by their Prime Minister's attempts to influence the appointments of brigade commanders. Then came his appointment to Second Army. In fourteen months he had jumped from major to major-general.[1] In effect he was Plumer's Chief-of-Staff. It was the start of a famous partnership.[2]

The much respected war correspondent Philip Gibbs was among those who were intrigued by the respective contributions of Plumer and his Chief-of-Staff to the successes gained by Second Army. Loathing the waste and horrors of what he had observed on the Western Front, after the war, when the censors could no longer blunt his pen, he wrote *Realities of War*, a book in which his disgust spilled out in a plethora of vivid strictures, some consequential, others less so. The incompetence of generals and the idleness and ignorance of staff officers were his main targets, but his sweeping reproaches were often much overstated: scapegoats were needed for the misery experienced by the fighting units, and the staff were readily available for the purpose. To write of the products of the Staff College as having 'the brains of canaries and the manners of Potsdam' was good fun but a little sweeping; to describe its system of training as 'hopelessly inefficient' was inaccurate.[3] Not without justification, Gibbs's main target was Gough's Fifth Army.[4] His inconsequence, however, lay in the liking and admirations he expressed for the many senior commanders and members of their staffs whom he met in the course of his work.[5] First among these were Plumer and Harington, of whom he wrote:

As there are exceptions to every rule, so harsh criticism must be modified in favour of the generalship of the Second Army – of rare efficiency under the restriction and authority of the General Staff. I often used to wonder what qualities belonged to Sir Herbert Plumer, the Army Commander. In appearance he was almost a caricature of an old-time British general, with his ruddy, pippin-cheeked face, with white hair and a fierce little white moustache, and blue, watery eyes, and a little pot-belly and short legs. He puffed and panted when he walked, and after two minutes in his company Cyril Maude would have played him to perfection. The Staff work of his Army was as good in detail as any machinery of war may be, and the tactical direction of Second Army battles was not slip-shod or haphazard, as so many others, but prepared with minute attention to detail. . . . How much share of this was due to Sir Herbert Plumer it is impossible for me to tell, though it is fair to give him credit for soundness of judgment in general ideas, and in the choice of men.

He had for his Chief of Staff Sir John (sic) Harington, and beyond all doubt this general was the organizing brain of the Second Army, though with punctilious chivalry he gave, always, the credit of all his work to the Army Commander. A thin, nervous, highly strung man, with extreme simplicity of manner and clarity of intelligence, he impressed me as a brain of the highest temper and quality in Staff work. His memory for detail was like a card-index system, yet his mind was not clogged with detail, but saw the wood as well as the trees. There was something fascinating as well as terrible in his exposition of the battle he was planning. For the first time, in his presence and over his maps, I saw that, after all, there was such a thing as the science of war, and that it was not always a fetish of elementary ideas raised to the nth degree of pomposity, as I had been led to believe by contact with other generals and staff officers. Here at least was a man who dealt with it as a scientific business, according to the methods of science–calculating the weight and effect of gun-fire, the strength of the enemy's defences and manpower, the psychology of German generalship and German units, the pressure which could be put upon British troops before the breaking point of courage, the relative, or cumulative effect of poison-gas, mines, heavy and light artillery, tanks the disposition of German guns, and the probability of their movement in this direction or that, the amount of their wastage under our counter-battery work, the advantages of attack in depth – one body of troops "leap-frogging" another in an advance to further objectives – the time-table of transport, the supply of food and water and ammunition, the comfort of troops before action, and a thousand other factors of success. . . .

After intense and prolonged work at all this detail involving the lives of thousands of men, he was highly wrought, with every nerve in his body and brain at full tension, but he was never flurried, never irritable, never depressed or elated by false pessimism or false optimism. . . .

There was a thoroughness of method, a minute attention to detail, a care for the comfort and spirit of the men, throughout the Second Army Staff which did at least inspire the troops with the belief that whatever they did in the fighting lines had been prepared, and would be supported, with every possible help that organization could provide. That belief was founded not upon fine words spoken on parade, but by strenuous work, a driving zeal, and the fine intelligence of a Chief-of-Staff whose brain was like a high-power engine.[6]

Brigadier-General Charteris, a professional soldier and Haig's senior intelligence officer, was someone else who contrasted Plumer and Harington:

They are a wonderful combination, much the most popular as a team, of any of the Army Commanders. They are the most even-tempered pair or warriors in the whole war or any other war. The troops love them. . . . The two men are so utterly different in appearance, Plumer, placid and peaceful-looking, rather like an elderly grey-moustached Cupid, Harington always rather fine-drawn and almost haggard. Neither has ever been known to lose his temper . . . nobody knows where Plumer ends and Harington begins.[7]

But Harington knew very well. The extent to which Plumer was responsible for the team's successes is a thread running through the relevant chapters of *Plumer of Messines*, his biography of his master. Published soon after its subject's death, ingrained loyalty combined with deep affection and respect inevitably resulted in an overly fulsome book, but this in no way blurred Harington's delineation of Plumer's qualities as a commander. When he took over his new job, he was, he wrote, 'soon to learn something of the Chief's methods and to this day I have never failed to try and follow them'.[8] At first Harington was somewhat overawed; he had, as he admitted, never learned to think in terms of 'Armies'. He was not alone in this. At the Staff College, which he had attended ten years before, no thought had been given to dealing with anything larger than the planned six-division expeditionary force. Now he was to be Chief-of-Staff of a force of four corps, an Army which was later twice to exceed thirty divisions and include three-quarters of a million men. One of the first things which impressed Harington was Plumer's thoroughness, especially the active interest he took in the supply and medical arrangements. His knowledge of administrative detail, Plumer was to inform his Chief-of-Staff, had been obtained during his time as Quartermaster-General at the War Office.

The morning he arrived Harington was able to observe how Plumer conducted his regular daily conferences. Attended by the heads of each branch of the staff and the various services and arms – medical, supply, ordnance, artillery, engineers and so one – they were a forum at which each man rendered an account of what had happened during the past twenty-four hours; there they learned about one another's problems and there Plumer issued his orders to them. All matters of importance had to be referred to him, Harington relates, and he kept the patronage of appointment firmly in his own hands.[9] And Plumer kept his finger on the pulse of everything; in no way was he a figurehead, gracing the bows of a ship steered by his Chief-of-Staff. To read Harington's *Plumer of Messines*, and his own autobiography, *Tim Harington Looks Back*, it is clear that Plumer was always in control and that his Chief-of-Staff learned much of his trade from his master.

At the end of these daily conferences most of those who had attended, including Plumer himself, did not return to their offices but got into their motor-cars or mounted their horses to visit the units, establishments or formations in their care. Their brief was to help. Plumer had, Harington emphasized, been a regimental soldier and never forgot it. He impressed upon us firmly that we were nothing but servants of the Troops and he never allowed an order to be issued without considering how it would be received by the regimental officer and soldier'.[10] Anthony Eden, who served as a staff officer at Second Army for a short time in 1917, confirms this, relating how Plumer adjured new staff officers to remember that they were the servants of the infantry.[11] Harington added his own weight. Speaking with some emotion to a gathering of war correspondents, whom he habitually took into his confidence, he told them that it had been his ambition 'to make cordial relations between battalion officers and the staff; and to get rid of the criticisms (sometimes just) which had been directed against the Staff'.[12] Trite though such sentiments may sound seventy years later, at the time they were fresh and inspiring. It was not an easy task. At any time and in any army the regimental officer or soldier is rarely in the habit of being polite about the staff. When food fails to arrive, when the guns are silent through lack of shells, when an undiscovered machine gun halts the advance, when a column of weary troops is turned around to march back by the way it has come, the staff is there to be blamed, regardless of whether the mishap or tragedy is within their control. The extent to which Plumer's staff officers managed to earn the confidence of those below them is singular.

In his attempts to keep in touch with all that was happening in his vast command, Plumer used a further instrument. To each of his corps he attached a young liaison officer, his special task to know each of the thirty or so infantry battalions in the corps and to spend at least two nights each week in the front-line trenches with one of them. The essence of their task was to be trusted and not treated as spies. Liaison officers were nothing new: both Wellington and Haig used them; as a brigade commander in Gallipoli Monash did so as well, and continued to do so when he moved to France as commander of the 3rd Australian Division.[13] But the close links established between the officers concerned and the units to which they were attached was something quite new. When the future Field-Marshal Montgomery took up the idea in the Western Desert in 1942, it was seen as a revolutionary and original concept, but he had, of course, observed the system in operation when serving as GSO2 in Plumer's IX Corps from July, 1917, onwards.

Although Plumer was to be remembered by those who served him as being unfailingly kind, just and fair, he was a strict disciplinarian; he may never have lost his temper, but he could deliver a formidable rebuke when need be. [14] He had no mercy for anyone who abused his good nature, nor would he hesitate to remove a senior officer who was succumbing to the incessant strain of the war. Provided, however, that Plumer had confidence in an individual, he would always support him: when, before Messines, he was pressed by GHQ to remove his artillery adviser, with good reason he refused to do so.[15] As even Harington admitted, there was a certain rigidity in his outlook, perhaps expressed in his hatred of the telephone (although he was not alone in his generation in this respect) and what could be an aggravating exactitude over punctuality at meals, foibles even then considered old-fashioned. His sense of humour could be mischievous, but he never permitted familiarity: a staff officer who might inadvertently refer to a fellow general such as Sir Henry Rawlinson or Sir William Birdwood by their generally used nicknames of 'Rawly' or 'Birdie' would earn instant rebuke. But under stress, he could show himself to Harington, and to others, as an emotional man, one who even had difficulty in restraining his tears.

By the standards of earlier wars, headquarters on the Western Front were unwieldy in size. Even so, Plumer's, like those of his fellow Army Commanders, consisted of only about fifty officers,[16] few enough to cope with so vast an organization, its problems complicated by the introduction of such new weapons of warfare as aircraft and tanks, gas and flame-throwers, wireless-telegraphy and large-scale mining, not to mention the many ramifications of the internal combustion engine. In the nature of things Second Army Headquarters was almost as static as a peacetime Command Headquarters in the United Kingdom. For most of the war it was housed in Cassel, some seventeen miles due west of Ypres, the larger part of its staff officers and their clerks working in what had been the casino, a building of startling ugliness which still disfigures the summit of Cassel Hill. One of several such bumps which rise unexpectedly from the Flanders Plain, Cassel Hill stands 500 feet above the disciplined farmlands that surround it, its wooded slopes intersected by small hedge-bound fields. Circling its upper slopes are the old castle walls which look down on the town's mediaeval streets. Besieged time and again over the years, its streets had often heard the voices of English soldiers, including that of the famous Duke of York who during the French Revolutionary Wars marched his men to the top of that very hill and then 'marched them down again'. From its summit, it was said, five kingdoms could be seen, those of France, Belgium, Luxemburg, England and God. Out of range of the German artillery, as the war progressed it was sometimes raided by German bombing-planes, forcing the staff to take refuge in the cellars of the old castle which the casino had replaced. That reluctant but conscientious and able soldier, Edmund Blunden, the poet, while attending a signal course nearby in 1917, describes its comparative tranquillity

> The road thither was secluded, and hardly anyone noticed the amazing fruitage of blackberries in the low hedges. . . . At the top, the cool streets of Cassel led between ancient shop-fronts and arches, maintaining in their dignity that war was nothing to do with Cassel. There was one memorable inn in whose shadowy dining-room officers from highest to lowest congregated. . . . Some confused noise of guns contested one's happy acquiescence.[17]

Plumer himself lived in a small mess, consisting usually only of Harington,

Major-General A.A. Chichester, his senior administrative officer, together with his Assistant Military Secretary and two ADCs. It was a small group of friends with whom he could relax and a place where he could entertain the continuous stream of visiting VIPs of all nationalities, a purgatory for their hosts and first experienced on such a scale on the Western Front. Plumer's temporary ADC, Lieutenant L. Parrington, elaborated in his diary upon Harington's description of their life.[18] With Plumer he spent his days on the continuous round of visits to units and establishments, corps and divisional headquarters, regiments and brigades at rest, railheads, ordnance depots, hospitals and all else for which his general was responsible. Lunch was usually eaten in the car, and in the evening Plumer returned to resume his never-ceasing office work, ranging from the examination of future battle plans to a letter of thanks, penned in his own hand, to a lady who collected money to send periodically a few dozen cases of Bovril to the troops of each of the British Armies in the field.[19] Among the time-consuming visitors Parrington met during his short tour of duty were Count Alex Tolstoy, together with several other Russians, among them a general responsible for his country's official press and a propagandist for an offensive in Salonika; there were several Italian generals and a Rumanian prince, who had to be well entertained as he was enthusiastic for his country to enter the war on the Allied side. Parrington noted Joffre's solidity and the fact that he lacked even a single word of the English tongue.

In 1915 Plumer's mess was housed in a square white château at the foot of Cassel Hill, where Maurice Baring, then Trenchard's staff officer in the RFC, heard nightingales sing in the garden and chatted to Plumer as he fed the ducks in his artificial pond.[20] Soon Plumer moved from this château to the Castle Yvonne, a small and characterless building, but just below his headquarters on the hilltop. From there he could look out towards Ypres and distinguish, on a clear day, the dark mass of the Messines Ridge beyond. The contrast between life in such surroundings and that of the frontline troops, even when they were out at rest, was indeed stark, but staff officers and their generals had to live and work somewhere, and the château provided the space required for transport parks, telephone exchanges and wireless telegraphy centres. But it was hardly surprising that Plumer had to work hard to attempt to reduce the inevitable alienation that resulted.

* * *

When the Somme battles of 1916 finally ended in November, swamped by the autumn mud, there was something of a respite around Ypres, if such a word can be applied to the life of the infantry, even in the so-called 'quiet' periods. Captain Walter Wadsworth was a Territorial field gunner, whose 55th (West Lancashire) Division had been moved to the Salient to recover from its losses on the Somme. The contrast moved him to describe Ypres, during the third Christmas of the war, as 'gently simmering in quite a holiday feeling'. The thermometer showed thirty degrees of frost, but canteens were handy and rations plentiful. With no more than a little regular shelling to endure each day among the suburbs of Ypres in which his battery was concealed, the war was not quite 'an unrelieved stretch of beastliness'.[21] Edmund Blunden, whose division had made the same journey, commented that 'the general silence and warlessness encouraged us to take life easy'.[22] It was one of the quietest times the Salient had known, but the frosts increased further the need for working parties, that never-ending curse of troops at 'rest'. The inundations along the Yser Canal, frozen into solid ice, were no longer a barrier to attacking infantry, so further widespread thickets of barbed wire had to be planted, digging being impossible in the frozen ground. But men were still being killed and wounded: shelling and raids, the proliferation of trench mortars, available now to both sides, and the mine warfare fought underground (of which more later) cost Second Army an average of 1000 casualties each week during the first five months of 1917.[23]

At the start of that year Haig had charge of sixty-nine divisions, five of them cavalry and two Portuguese, 'England's oldest ally' having been drawn into the conflict during 1915. Of these Plumer commanded a total of ten divisions, organized into four Corps, the II ANZAC, the IX, the X and the XVIII. But it was not just in its count of divisions that the BEF had grown in strength and power. Quantities of heavy artillery had begun to pour off the production lines, the total of such guns and howitzers having risen to 1157; in July, 1916, it had been only 761 and it was planned that by March, 1917, this figure would be doubled. By previous standards, ammunition was unlimited: 9 million rounds for the heavies were to be supplied during the first six months of the year.[24]

For two and a half years the French had carried the major burden of the war. As always, exact comparisons were almost impossible to make, but by June, 1916, their casualties on the Western Front numbered some 2½ million men, as opposed to rather more than 600,000 suffered by the troops of the British Empire.[25] It was hardly surprising then that the morale of both their civilians and their soldiers was faltering, and that one of the consequences should have been the sacking of Joffre in December, 1916. His successor was Nivelle, who had come to the fore when his French Second Army had twice counterattacked to good effect in front of Verdun; in both cases the assault had been supported by a massive

160

bombardment, and had been broken off as soon as its limited objective had been attained. What is more, Nivelle had accurately forecast what was to happen.

Nivelle possessed that accomplishment, rarer even among French generals than British, of speaking the other's language fluently; he could also make himself agreeable. At first he impressed the British, especially the civilians; Haig, after their first meeting, described him as 'straightforward and soldierly',[26] the highest praise he could bestow. Nivelle now promised his government that, by using his previous techniques, he could break through the German defences in an offensive lasting between twenty-four and forty-eight hours, a claim that Haig was not alone in treating with a certain scepticism. Nevertheless, Haig agreed to open a preliminary and secondary offensive in the Arras area eight to fourteen days before Neville attacked, its object to draw off the German reserves; he emphasized that this attack would be of short duration, Nivelle having promised that his offensive would either succeed or be abandoned after forty-eight hours.[27]

Joffre's departure coincided with that of Asquith, the British Prime Minister, whom Lloyd George had replaced in December, 1916, his predecessor's indecision, combined with the bloody stalemate of the Western Front having brought about his departure. The disparity of outlook between Haig and his new Prime Minister has already been touched upon. For the six months prior to attaining supreme power Lloyd George had held the portfolio of Secretary of State for War, but with the Somme offensive already under way, he had avoided any major clash with his military advisers. Like most of his fellow countrymen, he had been shocked by the successive battles on the Western Front, as each one seemed to end in a bloodbath with nothing gained. It was an unfamiliar experience for the British who had never experienced a major conflict on their own soil, and whose military sorties overseas, even those against Napoleon, had been fought by small professional armies. Unlike the British, the Continental nations and the Americans had already discovered, to their cost, the consequences of clashes between mass armies equipped with modern weapons. As that percipient German staff officer, Rudolph Binding, wrote in March, 1917, 'England has never waged wars in such a way that the soul of the people entered into them, and I do not believe that this is the case in this War. She fights without enthusiasm, as one fights against mice or other vermin, without putting one's heart into it'.[28]

So the new Prime Minister was grimly determined that he would not be responsible for further losses on the scale of the Somme. As he made quite clear to Haig when they met in London on 15 January, his method of winning the war was to attack on a 'soft' front. His problems, of course, were not just to find such an alternative, but to persuade his Allies, especially the French, to agree to such a dispersion of forces from the main battle front. It was unfortunate for future relations between the two war leaders that Lloyd George should, at this meeting, have committed the cardinal error of contrasting adversely the British Army with that of the French.[29]

The new Prime Minister also enthusiastically supported Nivelle's ambitious and optimistic plans. He went even further, intriguing with both Briand, the French Prime Minister, and with Nivelle himself to place the British forces in France and Belgium under Nivelle's direct command, and, in so doing, he neglected to consult either Haig or his own principal military adviser, Robertson, the GIGS. At a conference in Calais on 26 and 27 February, called ostensibly to discuss the breakdown of railway transport that had occurred in France, Lloyd George sprang upon the two soldiers his previously prepared plan that would have given Nivelle full operational command of the BEF, relegating to Haig what would have been little more than the functions of an Adjutant General – personnel matters and the like. The resultant strong protest produced a compromise whereby Haig was subordinated to Nivelle for no more than the duration of the coming offensive, an arrangement that was later to be further modified. To have set up a proper system of joint command, with both the British and the French forces serving under a common Generalissimo, would have been altogether different, and one that was to be achieved when Foch took command under the pressure of the disasters of 1918. The Calais plot would have relegated the British Army, then approaching parity with the French, to being no more than a contingent of their army; it was something that Nivelle was soon to make clear had been his intention. It had all been quite unnecessary, as Haig had always fallen in with Joffre's advice and requests, and he was to continue to show a similar cooperation towards Joffre's successors, including Nivelle. The sole outcome was that Haig and Robertson never again trusted the Prime Minister, while he, frustrated by working with military leaders in whom he had little or no confidence, withheld from them the full support they needed in order to win battles.

*　　*　　*

Nivelle's plans were to be upset by the Germans relinquishing the Somme battlefield to the Allies, the first and last large-scale, voluntary withdrawal by either side on the Western Front. As early as September, 1916, the Germans had begun work on what they called the 'Siegfried' and the British the 'Hindenburg' Line, twenty-five miles to the east of the eviscerated countryside that had been the Somme battlefield. It was not really a line at all but a belt of fortifications six to eight thousand yards deep, based upon concrete machine-gun posts covering wire obstacles, usually in three belts, each ten to fifteen yards wide. Starting their withdrawal in February, 1917, by 9 April the Germans were in their new defence positions. Behind them they left a desert of cratered roads, destroyed buildings, torn-up railway lines, and wells polluted but not poisoned; all the French civilians had been evacuated from the zone and the whole was well peppered with booby-traps. It was an early example of 'scorched earth'. Skilfully conducted, the German withdrawal met with little interference from either the British or the French forces, whose capacity to fight a mobile war had long before been smothered in the mud of the trenches.

As he had arranged with Nivelle, Haig opened his subsidiary attack in the Arras region with the Third and First Armies on Easter Monday, 9 April. It had been the worst winter of the century and the assaulting troops went forward through blinding snow and sleet. The main thrust was directed against the German positions just north of the Hindenberg Line, its object to drive towards Cambrai, so rolling up the new German defences. After three weeks of wire cutting by the artillery and a five-day bombardment by 2879 guns, one to each nine yards of front, the first day was a brilliant success. The highlight was the capture of Vimy Ridge by the Canadians and 51st Highland Division; from it the plain around Douai could be seen and the Messines Ridge dimly distinguished in the distance. Tunnels driven out from the labyrinth of cellars and caves which honeycombed Arras and its suburbs provided shelter for two of the attacking divisions before the attack and a safe passage for their infantry to their assault positions. Planning and execution had been near faultless: the British Army had put to sound use the lessons it had learned on the Somme. Prisoners poured back in droves to the freezing, windswept cages. Ludendorff was to describe the battle as seen by the Germans on the other side of the hill.

> The battle of Arras on 9 April was a bad beginning for the decisive struggle of this year. 10 April and the following days were critical. The consequences of a break-through of 12 to 15 kilometres and 6 or more kilometres deep are not easy to meet. In view of the heavy losses in men, guns and ammunition resulting from such a breakthrough, colossal efforts are needed to make good the damage. . . . A day like 9 April threw all calculations to the winds.[30]

But the prolonged British bombardment had enabled the Germans to pinpoint the place of the British attack and their reserves were so placed as to counter the British thrust. The first three days of fighting cost Haig only 13,000 casualties;[31] then German resistance began to stiffen.

Nivelle's complementary offensive on the Aisne began on 16 April. The conditions were the same as those endured by the British a week earlier. So frozen were the fingers of the wretched French African troops that their officers had to load their weapons for them. And the Germans were waiting, their counterattack forces poised. A week earlier a captured operation order had revealed the larger part of Nivelle's plan to them. As usually happened, the French broke through the enemy line at several points, but the massed German artillery crushed further advances. Despite the initial failure, Nivelle failed to abandon the attack after forty-eight hours and the losses mounted. His bombast shown for what it was, the French Government quickly sacked him and put Pétain in his place.

In a reluctant but vain attempt to help his ally, Haig maintained his pressure at Arras even after Nivelle's failure had become apparent. The fighting continued until 3 May and cost the British 160,000 casualties.[32] It was one of Haig's greatest errors of the war, attrition indeed but with a negative balance.

Nivelle's failure brought to a head the disgust of the French people with a war that had already cost them some million dead, apparently for nothing. Widespread strikes, accompanied by anti-war propaganda, proliferated. Far more serious was the collapse of morale in the French Army. Mutinies started to spread at the end of April, and, during the next five months 119 in all were recorded.[33] Some could be far worse than others: the soldiers of one unit might simply declare that they would hold their trenches but would not attack; in another they might march off towards Paris with the Red Flag flying in front of them. Trains were derailed, sometimes there were shots fired, but officers were seldom assaulted. For the time being the French Army was no longer a reliable instrument, and from then on the British played the major role on the Western Front. Pétain set to work with a will to reshape the French Army, but for the time being it was compelled to remain on the defensive, except for isolated attacks on a small scale. For good reason, the French never revealed the full extent of their misfortunes, either during the war or for many years afterwards. Only slowly did Haig become aware of what was happening, and much of what he did learn he withheld from the Prime Minister and the Cabinet, perhaps because he distrusted their ability to keep such a terrible secret, perhaps because he doubted whether he would be permitted to proceed with the offensive being planned in Flanders if French support were not forthcoming.

* * *

In order to discuss the genesis of this Flanders offensive, there is a need to go back to the early days of the war. Along the twenty-eight mile stretch of German-held sand-dunes which bordered the Belgian coast were the three ports of Ostend, Blankenberge and Zeebrugge, all used as bases for submarines and light surface craft. In December, 1914. Churchill, then First Lord of the Admiralty, had proposed a combined amphibious landing against Ostend, together with a coastal advance from Nieuport, the small town just above the mouth of the Yser, its object to clear the Germans from the coast. At the time, however, the British were far more concerned with defending the Channel Ports.

During 1915 and 1916 the German U-boat threat to Allied shipping gradually increased, adding to the Admiralty's continual concern with the problem of protecting the troops and supplies transported from England to France from the German light forces based so close to the cross-Channel shipping lanes. By the autumn of 1916 shipping losses were becoming serious with a total of 180,000 tons of British vessels sunk in December. On 1 February, 1917, the Germans openly declared their campaign of 'unrestricted' warfare, or the sinking without warning of neutral shipping as well as Allied. In April, 800,000 tons went to the bottom, 60% of the losses British; one in four of the ships which sailed from British ports did not return. Only six weeks' supply of food remained in a country which at the time depended for its survival upon imported food. In that dreadful month it was being questioned whether the Army could win the war before the Navy lost it.[34] The Admiralty was issuing dire warnings, and on 27 April Robertson wrote to Haig, 'The situation at sea is very serious indeed, and Jellicoe [First Sea Lord] almost daily pronounces it to be hopeless.'[35] To Haig himself Jellicoe stated that 'if the army cannot get the Belgian ports, the Navy cannot hold the Channel and the War is lost'.[36]

These early months of 1917 were, in fact, to be a period of almost unrelieved gloom for the Allies. In March the Russian Revolution was to explode upon a surprised world and the Czar was forced to abdicate; for the time being the Russian army fought on, but appalling losses had already broken its spirit and subversion instigated by the Soviets of Workers and Soldiers Representatives was to complete its collapse. The French army was for the time being near impotent, while the United States of America, which had entered the war on 6 April as a result of the 'unrestricted' submarine campaign, could do little until her manpower and industrial strength could be mobilized; the fear was that the war would be lost before this could be done.

As we have seen, soon after he took over as Commander-in-Chief Haig had examined the problem of clearing the Belgian coastline and at the same time cutting the German rail communications to the northern front, a possible preliminary to rolling up the enemy defences from north to south. Doubting the feasibility of a large-scale amphibious landing, he saw also that a major offensive from Nieuport was out of the question: north of the flooded fenlands between Dixmude and Nieuport there was only a two-mile-wide strip of dry sand-dune, a quite inadequate front from which to launch a major attack. The only sound way to attack was by means of a north-westerly hook from the area of Ypres which would by-pass the indundations, and Haig instructed Sir Henry Rawlinson to draw up plans for such an operation, in which the latter's reformed Fourth Army was to be used. Plumer's Second Army was to cooperate on Rawlinson's right, while a minor attack accompanied by an amphibious landing by two divisions would be launched on his left.

At a conference held by Haig with his Army Commanders on 13 January, 1916, Plumer, who knew every yard of the Ypres Salient, pointed out that the essential preliminary to any such operation must be the capture of the Messines-Wytschaete Ridge which formed the southern arc of the Salient and commanded the Gheluvelt Plateau to its north, which, in turn, would have to be taken before any deep thrust got under way. Plumer then emphasized that preparations for the capture of this Messines Ridge were already in hand and that they included the tunnelling of nineteen mines, upon which work had started six months before.

As it turned out, the large-scale fighting at Verdun and on the Somme pre-empted this northern operation, but Plumer continued with his preparations.[37]

When the Somme fighting at last died down, smothered by the mud of winter, the subject of this northern offensive was revived at the Chantilly Conference in November, 1916, at which the Allies discussed the series of major offensives that were to be launched the following year on the Russian, the Italian and the Western Fronts. After that conference, Haig instructed Plumer to submit fresh plans for this Flanders operation, which would be based upon thirty to thirty-five divisions being available for it. Plumer's proposals, submitted in mid-December, followed the lines of his earlier thinking, except for the requirement that the Pilckem Ridge, an almost indistinguishable feature just to the north of Ypres, should, in addition to the Messines Ridge, be captured as a preliminary to the main operation. As before, the use of two separate Armies was stipulated as being necessary, and Plumer suggested that his should undertake the main operation, with the other capturing the Messines Ridge beforehand. For this latter operation, he stated, only one month's notice would be needed.[38]

But Haig formed the opinion that Plumer's approach to the task was too cautious. In what was close to a rebuke, Kiggell, Robertson's successor as Chief of Staff, wrote to Plumer on 6 January, 1916, instructing him to recast his plans. In part, the letter read:

1. The operation north of the River Lys will not take place until after the subsidiary British attacks elsewhere and main French offensive operations have been carried out. It is therefore to be anticipated that the enemy will have been severely handled and his reserves drawn away from your front before the attacks north of the Lys are launched.
Under these circumstances it is essential that the plan should be based on rapid action and entail the breaking through of the enemy defences on a wide front without any delay.

2. The plan, as submitted by you, indicates a sustained and deliberate offensive such as has been carried out recently on the Somme front. In these circumstances the enemy will have time to bring up fresh reinforcements and construct new lines of defence.

3. The object of these operations is to inflict a decisive defeat on the enemy and to free the Belgian coast.

4. The immediate intention is to break through the enemy defensive positions on the approximate front Hooge-Steenstraat with the object of securing the line Roulers-Thorout and, by advancing in a north-easterly direction, to threaten the coast defences in the rear.
The Belgians and French will co-operate by attacking from Dixmude and Nieuport respectively.

5. The operations naturally divide themselves into two sectors and will be organized into two separate Army commands:
(a) The attack on the Messines-Wytshaete Ridge and Zandvoorde, with the object of forming the defensive flank for the decisive attack, will be carried out by the Southern Army.
(b) The decisive attack, from the approximate front Hooge-Steenstraat with objectives Roulers and Thorout, will be executed by the Northern Army. It is essential that this attack should be carried out with the least possible delay . . .

6. Will you please submit your plans by 31st January.[39]

Although Haig had been sceptical of the possible success of Nivelle's ambitious proposals, the enthusiastic confidence with which he had outlined his plans for his offensive had greatly impressed him.[40] Here was an operation of similar scope. In a deep offensive, the railway lines feeding the German forces in Flanders were to be cut and the coast was to be cleared. This was to be the decisive blow, carried out after Nivelle had drawn off a proportion of the German reserves. No more than a push was needed at the Belgian door for it to swing open.

But Plumer would appear to have been unimpressed. His fresh proposals, submitted to GHQ on 30 January, 1917, were, as the Official History suggests, 'more cautious than the instructions warranted'.[41] On the first day Plumer planned that the Southern Army should take the near crest of the Messines Ridge and the Northern Army the crest of the Pilckem Ridge; on the second day the rear slopes of the Messines Ridge, including Wytschaete village, were to be captured. Because there was unsufficient space to mass all the supporting guns and assemble the assaulting infantry, a gap of 2000 yards was to be left between the two Armies, running from Mount Sorrel to Bellewaarde Ridge; this would be dealt with by converging attacks by the two Armies after they had secured their original objectives. The Southern Army was then to occupy the whole of the Gheluvelt Plateau so as to protect the flank of the Northern Army as it resumed its advance. Wire-cutting and counter-battery work was to be spread over two weeks, but the artillery preparations for the first day's attack were to be extremely short.[42]

Whether Plumer consulted Haig before submitting this new plan, which bore such little relation to the instructions he had received, is not recorded. Even if he did, we see here an Army Commander confident indeed in his own judgement of how the operation should be tackled, ready either to sidestep Haig's instructions or to argue his case and win it. There is no hint of either 'rapid action' or 'breaking through without delay' in Plumer's plan. The doubts and uncertainties of the previous summer would seem to have been overcome, and Plumer was now ready to face up to his superior.

After what he had observed during the past two years, Plumer was clearly determined that lives should not be wasted without due cause. As Bean, the Australian Official Historian, remarked when discussing the Messines offensive, 'Both Plumer – as his white hair and patriarchal demeanour suggested – and his Chief-of-Staff, Major-General Harington, who was known to Australian leaders as a careful, helpful friend, were by nature prone to prudent measures.'[43]

Rawlinson, when consulted by Haig, agreed in general terms with Plumer's fresh proposals, but he emphasized even more strongly the need to seize and hold the Gheluvelt Plateau, behind which the enemy could conceal his massed artillery, before moving on beyond the Pilckem Ridge. In the end, after several weeks of discussion, a compromise was shaped between Haig and his two Army Commanders, but Haig was far from happy. Plumer and Rawlinson, both infantrymen and the only two of Haig's Army Commanders of that persuasion, were planning for a series of infantry battles, at least until the Roulers-Thorout line had been reached. An attempt at a rapid breakthrough of the type Nivelle was visualizing, with the Passchendaele Ridge reached almost at a bound, found little favour with these two rather more prudent generals.

The consequence was that Haig, impatient at the step-by-step tactics his two infantry generals were trying to impose upon him, turned elsewhere. On 30 April, he told Sir Hubert Gough, the Commander of the Fifth Army, that he had decided to use him instead of Rawlinson for the forthcoming Flanders offensive. A forty-seven-year-old cavalryman, Gough was a man after Haig's own heart. But by the time Haig made this change, he was conducting a *volte-face*. Nivelle's failure, combined with the heavy losses his own First and Third Armies had suffered in the attacks they had conducted at Arras to support the French, had demonstrated to him that the Germans were by no means yet beaten and that his ideas for the north had been over-optimistic. On 1 May he noted in his diary the outline of a letter he had that day sent by King's Messenger to the War Cabinet:

> The enemy has already been weakened appreciably, but time is required to wear down his great numbers of troops. The situation is not yet ripe for the decisive blow. We must therefore continue to wear down the enemy until his power of resistance has been further reduced.
>
> The cause of Gen. Nivelle's comparative failure appears primarily to have been a miscalculation in this respect, and the remedy now is to return to wearing-down methods for a further period, the duration of which cannot yet be calculated. I recommend that the pause which is forced upon us in vigorous offensive operations is utilised to complete measures for clearing the coast this summer. Success seems reasonably possible.[44]

Haig's plans had, in effect, been modified. It was to be attrition again in 1917, the 'wearing-down methods', with the breakthrough to clear the coast only 'reasonably' possible.

In his post-war denigration of Haig, Lloyd George made no mention of this memorandum written by Haig, but he reproduces in full the rather abrasive instruction sent to Plumer on 8 January which is discussed earlier, and which had, by May, been overtaken by events further south. It was to be one of the planks of Lloyd George's criticism of Haig for the failure of the Third Battle of Ypres, otherwise known as Passchendaele.[45] In the course of his polemics against Haig, Lloyd George wrote also in his *War Memoirs*, which were published after Plumer's death, that the Second Army Commander had 'deprecated' Haig's ambitious proposals; this could, of course, have been correct, but the Prime Minister quotes no evidence for the statement, nor does he mention the circumstances in which the alleged deprecation occurred.[46] Lloyd George went even further than this, stating that 'Plumer wished to treat it as an isolated operation and not as part of the general offensive in Flanders. To this last he was opposed although the War Committee was not informed of his doubts'.[47] Nothing in Plumer's reported statements or his actions lends any credence to this last comment. But, more than most autobiographies, Lloyd George's *War Memoirs* were an exercise in self-justification rather than historical precision.

Lloyd George had, in fact, given support to Haig's revised concept for the Flanders fighting. At a conference in Paris on 4 May between the military representatives of Britain and France, among whom was Pétain, appointed the previous day as Chief of the General Staff, it was agreed that there was now no hope of rupturing the enemy front, and that the object must be to exhaust his powers of resistance.[48] Later the same day and on the next, Lloyd George approved this policy at a general Inter-Allied Conference, the basis of which had been written into Haig's memorandum. 'The enemy,' the Prime Minister informed the conference, 'must not be left in peace for one moment . . . we must go on hitting and hitting him with all our strength until the Germans ended, as they always do, by cracking.'[49] The German loss of 45,000 prisoners on the Aisne and at Arras, Lloyd George submitted, must have induced pessimism among them. As for the time and place, and the methods to be adopted, he left these to the military, as he expressed it.[50] He did, however, insist that the French should continue to play a full part in the forthcoming battles. It is hardly surprising that all mention of this conference is omitted from his *War Memoirs*.

Two days later Haig informed his assembled Army Commanders that Nivelle's offensive had been halted, and that the Allied aim was now 'to wear down and exhaust the enemy's resistance by systematically attacking him by surprise'; when this had been achieved, the main blow was to be struck on the Ypres front 'with the eventual object of securing the Belgian coast and connecting with the Dutch frontier'. As the Arras operations were run down, troops would be transferred to the north where the fighting would fall into two phases: first, Second Army was to capture the Messines-Wytschaete Ridge about 7 June, after which the 'Northern operations' would start some weeks later.[51] It was a plan slower in operation and more limited in scope even than Plumer's of 30 January.

This was the chance for which Plumer had been waiting. Asked by Haig when he would be ready to attack, the firm answer came back, 'Today, one month, sir'. In Harington's words, 'We came back that day full of hope. The Second Army had its chance at last. We were going to be tried out. It was a wonderful month. Everything we wanted, we were given. Almost every day more guns, and more divisions, etc. arrived.'[52]

Not until 2 June, five days before Plumer was due to attack, did Pétain admit to Haig that, because of the lamentable state of his forces, the projected French attack to draw off the German reserves could not be launched. Nevertheless, Haig decided to allow the Messines attack to go ahead. A long visit to Second Army on 22 May had left him confident of success:

I saw Sir Herbert Plumer, commanding Second Army, at 9.45 a.m. for a few minutes. He is in very good spirits now that his Second Army occupies the first place in our thoughts! I find him a most pleasant fellow to work with and Harrington [sic] (head of the G.S.) and all his Staff, work very kindly with G.H.Q. All are most ready to take advice . . .

I dined with General Plumer at Second Army H. Qrs. in Cassel at 8 p.m.

On the whole there is a fine spirit in the Corps I saw today, but I felt that the leaders had been on the defensive about Ypres so long that the *real offensive spirit* had to be developed. I went into each Brigadier's plan today.[53]

It was perhaps a little condescending. Only grudgingly was Haig learning to appreciate Plumer's qualities.

Terraine has described Haig's method of command as 'Socratic'.[54] By question and answer he investigated the detailed intentions of his subordinates, avoiding friction and rancour, and suggesting changes when he felt them to be necessary, understanding that those who commanded must feel their plans to be their own. That was the theory but the fear in which those junior to him regarded him must have been an inhibiting factor. Plumer's methods were similar to Haig's but conducted in greater depth. Harington relates how he shaped his own plans in consultation with his Corps Commanders, and how they, in their turn, were encouraged to use the same methods with their Divisional Commanders, and so on down the line. Plumer was in the habit of elaborating these consultations during his daily visits to lower headquarters, so that all concerned felt that they had been given the chance of stating their case, even though they might disagree on points of detail with Plumer's final plan. Harington emphasized how such methods increased people's trust in Plumer, and he contrasted them with the lack of consultation in other Armies and the unfortunate consequences that followed.[55]

* * *

Other than the major amphibious landings of the Second World War, preparations have never been so comprehensive nor so prolonged as those for the Battle of Messines. First, there were the mines, the large-scale use of which will always be linked with this battle. Their employment was nothing new in war, dating back to the 8th Century BC Assyrians: to breach a city wall, a tunnel would be dug beneath it, the wooden supports then destroyed by fire and the wall above collapse. Gunpowder refined the art, but by 1914 the British Army had almost forgotten its techniques, siege-warfare being apparently a thing of the distant past. The new conditions on the Western Front and at Gallipoli were to bring about a revival of the skills, but those early mines were shallow tunnels, dug some fifteen feet below the surface and armed with a smallish charge. The Royal Engineers then proposed that deep mines should be excavated, ninety feet or so below the enemy trenches. Not until January, 1916, did GHQ give its official approval to the suggestion, but, by then, Plumer's sappers were already digging tunnels of this depth under the Second Army front. If the Messines attack had been launched, as originally planned, in the summer of 1916, four of these deep mines were ready for use; in the subsequent twelve months, the system was to be vastly expanded and elaborated.

The Royal Engineers had collected some officers and men with the required skills by combing infantry and other units, many of whom had been recruited from the coalfields. Others were enlisted direct from civilian life. One such unit, raised on 17 February, 1915, from the so-called 'clay-kickers', was the brain-child of an esoteric individual, Major J. Norton-Phillips, who had been with Plumer in both Matabeleland and the Boer War, and who travelled everywhere in France in his personal 2 1/2-ton Rolls Royce. The lot of these 'clay-kickers' was to dig the narrow tunnels required for underground cables and sewers, lying on their backs, each on a wooden frame, and kicking out the clay with a specially designed shovel. By 21 February that unit was already at work in France. Four days earlier, the British had fired a mine under Hill 60, the first of many; a few days later the Germans reciprocated. And so this underground war progressed, mining and counter-mining to destroy the opposing galleries and the men working within them, whose monotonous tapping could be heard in their trenches overhead and which caused terror when it ceased. It was a grim war, fought sometimes with picks and shovels in the foetid darkness when one side broke into the other's galleries. Gas was the other peril: depicted on the Scottish War Memorial in Edinburgh are the mice and canaries which were the tunnellers' friends.

By June, 1917, twenty-one large mines were ready on Plumer's front, some of them with shafts a quarter of a mile long. Mechanical diggers had been tried, but found wanting under battlefield conditions; they

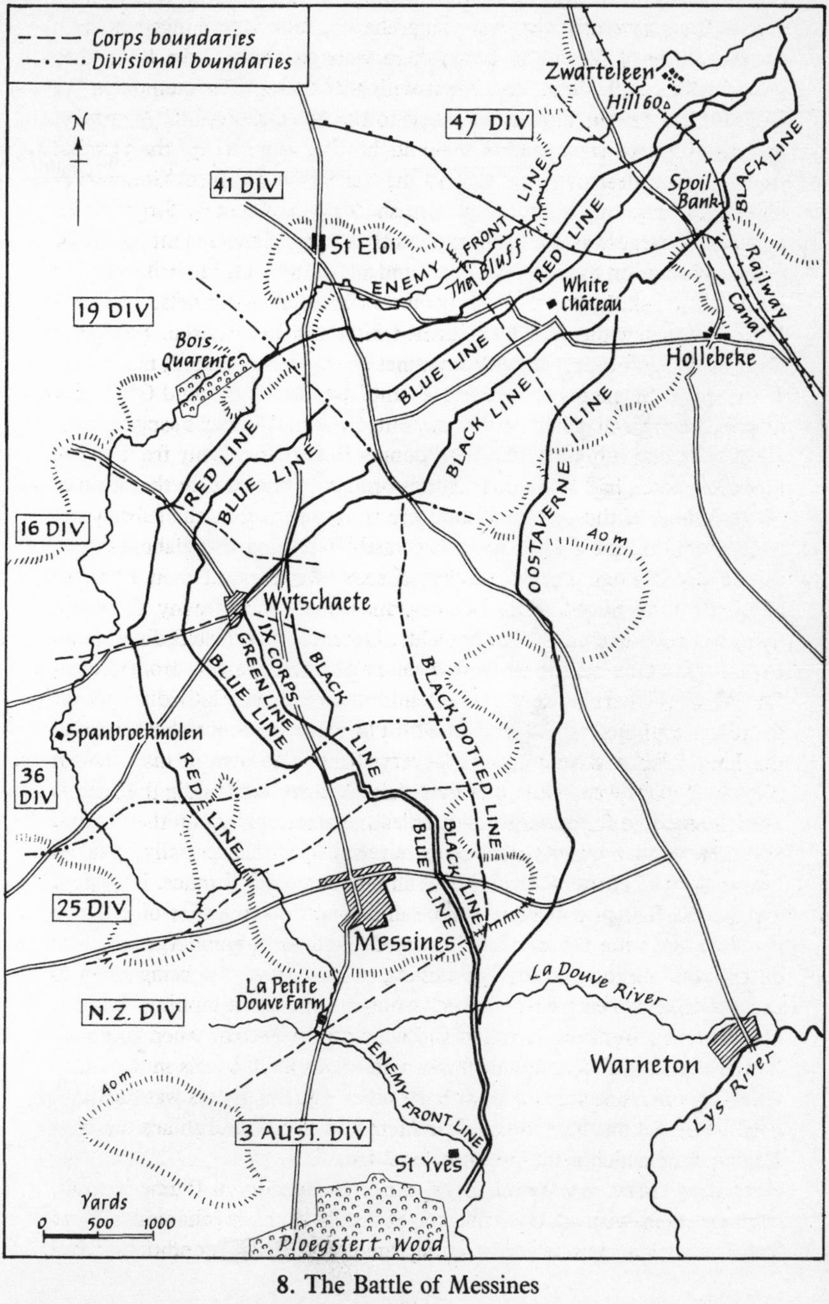
Corps boundaries
Divisional boundaries
N
Zwarteleen
Hill 60
47 DIV
41 DIV
Spoil Bank
BLACK LINE
St Eloi
ENEMY FRONT LINE
The Bluff
RED LINE
Railway
White Château
Canal
19 DIV
Bois Quarente
BLUE LINE
Hollebeke
BLACK LINE
OOSTAVERNE LINE
RED LINE
BLUE LINE
16 DIV
40 m
Wytschaete
IX CORPS
GREEN LINE
BLUE LINE
BLACK LINE
BLACK DOTTED LINE
Spanbroekmolen
36 DIV
RED LINE
BLUE LINE
BLACK LINE
25 DIV
Messines
La Douve River
La Petite Douve Farm
N.Z. DIV
ENEMY FRONT LINE
Warneton
Lys River
40 m
3 AUST. DIV
St Yves
Yards
0
500
1000
Ploegstert Wood

8. The Battle of Messines

remain entombed under Flanders' fields. The quantity of labour used was enormous, partly the consequence of the blue Ypres clay which, if casually dumped, would have revealed the digging to the enemy; instead it had to be packed into sandbags and carried back by working parties to be hidden in the woodlands. Countermining, together with the digging of underground shelters, used as many men as the offensive mining operations. On the Messines front alone, during the twelve months prior to the battle, 5000 yards of 6x3 feet underground passageways were excavated by pick and shovel. This was just part of the work of the Royal Engineers: 115 miles of broad-gauge and 85 miles of narrow-gauge railway were laid, the latter bringing ammunition right up to the positions of the heavy artillery. Water-storage, airfields, telegraph cable-laying, roads and hutments were other tasks with which they had to cope.[56]

The artillery preparations were just as far reaching. To support the attack, between one-half and one-third of the artillery supporting the First, Third and Fifth Armies was moved north, raising the total of howitzers and guns available to Plumer to 2266, one to each seven yards of front. 44,000 tons of ammunition were dumped, for the 18-pounders an average of 1000 rounds in each gun-pit.[57] During the previous three years there had been a revolution in the use of artillery. As the historian of the Royal Artillery on the Western Front has incontrovertibly put it, 'guns were the catalyst that made success possible'[58] in the siege warfare of 1914-1918. At its start there were few indications that this would happen. During 1914 the guns were used much as they had been in the Boer War, firing usually over open sights and fought in their sections or batteries. Communications were such that it was difficult to concentrate the fire of even two batteries; the skills of directing fire by forward observers working with the infantry and passing instructions back to the guns had not been adequately developed; the logistic back-up had not taken account of the large quantities of ammunition which would be needed; there was no way of grouping and controlling the guns of even a single division; and little thought had been given to cover from air observation, anti-aircraft defence or counter-battery work. As the war progressed all these problems were successfully tackled and overcome, while a number of scientific tools were introduced such as flash-spotting, sound-ranging and vastly better communications, together with improvements in the reliability of ammunition, especially fuses. By the Battle of Messines, it had become possible to concentrate the whole of the artillery under a single commander in the preliminary stages, and, by the year's end, the guns of an entire Army could open fire at H Hour without any previous warning, the registration of the guns by fire having become unnecessary. Local success could now be almost assured provided the infantry objectives did not lie beyond the range of the field artillery. If the enemy artillery could then be suppressed by counter-battery fire, and the field-guns could then be moved forward quickly enough to support successive blows by the infantry, enemy resistance could be worn down. It had, in fact, become an artillery war.

Plumer had also to obtain air superiority over the battlefield, although the term had yet to be coined. II Brigade RFC supported Second Army, and before the battle their aircraft had been increased in number to 300, almost double that of their opponents. From dawn to dusk the front was covered at 15,000 feet by continuous patrols of four to six 'scouts', while the actual assault area was further protected by planes flying at 10,000 feet, so providing a double layer of cover through which few hostile aircraft managed to penetrate. Every day the German defences were photographed, and eight captive balloons assisted the artillery observation aircraft. This information obtained from the air, together with that from all the many other intelligence-gathering agencies, was relayed by wireless, deep-laid cable or by messages dropped by the planes to the Second Army Report Centre, four miles behind the front.[59] And the internal combustion engine was in widespread use on the ground as well as in the air – extensively so, as is often forgotten: in Plumer's Army alone, there were more than 12,500 motor-vehicles, including 154 mobile workshops.[60] Warfare in 1917 was far from unsophisticated.

After Plumer's reputation had been firmly established, Harington was asked for his master's secret of success. The reply was 'Trust, Training and Thoroughness'.[61] These three precepts were linked closely together, each one reinforcing the others. 'Trust' and 'Thoroughness' have been described. The 'Training' Plumer organized for Second Army was as 'Thorough' as everything else and it reinforced the 'Trust' with which he was regarded.

The previous winter Plumer's staff had produced four training manuals for the use of his corps, one for the infantry, one for the engineers, one for the artillery, and one on communications. Instructions were based upon the lessons learned from the Somme, and subsequently the Arras fighting was to be dissected in similar fashion.[62] An enormous model of Messines Ridge and its defences was built, the size of two croquet lawns, and from the scaffolding that surrounded it every officer who was to take part in the attack was given the chance to study it. Even Blunden, cynical indeed after what he had seen and suffered, admired it, 'though whether from its charm as a model or value as a military aid' was uncertain; when prospects of the coming offensive reached his unit, 'people did not espouse these with the comparatively bright eye of the year before; 1917 was distasteful.'[63] Many of the infantry divisions involved also constructed models of their own areas so that the troops themselves could examine the ground which they would be crossing.

For the attacking units, the preliminaries were arduous. The front lines were thinned out, leaving only a single battalion to hold each divisional sector, while the rest either trained for the coming assault or toiled on working parties (among other tasks was the digging of six separate lines of trenches, each 100 yards apart, from which the assault was to be mounted). Anthony Eden described the training. Like Blunden, the twenty-one year old adjutant was a survivor. Smashed twice on the Somme, his Yeoman Rifles had twice been made up to strength with Londoners, and the battalion then spent a miserable winter just south of St Eloi. In the spring this unit was pulled back into a so-called rest area:

> We were now plunged into an intensive system of training such as we had never known. Though we did not realize it at the time, subsequent events proved clearly that every aspect of training as well as the operation itself had been carefully prepared by the army staff, closely supervised by Plumer, but under the direction of General Harington. . . . It was typical that during the training of our battalion Plumer himself inspected us at work, while Harington visited us several times.[64]

Eden's was one of over 100 attacking battalions. He rememberd the training as also having been an important morale-building exercise. The ground had been chosen to resemble so far as possible the country over which the battalion was to attack. With flags representing the creeping barrage, time and again the men rehearsed to a meticulous time-table until the rate of progress became almost automatic. First companies rehearsed, then battalions, then the brigade as a whole. Nothing was rushed. A thread connecting the memoirs of the soldiers of that war was the unpopularity of the training inflicted upon weary bodies supposedly resting from the front line. Before Messines, that training was accepted with just that little less ill-will.

8 Messines : The Battle

At 3.10 am on 7 June, 1917, as a grey dawn light began to filter across the countryside, nineteen mines, charged with a total of a million pounds of high explosive, exploded under the German positions along the edge of the Messines Ridge. Anthony Eden, whose battalion was one of those assaulting from St Eloi, a wasteland already shattered by the mining and counter-mining of the previous two years, was to describe what he saw and felt as the forward companies clambered out of their trenches:

> It was an astonishing sight, rising like some giant mushroom to a considerable height in the air before it broke suddenly into fragments of earth, stones and timber falling over a wide area. The whole ground heaved so violently that for a fraction of a second we thought we were over the mine instead of beside it. As the barrage opened simultaneously, the noise of the guns deadened all sound from the mine, except that we could hear, even above the crescendo, the screams of the imprisoned Germans in the crater.[1]

Private Norman Gladden's battalion attacked the equally devastated Hill 60. When the men moved forward in the darkness to their newly dug and shallow assembly trenches, they had been strafed by gas shells which 'whined over and struck the ground around us with their characteristically undecided thud', but they had done little damage; at one point in the march the reek of petrol indicated the presence of tanks, unseen and unheard. During that hardly bearable wait in the trenches for the first streaks of dawn to steal across the sky, all was quiet. The Germans had detected nothing. Then, as a voice cried 'Now',

> It was the hour. . . . The ground began to rock. My body was carried up and down as though by the waves of the sea. In front the earth opened and a large black mass mounted on pillars of fire to the sky, where it seemed to remain suspended for some seconds while the awful

red glow lit up the surrounding desolation. No sound came. My nerves had been keyed to sustain a noise from the mine so tremendous as to be unbearable. For a brief spell all was silent, as though we were so close that the sound itself had leaped over us like some immense wave. . . . There was a tremendous roar and a tearing noise across the skies as the barrage commenced with unerring accuracy. It was as though a vast door had been flung open, and the silence died within the instant. The skies behind our lines were lit up by the flash of many thousand guns, while above the booming din of the artillery rose the rasping rattle of the Vickers guns.[2]

To a German soldier who saw from a distance the entire spectacle, it appeared as:

nineteen gigantic roses with carmine petals, or as enormous mushrooms, which rose up slowly and majestically out of the ground and then split into pieces with a mighty roar, sending up multi-coloured columns of flame mixed with a mass of earth and splinters high into the sky.[3]

In Lille, fifteen miles distant, people rushed panic-stricken from their houses; even in London the shock was distinctly felt. Because, unintentionally, the explosions were not quite simultaneous, the last being nineteen seconds after the first, the effects upon the Germans were cumulative and the panic was increased by the ventriloquial character of the explosions, which appeared to spread and multiply their effects. Of those Germans who were far enough from the mines to survive, most were shattered, incapable of resistance. Some fled; some emerged from their trenches or concrete shelters dazed, shaking and cringing for mercy. The craters were as much as 300 feet in diameter and fifty to seventy deep, impeding the movement of the assaulting British units. Two mines failed to explode. One did so in 1955, causing no damage except to the fields of the grandchildren of the farmers who had tilled them forty years before; one still lurks deep underground, a constant threat.

Because the battle had been planned so long in advance and in such voluminous detail, the Operation Order, signed by Harington on 10 May, 1917, had covered little more than the proverbial sheet of foolscap, to which was attached a map showing the objectives of each corps, together with the designation and timing of each stage of the advance. It bears setting out in full:

1. Under instructions from the Commander-in-Chief and with a view to enforcing the enemy to withdraw reserves from the main battle front

1. The Battle of Tamai, 13 March, 1884.
From the painting by Douglas Giles.
"One longed to see active service but I have seen enough to last me some time." (p.8)

2. Canon's Park, Edgware,
bought by Sir Thomas Plumer in 1811. (p.10)

3. Photograph of Plumer
taken during the Matabele Rebellion. (Ch. 2)

4. The Duke of Connaught's staff at Aldershot, 1898.
Plumer is standing second from the left. On his left is Major the Hon. J.H. Byng. (p. 53)

5. 'Spy' cartoon of Plumer from *Vanity Fair* of 29 November, 1900.
Titled 'Self Reliant', the caption describes him as possessing pluck,
judgment, caution and self-reliance, and deserving all his success,
which he had won wholly off his own bat.

6. Drawing of Plumer
when commanding Second Army by Francis Dodd.

Ypern, 11.5 km.

St. Martinskirche in Ypern

Kirche in Ypern

Tuchhallen-Turm.

Baracke 0.3 km westlich
Höhe 37. · 5.1 km.

Drahthindernisse.

1030   1020   1010   1000

7. Ypres from a German artillery observation post.
Prominent landmarks are named. The only slightly damaged
buildings and the undamaged trees date the photograph
to the very early days of the war.

8. British mine exploding. (p. 177)

9. Messines Ridge seen from the British lines. (Ch. 7)

10. Captured German trenches on Messines Ridge. (Ch. 8)

11. British mine crater on Messines Ridge.

12. King George V visits Second Army.

13. Plumer in his Vauxhall staff car passes a French transport column.

14. Plumer taking the salute as his troops pass
over the Rhine bridge into Cologne after the Armistice.

15. General Officers of the First World War by John Singer Sargent.
Plumer is on Haig's right hand, Smuts on his left.

16. Plumer when High Commissioner for Palestine
with his wife and military staff. (Ch. 13)

17. Plumer laying foundation stone
of St. George's Chapel at Ypres in July, 1927. (p. 315)

18. Lord and Lady Plumer
arrive at an official engagement.

19. Plumer with his daughter
and granddaughter.

20. Low's cartoon of Colonel Blimp.

(Vimy-Arras), the Second Army will capture the Messines-Wytschaete Ridge on a date (Zero) which will be fixed later.

2. The troops alloted for the operations are:

    II Anzac Corps...............3rd Australian, New Zealand, 25th, 4th Australian Divisions.

    IX Corps......................36th, 16th, 19th, 11th Divisions.

    X Corps.......................41st, 47th, 23rd, 24th Divisions.

    Reserve Corps (XIV).......Guards, 1st, 8th, 32nd Divisions.

3. The objects of the operation are:

    (a) To capture the enemy position from St Yves to Observatory Ridge.

    (b) To capture as many as possible of the enemy guns in the vicinity of Oosttaverne and north-east of Messines.

    (c) To consolidate a position to secure our possession of the Messines-Wytschaete Ridge and establish a series of posts in advance.

4. The final objective of each corps is shown generally by a Black Line, the intermediate stages being shown by Red and Blue Lines, together with timings at each stage. It is imperative, in order to effect surprise and to capture enemy guns, that the attack should be pushed through without delay in one day.

5. The attack will be made at dawn (the exact hour will be notified later).

6. The initial advance will be assisted by the explosion of mines on each corps front. The mines will be fired at zero hour.

7. Two battalions of the Heavy Branch Machine-Gun Corps [tanks] will assist the operations.

8. The preliminary bombardment will be 5 days.

    The allotment of artillery to corps, the artillery policy to be pursued from now onwards, the method of carrying out the preliminary bombardment and the general artillery plan have been issued to corps concerned.

9. A subsidiary operation will be carried out by VIII Corps in connection with the above attack.

10. H.Q. Second Army will be at Cassel.

11. Acknowledge.

Issued at 9 p.m.

                                       C.H. Harington,
                               M.G.G.S. Second Army.[4]

Somewhat strange is the statement in the first paragraph that the operation was being carried out so as to enforce the withdrawal of enemy reserves from the main battle-front of Vimy-Arras. At the time that battle was, of course, at its height, but the remark could well have been inserted so as to avoid revealing Allied strategic intentions – the plan to transfer the weight of the offensive to the north.

Nine days later, on 19 May, Second Army issued a further order which extended the scope of the operation to include, at Haig's behest, the capture of the so-called Oosttaverne Line which ran to the east of the village of that name and took in much of the eastern slope of the Messines Ridge. The capture of this line, which involved at its deepest point a further advance of some 1200 yards, was planned for ten hours after zero; between then and the taking of the Black Line, which took in the eastern crest of the plateau, as much field artillery as possible was to be brought forward to give close support for the final phase of the battle, the positions of the guns having already been selected and the line communications laid.[5]

At the outset Plumer had under his command a total of five corps, while XIV Corps, the GHQ reserve, was held ten miles back, available if needed. Of the three assaulting formations, II ANZAC was to attack north-easterly to capture the eastern shoulder of the Messines Ridge, including the buttress formed by Messines village. IX Corps, in the centre, was to take the high ground around Wytschaete (or 'Whitesheet' as the British knew it); on the northern flank of the offensive was X Corps, its objectives the high ground which overlooked and commanded the devastated areas around St Eloi, Hill 60 and The Bluff, places of ill repute all of them. Further north still, II and VIII Corps were to hold the line from the north of Mount Sorrel to the Belgians at Boesinghe. Each assault corps was to deploy three divisions in the line with a fourth in reserve, and seventy-two of the new Mark IV Tanks had been made available to Plumer to deal with the concrete strong-points, the older tanks with their guns removed having the task of carrying petrol, ammunition and water to the forward units.

Plumer's artillery programme was based on what had been learned about the latest defence systems of the Germans, encountered during the Arras fighting and revealed in detail in a captured document, which, after translation, had been widely distributed. In outline it was as follows. The ever-increasing British and French superiority in artillery had persuaded the Germans that it was hopeless to fight a defensive battle in the devastated forward zone. This, then, they held lightly, with a stronger support zone further back, but the main strength of the defence lay in the succession of counterattack forces held ready to recapture any lost ground. Along the Messines Ridge, one three-battalion German regiment on average faced each of the nine assaulting British divisions. Only one battalion of each of these German regiments held the forward zone, which, stretching up towards the top of the plateau, was liberally sprinkled with those concrete machine-gun posts and defended shell-holes. In the second zone, on the top of the plateau, the front edge of which was the British Blue Line objective, was stationed the second battalion of each regiment, while the third was in reserve some two miles further back. Further back still were two further counterattack divisions, poised for use as the need arose.

The tasks of the British artillery were to destroy the German machine-gun posts, to blot out the wire entanglements, to harass communications and forward divisional supply routes, to silence the enemy artillery and to smash his reserves. As well as the 2266 howitzers and guns assembled for this purpose, 428 heavy mortars were available for use against the forward outposts. Further back, the RFC attacked rail centres and airfields, and machine-gunned and bombed the villages and hutments sheltering German reserves. The magnificent weather experienced during the week prior to the attack had provided the counter-battery and bombardment groups with perfect observation for their preparatory work, which had begun on 21 May instead of the five days before the attack originally stipulated.[6] During the afternoons of 3 and 5 June Plumer arranged for rehearsals of the barrages planned to cover the assaulting troops to be fired so as to trick the enemy into disclosing any still unlocated gun-positions, and he deployed the full strength of the RFC to spot them. Between 26 May and 6 June Second Army fired no less than 3 1/4 million rounds, and even that was one third less than the estimated expenditure. With preparations on such a scale, the only sort of surprise that could be achieved was to keep the Germans guessing when the blow would fall.

★ ★ ★

As the reverberations from the exploding mines told the men of the leading battalions of those nine assaulting divisions to clamber to their feet and start moving up the slope towards the German positions, a wall of steel fragments curtained them, the creeping barrage laid in front of them by two-thirds of the Second Army's 18-pounders; the other third, together with the 4.5 field howitzers, masked with standing barrages the strongpoints ahead. As if this were not enough, 700 heavy machine guns, using both direct and indirect fire, rained bullets ahead of the advancing troops; further ahead still, the heavy and medium artillery added their weight of shells, the counter-battery programme continuing for a full thirty minutes after zero-hour.[7]

Each infantryman should have known his individual task, rehearsed again and again. Clouds of dust and smoke from the explosions of the mines and the intense artillery barrage helped conceal them from the surviving German machine-gunners, but in the thick murk direction was sometimes lost, and compasses had to be brought into use. The tactics used by the infantry were those which had proved successful on Vimy Ridge; first conceived by a French Officer in 1915, they had been published in a booklet and adopted by the Germans who chanced upon a copy in a captured trench.[8] Leading assault groups with Lewis guns and rifle grenades bombarded the loop-holes of the concrete pill-boxes and the shell-holes from which enemy parties still resisted; at the same time other infantry groups infiltrated these defences, riflemen and bombers working their way from one shell-hole to the next; further back, mopping up parties cleared any enemy dugouts, their accompanying sappers making safe the proliferation of booby-traps with which the Germans sprinkled their abandoned shelters.

So it was that in thirty-five minutes, exactly upon schedule, the British infantry gained their first objective along the full front of the attack. In some places the fresh mine-craters impeded the troops as they advanced, but only in the very south was there a major hitch. There the 3rd Australian Division, commanded by Major-General Monash and fighting its first major battle, was harassed by gas-shells as it moved in four columns through Ploegsteert Wood to its assembly positions. Five hundred men collapsed, gasping and retching in the darkness, and a number of units were delayed, reaching their launching trenches only just before the mines exploded; despite this, the spirit and training of this raw division was such that its organization was hardly impaired, and its officers led their men straight up the slope into the attack. On the left of the Australians, the New Zealand Division encountered little difficulty, nor did the 25th Division, the non-ANZAC part of this Anzac Corps. It was much the same in the centre. Here the 36th Division Ulstermen and the 16th Division Southern Irishmen advanced together through the splintered tree-stumps of what had been fine woods around Wytschaete village; the Northerners suffered no losses at all at this stage of the attack, but the Southerners lost men from the blast of a mine fired just twelve seconds late, so catching them in the open. Further north still, in X Corps sector, all went as planned.

The sun was up, the prelude to another scorching day, and it was broad daylight when the Blue Line, the second objective, was reached. To gain it, the two support battalions of each of the eighteen assault brigades had leap-frogged through to breast the ridge, passing as they did so German bodies that were described as carpeting the ground. Stiffer resistance was met here, but still all went as planned. From the village of Messines the ground drops away sharply on three sides with a view extending from Armentières to Warneton and beyond into the German rear east of the Lys River. Here the New Zealanders faced the toughest job of the day, assaulting uphill into the heap of rubble that had been transformed into a fortress: wire entanglements and trenches encircled an inner keep of five concrete strongholds; the house cellars had been fashioned into reinforced dug-outs. Further north, along the Damm Strasse, a mile-long drive running from St Eloi to the White Château (both mere names now in the wilderness), the 41st Division also had a hard time, while the remains of the Château itself, the 47th Division's second objective, was twice assaulted before the survivors of the German garrison, fighting from the ruins with machine guns and stick grenades, could be persuaded to surrender. Here and there along the front, counterattacks by small parties of Germans were halted with little or no difficulty. The crust of the German defence had been broken. Captured documents later revealed that the enemy had planned on the crest of the ridge being held until the two rear divisions, earmarked for major counterattacks, could be moved forward.[9]

The Black Line, the next and the primary objective, lay 400 to 500 yards away across the largely flat and almost featureless summit plateau. A two-hour halt had been called so as to consolidate properly the Blue Line and deploy fresh battalions for the next assault. Strongpoints were quickly dug and wired, and machine guns were sited in depth in them. Carrying parties had struggled forward with the necessary wire and sandbags, and ammunition as well, some of them arriving only four minutes after the leading infantry had captured their objectives. As the work of consolidation progressed, the guns used for the creeping barrage continued to fire, dropping their shells 300 yards in front of the forward positions and sweeping backwards and forwards so as to trap any German units approaching to form up for a counterattack.

At 7 am the full force of the British artillery blasted forth once again and the infantry began to move across the plateau. Most divisions were now using their third brigades, and the tanks were in action as well, in ones and twos helping individual parties of infantry to crush pockets of resistance; forty-eight had been allotted for the day's fighting, but this was the first time they had been of any use as the carved-up ground in the forward zone had reduced their speed to about ten yards to the minute, instead of the expected three miles per hour. The hardest task at this stage was the taking of Wytschaete village, the highest point of the ridge, from which observation could be gained in every direction; its ruins, like those of Messines, had been transformed into a fortress. By 8 am, however, Irishmen of the 16th Division had stormed through the place and wiped out any survivors of the bombardment still resisting. Only in X Corps sector was there a check: in the vast heap of excavated earth known as Spoil Bank, north of the canal and beyond Hill 60, German defenders clung to their posts against repeated attacks by the Londoners of the 47th Division, and reinforcements even managed to survive the barrages to reach them.

By 8.40 am companies from the leading battalions had started to advance down the eastern slope of the Messines Ridge to the Dotted Black, or observation line, its purpose to allow the forward artillery observation officers to see more of the German positions in the valley below. This action foreshadowed the warfare of the future. Eight tanks supported the infantrymen as they moved down the slope behind the barrage, while scout aircraft, flying low, raked with machine guns any enemy they sighted. The Germans, by now demoralized, resisted only half-heartedly. By 9 am the British held the Messines Ridge from the Douve River to Mount Sorrel, and their artillery observers on the forward slopes were scanning the German rear areas. Behind was a ploughed-up wilderness, ahead a green and unspoilt countryside with the towns and woods of the Lys Valley visible in the far distance.

Two quite different accounts exist of Plumer's whereabouts when the mines exploded at 3.10 am on 7 June. First, there is the unlikely tale that he was celebrating in Skindles, the famous Poperinghe rendezvous for officers, named after the well-known Maidenhead hotel: there, two seconds before the explosions were heard, he is credited with having ordered another vermouth.[10] Harington's recollection was different. After seeking his bed at 9 pm with every loose end tied up, he had breakfasted with Plumer at 2.30 am, after which he walked up from the Château Yvonne to the top of Cassel Hill to watch the distant explosions. 'Not so the Army Commander. He was kneeling by his bedside, praying for those gallant officers and men who were at the moment attacking'.[11] Plumer's batman also has confirmed that it was his master's habit to pray before a big attack.[12] Imagination is needed to visualize the feelings of such a kind and devout man at the moment when thousands of young men are about to be killed as a consequence of the plan he has conceived and the orders he has given.

Harington relates that they met later in his office. When the news arrived that Messines Ridge had been captured, he remembered his general's hand on his shoulder and the tears in the old man's eyes.

That three-week period before Messines had been made unneedingly trying for Plumer. Senior officers, in the static conditions of the Western Front, too often performed their subordinates jobs for them, but Haig's 'Socratic' methods often verged near to interference. By the time Plumer issued his main operation order for Messines, the preliminary planning had been going on for months. Nevertheless, five days later, on 15 May, Haig was to direct that the scope of the battle should be extended by pushing on down the slope, past the 'Observation Line' to the 'Oosttaverne Line'.[13] This was a major change, one dictated by the desire to obtain a better view for the artillery observers, despite the unequalled observation both Messines and Wytschaete provided. This was not all. The British tunnellers under Hill 60 could hear Germans working so close to them that the noise of the windlass winching back the spoil was clearly audible. It is said that Haig, upon learning of this, lost his nerve (an unusual occurrence) and proposed that the charge under Hill 60 should be exploded ahead of time. Plumer, however, is reported to have demurred, confident that the Germans were not working fast enough to allow them to break through into the British tunnel before 7 June, and that, in the end, he made his point.[14] The sources for this tale have, however, proved elusive. It could well be another of the myths of the First World War.

Better authenticated is the report that, as late as 30 May, Haig held a conference to consider what might happen if the Germans should abandon their positions in the forward zone before the attack began. To avoid the possible waste of all the effort that had been put into preparing the mines, Haig proposed that they should be exploded before Zero Day and the craters occupied. Plumer objected, and he won. To retire from their forward positions to the top of the ridge was, in fact, something the Germans had considered but rejected.[15]

Previously, on 20 May, Haig had drawn up some notes for the guidance of Second Army in the coming battle. They were extremely detailed. After a number of paragraphs of a general nature, Haig posed a large variety of questions to Plumer's corps commanders, examples of which were:

Have you got the enemy's batteries accurately located? Are changes of position occurring, and, if so, in what manner? For example, is the enemy occupying alternative positions near vacated ones; is he re-occupying his old ones after a certain lapse of time, or do you see a general tendency to move his batteries back? Have you discovered any new positions in course of construction, and are they being camouflaged as they are made . . .? Have your Intelligence and Artillery Reconnaissance Officers detailed information as to where he is placing his machine guns, etc? How do you propose forming up the troops for the attack . . .? Have you a detailed plan for stopping the bridges over the RIVER LYS or CANAL D'YPRES, as the case may be . . .? Are your infantry trained to deal with low-flying hostile aeroplanes by Lewis Gun and rifle fire? Are you satisfied that the Inter-Corps and Inter-Division barrages are all co-ordinated and that, as far as possible, they meet with the views of the Divisional Commanders? Have you arranged your barrage in depth from the moment of the assault onwards? What is your plan for destroying the wire? Have you considered the number of guns that it will be necessary for you to allocate to counter-battery at zero?

The specific questions that followed for each of Plumer's corps were even more detailed: a minute cross-examination on how they were to capture specific objectives such as Messines and Wytschaete; how the River Douve and the Steenbeek were to be crossed; were the various counter-battery groups adequate and their positioning satisfactory? And so on for pages. For three full days, between 22 and 24 May, Haig visited the headquarters of the corps and divisions planning for Messines, working his way through the list and checking the plans of the various generals.[16] After consulting Plumer, he sacked one of the divisional commanders out of hand as a result of this cross-examination. This sort of thing was nearer to commanding three down than thinking two down, the received wisdom in military planning.

Haig's slightly condescending note that Plumer and his staff were most ready to accept advice[17] takes on a fresh meaning after reading these notes. At the end of that round of visits to the various headquarters, Haig recorded that Plumer had 'most cordially received' his suggestions, and that he had been able to tell him that the attack was the most carefully mounted he had known, and that Plumer and his troops were better prepared for their work than on any previous occasion in the war.[18] Clearly Plumer accepted this close supervision with outwardly good grace; of his inner feelings we know nothing. But after such meticulous and sound preparation, such detailed and last-minute interference can only have caused intense aggravation. Even more important was the effect such last-minute changes had on Plumer's subordinates. Revisions to plans followed one another, all the way down the chain of command. Only on 27 May did Godley, commander of II ANZAC, send out the last major alteration to his plan. It was hardly surprising that his divisional commanders blamed him for the changes,[19] and on that same day an exasperated Monash wrote to one of his brigade commanders, 'I have reason to believe that matters have at last reached finality'.[20]

Monash hardly fitted the mould of First World War generals. Many authorities paid tribute to him as the most creative general to emerge; others differed. In appearance this fifty-one-year-old militia officer, the son of German-Jewish immigrants, was in his quite different way as far removed from the typical British general as was Plumer. A brilliant and successful civil engineer, Monash combined the attributes of that profession with a deep knowledge of the theory of warfare. An able trainer, he was also a strict disciplinarian, a stickler for such matters as saluting and turnout, unpopular fads with his Australians. Overtly ambitious, he intrigued for honours and advancement, while denying that he did so – a not uncommon human failing. He commanded from his headquarters, rarely seeing anything of his troops when they were in the line, or even examining the ground over which they were to fight, content to work from his maps. His very Germanic attitudes are conveyed in this coldly calculated statement:

> If one stops to count the cost, or worry about the loss of friends and sorrow of the people at home, one simply could not carry on for an hour. The moment a man becomes a casualty, pick your man to take his place . . . it is the whole secret of successful leadership in war. The objective is everything – the means do not count.[21]

As an engineer he looked upon his troops as the raw materials with which he could build, and such raw materials must need be sound. The physical and mental welfare of his men was, therefore, always his care. Meticulous in everything – possibly pedantic – like Haig he usurped the functions of his subordinates: but, like both Haig and Plumer, he developed his plans by discussion. This stoutish, elderly-looking man, almost a caricature of the Jewish businessman, was popular with his troops, a popularity, like Plumer's, based upon confidence that they would be sent into battle properly prepared. He would become, in due course, a very able corps commander, but he was certainly not Lloyd George's greatest 'strategist in the Army'.[22]

To return to Haig. At 4 pm on that first afternoon, he was back at Plumer's headquarters* to congratulate him upon his success. 'The old man,' he wrote that evening in his diary, 'deserves the highest praise for he has patiently defended the Ypres Salient for two and a half years, and he well knows that pressure had been brought to bear on me to remove him from the Command of Second Army.'[24] Talking to Charteris that same evening, he described Plumer as 'his most reliable Army Commander', high praise indeed, as Charteris commented.[25]

Who wanted Plumer sacked? It is an intriguing question to which no satisfactory answer had been discovered. Harington, of course, had accused Douglas of being Plumer's only real enemy,[26] but Douglas had been dead since October, 1914. It would seem that he had another. It was certainly not Lloyd George, who at the time of Messines hardly knew him, and who was soon to consider him as a replacement for both Robertson and for Haig himself. Kitchener had refused to send him to France in August, 1914, but he did so a few months later, and he also had been dead for a year when Messines was fought. Lord Derby, the Secretary of

---

*Haig had established his own forward headquarters in a train, and he had followed the progress of the battle with a telescope from a hut prepared for him on the top of Mont Rouge, about two miles behind the battlefield.[23]

State, and Robertson, the CIGS, were the only other persons able to exert direct pressure upon Haig, but nothing at all has come to light to suggest that either of them might have been guilty. The only other possibility is perhaps Lord Haldane, the *eminence grise*, whose influence remained strong even though he held no office, and whose relations with Haig continued to be close. It is recorded that Haldane told Lloyd George that he thought little of Plumer's intelligence.[27]

★ ★ ★

The final phase of the Messines battle was an afternoon advance down the eastern slope to the Oosttaverne Line, and for this Plumer used the reserve divisions of each of his three corps. His original intention had been to press on to it from the Black Line without a halt, and with support provided from the twenty-four batteries of the reserve XIV Corps, well hidden and hitherto kept silent so as to escape attention from the German counter-battery artillery. 'Risks may and should be taken,' wrote Plumer to his Corps Commanders, 'in order to secure that line and capture the guns in the intervening area,' their number being estimated as 150. But his Corps Commanders persuaded him that such a rapid advance was ill-judged and could well clash with the inevitable German counterattacks. The result was that Plumer decided to wait until 1.10 pm before moving on, the delay making possible the forward move of forty field and a number of heavy batteries, some to already prepared gun positions at which ammunition had been dumped, and others into the previous 'No-Man's-Land' beyond the mine craters. Machine guns had also been placed in fresh positions to provide an overhead barrage, and twenty-four fresh tanks were ready to help the infantry forward. With the ground as it was after the mine explosions, all this forward movement of men, guns, horses and vehicles took longer than had been anticipated. So it was that at 10 am Plumer decided that two more hours would be needed for the preparations and that zero hour for the final assault would have to be postponed until 3.10 pm.[28]

It was ironic and tragic that the divisions that had attacked that morning had been rather too successful. Losses among the leading brigades had been estimated at 50% and among the reserve brigades that crested the ridge at 60%. Because casualties had been so very light, far too many troops arrived on top of the summit plateau to fall victim to the enemy defensive barrages. As the Official Historian wrote, because 'the unforeseen congestion was neither appreciated nor corrected, casualties now began to rise rapidly'. A German report recorded that 'crowds of British infantry were seen to take off their coats on this warm summer morning and begin to dig in along the skyline of the Ridge; working in their lighter-coloured shirt-sleeves, they made admirable targets for the machine guns'.[29] And so they did, even though they dug hard. A New Zealand Division Maori was seen to disappear completely below the ground within the hour. It was no longer necessary to persuade British troops to make use of their picks and shovels.

At 11 am formed bodies of German troops were seen crossing the valley bottom and starting up the hillside towards the British troops digging in, but the morning mist soon hid them from sight and the concavity of the slope masked them. Nevertheless, the artillery observers aloft managed to direct the British guns on to the advancing columns. Hastily organized, and sometimes mounted too late, these counterattacks all withered away before the combined British artillery, machine-gun and rifle fire, even before the intensive phase of the protective barrages could be brought to bear.[30]

An observer described the sunlit scene on top of the Messines Ridge before the attack on the Oosttaverne began:

> the aeroplanes wheeling, fighting in the brilliant sky; the German shells punching roan-coloured dust plumes from the ruins on the summit; lined-out working parties of New Zealanders furiously digging communication trenches up the slope; the Australians for the afternoon attack lining up on their flags, which, like those on a football ground, marked with each battalion's colours the line on which it was to assemble; tanks marshalling in the meadows; batteries of artillery racing up through the long grass, unlimbering, the teams trotting back with a jingle of chains, and the gun-crews later opening fire.[31]

Not mentioned were the parties of cavalry which had, in some areas, been more forward just in case the German resistance collapsed unexpectedly and completely.

As in all fields of human activity, things go wrong however thorough and efficient the preparations may have been, a statement of the obvious perhaps, but one often not perceived by uninformed commentators. Communications were the problem that afternoon of 7 June. Before the days of the man-pack radio, units on the move depended primarily upon runners or liaison officers for passing information. To find one's way in strange country and under heavy fire was both tricky and perilous: messages often failed to arrive.

The first to suffer because of this breakdown in communications was the right-hand of the two forward brigades of the veteran 4th Australian Division, brought forward from reserve to continue the attack on either side of the New Zealanders in Messines village. News of the two-hour postponement of the attack never reached the two leading battalions. While they lay out in the open, waiting for zero, casualties were heavy, but some men, wearied by the march up, still managed to sleep. On the IX Corps front in the centre, it was much the same. Because the converging morning advance had narrowed the front, only a single brigade of 11th Division was required for the afternoon attack, but the instructions for it to move forward to its assembly positions around Wytschaete village also went astray. Consequently its battalions were not in place until half an hour after zero hour. In the meantime, the Corps Commander, learning what had happened, ordered the still intact reserve brigade of the 19th Division to take on the job, but it had so little notice that it only just managed to get away as the creeping barrage opened up. Despite the chaos, this brigade did succeed in reaching the back of the Oosttaverne Line, but a gap was left between it and the Australians. Only in the north did the attack go according to the book: except around Spoil Bank, resistance in this area had all but collapsed, and two of the leading battalions advanced half a mile down the slope at the cost of only half a dozen casualties.

That 4th Australian Division was to have a hard time. During their long wait in the open, men of the leading units had watched the survivors of the German counter-attack seek refuge in the fortifications of the Oosttaverne Line, and they had also seen reinforcements arrive. Then, as they began to advance down the slope behind their creeping barrage, they were raked by machine-gun fire. Battlewise though they were, it was the Australians' first experience of blockhouse fighting. The struggle was savage. Covered by their Lewis guns and rifle-grenades, they set to work to clear the concrete pill-boxes with bayonets and bombs. Their Official Historian pictured, with unusual candour, what can happen in such circumstances:

The tensions accompanying the struggle around these blockhouses – the murderous fire from a sheltered position, followed by the sudden giving-in of the surrounded garrison – caused this year's fighting in Flanders to be marked by a ferocity that renders the reading of any true narrative peculiarly unpleasant. Where such tension exists in battle, the rules of 'civilised' warfare are powerless. Most men are temporarily half-mad, their pulses pounding at their ears, their mouths dry. The noblest among them are straining their wills to keep cool heads and even their voices; the less self-controlled are for the time being governed by reckless, primitive impulse. With death singing in their ears, the routing out of enemy groups from behind several feet of concrete is almost inevitably the signal for a butchery at least of the first few who emerge, and sometimes even the helplessly wounded may not be spared.[32]

In this sort of fighting, the right-hand Australian brigade carved its way to its objectives. The left-hand one fared the worst. Its right battalion was halted after it had lost all its company commanders; that on the left veered northwards to fill the gap left by the neighbouring corps, so creating a fresh gap between itself and its co-battalion. A British brigade major who watched it happening gave a further reason for the delays: some Australians were souvenir hunting.[33]

Despite these setbacks in the final stages of the first day's fighting, between sunrise and sunset Plumer's Second Army had won the most complete Allied victory since this siege-warfare had begun. Only the capture of Vimy Ridge by the Canadians earlier in the year could bear comparison, and that was on a far smaller scale. Not only had the Germans been pushed off the southern arc of the high ground that dominated Ypres and the countryside nearby, but the Second Army held the newly captured hills firmly and had repulsed without difficulty every German counterattack. The one disappointment, and that a comparatively minor one, was that only forty-eight German field-guns, nearly all badly damaged by shell-fire, had been captured; the pauses for consolidation had given the enemy time to pull back most of his artillery before the final British attack.[34] Nevertheless, the British counter-batteries had stamped out half of the German heavy artillery.[35]

The fighting was not yet over. The bitter struggle continued around Spoil Bank and on the ANZAC Corps front, some of whose Australian officers remembered the days and nights that followed the capture of Messines Ridge as some of the most harassing of the war.[36] It began on the first evening when a defensive barrage crashed down upon a battalion of the 4th Division in the Oosttaverne Line. It thereupon quit its trenches. A New Zealand unit on the ridge behind, thinking that all the Australians had retired, not just this single battalion, brought down further defensive fire upon the other nearby units. An officer who failed to stop the rot later protested that 'they would stand all the enemy fire you liked to give them, but they would not put up with being shelled by their own guns'.[37] Similar incidents happened in the IX Corps sector, and again during the subsequent two days, while the Australians lost more men trying to plug the gap on their left. It was all too typical of any battle anywhere.

Both the British and the Australian Official Historians blamed this confusion upon Plumer's caution. So as to ensure that the Messines Ridge itself, the feature of overriding importance, was retained against the formidable counter-attacks that had been anticipated, its defences had been planned to be independent of those of the Oosttaverne Line, by then held by what had been the reserve divisions. The result was that the staffs of the divisions holding the ridge were controlling the larger part of the artillery and machine guns which should have been supporting the troops in the Oosttaverne Line. It was the one serious and avoidable error in what had been an expertly planned battle, and it was a costly one, not corrected until 9 June. After years of static fighting, the staffs were unpractised in rapid reorganization and redeployment.[38]

For the Germans to have clung to their positions at the bottom of the ridge, closely observed and enfiladed from both flanks, was pointless. So, on 11 June, they slipped quietly away. When patrols finally established that their trenches and blockhouses were deserted, Plumer ordered a general advance to a slightly more secure line, and, in this way, the Battle of Messines finally ended.

The cost to the British had been 25,000 killed and wounded, half of them ANZAC. The losses on the first day had been reasonably small, under 11,000 as Haig noted with satisfaction in his diary,[39] with the greater part occurring through the overcrowding on top of the ridge and the errors in the organization of the defensive fire. In some units men could even feel that their losses had this time been worthwhile. Gladden's company of Londoners had lost forty of their men, but this private soldier recorded the pride of the survivors at having helped win what was being described as a great victory.[40]

The German losses were just about the same and included 144 officers and 7210 other ranks taken prisoner.[41] At the time the German propaganda machine depicted the battle as a costly setback for the Allies, but in retrospect their Official History admitted that Messines Ridge had been lost with 'dreadful casualties' and that 'French confidence began to grow again' as a result. General von Kuhl, Chief-of-Staff to Crown Prince Rupprecht of Bavaria, commander of the German Army Group in the north, described the battle as 'one of the worst tragedies of the world war'.[42]

The time taken and the resources used in preparing the mines inevitably raised the question of whether the effort had been worthwhile. The accuracy and weight of the artillery fire had been such that it is almost certain that success would have been achieved without the mines, especially as the German front line, in accordance with the new tactical thinking, was thinly held. Still, they had saved casualties, and their morale effect had been prodigious, not only among the Germans but among the British infantry also, their spirits lifted by the immensity of the explosions they had seen and felt as they got to their feet and started up the slope. Now, most of the craters are ponds, some attractively tree-lined, some used for watering farm animals. Only at Hill 60 have the craters failed to hold water; instead a peaceful hollow is enclosed by grassy parkland, a contrast to the trim Flanders fields nearby. The surface is pockmarked by the thousands of shells that continued to rain down on the area after the mines were blown, and below lie the remains of the men entombed by those and by earlier explosions. The Commonwealth War Graves Commission tends it all.

★ ★ ★

Harington noted that Plumer was bewildered by the telegrams of congratulation he received. The King, possibly a little cautious after so many previous disappointments, waited until 9 June before despatching his. Haig, in a lengthy Order of the Day, was generous:

> The complete success of the attack made yesterday by the Second Army under the command of General Sir Herbert Plumer is an earnest of the eventual victory of the Allied cause. . . . I desire to place on record here my deep appreciation of the splendid work done, above and below ground as well as in the air, by all Army, Services, and Departments, and by the Commanders and Staffs by whom, under Sir Herbert Plumer's orders, all means at our disposal were combined, both in preparation and in execution, with a skill, devotion and bravery beyond all praise.[44]

Liddell Hart wrote that Messines was a 'siege-warfare masterpiece' and that 'its perfect suitability of method at the time was overshadowed, and rightly, by its value as a moral tonic'.[45] For Robertson, writing three years after the war, it had been 'a masterpiece of modern tactics'.[46] Rarely sparing in his criticism of British generalship, Dr Bean, the Official Australian Historian, despite the losses suffered by his fellow-countrymen, wrote that

> the result was a revelation – how welcome only those who know can fully recall their own feelings at the time – that the British staff could plan and carry out a first-rate stroke with brilliant success. To the Australians who took part, the British higher leadership in the fight was as heartening as that in the Bullecourt operations had been depressing.

The rather surprised delight with which the British press greeted Messines was similar to its reaction to the news of the similarly unexpected victory at Alamein twenty-five years later. It was accurately described as the most sweeping and most brilliant victory won by British arms since the war began. Both during and after the war, the press was much criticized, sometimes with good cause, for its war reporting, but both the London and the provincial papers contained columns of, on the whole, well-written and well-informed descriptions of the Messines battle. W. Beach Thomas's four-column piece in the *Daily Mail* was military reporting of a standard seldom reached again during the subsequent fifty years. In many ways the accuracy was a tribute to Harington's handling of the correspondents, whom he had, as was his custom, briefed personally an hour before the battle, 'hiding nothing, neither minimizing nor exaggerating the difficulties and dangers of the attack', as Philip Gibbs wrote.[48] Noteworthy also was much of the comment on Second Army's strategy and tactics. The analysis by one writer of the reasons for the success – the limited objective, the use of the artillery, the cooperation of the aircraft and tanks – could well have been put together weeks rather than days after the events. Another percipient journalist emphasized that there had been much more to the victory than the use of mines. Here and there was a note of caution, as if the writer, with crossed fingers, was willing the Germans not to annul the gains by a decisive counterattack. It would, of course, be anachronistic to criticize the arrogant jingoism with which many of the reports were peppered.

Often the candour is surprising. One article, although enthusiastic about the hero of the day, describes Plumer as 'a plodder rather than a thruster, but the sturdy plodders are the men we want to lead us to victory'. Such a comment in the aftermath of a victory was indeed outspoken. Little had been heard of Plumer since Second Ypres in early 1915, when short biographies appeared in some papers and magazines to remind a new generation of readers of his exploits in Matabeleland and South Africa. For the time being his name was to be headlined more often than Haig's. One paper carried a complete page of photographs showing him looking equally 'Blimpish' whether dressed in hunting kit, service dress or undress uniform; among them was one of Lady Plumer busy 'directing affairs at a Y.M.C.A. hut in London'. Henceforth, the press had no call to remind its readership who Plumer was [49]

Over the years, only the Prime Minister belittled Plumer's victory. 'The capture of the Messines Ridge,' he wrote in his *Memoirs*, 'a perfect attack in its way, was just a useful little preliminary to the real campaign, an *aperitif* provided by General Plumer to stimulate the public appetite for the great carousal of victory which was being provided for us by G.H.Q.'[50] But, then, Lloyd George was getting at Haig.

* * *

In both 1916 and 1917 the plans for this northern offensive had emphasized the importance of gaining a footing on the western end of the Gheluvelt Plateau, above Mount Sorrel, as soon as might be after the Messines Ridge had been secured. It was an essential preliminary to any further and larger scale operations. On 24 May Haig had written to Plumer, making him responsible for exploiting any success gained by his Second Army; and on 3 June Plumer came back to his Commander-in-Chief, stressing that it was 'essential that the opportunity for exploiting a success should be taken advantage of at the earliest moment,'[51] and with this in view he had arranged for II and VIII Corps in the north of his sector to attack on either side of the Bellewaarde Lake with the high ground around Westhoek as their first objective. Both men seemed to be of one mind. To provide the extra artillery support that would be needed Plumer had arranged to transfer northwards from the Messines front sixty heavy and medium guns as soon as that operation had been successfully completed, a move that would take three days to complete.

When, however, on 8 June, patrols from these two northern corps reported strong resistance on the plateau above them, Haig asked for this next phase to be launched at once, but Plumer reiterated his request for a three-day delay in order to resite this artillery. The entry in Haig's diary for that day recounts what happened:

> General Plumer came to see me about noon after conferring with his corps commanders. The enemy having brought up reserves, the observation at Stirling Castle (south of Menin Road) cannot be captured without methodical preparation and systematic attack.
> I therefore decided that Gough should take over the troops on the northern sector of the Second Army front.[52]

It had been the opportunity Haig sought to pass responsibility for the next phase of the battle to Gough, in his opinion the more thrusting commander. That same day Haig ordered that II and VIII Corps should be transferred from Plumer to Gough, and he instructed the latter that 'as a preliminary operation to the main northern operation, the Fifth Army will prepare a plan for a minor operation to secure its right flank on the Ridge east of Ypres and with the object of gaining observation around Stirling Castle'.[53] There was no need for Gough to prepare such a plan. Plumer had, of course, already done so, and on 9 June he passed it over to him.

But nothing happened. When Haig held his next conference with his Army Commanders on 14 June, Gough reported that he had come to the conclusion that such a limited operation would leave his troops 'in a very exposed and difficult salient'. He then suggested that it would be wiser not to have such a preliminary operation at all, but to include the western end of the Gheluvelt Plateau in the main offensive. Haig approved the change, explaining that while the general British and French plan, formulated on

7 May, to wear down the enemy (attrition, in fact) still held good, the strategic object was the Belgian coast and the Dutch frontier; the first step towards this was, he hoped, to be the capture of the Passchendaele – Staden – Clercken ridge on 25 July, six weeks ahead.[54]

This failure rapidly to exploit Plumer's success at Messines while the weather held good was to have unhappy and costly consequences for the British Army. For the time being, the strategy of the limited offensive had been shelved. It was indeed ironical that an immediate and limited attack as Plumer had planned was both expected and feared by the Germans: on 9 June Rupprecht had noted in his diary that the whole of the high ground south of a line Zandvoorde-Hooge should be relinquished in anticipation of such an attack. Nevertheless, he did not withdraw the troops concerned, but on 19 June he was still expressing this fear that a succession of limited attacks on narrow frontages would eat up the German reserves and make possible a final British breakthrough on a wide front.[55]

9 Third Ypres

A commander-in-chief usually devotes nearly as much time and thought to coping with the authorities to whom he is responsible as he does to fighting his battles. If allies are involved, he will be even busier looking over his shoulder – and sideways. When Colonel Repington, by then military correspondent to *The Times*, suggested to Major-General Sir Frederick Maurice, Robertson's assistant at the War Office, that, in the aftermath of the war it would be found that fifty per cent of the time and energy of the soldiers had been expended on fighting their own politicians, Maurice countered that the figure was far too low; a university chair, he ventured, was needed 'to teach budding statesmen the rudiments of war',[1] a percipient forecast indeed. Of difficulties with politicians and with allies alike, Haig suffered rather more than his share.

The very day of the opening of the Messines attack, and just an hour after returning from congratulating Plumer upon his success, Haig learned from Pétain of further mutinies among the French troops. Two days later Robertson travelled to France, sent by the Cabinet to warn Haig of the perils of attacking without the full cooperation of the French; in so doing, he suggested that Austria would make peace if sufficiently harassed, and to this end Italy should be supported with artillery.[2] Haig's response to this warning was to reiterate his belief that the one plan for ending the war was to send to France without delay every possible man, gun and aeroplane.[3] Convinced that the war would be won only when Germany, the main enemy, was decisively beaten and that this could only happen on the Western Front, now that the Russians were almost out of the war, Haig became obsessed with this fear that his resources might be dribbled away to the Italian Front. His misgivings had the effect of further encouraging him to attempt to clear the Belgian coast: to remain on the defensive in the West would, as he saw it, increase the danger of his losing guns and troops to a theatre of war where they would probably be squandered by incompetent generals.

For five days, during the third week of June, while Gough was making his arrangements for the northern offensive, for which he had now been made responsible, Haig was in London talking to the War Cabinet. This compact body, set up by Lloyd George on 8 June to control the higher direction of the war, was a much-needed innovation. As well as the Prime Minister himself, its members included Lord Milner, Lord Curzon, Mr Bonar Law, the leader of the Conservatives in the coalition government, and Haig's old opponent from the Boer War, General Smuts, now a respected soldier and statesman of the Empire and rather more sympathetic than the others towards Haig's standpoint. At a series of meetings, Haig outlined his proposals, stressing three points especially: first, the need to clear the Belgian coast; second, the deterioration of the German Army, a subject upon which his senior intelligence officer, Charteris, had provided him with over-optimistic interpretations of otherwise accurate information; and lastly the danger of the Germans being about to transfer troops in appreciable numbers from the Eastern Front to his theatre. Against Haig's arguments for continuing the offensive in Flanders, the Prime Minister deployed his most lucid oratory, dwelling upon his fears that the British Army lacked the resources to succeed in such an enterprise and that the French Army was in such a poor state that it would not be able to play a proper part. Fearful of the further high casualties that would follow failure which would undoubtedly damage national morale, Lloyd George argued at length for the alternative strategy of making a start on the break-up of the Central powers by forcing either the Turkish or the Austro-Hungarian Empires out of the way: as a beginning, he proposed, 300 howitzers should be transferred from France to Italy so as to speed an Italian victory.

Underlying the stand made by the Prime Minister and those of his colleagues who supported him was the hope that their new American allies would arrive on the Western Front in large enough numbers to turn the scale in 1918. Why, then, not mark time there until they arrived? It was an alluring prospect. Winston Churchill, who returned to the Cabinet in July as Minister of Munitions, was a strong advocate of such a policy. Twice that summer he visited Haig in France, giving the Commander-in-Chief at tedious length the benefit of his strategical and tactical ideas. He was not always consistent. In June he forecast that the war would be brought to an end in August, 1918, but in September he admitted that both Lloyd George and he had doubts whether the Germans could be beaten on the Western Front. Haig countered by querying whether the French would 'quietly wait and suffer for a further year', and he noted also in his diary that Churchill possessed 'great brain power but his mind is quite unbalanced'. He feared also that Churchill's 'agile mind only makes him a danger because he can persuade Lloyd George to adopt and carry out the most idiotic policy'.[4]

By the time of these meetings with the War Cabinet, Robertson's thinking matched exactly that of Haig. Both soldiers pointed out to the Prime Minister that the Germans, making use of their interior lines, could move troops rapidly to the Italian Front when the need arose; only two railways ran from France to Italy, while the enemy had five. Moreover, if the Western Front were to be further weakened, there was a serious danger that the Germans themselves might break through. Then Jellicoe, the First Sea Lord, added his weight to the arguments of the soldiers by declaring that the war would, in any case, be lost in 1918 if the rate of shipping losses were to continue: Zeebrugge must, therefore, be cleared at all costs. It was a statement of doubtful validity, and one which the Prime Minister strongly challenged. In fact, in the following year the U-boat campaign was to be mastered, not by capturing their bases, but by introducing a system of convoys, long opposed by the Admiralty.

When Lloyd George realized how utterly opposed his military advisers were to becoming involved in an offensive in Italy, he suggested that Haig should confine himself to wearing down the Germans in 'Pétain-like' tactics with 'a push here and a push there'. This was, Haig rejoindered, exactly how he intended to conduct the offensive, a series of limited attacks which would not be launched without a reasonable chance of success. In the end the War Cabinet's approval was given, albeit reluctantly and hesitantly, the final written authority not being despatched to Haig until 21 July, by which time Gough's preliminary bombardment had been under way for three days. To the approval was added a *caveat* that the whole question would be examined again if the results of the offensive appeared unlikely to be commensurate with the losses incurred. Meanwhile, arrangements would be made to send troops to Italy in the event of the operations not succeeding.[5]

An entry in Haig's diary on 21 July reveals the reasoning that lay behind his determination to persist with his northern offensive. 'Even if my attacks do not gain ground as I hope and expect, we ought still to persevere in attacking the Germans in France. Only by this means can we win, and we must encourage the French to continue fighting.'[6] In these words Haig encapsulated his philosophy. He would break through if he could. If not, he would wear down the Germans by attrition.

In this hesitant way the battle commonly known as Passchendaele began. Officially and more accurately it was the Third Battle of Ypres, Passchendaele being only the name of a single village on the main ridge, but the culminating point of this autumn struggle.

The programme for the concentration of the fifty or so Allied divisions involved in the offensive had been arranged at the 7 May conference, two and a half months before. On 30 May Gough's Fifth Army Headquarters had moved into a château two miles outside Poperinghe and from there

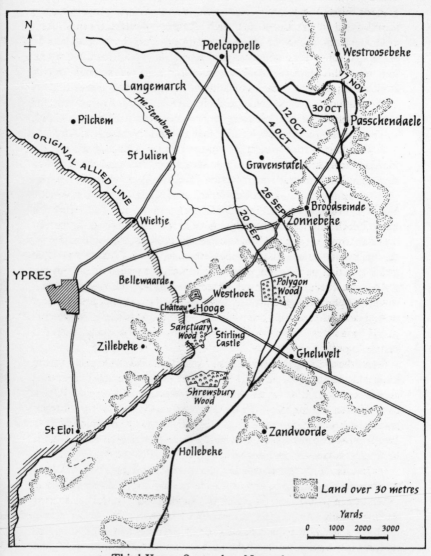

N

Poelcappelle

Westroosebeke

17 NOV

Langemarck

The Steenbeek

30 OCT

12 OCT

Pilckem

ORIGINAL ALLIED LINE

4 OCT

Passchendaele

St Julien

Gravenstafel

26 SEP

Wieltje

20 SEP

Broodseinde

Zonnebeke

YPRES

Bellewaarde

Westhoek

Polygon Wood

Château Hooge

Sanctuary Wood

Stirling Castle

Zillebeke

Gheluvelt

Shrewsbury Wood

St Eloi

Zandvoorde

Hollebeke

Land over 30 metres

Yards

0   1000   2000   3000

9. Third Ypres, September–November, 1917

Gough began to assemble his troops. First there were the four divisions of Plumer's II and VIII Corps, transferred to him immediately after Messines, and these were followed by a further four of Plumer's divisions at the end of June, together with two from the GHQ reserve. Six more arrived from Horne's First Army, and Plumer was also obliged to transfer half his artillery and all his tanks to Gough. Thanks to the complex railway system and the numerous and well-equipped camps and depots Second Army had constructed and developed around Ypres during the previous two years, this massive redeployment of hundreds of thousands of men and their equipment went as smoothly as such an upheaval ever does.

Further north still, General Anthoine's six French divisions covered Gough's left flank from Boesinghe to Steenstraat and King Albert's six Belgian divisions extended the line towards Nieuport, behind the Yser inundations. Between there and the sea Rawlinson's Fourth Army Headquarters, brought up from the Somme, commanded the five divisions that had assembled there during June and July for a simultaneous push along the coast. The main thrust of the offensive, as clarified in Haig's instruction of 5 July, was for Fifth Army first to secure the main Passchendaele-Staden Ridge; on its right it would be assisted by Second Army, while the French and Belgians would be cooperating on the other flank. This, Haig emphasized, was 'likely to entail very hard fighting lasting perhaps for weeks'. Afterwards exploitation would take place in the direction of Thorout, Ostend and Bruges, when opportunities for 'the employment of cavalry in masses is likely to occur'. Second Army, having covered the right flank of the Fifth, was to take over the defence of the main ridge as Fifth Army advanced and would be prepared in due course to push forward to the Courtrai-Roulers line.[7]

While the complicated preparations for this main offensive were in train, Haig ordered the First and Second Armies to carry out feint attacks in the directions of Lens and Lille respectively during June and July so as to distract the attention of the Germans, especially from the French front. Such operations tended to be expensive in lives and to achieve little, and so it proved for Horne's Army. Plumer, whose Second Army had been reduced to only twelve divisions, put this question to Haig at a conference on 14 June, pointing out that the extent of such limited attacks was dependent on the forces the Commander-in-Chief wished to expend upon them,[8] an elementary truth indeed but one that apparently needed voicing. As a result, Haig ordered Plumer to do no more than establish a sound defence line on his right. Godley's II ANZAC Corps had, in fact, been rather over-enthusiastically harassing the enemy, and Plumer had found it necessary to warn him that he did 'not wish your units to incur further casualties in these isolated attacks'.[9] Such feint operations by the two southern Armies achieved nothing. Although the German commander in the Lens-Lille area reported that he was sure that a major offensive was to be mounted towards Lens, Rupprecht disregarded his advice, certain that the British lacked the strength to mount two major offensives at the same time, and instead he moved ten divisions from that sector to Flanders.[10]

In the middle of these preparations, the British suffered a disturbing reverse. In Rawlinson's coastal sector, two divisions were making ready to advance along the sand dunes in conjunction with the amphibious landing over open beaches which was to take place at three separate points behind the German lines. The preparations had been thorough, in many ways foreshadowing the techniques of World War Two. The troops were to reach the shore from the monitors in which they were carried by means of bridges of floating pontoons, each 550 feet long and protected by bullet-proof screens; special tracks were carried to enable the accompanying tanks to mount the sea-walls. Experiments in the Thames Estuary had exceeded all hopes, but the Germans struck first, in what they described as a 'beach picnic'. The British defences, just taken over from the French, were inadequate to withstand a bombardment by 140 German Batteries, while most of Rawlinson's artillery had still to arrive. On 10 July the Germans overwhelmed the British positions north of the Yser Estuary. From the other side, Binding saw that:

All went well because it was well prepared. It had taken us long enough to learn that it does not simply do to order an attack for the next day, but *everything must be reconnoitred and prepared beforehand*.[11]

As the war progressed, both sides learned similar lessons by hard experience.

*   *   *

John Terraine, in his biography of Haig, wrote that 'The decision to entrust the main offensive in the Flanders battle to the Fifth Army under General Gough must be regarded as Haig's greatest and most fatal error.'[12] Haig may have thought of the youthful cavalryman as the thruster he was seeking, but he either forgot or ignored the fact that '16 years earlier, Colonel Plumer had the reputation of being the most rapid mover of the column commanders'.[13] The percipient Repington recorded the doubts he had expressed to Robertson as early as 5 July:

I said that I did not think that the choice of Gough for this particular operation was good, much though I admired his gifts. R. was inclined to agree, and wished that Plumer, who knew every stone in the north, had been placed in charge.[14]

Even Gough himself later admitted that Haig had been mistaken in not entrusting Plumer with the job, a man who had been on the Ypres front for so long.[15] But there was far more to it than local knowledge. Even more important was the skill Plumer had so recently demonstrated in his techniques for overcoming the German defences.

Gough was a shrewd general, personally popular, who cared for his troops, and who, unlike some, lived a spartan existence. His main fault was his failure to notice the defects of his staff, so marked that divisions showed a distinct reluctance to serve in Fifth Army. This was something that Haig failed to discover until towards the end of 1917, when he removed Gough's extremely unpopular M.G.G.S. and broke the news to Gough himself that divisions objected to joining his Army.[16] Walter Guinness, the future first Lord Moyne, was among those for whom such a transfer was unwelcome when the offensive was just about to start. His divisional commander, an outspoken officer, was of the same mind, having suffered from:

> Fifth Army methods the previous year on the Somme and lost no opportunity of rubbing in the inadequacy of our plans and arrangements. None of the lessons taught by Plumer's success seem to have been learned. The signal and R.E. arrangements were fearfully sketchy, nothing was thought out beforehand and everything was apparently left to be decided at the moment . . . . After the wonderful organization and devotion to detail which one had found in the 2nd Army, the 5th Army struck one as very haphazard in its methods.[17]

In addition to choosing the wrong man for the task, Haig committed a further and major error. He failed to insist that Gough should capture the high ground at the western edge of the Gheluvelt Plateau in a preliminary operation, using Plumer's II and VIII Corps, which had been transferred to him for this specific purpose. Moreover, he permitted Gough, in what the latter described as 'a slight change of plan',[18] to pivot on his left flank with the French instead of moving up on to the high ground through Gheluvelt and Broodseinde, the two most commanding places in the northern circle of hills, as he had been ordered.

Gough eventually evolved a plan which involved a four-phase attack on the first day, a maximum penetrations of 6000 yards, the third and principal objective of which was the German third line, in front of which lay the greater part of their field artillery and their counterattack reserves.

Once this was taken, the attack was to be extended to the fourth objective, the summit of the main ridge from the east side of Polygon Wood to Broodseinde; no settled pause was agreed upon before this fourth objective was tackled, and it was left to the individual divisional commanders to decide how far to go. Even more ambitious was the instruction that the advance was to be extended to Passchendaele and Poelcapelle if little opposition were to be met.[19] It was all somewhat vague. And, in its essence, it was a reversion to the methods that had failed on the Somme in 1916 – a deep advance with troops pushing forward as far as they could go.

Haig had strong reservations. Arriving back from England on 25 June from his discussions with the War Cabinet and only too aware that he lacked their full support, the head of his Operations Branch, the able Brigadier General J.H. Davidson, presented him with a succinct and well-argued paper that criticized Gough's plan. Instead, Davidson recommended, Gough should mount a succession of deliberate attacks, the depth of each limited to about a mile; in his opinion, only after a series of such blows had been delivered and the enemy counterattack forces repulsed, would German morale be such that exploitation could take place.[20]

Nevertheless, at a meeting with Gough and Plumer on 28 June, Haig gave his approval to the Fifth Army plan, reminding Gough of the importance of his right flank. Haig's diary reads:

> It is in my opinion vitally important to occupy and hold the ridge west of Gheluvelt in order to cover our right flank and then push it along to Broodseinde. The main battle will be fought on or for this ridge so we must make our plans accordingly. The main difficulty seems to be at the beginning of the attack, in advancing from a comparatively small salient to the attack on a wider area. I impressed on Gough the vital importance of the ridge in question, and that the advance north should be limited until our right flank has really been secured on this ridge.[21]

Despite this admonition, no change of any import was made in the Fifth Army plan. This failure to ensure that Gough should conform with his concept of how the battle should be fought is all but inexplicable. It contrasted also with the way he had so carefully supervised Plumer's attack at Messines.

Widely quoted has been the support Plumer is alleged to have given to Gough's plan for this deep first day advance. It has even been said that he went so far as to urge Gough to go all out for the final objective.

The sources, however, are questionable. The Official History, published over thirty years after the events it describes and after Plumer's death, records that:

> Sir Douglas Haig, after discussing Davidson's memorandum with him [Gough] and General Plumer at Cassell on 28th June, had, with General Plumer's support, allowed the Fifth Army scheme to stand; it seemed perhaps worth trying an all-out attack on the first day. [22]

The account written by Bean, the Australian Official Historian, written in 1932 goes even further:

> General Gough now urged that only the second objective should be aimed at on the first day . . . but General Plumer pressed for the deeper offensive, and his view was approved. [23]

But Bean's acknowledged source for the incident was Gough's own account of what had occurred, contained in his *Fifth Army*, published in 1931. It contains the following:

> Plumer was of the opinion that after so much preparation we should be allowed to go 'all out', but I was firmly of the opinion that the methodical advance and the limited objective was the sound policy. Haig eventually supported Plumer . . . . I think that the more cautious policy would have paid us better. [24]

The sources available to Edmonds in writing the British Official History have disappeared, but in many respects it is clear that for this volume he depended to a considerable extent upon Bean's excellent account of events. Nowhere in Haig's diary or letters has any reference been found to Plumer taking such a stand. [25] The sole authority for the incident does, in fact, seem to be Gough's own book, written in justification for his own failure at Passchendaele and before he had been cleared of the blame for what befell his Fifth Army in March, 1918. At the time of its publication, Plumer was a dying man, who, in any case, did not indulge in controversy with past colleagues.

It would indeed have been strange if Plumer had acted in this way. If he did do so, it was an abrogation of all he had learned at Messines, when he perfected the tactics used so successfully by Pétain and which Davidson was now recommending should be developed once again. A mutual respect existed between Gough and Plumer. At the time of the Curragh incident as a brigadier general, the young Gough, sick and disquieted at what had happened in Ireland, had written to Wilson at the War Office to say, 'We want someone here we can trust and respect. There is no one who would fulfil these conditions to anything like the same degree as Plumer. We feel we want someone here, who will not betray us again, and who will stand up to the Cabinet and protect us from its machinations'.[26] It could just be possible that Plumer, on good terms as he was with his fellow Army Commander, was reluctant to criticize the younger man's plans to Haig, but he was the last person to agree to something that could well involve the unnecessary squandering of life. Nor, as we have seen, was he averse in the summer of 1917 from expressing his viewpoint strongly when the need arose. It had been different in 1916, when he was under threat of dismissal, but by Third Ypres he had established his reputation as a battle-winning general, and with it his confidence. The accusations against him just do not ring true.

★ ★ ★

Gough was to be forced to seek several successive postponements to the approximate date of 25 July stipulated by Haig for the start of the main offensive. There were a number of reasons, among them labour shortages for building gun emplacements in the soggy ground and the late arrival of the heavy counter-battery artillery from the feint operations further south. Although outnumbered in guns by three to one, the Germans were all the time inflicting heavy losses both on the British weapons and on the men who served them, packed as they were within the Salient and under observation from the commanding ground to the west. Charles Carrington, who had survived for two years in an infantry battalion and who had been through the Somme, remembered thinking that 'the gunners, always in line, had a worse time at Passchendaele than the infantry, and the drivers, perhaps a worse time than the gunners. I cannot speak for the mules, splashed to the withers in sludge, except that dead mules were more conspicuous in the landscape than dead men'.[27]

The eventual report from Haig's artillery adviser that he was confident that the upper hand had been gained over the German artillery was to prove grossly over-optimistic,[28] as was the information Gough's subordinate commanders provided to Haig, those generals perhaps reluctant to express their doubts about so long and laboriously prepared an operation. After spending two days visiting these corps commanders, Haig told Gough on 21 July 'how thoroughly satisfied I was with all the preparations made by his subordinate commanders, and the confidence I noticed existed among all ranks'.[29] He was especially impressed by the assurance displayed by General Jacob, whose task it was to clear the Gheluvelt Plateau. Guinness thought otherwise. Although he regarded Jacob as a very good soldier, he described as 'arrant nonsense' the talk he gave before the attack in which he claimed that the Germans would be driven right out of Belgium during the next few days.[30]

Not for the first time the preliminary bombardment did its work only too well. Soon the Steenbeek, which ran down from the Gheluvelt Plateau to the east of Pilckem Ridge, and which lay directly astride Gough's line of advance, was a swamp of near liquid mud. Today, with the field drains in order and the becks running unimpeded, all work on the land stops when the rain starts; in a couple of days the earth on even the drier slopes took on the consistency of thick bean soup. The Royal Tanks Corps (as the Heavy Branch of the Machine-Gun Corps became at the end of the month) was especially unhappy about the state of the ground that July; 'Swamp Maps', sent daily to GHQ, were becoming increasingly more brightly coloured. Whether Haig ever saw them is not recorded. And the weather had not even broken, As the attacking infantry moved along the crowded roads up to the line, their main afflictions were the heat and the dust.

At long last, on 31 July, the great northern offensive began. Nine of Gough's divisions, together with two French ones on their left, started to fight their way forward in what was to be known as the Battle of Pilckem Ridge, an all but imperceptible feature as today one drives across it in a car. At first all went well. By mid-afternoon the two left-hand corps had reached the eastern slopes of the ridge and the Steenbeck at the bottom. There they beat off determined German counterattacks, and XIX Corps, the right-hand one, managed to cross the stream, although with heavy losses, partly the result of their supporting tanks getting stuck in the swamp. A gunner battery commander described what then happened:

About 2 pm an intense German barrage fell on our forward troops east of the Steenbeek; some from guns at Gheluvelt which enfiladed their positions as far north as St Julien. The 2nd Corps had unfortunately not been able to seize the Gheluvelt Plateau and rain and mist made aeroplane observation impossible, so counter-battery work was ineffecive. Shortly afterwards the Germans attacked and S.O.S. rockets went up. We answered and several more times as more rockets kept going up. I began to be a little alarmed about our ammunition situation. Our infantry were forced to fall back slowly to the Steenbeek, fighting every inch of the way and inflicting casualties. The Germans were stopped short of the Steenbeek but succeeded in recapturing St Julien. At 4 pm the drizzle turned to heavy rain and our infantry along the Steenbeek were up to their waists in water. At 6 pm the Germans, up to their knees in mud and water, made their last attack. They were stopped by the heavy S.O.S. barrage and withdrew up the slope leaving many casualties.[31]

As Haig had feared might happen, Gough's II Corps failed to secure the Gheluvelt Plateau, the patchwork of shattered woodlands – Sanctuary, Shrewsbury, Polygon and the rest, all names of evil repute – which the Germans had fortified into a near-impregnable bastion, some three miles square. Here again, the infantry reached the German first line, but again at severe cost, largely the result of the concentrated enemy artillery fire. Then, as had been forecast, the further the battalions penetrated, the stiffer became the resistance and the more frequent the German counterattacks. By midday it was obvious that the attack had failed.

Plumer's part in the day's fighting had been to launch a feint assault towards Warneton, pressing further down the eastern slope of the Messines Ridge into the Lys Valley. All but one of the outpost positions attacked was captured, but in some places the Australians and New Zealanders concerned seem to have once again tried too hard. As the Australian Official Historian expressed it:

> The protracted and rather costly nature of some of these operations drew criticism from the Second Army staff. But limited attacks against a somewhat shadowy outpost-line, close in front of an invulnerable position from which reserves would issue strongly supported by artillery, could not fail to be difficult. Undoubtedly they tied down for the time being some German artillery and potential reserve, although the German command was never in real doubt as to the true object and direction of Haig's offensive.[32]

With nothing gained, Second Army had lost nearly 5000 men. Again the pointless nature of most of these feint or subsidiary attacks had been demonstrated. During that and the subsequent two day's fighting, total British losses numbered 31,000, probably much the same as the German figures. The casualties were, as Haig informed the War Cabinet, 'slight for so great a battle.'[33] It was all a matter of degree. On the Somme on 1 July, 1916, in a single day the British alone lost 57,470 officers and men.

The driving rain that set in on the afternoon of 31 July continued, with intermittent breaks, for the next month. The countryside, which had still been green in July before the battle started, was soon ploughed into a swamp, 4000 yards wide, in which the flooded shell craters overlapped one another. The lines of trudging infantry, the supply columns and the batteries of guns were confined to a few duckboard tracks and plank roads, upon which the Germans concentrated their fire. To venture off them was to risk being drowned. Much has, of course, been written about this Flanders mud, but conditions on the Somme the previous winter had been just as bad. Edmund Blunden described these Somme conditions.

> It was blasted into a broad shapeless gully by intense bombardment, and pools of mortar-like mud filled most of it. . . . The wooden track ended, and the men fought their way on through the gluey morass, until not one or two were reduced to tears and impotent cries to God . . . the Schwaben Redoubt was an almost obliterated cocoon of trenches in which mud, and death, and life were much the same thing. . . . Men of the next battalion were found in mud up to the armpits, and their fate was not spoken of.[34]

On 10 August, during a short break in the weather, Gough made another attempt upon the Gheluvelt Plateau. The rubble that had been Westhoek village was occupied, but that was all. The failure was hardly surprising. The infantry were exhausted before they started, and the enemy artillery fire had been massed to cover this vital piece of ground, while Gough had dispersed his guns along the whole of his frontage in readiness for a renewed general offensive. Six days later he launched this second major push, which Haig had strengthened by transferring another three of Plumer's divisions to Fifth Army. Known as the Battle of Langemarck, its sole success was the capture of the village of that name. South of St Julien, no progress at all was made. Most of the units were quite unfit for the task, casualties and sickness having reduced their strengths by a third or so. One of the causes of this further repulse, as Haig complained, was 'commanders being in too great a hurry! Three more days should have been allowed in which . . . the artillery would have dominated the enemy's artillery and destroyed his concrete defences*'.[35]

After this Langemarck defeat, Gough continued to make further and usually ill-prepared attempts to claw more small segments of that morass out of German hands, but he was now acting against his better judgment. When he protested to Haig that success was impossible in such foul conditions, the latter insisted that operations must continue, explaining to him once again the strategic imperatives.[36] At the same time Gough agitated for

---

*After Messines, Plumer's name came readily to journalists' pens, whose heavily censored reports disguised the failures or near failures of these battles. 'PLUMER'S GREAT THRUST' aroused his wrath and with good reason. The upshot was a note from Harington to GHQ reminding those concerned that 'Sir Herbert Plumer hates publicity of all sorts' and that it should 'be made quite clear to the public that it is not his Army that is attacking'.[38] Whether he really disliked publicity is uncertain, but he had no desire to be credited with another's failures.

the Second Army to push forward also so as to draw off some of the German artillery fire from his front. This request was put to Plumer by Gough at a meeting on 24 August, chaired by Kiggell, Haig's Chief-of-Staff, whose master was absent in England. According to Gough, Plumer demurred, protesting that he had been in the Salient for two years, and that he 'had no intention of pushing himself into another'.[37]

Kiggell referred this dispute between the two Army Commanders to his Commander-in-Chief who returned later that day. Haig thereupon decided to pass the main role in the battle back to Plumer, whom he saw the next day. Second Army front was to be extended to the left as far as the Ypres-Roulers Railway, so taking in the Gheluvelt Plateau, and II Corps would be returned to Second Army. Plumer's objective was to be the Polygon Wood-Broodseinde Ridge. He was faced with capturing the objective that he had been only too ready to tackle after Messines if Haig had allowed him the necessary three days in which to shift some of his heavy artillery. In effect ten weeks had been lost.

In giving Plumer these instructions, Haig proposed that the village of Zandvoorde, lying a mile to the south of Gheluvelt, should be included in the attack, his reason being that enemy guns sited in the low ground east of the village could enfilade Plumer's main assault. By widening his front in this way, Plumer would make the enemy disperse his artillery fire and might mislead him about the principal objective of the British attack. Plumer disagreed, protesting strongly that to do this would create a greater degree of dispersal of his own resources than those of the enemy. He won his point, Haig conceding that Plumer should do no more than prepare plans to capture Zandvoorde, these to be put into effect only if it became impossible to take Gheluvelt without doing so.[39]

Four years after publishing his book *Fifth Army,* Gough told Liddell Hart that at this juncture in the battle Plumer complained that 'he had been fighting in the salient too long and stood out against taking part in the offensive'.[40] Again, nothing has been found to confirm Gough's comment. These uncorroborated statements by a man then elderly and bitter can only be suspect. Even if Plumer was reluctant to become more deeply involved in a campaign, the outcome of which appeared problematical, there is not the slightest doubt that over the coming weeks he was, as ever, to give Haig his complete and loyal support.

*   *   *

Having received his instructions, Plumer asked for three weeks in which to make his preparations for the attack. To this Haig agreed, but in the meantime he allowed Gough to attempt to try to gain further ground. It was an unfortunate decision. Gough launched a hapless operation, one recorded as ending 'in considerable further casualties and very little gain in ground'.[41] Altogether a bloody fiasco, in places the assaulting troops stood in torrential rain up to their knees in water for ten hours before zero hour. On 28 August Haig halted all operations on Fifth Army front until Second Army should be ready.[42]

Plumer needed this three week delay in order to move his troops, mass his artillery and complete the involved but essential administrative arrangements needed to assure success – the construction of the roadways and tracks to bring forward the massive quantities of ammunition and stores that were required, the burying of telephone lines (neglected by Fifth Army and one of the causes of their failures), and the laying of miles of light railway line. Twenty-six squadrons of the RFC were set to work to pin-point the German batteries and attack their rear areas; at the same time II Corps guns were being moved forward and Haig's other armies were being further stripped of artillery to reinforce Plumer. All this was helped by three weeks of dry and sunny weather which quickly turned the sea of mud into a desert of dust. An incidental effect of this pause in the campaign was that it deceived the enemy, Rupprecht's Chief-of-Staff, General von Kuhl noting in his diary that 'My inmost conviction that the battle in Flanders is at an end is more and more strengthened'.[43]

Plumer's plans for the capture of the Gheluvelt Plateau and the ridge beyond, submitted to GHQ on 29 August, after the usual discussion with his corps commanders, were for a Messines-like 'four-step' operation, but with a six-day interval between each 'step'. Integral to it was the limitation of each advance to about 1500 yards, so ensuring that the whole of the available field artillery could be brought forward for each successive phase. I ANZAC Corps was to replace II Corps Headquarters for the attack, but the now thoroughly shattered divisions of II Corps were, until just before it started, to remain in position and hold the line. To the south of these Australians would be X Corps, and Plumer's first 'step' would be launched on a front of only four thousand yards by two divisions from each of these two corps. On only half the frontage, twice as many troops would be used as on 31 July; twice the number of heavy and medium guns would be employed in the area, and the seven-day preliminary bombardment was to be on a scale never before experienced.

So far that summer the 1st, 2nd and 5th Australian Divisions of I ANZAC had been enjoying a much needed four-month period of rest and retraining after being continually in action on the Somme and in front of Arras. To bring the Corps up to the four divisions required, the 4th Australian was transferred from Godley's II ANZAC Corps, already fighting under Plumer, unwelcome news indeed for the men concerned, many of whom had been in action since April, during which time the Division had suffered 10,000 casualties. At the same time the rest of II ANZAC (the New Zealand Division and Monash's 3rd Australians) was withdrawn to Second Army reserve and was made up to its required four-division strength by the addition of two United Kingdom divisions, the 41st and 66th.

By this stage of the war these Australians and New Zealanders had confirmed their reputation as outstanding soldiers, a fact that owed something to their divisions fighting together, in their own corps, unlike the United Kingdom divisions which were continually shifted around the place; as with the Canadians, it was a palpable aid to efficiency and morale, an asset sometimes forgotten when discussing the fine qualities of these Dominion troops. As in the next war, the Anzacs were volunteers, men who reconciled with pride their growing nationalism and membership of the British Empire. Losses and reverses at Gallipoli and on the Somme had given them severe misgivings about the quality of British generalship and the capacity of some of the troops who had fought alongside them, doubts which they were not always backward in expressing. Plumer's handling of the Messines battle had, however, to some extent restored their confidence.[44] A happy relationship had also been established between the staff of Birdwood's I ANZAC Corps and Plumer's headquarters: typical of this rapport was a note penned by Harington to Birdwood's Chief-of-Staff when the preliminary work was at its busiest: 'The task in that area has been terrific. . . . We all realize what a hard time you have had and in what a splendid way you have dealt with it. . . . I won't worry you during the fight.[45]

Nor was it surprising that the morale of some of the United Kingdom troops was flagging by the summer of 1917. The August fighting had overtaxed tired and battle-weary divisions: in that month alone II Corps, in striving to capture the Gheluvelt Plateau, had lost 27,300 men; total casualties already numbered over 68,000.[46] Nevertheless, the Germans were suffering in the same way. For Kuhl,

> The Hell of Verdun was surpassed . . . in the water-filled craters cowered the defenders without shelter from weather, hungry and cold, abandoned without pause to overwhelming artillery fire.[47]

The thousands of British wounded shipping back across the Channel brought home the news of what was happening along the Steenbeek and up on the plateau. It had the effect of hardening the Prime Minister's opposition to an offensive which he had authorized only with great reluctance.

As the futile massacres of August piled up in the ghastly hecatombs of slaughter on the Ypres Front without achieving any appreciable results, I repeatedly approached Sir William Robertson to remind him of the conditions attached to the Cabinet's assent to the operation. It was to be abandoned as soon as it became evident that its aims were unattainable this year and our attention was to be concentrated on an Italian operation.[48]

At a meeting in London to which Haig was recalled on 4 September, Lloyd George reiterated these objections, but he in no way managed to shift Haig from his standpoint that the Germans must be fought in Flanders on ground where the British Army, together with its extensive and involved supply system, was established, and that a dispersion of resources to other theatres could allow the enemy to strike a possibly disastrous blow either at his own forces or at the French. But Haig won his point. A majority of the members of the War Cabinet decided that the offensive should be continued, but at the same time he was obliged to accept the loss of another 100 heavy pieces of artillery to the Italian front.

Disquieting also for Haig was the shortage of reinforcements A warning Robertson had given him in May that henceforth only 'scraps' of manpower were likely to be made available was near to being fulfilled. Time and again the rear areas in France had been combed for surplus men, but, as Haig was obliged to warn his army commanders, the infantry would be 100,000 men short of establishment, something which further damaged the morale of the men in the battalions. Competing, of course, were the demands from industry and agriculture, with the former seriously affected by widespread labour unrest. During 1917 almost six million working days were lost from strikes, a figure that can be put in perspective by comparing it with the strike-ridden early 1980s: only in 1985, the year of the Scargill coal strike, was the figure for 1917 exceeded.

Nevertheless, in one direction at least a glimmer of hope could be detected. Pétain was succeeding in reshaping the French Army. Those acts of 'collective indiscipline' had been quelled so effectively that the French were able to launch an effective attack at Verdun on 26 August. German losses were heavy, the French taking 10,000 prisoners on the first day. As Ludendorff, Chief-of-Staff to Hindenburg, who had replaced Falkenhayn in 1916, wrote, 'The French Army was once more capable of the offensive. It had quickly overcome its depression'.[50] There had also been heavy fighting at Lens, where the Canadian Corps, as part of Horne's First Army, had attacked in another attempt to deflect attention from Flanders. It was relentless attrition once again, as grim and wretched as anything the Canadians had so far experienced, even on the Somme.

But it was, in its way, successful. Canadian losses numbered over 8000, less than half those of the enemy.

*   *   *

Plumer's first 'step', in what was afterwards to be known as the Battle of the Menin Road Ridge, was fixed for 20 September. Three days beforehand, Haig visited the headquarters of the corps and divisions earmarked for the attack where he conducted his usual and formidable cross-examination. 'In every case,' he recorded, 'I found the officers full of confidence as to the result of the forthcoming attack. Every detail had been gone into most thoroughly and the troops most carefully trained. . . . Altogether I felt it was most exhilarating to go round such a very knowledgeable and confident body of leaders.'[51] The confidence shown was to be justified. His tour of Gough's area on the following day was rather less happy. 'I am inclined to think,' he wrote, 'that the Fifth Army staff work is not so satisfactory as last year.'[52] It was a fault of which he had become very much aware. Later that day Haig again visited Second Army Headquarters. 'General Plumer was in great spirits. I told him I had only small suggestions to offer as a result of my visit to his corps and divisions yesterday. Everything was quite satisfactory. I could only wish him great success and good luck.' But that slight deprecatory note was still there: 'The old man was full of good spirits and confident.'[53]

From the lessons of Messines and after discussion with his corps commanders, Plumer had evolved a rather more flexible method of tackling the German defences, those now sparsely-held forward positions, backed by belts of concrete pill-boxes with counterattack forces awaiting their opportunity as the attackers penetrated deeper into the maelstrom of artillery and machine-gun fire. As we have seen, for his main thrust, Plumer was to use four divisions, the 41st and 23rd of X Corps on the right, and the 1st and the 2nd Australians of I ANZAC on the left. Three bounds were chosen, each to be captured by fresh troops and each one shorter than the one before to allow for the increasingly greater difficulties which would be met: after the leading battalion of each forward brigade had taken the 800-yard-deep first bound, there was to be a forty-five minute halt for another battalion to pass through to the next objective, only 500 yards or so distant. A two-hour pause would then occur while the remaining two battalions of each brigade were brought forward for the final assault of only some 300 yards; here the major counterattacks by the German reserve divisions were likely to be met but the employment of the British reserves, to be held at each level, was left to local commanders to avoid the costly crowding which had happened on the ridge at Messines.

In the first assault, one or two lines of widely deployed skirmishers was to force the enemy to reveal any unpinpointed defences, which would then be dealt with by small parties composed of Lewis-gunners, rifle-grenade men and Mills-bombers; meanwhile similar groups would infiltrate between the strongpoints and mopping-up parties in the rear would cope with anything that had been overlooked.

During the first three weeks of September every unit had been given intensive training in these new methods. Among them was Private Gladden's battalion in the 23rd Division. A visit by Plumer in early August had warned Gladden and his comrades that the very pleasant period in rest which they had been enjoying was about to end. A little later they began to train for Menin Road. Taken to see the immense scale-model of the battlefield which had been built near Poperinghe, his reaction was that 'Although we had little stomach for our approaching glory, we certainly appreciated being brought into the picture and showed a great deal of interest in the demonstration. It struck me personally as a remarkable piece of work.'[54] Gladden was impressed also by the crowded camps, wagon-lines and store-dumps, everywhere he looked, an indication of the back-up behind them. Reconnoitring airmen brought to Binding, on the other side, news of these 'canvas camps of 200 or more big tents' which appeared overnight like mushrooms, and 'whole towns of new hutments'. He admitted to being scared, doubting whether they could withstand the odds. 'Verdun, the Somme and Arras are mere purgatories compared with this concentrated hell, which one of these day will be stoked up to white heat.'[55]

The enemy planes were also bombing the British rear areas, flying in sixteen-strong formations and using a new and especially unpleasant anti-personnel bomb. Gladden's battalion was among those which suffered, and he 'was not sorry to leave such a hot-spot for the line on 18th September'.[56] He quickly changed his mind, as soldiers do. After passing through the serrated ruins of Ypres, they approached the ridge where 'All around us stretched a morass in graduations of grey and black which looked like some petrified inferno from Dante. . . . Peril threatened everywhere off the tracks. . . . In the hollow lay the derelict corpses of a couple of tanks . . . hopelessly bogged down and badly shattered.' A sergeant and a private of Gladden's company slipped off the greasy duckboards, never to be seen again.[57] Blunden, who made a similar journey, described the plank-roads as being 'at once the salvation and the slaughterhouse of the forward areas of this battle',[58] targets as they were for the German guns.

After a day spent under steady bombardment and sniper fire in an old German strongpoint, Gladden's was one of dozens of infantry battalions that moved forward on the evening of 19 September to their final assembly positions. Soon everyone was soaked: the weather had broken yet again. It alarmed Gough, whom Haig had placed under Plumer for last-minute decisions; around midnight he telephoned Plumer to suggest a postponement because of the foul conditions. Plumer straightaway consulted his corps and some of his divisional commanders, whose response was mixed.[59] Birdwood, whose Australians had a major role, was in no doubt what should be done. In a letter written four days later to Colonel Clive Wigram, the King's Assistant Private Secretary, he recounted how he had spent a very anxious night. 'As rain came on at 10 p.m. Sir H. Plumer called me up, asking what I thought of postponing the operations, as the 5th Army suggested we should do so. I strongly opposed this.'[60] It was, of course, as Plumer told Repington afterwards, difficult to cancel an attack any later than 7 pm; by that time the troops would be moving forward to their final positions.[61] As it was, having obtained quite an optimistic forecast from the meteorologist, Plumer decided to go ahead.

The Official Historian remembered that 'The order and silence of the approach march impressively confirmed the excellence of the arrangements'.[62] The inevitable errors that occurred had no effect on the outcome of the operation and harmed only unfortunate individuals directly concerned. In places tapes for the leading battalions had been laid out in 'no-man's land', 150 yards behind the line of the opening barrage, while the units for the second phase waited to advance from the British front-line positions. Close-packed in this way, it was a daunting moment when, just before the 5.40 am zero, white rocket flares lit up the centre of the ANZAC sector and the German artillery crashed down. But, before serious damage could be done, the British batteries drenched the German gun-positions with gas-shell, the barrages opened, and the men lying among the craters rose to their feet to materialize, as a German diarist wrote, 'like spectres out of a mist'.[63]

There was no way the Germans could stop these Australian 'spectres'. Although the ground surface was slippery after the rain and the flooded shell-craters were death traps, three weeks of sun had hardened everything underneath except in the valley bottoms. The force of the seven-day artillery preparation and the complexity of the barrages were unprecedented. The field artillery had laid two belts of fire ahead of the advancing troops, one of shrapnel and one of high-explosive, each lifting fifty yards every two minutes; ahead of this barrage crept two separate belts of heavy and medium howitzer fire, and between the two there was yet another barrage laid by 240 medium machine guns. Caught either in their shelters or just as they emerged, the demoralized survivors of this crushing fire were not slow to surrender.

On the far left the 2nd Australian Division gained its second objective with hardly a shot fired, but elsewhere the struggle was bitter. Gladden, whose battalion lost all its company commanders, lay miserably in a shell-hole that night reflecting that they had gained their objective only because 'The enemy's barrier of steel and concrete had been pierced, or rather smashed open, by our artillery and occupied by our puny selves',[64] an apt summary of Plumer's tactics. As against this, a Green Howard battalion of the same division, which suffered heavily as it approached the second objective, discovered that the German dugouts had hardly suffered from the bombardment, but that several parties of the enemy emerged from them waving pieces of white cloth that had clearly been prepared beforehand; by the end of the day the Green Howards had lost two-thirds of their strength.[65]

At about 7.45 am, as this second objective was being consolidated, a south-westerly breeze rolled away the morning mist to reveal, in bright sunlight, the plateau around Broodseinde, still far away across the wilderness of shell-holes and tree stumps. It was the time for the pause of two hours, during which the two reserve battalions of each assaulting brigade moved forward and the final assault, under cover of a fresh barrage, was launched. As had been accurately forecast, the fighting was still more severe, but within another half-hour the job had been done. Only on the right of the main assault was success incomplete. There the 41st Division failed to carry the maze of concrete dugouts and pill-boxes known as Tower Hamlets, a hardly perceptible spur of land between Gheluvelt and Zandvoorde on the eastern slope of the main ridge. Further south still, Plumer's 39th and 19th Divisions, protecting the flank of the main assault, edged forward too, but suffered quite heavily in so doing. To the north Gough's Fifth Army, which also had pressed forward to conform with Plumer's advance, gained all its objectives.

Then came the expected German counterattacks. To halt these, Plumer's preparations had been as meticulous as those for the assault. He had correctly anticipated that the major test would be to hold the ground he had captured. With the final objective only thinly held as an observation line, his main resistance was centred around the second objective, in and among the captured concrete defences and fortified shell-holes; continuous lines of trenches were avoided, as they had been by the enemy. Because forward telephone cables were nearly always cut by shell fire, a complicated system of signals had been organized, using Lucas lamps, flags and firework rockets; these were supplemented by pigeons, runners and message-carrying dogs; at each brigade headquarters and at some artillery observation posts wireless sets had been set up. The result of all these well-planned preliminary arrangements was that when, during the late afternoon, the German reserve divisions were seen to approach, artillery and machine-gun barrages were brought down to smash their regimental columns long before they reached the British defences. Only on the very left of the Fifth Army did any counter-attack succeed in recovering lost ground.

The victory was complete. The battle had gone almost exactly as planned. Ludendorff summed it up: 'The enemy's onslaught on the 20th was successful, which proved the superiority of the attack over the defence. Its strength did not consist in the tanks; we found them inconvenient, but put them out of action all the same. The power of the attack lay in the artillery.'[66] German losses during the day's fighting have not been recorded, but over 3000 prisoners had been taken; on the front of the 23rd Division alone, 1000 German bodies were buried. But British casualties were not light either, numbering 20,000 in all on 20 September and during the next five days, 12,000 of them in Plumer's army.[67] On both sides the artillery had caused the most damage. Blunden's battalion lost 280 men in four days, nearly all by shell-fire, in just holding the ground gained by other units of 39th Division. The men were frozen by night and roasted by day and water was scarce. 'The guns of all calibres poured their fury into our small area. It was one continuous din and impact. The trenches immediately about our pill-boxes were already full of bodies. . . . The Aid-Post was hit, and the doctor continued to dress the wounded at incredible speed.'[68]

Yet even in those so-called 'quiet' periods, the toll continued: during Plumer's three weeks of preparations for the Menin Road, the killed and wounded in Second Army had totalled 6000.

On the same evening of 20 September, as soon as Plumer learned that the German counterattacks had been beaten off, he issued a warning order for the start of the second 'step', an advance of a further 1000 yards by I ANZAC to clear Polygon Wood and the western half of Zonnebeke village on 26 September. Again Gough's troops and the rest of the Second Army were to so conform as to avoid the Germans concentrating their entire strength against this vital sector. The crucial aspect of Plumer's preparations was the shift forward of his artillery across the churned-up ground, a task that had begun on the afternoon of the Menin Road battle. Fine weather and a drying breeze ensured that the move was completed within the five days, despite the incessant and accurate shelling. Early on 25 September fresh divisions were brought forward to relieve those exhausted by the earlier fighting and, as the last of these reliefs were taking place, that of the 23rd by the 33rd Division, the Germans counterattacked again. They were repulsed, but only after the incoming division had been hit hard and disorganized just as it was due to attack.

The 4th and 5th Australian Divisions were the spearhead of Plumer's fresh thrust across the plateau. As their leading infantry moved off at dawn on 26 September, in what was to be remembered as the Battle of Polygon Wood, as at Messines the shell-bursts raised a dense wall of dust which hid the advancing men from the enemy machine-gunners. (Third Ypres was by no means all mud.) The day's fighting was to be a near replica of the previous battle. Polygon Wood and the western part of Zonnebeke were cleared as planned; on the right the 33rd Division, still recovering from its vicissitudes of the day before, failed to keep pace with the Australians, but this did not affect the outcome. During the afternoon defensive barrages again crushed the two waves of German counterattacks. And, once again, away on the right, Tower Hamlets proved too hard a nut; impregnable is an over-used word, but the fortress built on this gentle spur seemed to be so.

The German defence system, based on thinly held forward positions backed by massive counterattack forces, had failed against Plumer's sledge-hammer tactics, his 'planned lurches' as Captain Carrington, who took part, described them.[69] At Polygon Wood Plumer's main thrust had overrun two enemy divisions and smashed two more in the counterattacks that failed – 'their attack power lamed', as the German Official History put it.[70] This defeat led to a major change in German tactics, a reversion to earlier methods. Because their counterattacks had rarely been launched in time to hit the British as they were fighting their way on to their objectives, the time at which they were the most vulnerable, the Germans decided to delay their ripostes for a day in the future so that systematic artillery preparations could be made. It had been the old story of attacks that were too hastily organized meeting with failure. The corollary of this change of method was that the German forward positions had to be strengthened so as to delay the first onrush of their enemies, so placing more men in danger from the crushing power of the British artillery preparations. This change of tactics did not long stay secret; on 5 October a German order was captured describing it.[71]

Plumer's next 'step' was the capture of the eastern end of the Gheluvelt Plateau and the village of Broodseinde on the summit of the ridge. For this II ANZAC was brought forward from reserve to relieve Gough's V Corps, so extending Plumer's responsibility northwards and further reducing the size and the task of Fifth Army. For the main thrust the 1st and 2nd Australian Divisions of I ANZAC Corps, together with the 3rd Australian and the New Zealand Divisions of II ANZAC, were directed against Broodseinde and the Gravenstafel spur; with four more divisions attacking to the south of the Australians and New Zealanders, and four of Gough's directed towards Poelcapelle, twelve divisions in all were being used on a front of 14,000 yards.

It was another hammer blow, the tactics used, with one exception, for this Battle of Broodseinde, being the same as for Plumer's two earlier 'steps'. In this siege warfare surprise was an elusive quarry, anything more than the day and time of an operation being all but impossible to disguise. In an attempt to achieve at least this, Plumer had limited his bombardment to a single day at Polygon Wood as opposed to the week of the Menin Road battle. For Broodseinde he abandoned it altogether except for counter-battery work and the destruction of individual strong-points. Instead, from 27 September onwards, a number of full practice barrages were fired.

Yet again, nearly everything went as planned. With one or two exceptions, all the objectives were reached. Almost everywhere, however, this third 'step' on 4 October resulted in even more bloody fighting. As they awaited zero hour, I ANZAC's forward battalions suffered badly from a heavy German bombardment and, when at last they were allowed to clamber to their feet, straightaway they ran into German troops advancing towards them. At the sight of the Australian bayonets, most of the enemy infantry fled, running back in the half-light through the sheet of flame that marked the Australian barrage. The shelling under which the Australians had lain before zero had not been a German defensive barrage, called down upon them because they had been spotted, but the preliminaries for an attack by the other side which, by coincidence, had been launched at exactly the same time.

Fighting their way forward, both ANZAC Corps gained the ridge-top, from which German gun-teams could be seen limbering up and galloping back across the still green fields below. The Australians and New Zealanders had reached the British battle-front of the winter of 1914-15 and, as they feverishly tried to get below ground to escape the enemy shelling, their shovels everywhere turned up scraps of old khaki uniforms. Losses during the day had been high, but so had those of the Germans. Second Army alone had taken more than 4000 prisoners; the German dead littering the battlefield lay thicker than had ever before been seen.[72] It had been an overwhelming victory. Plumer, even with Messines in mind, described it as 'the greatest victory since the Marne'.[73] Ludendorff admitted to it having been 'extraordinarily severe, and again we only came through it with enormous losses. It was evident that the idea of holding the front line more densely, adopted at my last visit to the front in September, was not the remedy'.[74] Lloyd George, on the other hand, was afterwards to enquire '. . . the Broodseinde victory, as it was called. Who remembers the name now? (Try it on one of your friends).'[75]

It was to be the last of Plumer's unqualified successes of 1917. During the day the weather broke and that afternoon the evacuation of the

3rd Australian's wounded broke down as the stretcher-bearers struggled through the mud with their pitiful burdens; wounded lay about
unattended in the morass outside the packed pill-boxes used as dressing
stations; under the weight of the traffic the planked roadways collapsed,
guns and ambulances slipping off the greasy surface into the bog. It was a
foretaste of what was to come, 'all-in wrestling in the mud' as Carrington
remembered it all.[76]

★   ★   ★

Despite the lateness of the season, Plumer's successes at Menin Road and
Polygon Wood had encouraged Haig once again to consider the possibility
of a breakthrough. On 28 September he had told Plumer and Gough that
the next phase would be launched on 10 October, once Broodseinde was
taken, and that they would then attempt finally to clear the Passchendaele
Ridge. It would, however, be a less strictly limited operation, aimed at
exploiting either towards Moorslede or Roulers, and employing tanks and
cavalry.[77] Haig then asked the two army commanders to submit their
requirements in men and material for the battle. In his reply, sent two
days later, Plumer suggested that it would be premature to consider such
an exploitation, and that a further series of step-by-step operations were
needed to clear the Passchendaele-Westroosebeke Ridge. The next day
Gough made a similar response.

Haig's comment on these submissions was that he had not meant that
exploitation would necessarily follow the 10 October attack, but that he
wanted arrangements made so that opportunities could be taken when
offered. At a further meeting on 2 October he explained that he was anxious
not to repeat the mistake the Germans had made on the same battlefield on
31 October, 1914, when they failed to take advantage of the exhaustion of
the British forces. He also told them that he was concentrating everything
he could for the Ypres offensive which would continue *so long as weather
conditions permitted:* six divisions would reinforce Fifth Army from other
sectors and four would join Plumer. For the possible exploitation, the
reserve divisions of Second Army, held fifteen miles back, would be ready
to entrain on 10 October; two tank battalions would be alloted to Second
Army and three to the Fifth, and, in addition, a cavalry division would
be ready to operate with each of Plumer's corps.[78] Haig's diary note of
this meeting, made that evening, reads in part:

I pointed out how favourable the situation was, and how necessary it
was to have all necessary means for exploiting any successes gained on
10th, should the situation admit, e.g. if the enemy counterattacks and is

defeated then reserve brigades must follow after the enemy and take the Passchendaele ridge at once. Both Gough and Plumer quite acquiesced in my views, and arranged wholeheartedly to give effect to them when the time came. At first they adhered to the idea of continuing our attacks for limited objectives.[79]

When news of the success of Broodseinde reached GHQ on 4 October Haig immediately sent Charteris to Plumer to discuss the possibility of launching this exploitation straightaway. Plumer demurred. He was aware that there were still eight German divisions in close reserve behind the battle sector and another six nearby, and he reminded Charteris that the Commander-in-Chief himself had stressed that no exploitation should be attempted until the German counterattacks had been beaten off; further-more, the German artillery fire was undiminished and he would need to bring forward his own guns through the two-mile-wide slough before any-thing more could be attempted. Before he saw Charteris, Plumer had, in fact, directed Birdwood to push I ANZAC eastwards towards a small spur, just beyond Broodseinde, but his Corps Commander had immediately objected on the grounds that the fighting had been stiffer and casualties greater than had earlier been believed; he insisted, above all, that some guns must be got forward before anything further was attempted. Plumer accepted Birdwood's advice. This spur and Passchendaele could almost certainly have been occupied during the day, but the German reserves would just have surely recovered the ground.[80] Later that afternoon Haig discussed progress with his two Army Commanders in the house into which he had moved at Cassel, adjacent to Plumer's own headquarters. Here Plumer emphasized that only the leading enemy divisions had, as yet, been encountered. Charteris disagreed with him, but any question of immediate exploitation was, nevertheless, dropped.[81]

Haig now either forgot or ignored his own warning that the offensive would continue *so long as weather conditions permitted*. It was another major error. The rain, often torrential now, continued. On 5 October Birdwood protested to Plumer that, so far as his Corps was concerned, any far-reaching proposals for exploitation were not practicable, as neither the light railway nor the Westhoek-Zonnebeke road could be completed in time to carry the quantity of heavy and field artillery ammunition required.[82] On no part of the Second Army front was it now proving possible to move guns through the morass, and the mules carrying ammu-nition were taking between six and sixteen hours for what should have been an hour's journey; shells arrived coated with slime and had to be cleaned by already exhausted artillerymen. Everywhere the misery was complete. The truth of Napoleon's reputed adage was again being demonstrated that 'The first quality of the soldier is constancy in enduring fatigue and privation. Courage is only the second'. At Plumer's headquarters no one had any illusions about the true conditions. Harington himself, just after the capture of Broodseinde, had visited the Passchendaele front under the most shocking circumstances.[83]

It was, then, hardly surprising that, at a conference on 7 October, both Gough and Plumer should have informed Haig that they would welcome the closing-down of the campaign, although they were willing to proceed if ordered to do so. Haig refused, his grounds being that the longer the operation was postponed, the better prepared would be the German defences and reserves; at the very least he intended to gain the full length of the main ridge and its drier ground before the onset of winter proper so as to avoid the troops sitting for months in the morass of the lower slopes and under full enemy observation.[84] In this view he persisted despite having learned four days earlier that the War Cabinet was instructing him to take over a further stretch of the line from the French, a 'great bombshell' as he described the news.[85]

The main weight of this renewed attack, brought forward to 9 October, again fell on Plumer's two ANZAC Corps, but in this assault II ANZAC used the attached 49th and 66th United Kingdom divisions, the troops who had fought at Broodseinde having been pulled back into reserve. With I ANZAC still on the left, the plan was for the leading brigades to pursue the enemy beyond Passchendaele, still more than 2000 yards away, and to drive him off the slopes to the north and east of that village. At the same time Fifth Army was to close up to the main ridge at Spriet, much the same distance away. On 12 October a further blow would be struck to take Westroosebeke, at the northernmost point of the ridge.

On 8 October, the afternoon before, Haig saw Plumer again at Cassel:

It was raining and looked like a wet night. He [Plumer] stated that 2nd Anzac Corps (which is chiefly concerned in to-morrow's attack) had specially asked that there should be *no postponement*.[86]

Godley was, of course, II ANZAC's commander. Birdwood, on the other hand, was hoping for a postponement; in Gough's army it was the same, one corps commander in favour of putting the attack off, one against. Plumer's own views on the subject have not survived. There are indications, however, that success may have engendered over-confidence in the Second Army. The Australian Official History contains the following:

Notes of an address given by General Harington to the war correspondents on the eve of this attack show that the recent successes were proudly attributed by him to the methods pursued by the Second Army, and that, whether the Fifth Army thought differently or not, the Second Army was set upon making the attack. It still hopes that after one or two more strokes the cavalry might be put through, and, though ill-weather was almost certain, considered the attempt worth trying. The sandy crest of the ridge, Harington said, was 'as dry as a bone'.[87]

To some of those who listened the brilliance of the Second Army's success appeared to be tempting its leaders to forsake its tried methods.[88] Whether this address was an accurate reflection of Plumer and Harington's views, or whether Harington was merely giving public support to Haig's policy and showing the public pre-battle confidence to be expected at such a time, is not and probably never will be known.

So began the unhappy slaughter of the final phase of Third Ypres, the attempts to capture the rest of the Passchendaele Ridge and possibly break through as well. The entire Steenbeek valley, the ground that now lay to the rear of II ANZAC, was, in the words of the chief engineer of one of the divisions, 'a porridge of mud'.[89] Through it the two ANZAC Corps had failed to move more than a few of their guns: some of them were firing at maximum range and most from hastily constructed and unstable gun-platforms. In such conditions it had been estimated that the assaulting brigades would need five hours to cover the two and a half miles to the front line; some took ten hours and arrived utterly disorganized and exhausted, to be pushed into the attack too late to obtain protection from what was a weak and inaccurate barrage.[90] Not surprisingly the attacks on 9 October failed nearly everywhere and with heavy casualties. Only on the very far left of the Fifth Army, where the approaches to the main ridge had been far less damaged, did the Guards Division and the First French Army gain their objectives.

It was all to happen again three days later. Acting on misleading information provided by Godley on the evening of 9 October and sent back when the situation had not properly clarified, Plumer informed GHQ that II ANZAC had gained 'a sufficiently good jumping-off line for the next attack on the 12th', when, he added, there was every hope of capturing Passchendaele.[91] Haig's three major misjudgements have already been described. This was Plumer's notable error of the battle.

When the 3rd Australian and the New Zealand Divisions relieved the shattered 49th and 66th on the morning of 11 October, conditions were horrific, even by the standards of the Salient:

The sodden battle-ground was littered with wounded who had lain out in the mud among the dead for two days and nights; and the pillbox shelters were overflowing with unattended wounded, whilst the dead lay piled outside. The survivors, in a state of utter exhaustion, with neither food nor ammunition, had been sniped at by the Germans on the higher ground throughout the 10th.[92]

It required sixteen men to handle a laden stretcher across the mile of mud to a duckboard track leading to a dressing-station. The Germans noted that effective counter-battery fire had almost ceased; ahead the ANZACs could see almost undamaged wire and pill-boxes lying between themselves and Passchendaele.

As the rain once more began to fall, Gough again telephoned Plumer to propose a postponement, but Plumer again, after consulting his corps commanders, decided to carry on. Again the barrage was inadequate, giving the impression of being no more than casual shelling. For all that, a handful of Monash's 3rd Australians did manage to reach the church at Passchendaele, but they did not stay there. Another severe setback had been suffered, despite the magnificent courage shown by the ANZACS; Godley's Corps alone suffered another 6000 casualties that day: by the end of Third Ypres 38,000 Australians had been killed, wounded or drowned.[93] Monash was justified when he wrote to his wife that men were being sacrificed in 'hair-brained ventures, like Bullecourt and Passchendaele', and that no one in the War Cabinet protested because Australia was not represented.[94] So encouraged had the Germans been by their success on 9 October that they had not even thought it necessary to relieve their forward divisions before this renewed British assault hit them. Haig's diary entry for 12 October was terse:

Second and Fifth Armies continued their attack at 5.25 this morning. Troops reached points of assembly up to time in spite of the very bad state of the ground. Owing to the rain and bad state of the ground, General Plumer decided that it was best not to continue the attack on the front of his Army.[95]

The following day Haig, Plumer and Gough were unanimous that the next attack should be launched only when there was a fair prospect of fine weather. Plank and sleeper roads must be completed to bring forward the guns.[96]

* * *

Third Ypres was not yet over. Fresh troops were available in the shape of the Canadian Corps; these, Haig decided, should be placed under

Plumer after Kiggell revealed to him that 'the Canadians do not work kindly' with Gough.[97] Arrangements were made for them to take over from II ANZAC about 18 October, and Plumer's tried tactics of three short advances with an interval between each one were again to be used. Fortunately the weather was again to improve in mid-October, so helping the road-building forward, but conditions were still foul. In the Steenbeek valley the Germans drenched everything with a combination of sneezing and mustard gases: the first obliged men to remove their respirators, so allowing the second to attack their eyes and throats, as well as burn bodies and contaminate gun-positions and bivouacs. As a result, some thousands of men working in the rearward areas were disabled.

Nevertheless, by 21 October the guns were in position and systematic wire-cutting and counter-battery work could begin. Five days later two Canadian divisions started to batter their way up the slopes towards Passchendaele, attacking across the ground where II ANZAC had twice previously failed. Adequate preparations had, however, now been made, and in bitter but often confused fighting the right-hand division reached its objectives; on the left another division only got half-way up the slope against even more stubborn opposition. Rain, which again broke out during the morning, produced conditions similar to those experienced by the Australians, the Canadians on the lower ground sometimes struggling waist-deep in water. Even so, the German counterattacks were beaten off and forward Canadian positions established on higher and drier ground. It had, as their Official Historian put it, been 'a satisfying but costly beginning'.[98] Four days later the same two divisions attacked once again and reached their objectives, only some 800 yards away; four separate and major counterattacks were repulsed by the use of artillery and machine-gun barrages alone.

After this second Canadian 'step', Haig ordered Plumer to take over XVIII Corps on the Canadian left from Fifth Army, so leaving Gough with the rump of a single corps to command. Counter-battery work was now intensified and, on 6 November, two fresh Canadian divisions attacked. Plumer's third 'step' was a complete success. In the early hours of the morning, the leading Canadian battalions were streaming through on either side of Passchendaele, bayoneting any German survivors.

Four days later the Canadians extended their hold on the ridge. Westroosebeek, just a mile beyond Passchendaele, was never reached. On 12 November Haig closed the battle down, finally relinquishing his hopes of occupying the entire ridge before the winter; any question of exploiting towards the Channel Ports had disappeared after the October failures. The final three weeks' fighting had cost the Canadians 12,403 casualties, of whom only twenty-one had been prisoners captured by the

Germans.[99] The latter was an astonishingly low figure and a tribute to the way these Canadians had fought.

Plumer never saw his battle end. By 9 November he had left the Western Front and his Second Army to take charge of the British forces in Italy – of which more later.

* * *

For Lloyd George Third Ypres, together with the Somme and Verdun, would

> always rank as the most gigantic, tenacious, grim, futile and bloody fight ever waged in the history of war. . . . The tale of these battles constitute a trilogy illustrating the unquenchable heroism that will never admit defeat and the inexhaustible vanity that will never admit a mistake.[100]

Certainly at Third Ypres the heroism of the fighting men had been remarkable, even though it often flagged, as heroism does. But anyone who had fought on the Eastern Front, in the French offensives of 1914 and 1915, along the Isonzo River in Italy or even in the American Civil War, might have queried the Prime Minister's other superlatives. But then he was a Welshman with a way with words, not a student of military history, and he was intent on retrieving his own reputation and damning that of Haig.

The Official History was blunt and accurate. 'No great victory had been won.'[101] Haig had not broken the Flanders deadlock nor cleared the Belgian coast. Whether he won the battle of attrition is arguable. In almost five months of fighting he lost almost a quarter of a million men; of these 82% were to return to duty, either with fighting units or at the rear.[102] German losses were probably much the same, but they may have been greater; the figures are still a matter for acrimonious dispute.[103] One of the military myths debunked by John Terraine is that, during the present century, the attacker has always suffered more severely than the defender.[104] By the middle of 1917, artillery, and not the machine gun was the main killer on the Western Front, and the British and French artillery techniques were more sophisticated than those of their opponents and by then they possessed the greater resources.

With good reason the name Ypres encapsulates the waste and horror of war. But that melancholy figure of a quarter of a million British dead and wounded should be put into some sort of perspective. It was no more than Haig had expected. On 19 June he had warned the Prime Minister that he had estimated that casualties on the Western Front would be 100,000 monthly, although he hoped that the figure might be less.[105]

During the same period of time, on the Somme during 1916, losses had totalled 400,000. Six weeks in front of Arras had cost yet another 160,000. During the whole of that year battle losses numbered 800,000. Even by World War Two standards the casualties at Ypres were not inordinate, 2121 daily as opposed to 3552 in Normandy for the Allied Forces during June, 1944.[106] But, in the words of the Official Historian:

> The casualties alone do not give the full picture of the situation; for, apart from actual losses, the discomfort of the living conditions in the forward areas and the strain of fighting with indifferent success had overwrought and discouraged all ranks more than any other operation fought by British troops in the war, so that . . . discontent was general.[107]

Philip Gibbs, who saw it all from quite close quarters, wrote in much the same terms:

> Our men were too sorely tried. For the first time the British Army lost its spirit of optimism, and there was a sense of deadly depression among many officers and men with whom I came in touch. They saw no ending of the war, and nothing except continuous slaughter, such as that in Flanders.[108]

On the other side, Kuhl wrote of 'the greatest martyrdom of the war'.[109] It was that for all who were there. Yet another statistic helps place this Flanders carnage in focus. On the Western Front as a whole one in four of the British dead had no known grave. Around Ypres the figure is one in three, a measure of the extent this small area was harrowed again and again by high explosive and the older graves churned up.

It was hardly Lloyd George's accusation of 'inexhaustible vanity' that impelled Haig to persevere as he did at Passchendaele. Certainly he was stubborn, but this can be a virtue and is a quality often found in successful men. Hindsight allows us to catalogue Haig's errors, possibly three in number. For the main offensive, he chose Gough instead of Plumer, who, despite his recent showing at Messines, had still to win Haig's unstinted confidence. Second, there was his failure to ensure that Gough carried out his instructions to put his full weight against the Gheluvelt Plateau in the opening stages of the offensive. And lastly there was Haig's error in ignoring his own admonition against continuing the campaign after the weather had finally broken.

Like Haig, Plumer made his mistakes, especially in his handling of the ill-conceived and executed attacks by the ANZAC Corps on 9 and 12

October, in which the objectives were too optimistic and his confidence in the ability of the troops to cope with the impossible conditions misplaced. Perhaps he should share a part of the blame with Haig for failing to halt the offensive. Both Gough and he had told Haig on 7 October that they would welcome an end to the campaign, but this Haig refused. Should he have pressed his point to an offer of resignation? But this was not in Plumer's make-up: his code was one of complete loyalty to his Commander-in-Chief.

Afterwards Lloyd George accused Haig of carrying on with the campaign despite the opposition of 'all the Generals' engaged.[110] About Plumer's attitude, he was specific: he was opposed to a general offensive in Flanders.[111] In discussing the many shortcomings he had detected in Haig, Lloyd George made much of Plumer's letter to Haig of 30 September, which was said to have thrown 'cold water on his [Haig's] hopes!'[112] Yet this letter, so far as is known, was merely Plumer's statement that he considered exploitation at that stage of the battle would be premature, and that, before this could happen, the main Passchendaele Ridge would have to be taken by a series of 'step' attacks. Harington, incidentally, doubted whether Plumer ever wrote this letter as he did not see it and he claimed that he handled everything that passed over Plumer's desk.[113] The evidence for it depends upon the Official History and Gough's *Fifth Army*, probably the source for the statement made in the Official History.

Harington was especially incensed that Lloyd George should have suggested that Plumer was not loyal to Haig. In asking Edmonds for his advice on *Plumer of Messines*, he said:

> My job begins and ends with clearing Plumer from L.G.'s assertions that he disagreed with Haig over Passchendaele as he certainly did not. Lady P, I understand, does not even want that done as she knows of his utter loyalty but that is not the point – The public must also know and will expect something from me.[114]

At the time Harington wrote this, in the early nineteen-thirties, when criticism of Passchendaele was at its peak, it would have been easy for him to have glossed over Plumer's support for Haig and allowed Lloyd George's assertions of opposition to stand unchallenged. Instead, he went out of his way to emphasize, both from his own intimate knowledge of Plumer's thought processes and from his reading of his chief's letters to Lady Plumer, that it was

> inconceivable to me that his agreement with the views of the Commander-in-Chief was anything but one of '*utter loyalty*' and desire to carry out

his Chief's orders to capture Passchendaele . . . he never gave thought to stopping and turning back.[115]

After the weather broke again on 4 October Plumer did, of course, advise Haig to stop. But the last thing he would have done was to criticize Haig subsequently to Lloyd George for failing to accept his advice. Loyalty, in Plumer's book, even to a man he probably knew or suspected disliked him, was paramount.

10 Italy: The Reluctant Commander-in-Chief

For the past century the Italian Army has suffered from a bad press. Ridicule met its first and disastrous attempts to win a colonial empire by invading Abyssinia in 1896; its more successful campaigns in the next century aroused mere disgust. The reluctance of Italian soliders, dragged into World War Two on what was clearly the wrong side, to get themselves killed on behalf of German allies whom they both feared and hated was reflected in the ease with which they often surrendered. 'Still, it was little more than the world expected. Their reputation bore the stigma of their rout at Caporetto in October, 1917, a byword for military poltroonery. The real story was somewhat different.

Italy's entry into the First World War happened as a result of hard political bargaining with both sides. At the outset she was still nominally a member of the Triple Alliance, the secret treaty of 1882 directed against France and hatched in collusion with the German and Austro-Hungarian Empires. A growing sympathy with France and fear of Austria, her traditional enemy, with which was combined greed for territorial expansion in the Trentino and Trieste areas, brought Italy into the war in 1915 on the Allied side, the formal Pact of London having described in detail the help to be given her and the subsequent carve-up of territorial booty. With Russia close to defeat and most of northern France and Belgium in German possession, and likely to remain so, Italy's politicians could perhaps have chosen a better moment to enter the war.

Except for a six-mile coastal strip near the Adriatic, the entire 375-mile frontier between Italy and Austria was guarded by the high Alps and their rugged outliers on Italy's eastern border. Geography favoured the Austrians. The Venetian province east of the River Adige formed a dangerous salient, vulnerable to any Austrian offensive out of the Dolomite mountains of the Trentino. However, the main Italian Army faced its eastern frontier, and, at the start of the war, pushed forward to the deep gorge of the River Isonzo, on either bank of which high limestone ridges towered 2000 feet or more above its rushing blue waters. For the next

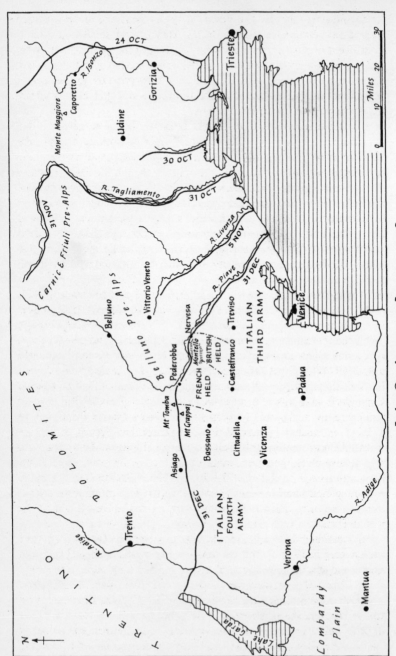

10. Italy, October, 1917–January, 1918

twenty-nine months the two armies grappled with one another in this rugged and inhospitable country, each at times carving small mountainous salients out of one another's lines, but always at prodigious cost. In what were to be known as the eleven Battles of the Isonzo, the Italians took the offensive on eleven separate occasions. In proportion to the total of population, the half-million Italian war-dead was to match exactly that of the white races of the British Empire.

Why these mainly illiterate Italian peasants fought so gallantly is a question hard to answer. Understanding little or nothing of what the war was about, the manipulation of their politicians could as well have committed them to one side as to the other. Although the Austrians were the traditional enemy of this new Kingdom of Italy, a country with little more than half a century's history behind it, they no longer menaced its independence. The Italian officers were brave enough, but few understood how to care for their men; equipment was poor, although so was that of the Austrians; staff-work was usually abysmally bad, while the artillery was inadequate in calibre and quantity, its ability to co-operate properly with the infantry almost non-existent.[1]

The eleventh Italian offensive along the Isonzo cost 166,000 casualties in August, 1917, almost double the Austrian losses. It was small wonder then that morale both on the home front and in the army neared breaking point, the consequence of what seemed to be an endless and pointless war, conditions which a most effective German propaganda machine exploited to the full. What the Allied leaders had feared then came about. Despite the British pressure at Passchendaele, the collapse of Russia allowed Ludendorff to release his small general reserve of six divisions (later reinforced by a seventh) to prop up the shaky Isonzo front. On 24 October, in what was intended to maim rather than destroy the Italian threat, the now combined German and Austro-Hungarian forces launched an offensive along the entire length of the Isonzo, its main thrust in the Caporetto area, a quiet part of the line held by IV Italian Corps, some of whose regiments had been made up to strength with mutinous munition workers, recently called to the colours after a civilian revolt against the war in Turin.[2]

Panic resulted from a gas attack, against which the Italian respirators were largely ineffective, and the isolation felt by the poor-quality troops among the strange mountains. Through the resulting gaps in the front of IV Corps, the German battalions wormed their way, their infiltration tactics decisive in their results. A certain Captain Erwin Rommel greatly distinguished himself as a member of one of these effective German units, winning the Pour la Mérite, the German equivalent of the Victoria Cross. Amid the increasing confusion, General Cadorna, the Commander-in-Chief, on 26 October ordered his armies to pull back behind the Tagliamento River, but, by then, his Second Army, of which IV Corps formed a part, was disintegrating, the consequence of poor orders, inadequate supervision and faulty dispositions, rather than treachery or the reluctance of the soldiers to fight.[3] Road were jammed by refugees and vehicles, there was no form of traffic control, and discipline was collapsing with men pillaging, throwing away their weapons and sometimes making for their homes. A brief halt was made on the Tagliamento, but the enemy crossed the river on the night of 2 November, and Cadorna was forced to order a further retreat to the River Piave. There the pursuers were obliged to call a halt, the unexpected speed of their advance having outrun their supply services. Throughout the Italian retreat the Duke of Aosta's Third Army, on the right of the Second, had pulled back in good order, and it now became the mainstay of the defence of this new Piave front, 100 miles shorter than that of the Isonzo.

The British Prime Minister was only too ready to respond to the Italian call for help that followed the *débâcle*. The French had already reacted, four of their divisions having started for Italy on 31 October. The War Cabinet now instructed Haig to select two good divisions to move straight away to Italy under a corps commander, who should be 'a good man'. Obeying his orders, Haig chose two sound divisions, the 23rd and the 41st; these he put in charge of Lieutenant-General the Earl of Cavan, whom he rated as the best of his corps commanders. At the same time he protested to Robertson, the CIGS, that the loss of this Corps might jeopardize his operations in Flanders.[4] Sound arrangements had already been made provisionally for the movement of troops across France and Italy by rail and road, and for establishing the necessary administrative superstructure. On 1 November the first British troops wiped the Flanders mud off their boots and entrained for what held out every prospect of being a far less insalubrious war.

* * *

Lloyd George had proposed to M. Painlevé, the newly appointed French Prime Minister, in mid-October, 1917, that a permanent military staff should be set up to study the war as a whole and to advise on inter-Allied strategy, a major step towards unity of command. The problem of helping Italy now provided him with the opportunity he sought to get things moving. At Rapallo, on 5 November, the Prime Minsters of the three countries concerned met together, accompanied by their military advisers, among whom was the now Lieutenant-General Sir Henry Wilson, selected in advance as the British Military Representative to serve on the new body when it was set up. The Tagliamento line had by then been broken, the result being that the British and the French readily agreed to the Italian request for yet further help; Lloyd George announced that he would send two further divisions, and more if need be, as did the French. At a later session, at Painlevé's proposal, the Supreme War Council (often known as the Versailles Council) came into being, its charter to effect unity among the Allied powers.

At the same time as he agreed to send these further divisions to Italy, Lloyd George decided also to release Plumer to take command of the British forces there, and he also issued instructions that Plumer could take with him Harington and any other staff officer he wished so that he would be able to get to work straight away with men he knew.[5] With the final assault on Passchendaele under way, Haig was far from pleased. 'Was ever an Army Commander and his staff,' he reflected, 'sent off to another theatre in the middle of a battle?'[6] Haig's staff officer, Charteris, also commented on the sudden move, the note in his diary reflecting as well the current disenchantment with the reported behaviour of the Italian Army:

They say the lower classes in Italy want an end to the war at any price. Anyhow, Plumer is the very best man we could have sent to pull them together. His departure makes a big difference as regards our next operation, which, however, may not come off.[7]

Aggravated at losing Plumer in this way, Haig recommended that another of his Army Commanders should go instead, but it was not to be.[8] Nor did Plumer want to leave. On 7 November he wrote to his wife:

I have just received a great shock. I have been ordered to go to Italy to assume command of the British Forces there. I am very sick about it and do not want to go in the least.[9]

The next day he wrote again saying that the more he thought about the move the less he liked it, and that he simply loathed leaving Second Army, the idea of which made him feel very depressed.[10] To Haig he emphasized his sorrow at leaving, and he also told his Commander-in-Chief that he thought it a great mistake to send so large a force to Italy.[11]

Harington related how Plumer broke the news to him:

I went up to his room where he was sitting with a telegram before him. He just looked up and said: 'You and I have got the sack. We are to hand over to General Rawlinson at once.' I confess I was staggered at what seemed a great injustice to my Chief. Then he added: 'We are to go to Italy at once.' No doubt the telegram had been a great shock to him, so with his keen sense of humour he thought he would just play it off on me.[12]

Keen indeed, but perhaps just a little quirky at times.

As he changed trains en route for Italy in Paris on 11 November, Plumer was summoned to the Hôtel Meurice to meet his Prime Minister who was on his way back to London from the Rapallo conference. Present at the meeting were Painlevé and the future Lord Hankey, the Cabinet Secretary. Harington, who was also there, remembered Lloyd George's insistence on the necessity of restoring the Italian Front, and his keenness to remove as many troops from the Western Front as Plumer could wish.[13] Lloyd George's account of the meeting, published after Plumer's death, read:

He [Plumer] did not conceal his satisfaction at the prospect of exchanging the Flemish swamp where he had been fighting a characteristically stubborn battle for the more genial surroundings of his new command. His delight, I felt certain, was not prompted merely by climatic reasons. He had no responsibility for initiating the campaign in Flanders and it was quite evident that his heart was not in it. In Italy he won the respect and goodwill of all with whom he came into contact, and justified to the full the reputation he had already won as one of the best soldiers in the British Army.[14]

It hardly rings true. All the evidence indicates that, far from being glad to leave Flanders, the opposite was the case. Plumer's letters to his wife demonstrate the shock and reluctance with which he received the news; nor were they written with a view to subsequent publication. And they are only a part of the evidence. Even if he had been opposed to leaving Flanders, he would hardly have told the Prime Minister so, especially with both Painlevé and Harington present at the meeting. Perhaps an injudiciously humorous comparison between the climates of Flanders and Italy were either misunderstood or deliberately misinterpreted by the Prime Minister as a part of his campaign to justify his own judgments and disparage those of Haig.

* * *

The instructions Plumer received in his new rôle from Robertson were to regard himself as a completely independent commander, with the proviso that, so as to cooperate effectively, he was to conform to the wishes of the Italian Commander-in-Chief regarding the disposition and employment of his forces; if, at any time, he was asked to carry out an operation which, in his opinion, unduly endangered his troops, he was to represent the fact to the Italians, and, if need be, refer the matter to London. He was also to report upon what reinforcements he thought might be needed.[15]

After stopping at Mantua to talk to Cavan (among whose staff captains was the future King Edward VIII, still fretting at being kept out of the front line), he continued his journey to the Italian GHQ at Padua, where he found a galaxy of Allied generals. Received by the King of Italy, he then met Wilson, Foch, now Chief-of-Staff of the Army and representing the French Government, and Weygand, Foch's principal assistant. Here also was General Diaz, who had replaced Cadorna the previous week, pressure from the British and French Prime Ministers having hastened the latter's departure. A member of the Neapolitan bourgeoisie, Diaz was a very different man from Cadorna who belonged to the Piedmontese military aristocracy, a class described by an Italian officer who served alongside the British and wrote a history of the campaign as one 'that tended to forget soldiers were human beings and regard them as military machines'.[16] In no way a charismatic commander, Diaz was a most able staff officer, sensible and prudent, and very ready to work with his British ally. His Chief-of-Staff was to be a rising young Italian lieutenant-general, Badoglio, the future conqueror of Abyssinia and leader of the conspiracy that was to depose Mussolini. He and Harington were to hit it off well and become great friends.[17] Also at Padua was a British brigadier-general, the representative of the CIGS, whose services Plumer straightaway dispensed with on the unarguable grounds that to disagree with him would be unpleasant but that if they agreed there was no point in the brigadier-general being there.[18]

The worst was already over when Plumer arrived. The Italians were firmly in place along the Piave, defending a shorter line against an enemy who had overreached himself, credit for which is due to Cadorna, a clear-minded and unflappable general, despite his many other defects. And help was at hand: the first two French divisions had already arrived; Cavan's Corps was to complete its concentration around Padua by 21 November, and another corps was preparing to entrain from France. Although still very nervous, the Italians had recovered without any help from their two Allies, other than the British and French medium and heavy artillery that had been sent during the spring and the summer.* Even today we read about the 'destruction of the Italian armies' at Caporetto, certainly the fate

---

*Between April and August a dozen French medium batteries, together with one heavy and sixteen medium British batteries, arrived in the theatre, but during August all but six of the British batteries were withdrawn.

of one of their armies, the Second in the centre of the Isonzo front, but elsewhere their soldiers had stood their ground and fought well. Harington was among those who vehemently denied the accounts of the Italian retreat having been halted by the arrival of the British and French divisions.[19]

The principal cause for concern in mid-November was the possibility of the enemy breaking out from the Dolomites to take the defenders of the Piave in their rear. The first such attack was launched on 10 November, but was halted after six days of heavy fighting when the invaders' supply arrangements collapsed. Casualties among the German and Austrian divisions concerned were heavy, but the *Commando Supremo*, still concerned by this threat to its rear, told Plumer on 18 November that their positions in the mountains might have to be abandoned. Winter was on the way. After calming down his rather excited informants, Plumer promised to send a member of his staff up into the mountains to report. By the time this officer reached the Asiago Plateau all was again quiet, but he reported that, although the Italian troops there were in good shape, too many of them were looking over their shoulders to see if their neighbours looked likely to disappear.[20] Nevertheless, the Italians managed to fight off another attack in the Monte Grappa sector, at the northern end of the Piave line, although they lost Monte Tombe, at the easternmost end of the Monte Grappa; they also stopped without difficulty further and half-hearted probes by the now half-starved Austrians along the Piave.

The general uneasiness is reflected in Plumer's first, and slightly ambivalent, report telegraphed to London the day after he arrived in Padua and based upon what he had learned from those he had met. 'The situation in general,' he said, 'is tactically such that there would be no cause for anticipating more than local loss of ground, if it were not for the probability that one or two local reverses would mean a general abandonment of the line now held . . . but if the Italians can hold their present [Piave] line until we and the French are on the Vicenza Line, we should be able to hold that for some time, cover any retirement of the Italians if one is made, and possibly deliver a counter-stroke.' Plumer went on to ask that two more divisions should joint the first four, together with a brigade of cavalry.[21]

Ten days later Harington could be rather more positive. A personal letter to Maurice, the Director of Military Operations at the War Office, is informative about the problems faced by a Chief-of-Staff at such a time:

I hope to start shortly sending you a proper weekly letter. Our Staff are gradually turning up but I still have only one clerk and one typewriter. However, we are very happy and things improve daily. Luckily we are all built to see the funny side of things. I don't know how some of these nations ever get any work done. Sir Herbert and I have attended conferences every single day up to today and we have certainly got some system into what is required and what we are going to do, yet everyone talks at the same time. No one takes any notes except myself. They airily say, move here and move there, and have little idea of what staff work is entailed. I thought I had a pretty good experience of boundaries and areas, but these people beat everything. The French are awful pinchers and up till now have had 3 Commanders and 3 Staffs (Foch, Fayolle and Duchesne) who all promise different things. The Italian Staff write volumes and the French much the same. I met an unfortunate man who was told off to arrange for five Corps to move S.W. through our advance and 200,000 men to move due South also across our march!

Last night after all arrangements were made for us and the French to cross the BRENTA today to get up close in case of trouble, the Italians of course found that they could not possibly clear their own troops. However, it is all in the game and now we have got anchored at last and a direct wire to Radcliffe [Brigadier-General Delmé Radcliffe, the Head of the British Military Mission with the Italians] and our advanced branch with the Italians, and also to Cavan. I don't care if it snows. It was awful motoring about 200 miles a day seeing all these people and then feeling that one had no means of communication at all. The Italian atmosphere is improving daily. Our parties from their front line all report well and there is no doubt that the move up of the British and French is doing great work.

It was not pleasant when we were behind. Now we can say: "Here we are, what is the best we can do for you?" We have made many proposals but there is no doubt that the one selected is the right one – viz. for us and the French to take over from NERVESA to PEDEROBBA (British from NERVESA to CIANCO). We go in opposite the Germans and that is what pleases them. . . . Two divisions (23rd and 41st) in line; 1 Division (48th) in Reserve about CASTELFRANCO; Haking's Corps (7th and [?]th) south of CASTELFRANCO between that and BRENTA, ready to go either way. The French will be on our left about BASSANO and CITTADELLA. We shall then be all right.

The next thing is to help the Italians with their training and schools. The junior officers know nothing and have no authority. They say they can't ask the men to do more than half an hour's work a day. The men look well and of good physique. They only want teaching and handling I have great hopes that we can made a job of it for you. Diaz likes Sir Herbert. Diaz is a quiet little fellow, not much personality. He is finding his feet more daily. He was quite overawed by the task and went through a bad time.

We work in very well with him and with his staff . . . I think now that

Foch has gone and we have a settled policy for French and British to carry out we shall get along. . . .

Our one object is to make a job of this as economically as we can and then you can get us back to Flanders.

Queries about routine aggravations such as temporary ration allowances and the titles of the force filled up much of the rest of the letter.[22]

A few days after he wrote to Maurice, Harington suffered a very close shave. Before the arrival of the Germans there had been a mutual under-standing between the Austrians and the Italians that towns would not be bombed, but the Germans changed all this. On 29 November they bombed Padua. Harington, who invariably returned to his office after dinner, was suffering from a very heavy cold and Plumer ordered him to bed. A bomb destroyed his office, killing a sentry and wounding one of his clerks.[23]

Plumer confirmed his need for the two extra divisions in a personal letter to Robertson, dated 16 November, in which he joined Harington in complaining that the 'French command situation is curious. I believe Foch is in command. I thought Du Chesne [sic] was until yesterday'[24] (one week later Foch had left).* Robertson's response was tetchily terse. Deploring the fact that he would not get anything back that might be sent to Italy, he objected strongly that Plumer should have told the Italians and the French that six British divisions were to arrive; at the same time, he admitted that Plumer had been instructed to ask for what was needed. He then went on to say that he trusted Plumer 'not to send at any future date, at any rate officially in the first instance, anything tending to imply that you think that the war can easily and properly be won by sending more troops from the West Front to Italy'.[25]

Plumer's reply to the CIGS's letter merits quoting at length:

Dear Robertson,

In the two or three letters I have sent you I have tried to keep you informed of the trend of events here and the general situation, but your letter of the 26th November, which I received only yesterday, requires a separate answer.

Before I came out here my own personal opinion was, as I said at ST. POL, that from the military point of view only it was a mistake to send British troops to Italy at all. You pointed out that there were other

---

*A typed copy of this letter, together with the one from Harington to Maurice, also typed, reached the CIGS's desk because the DMO had decided that the poor handwriting was 'so difficult to read'.

240

considerations which could not be ignored and that the Government had decided to send them.

Very soon after I came out here I came to the conclusion that if the troops sent were to fulfil their purpose they must be such as would afford practical material assistance to the Italians. When we arrived here the Italian Commanders and troops were only just beginning to recover from the shock of their enforced retreat. They had halted mainly because the pressure of pursuit had abated but they believed that abatement was only temporary, and they had little confidence in themselves or each other. A further serious pressure would probably have caused another retirement and this would have involved the loss of VENICE and the Venetian Provinces. As soon as it had been decided that French and British troops were to be sent to Italy information to that effect was circulated amongst the troops and they were told repeatedly that assistance was being sent to them and that if they held on for a few days relief would be forthcoming.

Foch and Wilson, who were here at the time, very rightly decided that the utmost the French and British troops could do at the outset was to occupy a line of hills N. and S. of VICENZA where in case of a retirement of the Italian troops from the PIAVE a stand could be made.

As the days went by and no serious attack was made on them the Italians recovered confidence but all Commanders declared that their troops were very tired, that they had no others to relieve them and that those in the line could not hold on indefinitely or indeed for any length of time. It is quite true that with proper organization and a sound system they should have been able to furnish reliefs themselves, but it would not have been much use telling them this: they wanted troops then, not lectures.

I believe that if the Italian troops had thought that then we were only going to give "moral" support and not practical relief, they would have given way.

It became evident then that if the PIAVE line was to be held the French and British troops must go into the front line as soon as possible. This was all the more necessary because of the reports which were being sedulously put about by German agents to the effect that the Allied troops had come to consume all the supplies in the country but had no intention of taking any part in the fighting. I have explained the various proposals which were made with regard to the particular sector we were to occupy which resulted in the selection of the two North-Eastern sectors.

There hardly seemed any alternative as a matter of fact, but having accepted this it would not have been wise at the time to have taken the Sector over with very little force in reserve and as time was an important factor I asked for the extra Divisions so as to have a reserve if things went wrong and afterwards to be able to take over the front of two Italian Corps which would afford the Italians the relief they looked for. . . .

I hope and believe that it will be possible to have our stay here regarded as a temporary one and I think this should be made clear in any statement of policy made in England.

As I told you I have based my requirements on a six-months' residence only and a supply of one month of everything in the country. . . .

Our policy should be, I think, while we are here to do our best to set an example of organization, training, etc., which we hope the Italians will imitate. To get them to do this we must show that we are ready and anxious to take our full share of any fighting that comes along.

I am as fully convinced as I ever was that the correct strategy is to continue the offensive on the Western front and I do not in the least believe in an offensive on a large scale being practicable here. I think however, that the Italians should be encouraged to make preparations to assume the offensive themselves in the spring and recover some of their lost territory, which they should be perfectly capable of doing. *I need hardly say that any views which I may express either privately or officially will be my own, for what they are worth.* [Ed. italics] . . .

I have not been long enough in the country or know enough of the people to give any real opinion but the impression seems to be that the magnitude of the defeat they have had has touched the pride of the people very keenly and turned the sentiments in favour of peace which were evidently pretty general into an increasing determination to continue the war.

Yours sincerely
Herbert Plumer.[26]

Harington, who appears to have kept little in the way of written records, other than copies of operation orders and suchlike, incorrectly claimed that Plumer only rarely put pen to paper himself;[27] this letter, typed though it was, and not handwritten, clearly bears the imprint of the signatory's own hand. From its tone and content, Plumer had, not surprisingly, been irked by Robertson, especially by the suggestion that he should be careful what he said in his reports to Whitehall about the future conduct of the war. The letter provides further evidence to refute Lloyd George's claim that Plumer had been glad to leave Flanders, and it also reveals the writer's anxiety to see his divisions returned to the Western Front as quickly as possible. The possibility of using the Prime Minister's support to win fame for himself in an independent command by conducting a successful offensive south of the Alps at no time occured to Plumer. He was no empire builder, intent on personal aggrandisement.

Plumer's letter was also a useful corrective for a CIGS whose views on the Italians were a little simplistic. In a letter to General Milne, commanding in Salonika, Robertson had written:

> The Italian débâcle was unpardonable and was brought about purely by the refusal of the troops to fight. They were far superior to the enemy and the latter made no really big attack. In fact downright treason started the business and then the Italian Command and Staff were unable to handle the situation. But it was a very difficult one to deal with simply because the troops and the country have generally been saturated by a vigorous and invidious German propaganda.[28]

* * *

Plumer's well developed diplomatic skills were given full rein in encouraging and assisting the crestfallen Italians to stand upon their own feet once again. They were a proud race and needed handling with great tact. As Luigi Villari wrote:

> Relations between the Italians and the Allies were not always easy. Some of the Allied troops, especially the French, assumed occasionally a certain air of superiority as saviours of the Italian front, although it must be said that this was not the attitude of the commanders and other responsible leaders. The enemy frequently dropped fly-leaves on the Italian lines in which it was stated that the British were masters in Italy and were shooting down Italian participants in worker peace demonstrations. Lavish equipment also caused jealousy.[29]

Plumer's studied endeavour to show the Italians that he regarded them as equals was probably the source of the immense confidence they placed in him, and it also did much to restore their confidence in themselves.[30] His handling of Diaz was especially deft. When inviting him to visit the British sector of the front, Plumer stressed that such a visit by an Italian Commander-in-Chief (he was not) would greatly please the troops and give them confidence. Diaz was highly flattered.

What the Italian general saw astonished him. Despite all they had gone through, the Italians had learned little about modern warfare. Their front lines were crammed with infantry, with practically nothing in reserve, a system that wore out the troops and provided fine targets for the enemy artillery. At the hinge of the front, where the mountains met the Piave, was the Montello, an isolated and commanding flat-topped hill, some seven miles long and four deep, overlooking the river. It was here that the British first took over a stretch of the line, and they discovered that the Italian defences were based upon a line of trenches running along the Piave. Straightaway the British divisions thinned out these forward positions and built for themselves on the plateau above shell-proof dugouts and machine-gun emplacements in depth, making use of the concrete that was available. Diaz's visit was, in effect, a demonstration of how a position should be held. He said nothing, but afterwards the British noticed how the nearby Italians were beginning to improve their defences.

The hard core concealed beneath Plumer's normally affable exterior could be shown when need be. When, in December, the enemy renewed their attacks in the Trentino, intent upon reaching the plains before winter set in properly, Diaz lost his nerve and informed Plumer that a further retreat to a still shorter line would be necessary, perhaps even to the neck of the Italian peninsula so as to cover Rome. To this Plumer replied that he would continue to hold the Montello. Diaz, assuming that the interpreter had failed in his task, explained matters again and at great length, pointing out that if the British were to remain where they were, they would be isolated and cut off. Plumer's only response to this was to say that he quite understood what he was being told, but that he saw no reason to retreat. And that ended the matter.[31]

Although Plumer was convinced that one of the worst defects in the Italian Army was its neglect of training, he moved circumspectly. Italians were made welcome as students at the wide range of training schools the British established in the rear areas; there every specialist skill was taught from camouflage to anti-gas defence, from musketry to minor tactics, and from gunnery to signalling. Willing though the Italians were to learn, it was vital to avoid their feeling that British methods were being forced upon them, and, to avoid this, British instructors were impressed with the importance of avoiding any suggestion of superiority. Also, in a tactful manner, the British sent their students to Italian schools, but here language was a problem.

There was little Plumer could do to repair the deficiencies in Italian staff work. As he reported to the War Office in January:

The Italian staff officers are exceedingly easy to work with, and try in every way to help: but their knowledge of staff work is so theoretical that they do not understand the practical difficulties of their orders. Paper is the ruling factor, and they agree to things and issue orders which cannot be carried out, and this has been the chief defect in their operations. All staffs are inclined to think that once an order is issued it is as good as done, which is far from being the case, and staff officers do not go out and see that the orders are being carried out. They are generally speaking not active and do not visit the front line enough. I think in this respect they have been much impressed by the frequent visits of British commanders and staffs, and that this will have a good effect. There is a lack of co-operation between their General Staff and the other branches.[32]

It was a tidy summary of the essentials of staff work.

News of the way in which Plumer was handling the Italians so diplomatically fast found its way back to London. On 28 December, in a letter congratulating him upon the award of the GCB, Robertson added, 'From all accounts I receive you seem to be getting on well with Diaz, who however does not seem to be getting on well with the Frenchmen. The latter are a queer lot.'[33] Ten days later he repeated the sentiments, remarking that 'You seem to be getting on admirably with your Italian friends and I have no doubt you will continue to do so'.[34] The historian, G.M. Trevelyan, in charge of an ambulance unit of the British Red Cross on the Italian front for much of the war, described Plumer as one of England's 'best loans' to Italy.[35] The goodwill he engendered was certainly reciprocated: from their side, the Italians did all they could to help the British. Seldom have two allies rubbed together so well.

* * *

At the time Cavan's Corps took over the Montello two French divisions had also moved into the line, in the hills facing Monte Tombe, immediately to the north of the British. By then there were five British and four French divisions in Italy, the arrival of a sixth British division having been delayed. This came about as a result of the eventual British reverse at the Battle of Cambrai during November. In the course of a massed tank attack, the first seen in war, in which the armour moved ahead of the infantry and surprise was effected by dispensing with a prior bombardment, the German defences were overwhelmed. When the lack of adequate reserves with which to follow up the success turned a brilliant victory into a grave setback, Plumer had written to Robertson that 'the situation in France must take precedence of everything but I hope that the delay will not be a long one. It is difficult to make the Italians understand that we are not "hanging back". A "tired" division would do.'[36] This sixth division never did arrive in Italy. On 21 December the 'Supreme War Council decided that no further men or guns should be removed from the Western Front.

Worries about the situation around Asiago, to their north, prompted Plumer and the French general, Fayolle, to concoct a plan on 7 December for the use of their reserves, first to block and then to push back any enemy penetration from the mountains into the Lombardy Plain. Two groups were to be formed, each composed of a mixture of British, French and Italian divisions; one was to operate east and one west of the Brenta River, the former commanded by Plumer and the latter by Fayolle. It was a complicated scheme, but one dictated by the positions of the British and French divisions already in the line. It seems that agreement to the plan was reached without dissent, and Diaz accepted it as soon as it was put to him.[37] At the same time a start was made on the construction of two major defence lines, parallel to the Alps and sited so as to block any enemy advance southwards.

As Harington had hinted in his letter to Maurice, the matter of command in Italy was not an easy one. Foch had tried to persuade Robertson to place the British force under Fayolle, who had previously commanded a group of armies in France, so as 'to unite the two Armies, French and British, sent beyond the Alps under one command'. Robertson's refusal was blank. Not only was it impossible, he replied, to place such a brilliant commander as Plumer in a subordinate position, but he had already been given complete independence of command.[38] Nevertheless, there was surprisingly little friction on the spot despite the problems inherent in having the independent British and French forces operating in another ally's country.

After the misery of Flanders, life in Italy for the British was in every way far less unpleasant. Compared with even the 'quiet' times in France, casualties were light, numbering only 279 in killed and wounded in the two front-line divisions during December when no major engagement was fought. It was hard work constructing the new rear defence lines and improving the positions on the Montello, but there was still time left over for a little rest and relaxation. Until February, the Italian winter days were often a joy, sunny and cold, but with bitter nights; even in the front line though, most men had a roof of sorts over their heads. Vermouth by the tumbler provided some sort of substitute for beer, and despite its ample supply the Italians were to be surprised by the good behaviour of this foreign army. A letter from an Italian officer to a compatriot described the British troops as:

. . . marvellous. I am not speaking of their discipline which is perfect, but of the singular delicacy of feeling which distinguishes officers and soldiers . . . Their cleanliness is so great that you would not find a straw on the ground . . . they do not leave any trace of their passage. No one even takes a glass of water without leave.[39]

Possibly a little over-stated, but there does seem to have been very little trouble.

Plumer and Fayolle had to refuse a request for their troops to operate in the high mountains because the right clothing and equipment could not be provided in time – not that the Italian troops were especially well equipped. Plumer had straightaway ordered what was needed from the War Office, to the consternation of the QMG who told the ubiquitous Repington that Plumer was 'indenting for all kinds of strange new things for Alpine warfare, of which the W.O. have not even samples, and that it would take three months to have any one of them ready'.[40] The War Office did better than this. Before spring arrived, the British divisions had received, among other outlandish articles, as yet unknown except to a small and exclusive coterie of mountaineers, over 30,000 pairs of crampons and the same number of alpenstocks, as well as adequate supplies of fur sleeping-bags, boots and hoods.[41]

The arrival of proper winter weather in mid-January rendered impractical large-scale operations in the Dolomites. With this major threat from the north removed, at Plumer's suggestion the grouping plan was abandoned, so enabling XI Corps to enter the line on Cavan's right and relieve a further body of Italians. For the next few months it was stalemate, with fighting largely confined to artillery duels across the shallow Piave which varied in width from 800 to 2000 yards. Across the river raiding parties either waded or were pulled in boats by men stripped to the buff and coated in oil; on their return hot blankets awaited the frozen participants. During this time, the only serious fighting occurred on the French front. Here, at the end of December, in a perfectly planned attack against Monte Tombe, a French division inflicted over 3000 casualties on its Austrian defenders at a cost of 259 of their own men, a factor of twelve to one in their favour. The operation, Plumer decided, had much encouraged the Italians.[42]

* * *

Further intrigues against Haig had been stimulated by the setback at Cambrai that had followed so closely the losses of Third Ypres. For the time being Haig's apparently unassailable public prestige obliged Lloyd George to limit himself to making inroads against his Commander-in-Chief's staff. Although Haig defended him for rather too long and too loyally, Charteris was the first to go, sacked in late December under pressure from the War Cabinet; even the charitable Plumer had been driven to criticize the unfailing optimism of Haig's senior intelligence officer.[43] Next to go was Kiggell, whose health had been failing under the strain, and the CGS was followed by three more senior members of

Haig's staff. It had been nearly a clean sweep of the top men, carried out in a matter of weeks, but Haig was the Prime Minister's real target. On 19 January he despatched Smuts and Hankey to France on an overtly routine visit, its real purpose to look around for the best replacement for the Commander-in-Chief. Their report disappointed the Prime Minister. A number of generals had been considered, including those serving in other theatres, Allenby, Cavan and Plumer among them. Of the contenders, Plumer was easily the favourite. A brigadier, fresh from the front, had confided to the Prime Minister that 'Plumer as C-in-C would be worth ten extra divisions', a remark that Lloyd George though extravagant, but which demonstrated to him that 'any change which brought Plumer to the front would be popular'.[44] Lord Milner was grudgingly to suggest to the Prime Minister that if Haig should fail to obey orders about creating a General Reserve, 'The Army would be quite happy, if the worst came to the worst, with Plumer and Harrington [sic]'.[45] Charteris, who had seen which way the wind was blowing at the time he was sacked, had tipped either Plumer or Allenby as Haig's replacement,[46] Allenby having just occupied Jerusalem to the delight of the Prime Minister.* Wilson had no doubt what should be done. After he had written to congratulate Plumer after Messines, he had noted in his diary, 'I wish he were C.-in-C. He has twice Haig's brain and just as much character'.[47]

However, Lloyd George held his hand, doubtful about who could replace Haig. As he afterwards wrote:

Who could be put in his place? It is a sad reflection that not one among the visible military leaders would have been any better. There were amongst them plenty of good soldiers who knew their profession and possessed intelligence up to a point. But Haig was all that and probably better within his limits than any others within sight.[48]

Having decided not to remove Haig, Lloyd George's next target was Robertson, his CIGS. During the previous October he had sought advice from both Sir John French, who was commanding Home Forces, and Henry Wilson upon the future conduct of the war, an act that brought Robertson close to resigning. Haig had, however, dissuaded him after receiving a letter from him with the *cri-de-coeur* that the Prime Minister was 'out for my blood very much these days. Milner, Curzon, Cecil,

---

*Hankey had met both Plumer and Allenby during a visit to France with Asquith in September, 1916, and had formed the opinion that Plumer was 'rather a stupid man' and Allenby 'not very impressive', both of which judgements he afterwards substantially amended.[49]

Balfour, have each in turn expressly spoken to me separately about his intolerable conduct during the last week or two . . . I am sick of this d – d life.'[50]

It was not a sound way to run a war. Lacking confidence in the advice he received from his principal military adviser, whose ideas were so completely contrary to his own, the Prime Minister sought for ways of bypassing this rough-hewn and irksomely outspoken soldier. He was to prove easier game than Haig. The opportunity came about in this way.

On 21 January the Military Representatives at the Supreme War Council were to propose that, as no decision was likely to be reached in the West during 1918, a knock-out blow should be delivered against Turkey during the current year. Two days later, they produced a further recommendation that a General Reserve should be established for use on the Western Front and in Italy. Superficially it was a sound idea, but the difficulty lay in implementing it unless an Allied Generalissimo were to be appointed. Based upon a resolution drafted by the British Prime Minister and accepted by the Council, the eventual solution to the problem was to set up an Executive Committee, composed of the Military Representatives with Foch as its President; this Executive Committee would then decide upon the composition, handling and positioning of the General Reserve. It was command by committee, against whose majority decisions a national member could do no more than protest to the Supreme War Council itself, an impossibly cumbersome procedure in a military emergency.

Robertson, who had favoured measures that would lead to unity of command, had no objection to the appointment of a Generalissimo to coordinate Allied strategy and control a central reserve, provided that the right man could be found. The outcome being what it was, however, he was insistent that the Commanders-in-Chief should receive orders from one source alone, and not from the Executive Committee as well as their own national Chiefs-of-Staff, of whom he was, of course, one. This could be made possible by ensuring that the Executive Committee was staffed by these Chiefs-of-Staff, a measure which both the French and the Americans had adopted. But the British representative was the clever and subtle Wilson, a man whose ideas were at the time wholly at variance with those of Robertson and Haig, who usually made common ground on strategic questions.

The outcome of all this was that when he returned from Versailles to London Lloyd George offered Robertson two equally unpalatable alternatives. Either he could remain as CIGS, but with his operational powers so limited that he would no longer be responsible for issuing orders to the various British Commanders-in-Chief, or he could change jobs with Wilson at Versailles. The so-called 'Welsh Wizard' had deftly out-manoeuvred him: in either case Wilson would have the major, and probably final, say in strategic matters.

Because he was not prepared to operate a system which he judged to be basically unsound, Robertson was dismissed. Rawlinson was sent to Versailles, and Wilson became CIGS. Haig, whose views in general matched those of Robertson, confined himself to smoothing matters over, rather than supporting the colleague with whom he had worked so closely for so long. If he had done so, he might have saved Robertson, but he rightly gave himself credit for avoiding a major conflict between the politicians and the soldiers,[51] an outcome that could have proved disastrous for the country.

The Prime Minister's account of the appointment of Robertson's replacement is not entirely accurate. It reads:

In the circumstances I thought it desirable to offer the post to a soldier who commanded the respect and confidence of the whole Army without distinction of rank and of the nation without reference to party. I therefore first of all offered it to Plumer, who was then in command of the British Army on the Italian Front. I had consulted Haldane, who knew the Army well, and he warned me against Plumer. He was fully alive to his fighting qualities, but thought little of his intelligence.* He considered him quite unfitted for the duties of Chief of Staff. Plumer, however, settled the matter by declining the post. He made it clear that his sympathies lay with Robertson. I am not sure whether he decided on merits or out of personal loyalty. There was no other obvious alternative.[52]

The Prime Minister first choice for the post had, in fact, been Wilson, but he had changed his mind, probably as a consequence of a conversation with Haig, who had warned him bluntly of the Army's distrust of Wilson.[53] This the Prime Minister would appear to have taken seriously, for it was then that he offered Plumer the job, telling Robertson that he could go to Italy in Plumer's place.[54]. To yet further complicate matters, when Wilson

---

*How much Haldane influenced Lloyd George's thinking on this matter is uncertain. The Prime Minister's admiration for Plumer is manifest from the contents of a note made by Lord Stamfordham, Private Secretary to King George V from his accession until 1931, and, as with most other men who held this office, a person of infinite sagicity who exercised great influence. In an hour-long confrontation on 22 January, Lloyd George had been asked to explain to Stamfordham the then current press attacks upon Haig and Robertson and had 'opened his heart' about the shortcomings of the generals: Robertson had 'never commanded a battalion . . . and never originated a strategic plan'. Of them all, the Prime Minister praised only Plumer, who, with Harington, made 'a perfect combination – the only General in whom the troops have implicit confidence'.[57]

was called to London on 10 February for consultations he learned that the Prime Minister still had in mind the possibility of Plumer replacing Haig, with the last-named becoming CIGS.[55] Haig's departure from France was still a matter for speculation the following month.[56]

Why did Plumer refuse the Prime Minister's offer? The Official History states categorically that it was because he disagreed with 'the scheme for the command of the reserve'.[58] This is also the reason Lord Derby, the Secretary of State for War, gave to the King when he told him that Plumer had refused the offer 'practically for the same reasons as those of Sir William Robertson'.[59] But there is small doubt that loyalty was also a crucial factor in Plumer's decision, as the Prime Minister suggested – loyalty to Haig and loyalty to Robertson, with both of whose views on the conduct of the war he agreed completely. Combined with this could also have been a sense of duty towards the men he commanded in the field: an officer of Plumer's mould does not relish being removed from his troops at a time of crisis, and a deepening crisis was looming for the Allies in the early weeks of 1918. Perhaps also he saw his talents lying in command in the field, rather than the politics of Whitehall, a place that carried unhappy memories for him.

Harington's accounts of the events is relevant:

When I returned to Italy I was sent for to the War Office* and told confidentially that a wire had been sent to General Plumer, offering him the post of CIGS in succession to Sir William Robertson, but there was a snag in it as it only gave him some restricted powers, and not an entirely free hand. On this I wired to General Plumer and I asked him to await my arrival. He met me at Milan and I asked him if he had got the War Office wire; he said; 'Oh yes, and I answered it at once.' On enquiring what he had said, he replied: 'Refused, of course'. He had seen the snag all right.[62]

Someone, most likely either Robertson himself or Derby, who had taken over the War Office on the formation of the coalition Government, had made use of Harington's fortuitous presence in London to warn Plumer of

---

*Again Harington's memory is faulty. He dates this incident to Christmas, 1917, when he was on leave in London. This could hardly have been correct, but he was home for a War Cabinet meeting in February. While lunching with the Prime Minister and Hankey, he was taken aback by the former's question, 'Now, General, tell us how you would win the war'. Replying that he hoped that the then dormant operations on the Western Front would succeed in the spring, was, he knew, quite the wrong thing to say, and he was soon shown the door.[60] According to Hankey, Lloyd George was considering Harington as a possible successor to Robertson, but he had in his reply failed 'to take a wide enough view'.[61]

the pitfalls of the offer, either for his protection or in the hope that a united front would be shown against what was an unworkable arrangement, or possibly for both reasons. Hankey was percipient. On 15 February he noted in his diary that the Prime Minister had 'wisely' asked him to see Derby's draft telegram offering Plumer the appointment; finding it 'quite calculated to make Plumer refuse', he redrafted it for Derby. Hankey thought that Plumer's eventual reply, couched in terms of general support for Robertson, looked 'suspiciously like a "rig" by the great General Staff Union'.[63]

Yet another reason has been suggested for Plumer's refusal. Nearly thirty years later, Lieutenant-Colonel W. Robertson (no connection with either his namesake in the Army or the official with whom Plumer was to work in Malta), a senior member of his staff who saw much of him, told Edmonds that Plumer had refused the offer 'not only because he disliked working with politicians, but also because he was reluctant to undertake the distasteful duty of removing D.H. from his command'.[64]*

* * *

One consequence of these changes at the top was Plumer's return to France, insisted upon by Haig as a *quid pro quo* for the loss of Rawlinson to Versailles. At the same time there was a need to reinforce the Western Front because of the German offensive that threatened there. Asked by the War Cabinet whether he would prefer to have two British or four Italian divisions from Italy, Haig chose the former. The upshot was that, on 18 February, Plumer was told to return two of his five divisions to France; the very next day he received further orders to hand over command to Cavan and leave himself, together with the bulk of his staff. It was exactly what he wanted.

The Italians protested the loss of these two divisions, and with good reason as the British War Cabinet had acted unilaterally without reference to the Supreme War Council. In fighting what was clearly a losing battle, the Italian Foreign Minister suggested that French rather than British divisions should go as the latter were so popular and had exercised such a good effect on Italian morale.[65] Whether he displayed similar tact when dealing with the French is not revealed. Be that as it may, during March

---

*There is an epilogue to Lloyd George's vendetta with these senior military advisers. Talking to Edmonds just before World War Two, he admitted that he could have misjudged both Haig and Robertson. His excuse was that he had kept no notes or diaries, and that he had relied for the 'Passchendaele' chapters of his *War Memoirs* on a 'then well-known military publicist who had assisted him'. This, of course, was Liddell Hart. Perhaps the old statesman was telling the truth. Who knows?

three of the six French divisions left as well, together with a further British division during April. This left Cavan with two divisions to help stem, in company with the French, a major Austrian assault on the Asiago Plateau in June, and then give important help to the Italians in their final victory that brought to an end the war south of the Alps.

When he was sent off to Italy, Plumer, like Harington, had not had a break since Third Ypres, but, unlike his Chief-of-Staff, Plumer failed to get home during his time in that country. Perhaps it was inequitable, but it was certainly sensible that his wife should have been allowed to join him there for a short stay. Together the two of them spent an idyllic ten days in a loaned villa in Portofino, from where they were able to visit British wounded in hospitals in and around Genoa. It was during this break that his orders for France arrived, and they then paid a round of official and semi-official farewells in Rome that included visits to the Queen and the Queen Mother.[66]

In the meantime, with the Italians doing everything they could to retain Plumer's services, the War Cabinet delayed his departure but failed to inform or consult Haig. The result was an exasperated protest from the Commander-in-Chief in which he pointed out that he had released Rawlinson on condition that Plumer returned to the fold as quickly as possible. Six days later, on 10 March, 1918, Plumer at length took train for the Western Front.[67]

11 Victory

Accompanied by Harington and a few other picked staff officers, Plumer arrived back in Flanders on 13 March, 1918, his sixty-first birthday, to take charge once again of that familiar Ypres Salient, the battleground with which his name was already inextricably connected. That he should command in that area if his return was not too long delayed was a promise Haig had made to him at the time he left for Italy.[1] The designation of the Army Headquarters at Cassel was now switched back from the Fourth to the Second, thereby reversing the change that had been made when Rawlinson took over from Plumer: on that Western Front, the titles of Armies were in effect the personal fief of their commanders.

Plumer's return was welcomed by everyone. Haig, who had been agitating for this to be speeded up,[2] wrote that it was 'a great satisfaction to me to have you again at the Head of an Army here',[3] sentiments that were not a mere formality. Birdwood, whose Australians were again holding the high ground around Messines and Wytschaete, and who regularly exchanged letters with Clive Wigram, the King's Assistant Private Secretary, wrote how heartily welcomed Plumer would be and how everyone had the greatest faith in him.[4] The press churned out the routine eulogies on the returning hero.

Five days passed before Haig, on 18th March, was able to visit his newly returned Army Commander, during which time nothing appears to have been done properly to brief Plumer on the changes that had occurred since he left. Haig noted:

> Plumer has not yet realized that the situation on this front has much changed since he left here in November for Italy . . . Plumer would like to continue the attack in Flanders like last year, but neither our manpower situation, nor the increased strength of the enemy, justifies our attacking on the offensive.[5]

This was certainly so. Since December the prospect of an overwhelming

German offensive had loomed. Since the Russian Revolution had brought the war in the East to an end, the Germans had been able to transfer forty-two divisions to the West, so tipping the balance decisively in their favour. By early March, 170 Allied divisions faced 192 German, and by far the most vulnerable section of the front was that held by Haig with a total of sixty divisions, most of them understrength and two of them Portuguese. In the far south Gough's Fifth Army covered forty-two miles with a mere twelve divisions. A large part of this front had been taken over from the French during the latter part of January, a decision made by the Military Representatives at Versailles without reference to Haig.[6] Against the Fifth and Byng's Third Army on its left, the GHQ intelligence staff, ably trained by Charteris, had forecast with complete accuracy that a major German offensive would be launched. The day after Haig talked to Plumer the time as well as the place was revealed by prisoners and deserters. It would start the following day, 20 March, or possibly the day after that.

By 1918, the British defences were based upon three zones, the 'Forward', the 'Battle' and the 'Rear', each organized in depth and consisting of mutually supporting posts, sited for all-round defence and protected by continuous belts of wire, with counterattack forces held ready to halt any penetration. That, at least, was the theory, but, in Gough's Army especially, the troops were grossly over-extended and the field defences were in a sad state. The successive British offensives of 1916 and 1917 had involved the massing of both troops and labour at the sectors to be attacked to the detriment of the garrisons in the other parts of the line; as a consequence the latter were so weakened that they could cope only with routine work and had nothing to spare for improving their defensive positions. Particularly badly neglected had been the part of the Fifth Army front acquired from the French. There the 'Battle' and the 'Rear' Zones were little more than optimistic figments; in some places old defence works had even been filled in and the land returned to cultivation.[7] Furthermore, after the 1917 battles, the troops were physically and mentally weary, while the vast quantity of labour needed to remedy the defects in the defences had impaired both the rest and the training they so sorely needed.

Haig also had to cope with a general shortage of men. Bitter at what he saw as the fruitless sacrifice of life during 1917, the Prime Minister was deliberately withholding reinforcements so as to ensure that the British Army remained on the defensive on the Western Front, waiting for the Americans to mass in France for what would be the decisive war-winning campaign of 1919. Even though there were a million and a half soldiers in the United Kingdom at the start of the year and nearly a million more overseas in other theatres of war – and that excluded Indian and Colonial troops – Haig's divisions were starved of men despite the developing threat. Even worse, their establishment had been reduced, and that without reference to him. The War Office, on 10 January, had ordered that the infantry in each division should be reduced from twelve to nine battalions, a measure that meant disbanding 145 battalions; not only had fighting strengths been cut, but complicated problems of movement and reorganization resulted at the very worst time. As a war leader who could inspire the nation, Lloyd George was matched only by Churchill a quarter of a century later. But his continuing interference with military dispositions, especially the flow of reinforcements to France, came near to bringing his country to defeat.

The long-awaited blow fell on 21 March. Just before 5 am a ferocious bombardment from over 6000 guns and including a high proportion of gas crashed down upon a fog-blanketed countryside. Against the twenty-six divisions of the Fifth and Third Armies, the Germans had massed a total of sixty-three, in addition to the eleven which were already holding the line. Stumbling through the darkness, and further blinded by their respirators, the British reserves began immediately to man their fighting positions. Then, at about 10 am, the leading German infantry were discerned approaching through the murk. Inexperienced young subalterns in charge of half-trained platoons gallantly fought on in the isolated posts of the 'Forward Zone', 'blobs' as they were known to the critics of the system. The defensive artillery fire was dislocated by shattered telephone wires and SOS flare signals hidden by the fog. By that night the Germans had overrun the 'Forward Zone' and, in many places, the 'Battle Zone' as well.

The assault persisted without let-up. In forty-eight hours the Fifth Army had been pushed fifteen miles back behind the Somme. The incredible had occurred. The Western Front seemed to have collapsed. With a mere eight divisions in reserve, two behind each of his Armies, Haig had nothing worthwhile with which to check the German flood. Nevertheless Haig and Pétain had arranged to reinforce one another's front if the need arose, even though Versailles had yet to put together its planned General Reserve. With forty divisions in reserve, Pétain was well placed to help, but a clever German deception ploy intensified his fears of being attacked in the Champagne and so delayed his sending a force to help plug the gap on Haig's front. Such an outcome had been forecast by the Chief-of-Staff of the German Eighteenth Army who wrote, 'It need not be anticipated that the French will run themselves off their legs to the help of their Entente comrades'.[8]

Only one other source of troops was available to Haig. On the evening of 23 March, a very worried man, he met Plumer. Without demur, his Second Army commander straightaway agreed to release from his front the best troops he possessed, four Australian and the New Zealand divisions, together with a fully fit United Kingdom division, his one proviso being that the Belgians should agree slightly to extend their front.[9] Haig's gratitude is discernible from the entry he made that night in his diary:

> I arranged with Plumer to *thin down* his front; when he has done this I shall be glad to see the Divisions set free near the Somme. It is most satisfactory to have a Commander of Plumer's temperament at a time of crisis like the present.[10]

As the Australian Official Historian expressed it, Plumer as always rose to the occasion.[11] Charteris, still serving at GHQ, but no longer in charge of intelligence matters, said much the same, commenting that, as usual, Plumer had 'played up'.[12]

Harington's account of the incident is more detailed:

> How well I remember the Commander-in-Chief's words, 'What can you do to help?'
> I may mention that we then had fourteen divisions in the Second Army, all in good condition. This was the number we had taken over on our return from Italy the previous week. We still held Passchendaele. The Messines-Wytschaete Ridge was held by three Australian divisions.
> I am the only living witness of this scene.
> The older man (Plumer) with his hand on the younger man's (Haig's) shoulder just ready to give the maximum and more to help his Chief. His answer, 'I will give you twelve divisions in return for tired ones.'
> To me it appeared impossible.
> The Commander-in-Chief was obviously moved by it and said, 'That means giving up Passchendaele.'
> 'Not a bit of it,' replied my Chief without a moment's hesitation. I can see the look of gratitude in Sir Douglas Haig's eyes as he saw us off in the car to return to Cassel.[13]

Faulty though Harington's memory could be (he dates this story incorrectly), it has the ring of truth about it.

Pétain at first reacted much as he did in similar circumstances in 1940. On 24 March Haig judged him to be 'much upset, almost unbalanced and most anxious',[14] a verdict Clemenceau, his Prime Minister, was to corroborate two days later.[15] What most alarmed Haig was his discovery that Pétain had instructed his reserves to fall back towards Paris if the Germans advanced further, so opening a gap between the Allies. The full force of the German armies could then be concentrated against the British to press them back against the Channel Ports and thence into the sea.

Haig perceived both the danger and its remedy. His solution was pragmatic, dictated not by principle but by necessity. Only with a Frenchman coordinating the armies of the three Allies on the Western Front could Haig be sure that the French would fight for Amiens, the communication centre of the northern sector, rather than retreat in a south-westerly direction towards Paris. It was at his behest that there gathered at Doullens on 26 March the main Allied leaders: Poincaré and Clemenceau, President and Prime Minister of France, Foch and Pétain, Wilson and Haig, together with Lord Milner representing the British War Cabinet. Without acrimony there were placed in train the measures that led to Foch being appointed Generalissimo.

Foch did order the French reserves to cover Amiens, and the Allied line held. On 5 April Ludendorff abandoned the offensive; his success had been greater than anything experienced by either side since 1914, but he had gained no strategic objective. Once again it had not been possible to maintain momentum. Guns and transport could not be shifted rapidly over countryside the Germans themselves had devastated as they retreated towards the Hindenberg Line. After sixteen days' fighting, the troops were tired, but even worse had been the steady deterioration in their morale as they advanced. Special battalions of 'storm troops' had led the advance, but the rest of the infantry had been milked of their best men to form them, an error the British made in the next war with their proliferation of 'Special Forces'. In Germany families were starving, the consequence of the harsh Allied shipping blockade, and the belief that their enemies were similarly suffering was rudely dispelled. Binding saw what happened:

We are through at last the awful crater field of the Somme. After twenty-five miles of unbroken waste . . . we are already in the English back areas, or at least rest-areas, a land flowing with milk and honey. Marvellous people these, who will only equip themselves with the very best the earth produces. Our men are hardly to be distinguished from English soldiers. Every one wears at least a leather jerkin, a waterproof short or long, English boots or some other beautiful thing. The horses are feasting on masses of oats or gorgeous food-cake. [16]

German propaganda had back-fired. Soon discipline collapsed as well. Outside Albert, Binding discovered that his division had, for no clear reason, halted. Then he saw:

Men driving cows before them; others carrying a hen under one arm and a box of notepaper under the other. Men carrying a bottle of wine under their arm and another open in their hand . . . Men dressed up in comic disguise . . . Men staggering. Men who could hardly walk.[17]

But by then the Fifth Army as such had ceased to exist. 1000 guns and 70,000 prisoners had been taken; British losses in killed, wounded and gassed were even higher.[18]

For such a disaster a scapegoat was required. Rightly or wrongly, and against Haig's protests, the War Cabinet ordered that Gough should be the sacrifice.

★ ★ ★

Without pause, Ludendorff let loose a fresh offensive, this time in Flanders, the sector he would have preferred to tackle first, as success there would have driven the British Army back against the Channel coast. And, facing as they were the larger number of German divisions, by the spring of 1918 the British had become the major partner in the Entente. However, the countryside around Ypres in March was thought to be still far too wet for a major offensive, and Picardy was chosen.

When, on 26 March, Ludendorff's staff advised their general to shift the offensive from Picardy to the north, his success tempted him to continue his attack against the British Third and Fifth Armies despite his mounting losses. The result was that in the end he could find only twenty-one divisions to reinforce his northern army group, only one third of the force envisaged when the original plans had been concocted back in January [19] But the bulk of the German artillery could be moved as well as these extra divisions, and this should have been enough: the calibre of the opposition in the Second Army by then could hardly have been poorer.

The reason for this state of affairs was that Plumer had been obliged to send south all but three of his original divisions, and he had received in return from the Third and Fifth Armies shattered formations, mere skeletons of divisions that had lost seventy to eighty per cent of their infantry. To his south, Horne's First Army was in nearly as sad a state. In both armies the divisions had been brought up to strength with drafts of nineteen-year-old lads, half-trained and stiffened by a handful of returning and often discouraged wounded men. To the Australians, whom they relieved in the line, they appeared like pink-cheeked, soft-chinned and dazed children.[20] Some of these drafts had joined their units while they were on the move; few of the newly arrived officers and NCO's knew one another; fresh command teams had often to be built from scratch. Clothing, weapons, transport and horses needed to be replaced, machine

259

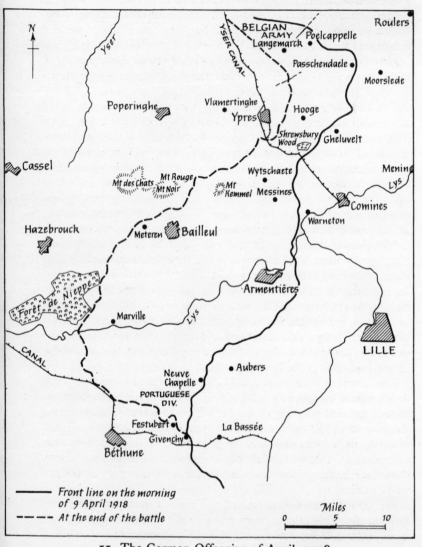

N

Roulers

Yser

BELGIAN
ARMY
YSER CANAL
Langemarck
Poelcappelle

Passchendaele

Moorslede

Poperinghe

Vlamertinghe
Ypres
Hooge

Shrewsbury
Wood
Gheluvelt

Cassel

Wytschaete
Menin

Mt des Chats
Mt Rouge
Mt Noir
Mt
Kemmel
Messines

Lys

Comines

Hazebrouck
Meteren
Bailleul
Warneton

Forêt de Nieppe

Armentières

LILLE

Marville
Lys

Neuve
Chapelle
Aubers

PORTUGUESE
DIV.

CANAL

Festubert
Givenchy
La Bassée

Béthune

⎯⎯⎯ Front line on the morning
of 9 April 1918
- - - - At the end of the battle

Miles
0   5   10

II. The German Offensive of April, 1918

and Lewis-gunners trained, and their weapons had to be calibrated; some divisions lacked their integral artillery, and in others their batteries arrived only on the eve of the battle in which they were to be engulfed.[21] Unlike Picardy, however, the defences were quite sound. In part, they had been occupied since the winter of 1914-15, and they bristled with those 'blobs' – concrete posts, belts of wire, switch lines and gun positions soundly constructed for all-round defence.[22]

Horne's sector was, however, badly flawed. Between Armentières and Béthune two Portuguese divisions had stagnated for over six months in what was about the quietest sector of the British front. 'Britain's oldest ally' had loyally placed her troops at the disposal of the Entente, but it was another matter to persuade her soldiers to die for a cause that meant nothing to them, their enemy a country of which most of them had never even heard. Another problem was that their officers had little rapport with their men, and some had strong German sympathies. It was sadly true, as Haig put it, that they were 'a wretched lot and hardly worth their food here'.[23]

Well aware of this weak link and also of the coming German offensive, by 8 April Horne had withdrawn one of these two Portuguese divisions and the second was in the process of being relieved. Upon it on the morning of 9 April fell the full weight of four German assault divisions. Hardly surprisingly few Portuguese waited for the German bayonets; most departed westwards, some discarding their boots so as to run the faster. To their north, a British division which had been mauled during March gave way as well, but around Givenchy, on their other flank, the 55th (West Lancashire) Division held its ground and continued so to do. It was the start of the Battle of Lys. By nightfall the Germans had carved a salient six miles deep out of the First Army front.

That afternoon Haig's appeal to Foch for help produced no more than the promise to hold four French divisions behind Amiens, ready to move north if the need arose. Again thrown back on his own resources, again Haig turned to Plumer, who, without argument, agreed to send Horne two of his three sound divisions, the only ones not to have been through the maelstrom of the March fighting. Both were in corps reserve and that night three brigades were being bussed south to help plug the gap in Horne's line.[24]

The next day the fighting spread to Plumer's front. After the now standard short but intense bombardment, the Germans renewed their drive against the First Army in the direction of Hazebrouck, the railway centre upon which the British depended for half their food and munitions; at the same time they extended their attack northwards as far as Shrewsbury Wood, a mile north of the Ypres-Comines Canal. Against three of Plumer's half-strength divisions holding a 17,000 yard front, the Germans flung seven fresh divisions. Infiltrating through the thick mist (it was the same nearly every morning), they crossed the Lys, took Messines and drove its defenders back to the outskirts of Wytschaete. The First Army was forced to evacuate Armentières, but during a day of successive fighting withdrawals the two armies managed to maintain contact with one another. As had happened over the same ground in 1914, a miscellany of small improvised units – this time Australian Tunnelling Companies, Reinforcement Units (one commanded by a sixty-five-year-old 'dug-out'), dismounted Tank Corps Lewis-gunners, instructional staff, grooms and orderlies – puttied up the gaps as they occurred. During that and on each successive day, Plumer managed to visit every divisional and some of the brigade headquarters involved. 'It was hard to exaggerate,' one of the divisional commanders afterwards recorded, 'the good these visits did in cheering us all up, giving us information and creating an atmosphere of confidence and encouragement.'[25]

That night Foch agreed to reinforce the British front with four infantry and three cavalry divisions, and Haig had already stripped the still-threatened Somme front to send two cavalry and an infantry division to Horne, and the 5th Division, just back from Italy, to Plumer, together with the 1st Australian from GHQ reserve to cover Hazebrouck. Even so, there was no chance of these troops arriving in time to help halt the German advance on 11 April. As the enemy still continued to press ever nearer to Hazebrouck, Haig that day issued his renowned 'Backs to the Wall' message, penned in his own hand, and the only order of its type he ever wrote:

Three weeks ago to-day the enemy began his terrific attacks against us on a fifty-mile front. His objects are to separate us from the French, to take the Channel Ports and destroy the British Army.

In spite of throwing already 106 Divisions into the battle and enduring the most reckless sacrifice of human life, he has as yet made little progress towards his goals.

We owe this to the determined fighting and self-sacrifice of our troops. Words fail me to express the admiration which I feel for the splendid resistance offered by all ranks of our Army under the most trying circumstances.

Many amongst us are now tired. To those I would say that Victory will belong to the side which holds out the longest, The French Army is moving rapidly and in great force to our support. There is no other course open to us but to fight it out. Every position must be held to the last man: there must be no retirement. With our backs to the wall and believing in the justice of our cause each one of us must fight on to the end. The safety of our homes and the Freedom of mankind depend upon the conduct of each one of us at this critical moment.[26]

For civilians at home and rear area troops this was inspiring stuff. Many of those at the front, who heard it in time, still marvelling at their continued survival, thought differently. Godley recorded that his ANZACs treated the message with 'considerable amusement', knowing that they had had 'their backs to the wall since March, and did not need to be told it!'[27] But another reliable and Australian witness claimed that the appeal achieved exactly the results intended[28] (It is hard to say more). After seventy years it is not easy to capture the exact echoes, but those who remember the response evoked by Montgomery's inspirational battle cries may wonder if Haig's appeal did not strike a similar but muted chord.

The crisis of the battle was delayed until 12 April, the day Plumer took over Horne's northernmost corps, so extending his front to a point two miles north of Marville. By that night the Germans had deepened their salient by a further four miles to reach within four miles of Hazebrouck. In front of the town Plumer deployed the 1st Australian Division, now under his orders. This magnificent formation, sent south from the Messines Ridge in March, had fortunately been returned to him intact, and, like its fellows, it was still thirteen battalions strong. Together with the 5th British, also fresh and at full strength, it held Hazebrouck, but only just.*

So as to scrape together a few reserves by straightening the line, Plumer had already begun to thin out his troops along the Passchendaele Ridge and pull back a part of their supporting artillery. Plans for such a contingency had been laid the previous January.[30] Not until 14 April, however, did he finally accept the need to abandon the Ypres Salient completely, and then only reluctantly and after pressure had been exercised by both Harington and Haig.[31] It had been galling enough to lose the Messines Ridge; Harington described his anguish at relinquishing the rest of the ring of hills around Ypres, won by his troops at such terrible cost the previous year. When his Chief-of-Staff finally insisted that the time had come to quit the Passchendaele Ridge, Plumer at first refused point blank, walking out of the room. But a few minutes later he returned. 'You are right,' he

---

*Indiscreetly perhaps, but with much justification, Plumer afterwards congratulated its senior officers. 'You know, gentlemen,' he told them, 'that it is not my practice to make eulogistic speeches – there will be plenty of time for that after the war. At the same time I would like to tell you that there is no division, certainly in my army, perhaps in the British Army, which has done more to destroy the morale of the enemy than the 1st Australian Division.'[29]

told Harington. 'Issue the orders.'[32] It was about this time of crisis, when defeat could well have resulted in losing the war, that Harington reported to Plumer that his Second Army was in three pieces. 'Well, that is better than being in four,' was the laconic response.[33]

That tricky withdrawal was not only conducted faultlessly, but it had the effect of frustrating the attack the Germans were preparing against the Passchendaele Ridge. By first light on 16 April Second Army was defending a tight perimeter around Ypres city, its 'Battle Zone' along the ramparts and the Yser Canal. Two days before, as a result of German air attack, Second Army headquarters had been obliged to shift back to Blendesques, leaving only a small operational staff at Cassel.

On 17 April the Germans switched the weight of their attack against the chain of hills that ran westwards from Messines and Wytschaete towards Mounts Kemmel, Rouge and Noir, all, like Cassel, prominent features jutting out of the plain. It ended in disaster. Deftly sited British machine guns, firing in enfilade, slaughtered the assaulting German infantry. So severe was their repulse that Rupprecht, still in command on this northern front, considered breaking off his offensive, but in the end it was renewed the following day. The result was the same.[34] Then, for a week, there was a lull.

*   *   *

Let us go back for a few days. By 14 April two divisions of French infantry and three of cavalry had arrived in Flanders to be placed under Plumer's command. Even so, Foch's approval was needed before he was allowed to use them, a stipulation ignored by the local French commander who, on 15 April, brought the guns of his divisional artillery into action to support the hard-pressed British. By then the condition of Second Army had become serious indeed. That same day Wilson, again visiting the battle-area, had a long talk with Plumer who confided in him that he would not be able to hold the line of the hills much longer if the Germans were to attack again. 'He can't trust his troops,' recorded Wilson; they were untrained and, 'although as brave as possible, simply don't know their business'.[35] It was not the kind of admission that Plumer, or anyone else, cared much to make. Wilson then saw Foch. That day Wytschaete had fallen, and he was obliged to listen to Foch's complaints that the British were not handling their troops properly. The CIGS's unarguable rejoinder that Plumer's troops were both exhausted and insufficient was merely brushed aside.[36] Visiting Second Army to find out for himself what was happening, this former *professeur* of the *Ecole Superieure de Guerre* proceeded to entertain Plumer to an hour-long discourse on the tactical methods by which Mount

Kemmel should be held.[37] This sort of behaviour was not unusual. General de Mitry, who was to take command of *Détachement d'Armée du Nord* (or D.A.N.), as the French forces with Plumer were to be termed, complained to Haig that lectures upon strategy from Foch were inseparable from his conduct of the battle.[38]

By the time Foch delivered this aggravating homily to Plumer, he had, in fact, released the reserves to his use, proclaiming the fact with the exuberant Gallic signal that it was 'the duty of the French troops to hasten to the battle where it is engaged'.[39] To husband his reserves, Foch tended to counter Haig's appeals for help during those German spring offensives by inferring that it was Haig's task to hold his front with his own resources, and that, in any case, too much could not be asked of the French divisions. It was harsh but not unsound generalship. During both March and April the British Army did manage to stave off disaster before French succour came, albeit at desperate cost. By that spring Pétain had performed a near-miracle in nursing his divisions back to something like their old form. The 1917 mutiny had been a protest against their gross misuse rather than the war as such; during 1918 the French frequently, but not always, fought as well as they had done during the first three years of the war.

Given full control of the D.A.N., Plumer directed two of its divisions, in conjunction with their neighbouring British formations, to counterattack to recover Meteren and Wytschaete, both in enemy hands. In the south of his front, the leading French division merely went to ground when it reached the British lines opposite Meteren, while, in the more northern attack against Wytschaete, the second of the two, after a series of postponements, never even started.[40] But the next day units of this formation did help in that stirring defence of Kemmel Hill, and on 18 April it began to take over this section of the front from its few surviving British defenders. There were not many left: by then the fighting strengths of the Second Army divisions averaged only 5500, one-third of their proper establishment.[41]

As the French relieved Plumer's exhausted divisions around Mount Kemmel, the Belgian Army took over a further stretch of his front in the north. Meanwhile, the Germans were making their preparations for yet another attempt against the steep and wooded slopes of Mount Kemmel itself, from which the entire Messines Ridge can be overlooked on a clear day. On 25 April they attacked once again on a 16,000-yard front, aiming their main blow against Kemmel. It took them just an hour to clear the French off the hill, some of whom had started for the rear long before the German infantry arrived; 6500 stayed to surrender.[42] Up here in the north the *poilu* often showed a distinct disinclination to lose his life in defending

Belgium, however gallantly he might fight for *la patrie* elsewhere.* With the enemy now holding the high ground above them, the British troops on the left of Mount Kemmel were obliged to fall back as well as form a defensive flank. It was a near disastrous situation.

As soon as Plumer learned what had happened, he drove forward to de Mitry's headquarters to arrange for this vital piece of ground to be recovered. One French and one of the badly depleted British divisions, both under French command, were detailed for the task, but the affair was to be sadly muddled. The barrage was feeble and thin, once again the French failed to venture beyond their own front line, and the British infantry took only their first objective. One British battalion commander even went so far as to make a written protest at what he described as 'this discreditable affair'.[44] Again it had been shown that the tactics of holding positions lightly, with counterattack forced poised to recover them if lost, would succeed only if the reserves involved were both fresh and determined.

On 29 April the Germans made what was to be their final attempt to smash their way through. It failed. General von Kuhl placed it all in perspective:

> The storming of Kemmel was a great feat, but, on the whole, the objective set had not been attained. The attack had not penetrated to the decisive heights of Cassel and Mont des Cats, the possession of which would have compelled the evacuation of the Ypres Salient and the Yser position. No great strategic movement had become possible; the Channel Ports had not been reached . . . The second great offensive had not brought about the hoped-for decision.[45]

If Plumer's depleted divisions had failed to prevent that German break-through to the Channel Ports, the war would almost certainly have been lost.

As so often happens, too much of Plumer's time during the Battle of the Lys had been spent in placating and encouraging an ally with whom relations were, more often than not, badly strained. There is a certain understatement in Haig's comment to Wigram, written on 18 May, that 'The French have been very trying and poor old Plumer has had a most anxious time!'[44] The Belgians had proved far easier to work

---

*So as to encourage the French (as Haig put it), on 1 May he asked the Secretary of State to send him 100 DSOs, 200 MCs and 300 MMs as soon as possible for the French troops fighting under Plumer.[43] In that war such decorations were scattered around Allied armies with a lavish hand, in stark contrast with their sparse distribution in subsequent wars, not just to Allied, but to British officers and men also.

with, as is brought out in a letter from the Earl of Athlone, the head of the British Military Mission to King Albert's Headquarters, written to his brother-in-law, King George V (addressed as 'Dearest Georgie'). In it he describes how Plumer's II Corps liked having Belgians next to them, and that neither King Albert nor his people desired to have the French alongside them. The Belgians, he told the King, would 'do anything for General Plumer'.[47] The writer continued:

> I am afraid that the chief trouble in 2nd Army is the fact that the French had been dragged up to help us out. They were of course furious about the 5th Army show and pretend that they cannot rely on us. Anyway they have lost Kemmel which, in spite of gas shells, should have been held for ever, and when told to carry out a counterattack did not start with our 25th Div as the preparation of the artillery plan was not good enough for the little people.

This disdainful reference to 'the little people' matched the scorn of the French for the British reverses. However, after Kemmel it was noticed that the officers of the D.A.N. no longer spoke contemptuously of the British failure to stop the Germans.[49] Such is life when fighting with an ally. When things go wrong, the other country is inevitably denigrated.

* * *

During the recurrent crises of the Flanders fighting that spring, Haig had usually left Plumer alone to cope with his own problems, rarely offering advice. He had learned to trust his Army Commander's judgment and appreciate his other great qualities, but his habitual use of the term 'old Plumer' (as in that letter to Wigram) seems deprecating rather than affectionate. Plumer did look old, but this habit of dwelling upon his age, only four years more than his, may even have been deliberate. During the first half of 1918 his position as Commander-in-Chief was at no time secure, and Plumer, as he well knew, was the man most likely to succeed him. Repington's diary reflects the gossip that was current in high places. In commenting upon French's move to be Viceroy of Ireland (an appointment in which the writer wished him joy), Repington noted that 'One plot is for Haig to be recalled and put in French's place [as Commander-in-Chief of the Home Forces] and Plumer to have the command in France';[50] two months later he learned from an old brigadier-general friend that 'Plumer is considered a lucky general by the troops. Haig has the Army's confidence, but they seldom see him. He would prefer Plumer if there were to be a change.'[51]

Haig had brought the matter to a head in a letter to Lord Derby, still Secretary of State for War, written on 6 April. In it he protested that, although he was ready to continue as long as the Government so wished, 'I have more than once said to you and to others in the Government, the moment they feel that they would prefer someone else to command in France, I am prepared to place my resignation in your hands.'[52] It was the opportunity for which the Prime Minister had been waiting, but he needed support. Wilson, when asked whether Haig should be taken at his word, advised against so doing on the grounds that there was 'no really outstanding personality to succeed him'.[53] And so Lloyd George held his hand. If he had decided to rid himself of the Commander-in-Chief in whom he had so little confidence, there is little doubt that Plumer would have been chosen as his successor. That successful defence of the Channel Ports had further enhanced his reputation with the Prime Minister. A revealing anecdote, related by Frances Stevenson, then his secretary and later his wife, tells how, at the height of the April battle, Lloyd George and Hankey went together to St Anne's, Soho, to hear the Easter Passion music; on entering the church they were greeted with the words 'O Lord, make haste to help us', remembered as singularly appropriate when, on arriving back in Downing Street, the two men learned that Plumer had halted the Germans.[54] A fervent admirer of the American General Stonewall Jackson, Lloyd George afterwards wrote that 'the only Army Commander in France who commanded that kind of confidence in his men was Plumer'.[55] Yet the Prime Minister had probably acted with wisdom in accepting Wilson's advice to leave Haig where he was. As the Official Historian summed the matter up, 'The Army had . . . extraordinary faith and confidence in Haig, and his supercession, even if he had been succeeded by Sir Herbert Plumer, might well have destroyed its faith in itself and in ultimate victory.'[56] Within six months the war was to be over, and Haig had been primarily responsible for the Allied victory. That spring such a prospect was near fanciful, but Haig was grimly intent upon finishing off the Germans during 1918 before another winter, combined with dwindling manpower, reduced the British Army to impotence. Because of this, he was especially exasperated by the plans being compiled in Whitehall for the campaigns of 1919 and even 1920. To await the deployment of the Americans was, in his view, to risk defeat in the meantime.

* * *

Even though they had been halted by Plumer at the Battle of the Lys, the Germans did not let up. With more than half the French reserves sucked up to Flanders, they again attacked in May in the area of the Chemin des Dames, in what was to be a diversion for a renewed offensive in June against the British, now, in the opinion of the German General Staff, their main enemy.[57] Succeeding beyond all expectations, in six days this offensive surged forward for forty miles, reaching Château Thierry on 3 June. Paris, only fifty miles distant, was once again menaced. That day Haig instructed Plumer to have plans ready to fall back to cover Dunkirk in the event of the French calling for help from the north to protect their capital.[58] But Ludendorff had once more overreached himself.

An American division, the first to be engaged in a major battle, had fought well alongside the French in helping check this German offensive. The build-up of the United States Army had been slow. It was thirteen months since their country had been drawn into the war; by comparison thirty British divisions were in action by September, 1915, although conscription had not been introduced, something the Americans brought into force three weeks after they declared war upon the Central Powers. Even though, by the summer of 1918, American troops were crossing the Atlantic at the rate of 100,000 each month (the figure doubled during July and August), they still had to be organized into an operationally effective army. Especially serious was the shortage of trained staff officers; and their French and British allies were obliged to supply them with every gun and tank they used, as well as half their aeroplanes. Training was rudimentary, except in their individual skill-at-arms, and French and British cadres were helping them to remedy defects. Although they knew little, as ever these Americans were keen to learn, and they learned fast. Above all, their quality was magnificent, evoking memories of the men of the original Kitchener Armies of 1915 and 1916. Come what may, their commander, General John J. Pershing,* was determined that they would fight as a national American Army, and he had successfully resisted their being frittered away to plug gaps that occurred in the line, either as units or as complete formations. So it was that, in early August, the First American Army, one million strong and formed into twenty-seven large divisions, had gathered around St Mihiel. By then, however, it seemed that the best of the campaigning weather might almost be over.

By then the French had turned the tide in the south. Benefiting from lessons they had learned in May, on 15 July they repulsed a fresh German offensive, mounted by fifty-two divisions operating on either side of Rheims in an attempt to enlarge the Château Thierry Salient. Three

---

*When Haig first met Pershing in July, 1917, he had been unimpressed by the staff officers accompanying the American general. An exception had been a Captain George S. Patton, described by Haig as 'a fire-eater who longed for the fray'.[59]

days later they counterattacked in what was to be remembered as the Second Battle of the Marne. By 4 August they had eliminated this salient and captured 30,000 prisoners and 793 guns; in all, another 138,000 casualties had been inflicted upon the Germans. It was the turning point of the year. As Ludendorff's armies melted away, his already delayed plans for moving his reserves north for a decisive battle against Plumer were, of necessity, abandoned. British, American and even Italian divisions had fought in the Battle of the Marne, but it had been the renaissance of the French Army.

★　★　★

Assisted by Foch's wholehearted support and cooperation, Haig was now to fight the winning series of battles of the war. Theirs was a fine combination of talents, brought together at a time of crisis and, by then, fused for the final winning campaign. Foch's part was to obtain agreement on the course of action to be followed, using persuasion rather than direct orders, and to move his reserves so as to give effect to that policy. Unlike the supreme commanders of World War Two, he operated with a staff of only some twenty officers, his methods, to quote Terraine, 'inspirational, not administrative'.[60]

Confident in one another and in the future, on 16 May Haig and Foch had discussed plans for taking the offensive, and, when the Second Battle of the Marne was almost won, Foch announced to the Commanders-in-Chief of his three Allied Armies that the defensive strategy forced upon them by the overwhelming German numbers could be abandoned. The offensive could now start, its first and most urgent task to make safe the lateral railway that ran behind the Allied front. The British part was to free Amiens and the Paris-Amiens railway from the threat of a further offensive in Picardy; for this he was to use Rawlinson's Fourth and the French First Armies, both operating under his command.

Haig struck his blow on 8 August, a complete surprise despite the size and complexity of the arrangements. That night his two Armies had surged eight miles forward and inflicted 27,000 casualties upon the enemy. It was, wrote Ludendorff, 'the greatest defeat which the German Army had suffered since the beginning of the War'.[61] When the pace of Rawlinson's advance began to slacken three days later, Haig halted him and the French, ordering Byng's Third Army on the left to enter the battle. Haig's decision produced one of several confrontations between him and Foch, his superior clinging with fervour to his belief that offensives must never be halted, despite the cost. But Haig won his point. With Foch such disputes could occur, but his character and reputation were such

270

that relations between him and the Allied Commanders-in-Chief never suffered irreparable damage.

Second Army's part in these early stages of Haig's offensive was small. During June and July its seventeen divisions had been preparing for the German offensive that was expected when the Chemin des Dames battle ended, but Plumer had been working without the help of Harington, whose excellence had been recognised by his promotion to lieutenant-general as Wilson's deputy at the War Office. The French counter-offensive then changed everything. Plumer's intelligence staff first noticed that German reserve divisions were disappearing southwards and that the preparations that were in train for an attack on Second Army front had ceased. Small local withdrawals started, and these Plumer's divisions and those of the Fifth Army (reconstituted and now operating on Plumer's right) were ordered to follow up, acting when need be on their own initiative.[62] With the start of Haig's main offensive, these forward movements quickened, Plumer capturing the Outtersteene Ridge, the only high ground still in German hands south of Bailleul, in a small set-piece battle on 18-19 August. Three days later, Haig ordered all his Army Commanders to push ahead. 'Risks that a month ago would have been criminal to incur', he declaimed, 'ought now to be incurred as a duty.' Nevertheless, Plumer continued to conduct his advance in a careful and methodical manner, opposed on his front by a still resolute enemy.[63] As always he was intent on conserving the lives and the morale of his men, but by 7 September he had cleared the Lys Salient; once again evocative names such as Ploegsteert, Kemmel and Bailleul were headlined in the British press.

Until the last days of August, when they were moved south to join Pershing, two American divisions had been serving under Plumer. Once again, his touch was just right, their commander, Major-General John O'Ryan, writing how Plumer '. . . became a very good friend of the 27th Division, and all in the division who had the good fortune to make his acquaintance will always remember his kindness of heart and his interest and confidence in American troops'.[64] Methods differ. To American officers the British have, oddly enough, always seemed a little informal. The warning order given by Plumer for a small-scale American attack consisted of a remark made casually after tea, 'Oh, by the way, O'Ryan, how would you like to have a go at our friends on the Ridge?' O'Ryan, in replying that the Americans were there for that purpose, was then told to have a word with Plumer's Chief-of-Staff, whereupon he discovered that the details of the plan and the tentative corps order were already available for discussion and questions.[65]

By then learning fast, but still far from well trained or organized, the Americans cleared the St Mihiel Salient on 12 September, an inspiring passage-at-arms; and, as summer moved into autumn, both they and the French struck as the occasion warranted, drawing off the enemy reserves from Haig's main battleground. Upon Haig's tried but weary armies was falling the principal task of keeping up a steady and relentless pressure against the now retreating Germans. By August's end, the Third Army offensive from Albert, supported by the Fourth and First on its flanks, had brought the British up to the Hindenburg Line, but casualties had again been fearsome – 190,000 in five weeks. Such losses again alarmed Whitehall, and on 28 August Wilson warned Haig that the War Cabinet would become anxious if further heavy punishment was incurred in attacking the Hindenburg Line without success.[66] Lord Milner, who had replaced Lord Derby as Secretary of State,* reiterated the warning later in the month, expressing the fear that there might not be enough recruits available for the 1919 campaign.[67] Despite Churchill's habit of handling 'great subjects in rhythmical language' and becoming 'quickly enslaved by his own phrases', as Lord Esher had put it to Haig,[68] the latter developed both respect and regard for the future war leader as time went on, but his planning, as Minister of Munitions, for a 1919 or even a 1920 campaign added to Haig's exasperation. His violent reaction to Wilson's telegram, 'What a wretched lot of weaklings we have in high places at the present time', could be forgiven with victory all but in his grasp.[69]

* * *

The part played by Plumer in the war's final battles was dictated more by politics than strategy. With all but a small corner of their country occupied since 1914, the Belgian Army had no way of replacing its casualties. Its twelve infantry and two cavalry divisions had, as a result, experienced a comparatively quiet war, but, in late August, King Albert pressed that his soldiers should take a proper part in the forthcoming liberation of their country. The upshot was that Foch, on 2 September, requested that the Belgians, the Second Army, and the six French divisions (three of them cavalry) in Flanders, should between them recapture the Passchendaele – Clercken Ridge, so extending the Allied offensive northwards from the River Lys. This would coincide with an attack by the British First and Third Armies towards Cambrai, and the assault by the Fourth Army on the ten-mile-deep belt of fortifications of the Hindenburg Line.

---

*Dismissed by Hankey, as 'a flabby jelly' and 'a poor wobbly thing', Derby would have been removed earlier but for the fear that his departure might produce a resignation statement that would have made public the opposition of Haig and Robertson to the Versailles arrangement.[70]

Plumer had different ideas about how the northern flank should be tackled. It was apparent to him that the Germans were preparing for further withdrawals from both the Lys Valley and from the Passchendaele Ridge itself, so he wished to press on east through Wytschaete and Messines, thereby bypassing the worst of the ravaged ground east of Ypres. However, Haig overruled his protest, pointing out that the first thing was to get the Belgians moving, to which Plumer responded that he had every confidence that their troops would do well once they had started.[71] Plumer then learned that, for the coming offensive, King Albert was to be placed in nominal command of all the Allied troops in Flanders, which would be known as the Group of Armies of the North (or G.A.N.). In reality, in the Continental manner, command would be exercised by his Chief-of-Staff, the French General Degoutte, whose Sixth Army had played a major part in the recent French counter-stroke. An obituary described Degoutte as 'placid in countenance and spectacled; in spite of a military moustache he gave the impression of a scholar with a dash of a man of the world who knew his own mind, which, indeed, sums up his real nature.'[72] As the British Official History tersely recorded, Degoutte failed to exercise much influence on either the King or on Plumer: the latter, its author noted, required no mentor.[73]

Nine Belgian divisions were given the Passchendaele-Clercken Ridge as their objective, with six of Plumer's now depleted Army, only ten divisions strong, attacking on the right of the Belgians, their task to form a defensive flank along the Lys River. 'Going dead against the expressed opinion of General Plumer,' as the Official History put it, 'it was laid down that it was not necessary to attack the Wytschaete-Messines area.'[74] Far from needing a mentor, it now fell to Plumer to remedy faulty staff work in the G.A.N. and to carry out much of the essential coordination necessary between his own Army and the Belgians, especially the scope and the details of the artillery programmes.

The attack, launched on 28 September, was a complete success. Secrecy was achieved.[75] The German defences were formidable, but thinly held by infantry, many of whom had lost the will to resist. That ridge of land of bloody memory, around which so many hundreds of thousands of British, French, Belgian and German soldiers had died, was carried by King Albert's men with comparative ease. Those Belgians were fit and mature men, their units spared the carnage of the previous four years.

At 7 pm that evening Plumer issued his orders for the next day's advance, naming the Wytschaete–Messines Ridge, Warneton and Comines among his objectives. A little later there arrived a lengthy instruction from Degoutte, ordering the attack to be continued during the night and numbering among its objectives places already taken by the British.

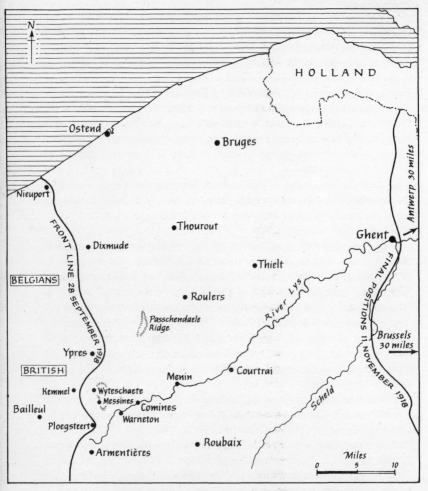

12. The Final Offensive in the North, 1918

Plumer read it carefully, but then ignored it, seeing no reason to modify the orders he had already sent out. Included in Degoutte's instruction were arrangements for French reserve divisions to support the next day's attack, but again, nothing was seen or heard of them.[76]

The following day the success was to be repeated. A night of near-torrential rain, which reduced the battlefield to its customary slough, slowed everything down, and the inexperience of staff officers coping for the first time with this unfamiliar open warfare caused further delays. Nevertheless, the whole of that dominant ridge of hills that encircled Ypres was, by the evening, back in Allied hands; in the south the British had reached Warneton on the River Lys, and the Belgians had reached to within two miles of the vital Roulers railway junction.

Great plans were laid for next day. A '*groupment d'exploitation*' under French command was to be put together, its components two Belgian and three French infantry divisions, together with heavy artillery and French cavalry. In stirring words, Degoutte instructed its commander to continue the pursuit by day and by night, regardless of the fatigue of the troops. But the force never made its appearance, nor had Degoutte made any administrative arrangements for its support. The rain did the rest. There was chaos in the rear of the Belgians, whose lines of communication stretched back through the quagmire of four years of destruction. And, in addition, the Germans somehow found six divisions with which to bolster their defence.[77]

The fatuous orders that emanated from Degoutte's headquarters continued to plague Plumer. On 1 October Second Army was ordered to break through that very night, instructions that Plumer again ignored.[78] It is far from clear whether this sort of thing was merely Degoutte's Pavlovian reaction to the offensive doctrines upon which he and his fellow French generals had been raised, or whether he was placating Foch's insistent pressure for further advances. What was now clear, however, was the need for a pause before another move forward could be undertaken. High expectations had again been smothered by the absence of a suitable weapon to exploit the initial breakthrough.

There had, however, been one breakthrough in tactical doctrine. On 2 October, at the request of the Belgians, eight aeroplanes dropped thirteen tons of supplies to 15,000 Belgian and French troops, starving in the forward areas because their transport could not penetrate the morass of mud. This use of air-supply was an early harbinger of a battle-winning weapon of World War Two, but one to which post-war armies paid no significant attention. In this respect Plumer was ahead of his time. Despite the poor impression he had made two years before upon Thomas Hughes, that young pilot, he was alive to the potential of this new weapon. Marshal of the Royal Air Force Sir John Slessor, writing twenty years after the war in which he first made his name, remembered how:

During the last great German offensive of March and April, 1918, which looked so mortally dangerous, both General Nash, in charge of railway transportation at GHQ, and General Plumer, in command of the Second Army, which was bearing the brunt of the attack, pressed urgently for concentrated bombing of vital points of the German supply system to help slow down the enemy advance. Plumer in particular was emphatic that an essential condition of success was the concentration of all available aircraft continuously on the minimum number of points where the greatest dislocation could be produced.[79]

After that essential pause to sort out the administrative confusion that had halted the northern push by the Belgians and the French, the offensive by the G.A.N. got under way again on 14 October. Meanwhile, Rawlinson had breached the Hindenburg Line and the Allies were on the move all along the front, but against resistance that was often still dour. Although Haig was no longer in command of Second Army, he had emphasized to Plumer that his role was still that of flank-guard to the Belgians and French, and that he should not push his advance-guards across the River Lys unless the Germans were seen to be falling back; he also warned him that his main task was to press on north of the river and eventually cross it east of Courtrai so as to link up with the rest of the British Army around Tournai.[80]

Second Army took two days to cross the flat Lys Plain and close up to the river. On its left the Belgians kept pace with it, but the French, who were now in a section of the line between the two Belgian armies, made but feeble progress, as their official account of the fighting has admitted.[81] So dissatisfied was King Albert with their progress that, on 17 October, he ordered Plumer to relinquish his role as flank-guard: instead he was to cross the Lys and push eastwards as rapidly as he could. The order arrived too late. As had now become almost a habit, Plumer had ignored his original instructions and the warning he had received from Haig. His advanced guards had crossed the river two days earlier. By the time he had received the order, the major part of two of his corps were on the other side of the Lys, pivoting on Courtrai in a wide flanking movement towards Roubaix, which fell to him on 19 October. Plumer continued to disregard his orders in this way. Those he had received on 17 October had stipulated that his three northern corps were not to make any extended move, but to rest and economize their troops.[82] Instead, by 19 October, he had also occupied Courtrai. Haig, for his part, seems to have accepted what was happening. He noted in his diary on both 15 and 16 October that Second Army was doing well.[83]

There was still plenty of hard fighting ahead for Second Army. As it continued to advance across the watershed between the Lys and the Scheldt, its leading troops, between 20 and 27 October, encountered many small farms and labourer's cottages converted into strong points, so creating problems for both regimental officers and the staff, whose training and experience were rooted in the static warfare of the past four years. Filled with immature and often raw drafts, it is a wonder that the units kept moving at all, but move they did in that final surge, arguably the greatest victory in British military history. Even though much of the German infantry had lost the will to resist, their machine-gunners and artillery men usually fought doggedly on, regardless of the fact that the war was clearly lost. Between 27 September and the war's end they were to exact a further toll of 100,000 of Haig's infantrymen, 17,000 from Plumer's Army.[84]

Of the disputes that occurred between Foch and Haig in these final few months of the war, the last was probably the worst, its cause Plumer's Second Army. Although Haig had readily agreed to its being detached to the G.A.N., by September he had become increasingly aggravated by the arrangement which had relegated Plumer to a secondary role while the Belgians and French made their slow progress towards liberating Brussels and Antwerp, strategically quite the wrong axis. When, on 24 October, Haig requested the immediate return of Second Army so that it might join his others in his coordinated drive eastwards towards Germany, Foch refused flatly. As Haig saw it:

Foch declines to return the Second Army to me because of the political value of having the King of the Belgians in command of an Allied Army, when he re-enters his capital, Brussels! His real object is to use the British Second Army to open the way for the 'dud' Divisions (of which the rest of the King's Army is composed) and ensure that they get to Brussels. France would then get the credit for clearing Belgium and putting the King back in his capital. De Goutte [sic] is nominally Chief of Staff to King Albert; really he is the Army Commander.

I explained the military reasons why my Second Army must now be under my orders. If there were political reasons requiring the Second Army to remain under King Albert, then the British Government must direct me on the subject. Until I was so informed, I must continue to view the situation from a *military* standpoint, and insist on the return of Second Army without delay. F. asked me to submit my request in writing.[85]

In the end, after Milner had brought pressure to bear upon Clemenceau, Foch capitulated and with good grace. It was agreed that Second Army would revert to Haig as soon as it reached the Scheldt, and this it did by the end of the month, with the French and Belgians lagging still further behind. As the Official History expressed it, 'What success had been achieved fell to the flank guard and not the main attack.'[86]

On reaching the Scheldt, Plumer's problem was to cross a broad water-way whose canalized course was widened by the numerous original loops of the river and a mass of drainage canals. A major river-crossing had to be mounted, an operation which required a mass of bridging material and every gun that could be dragged forward. Plans were laid for the crossing to take place on 11 November, but three days beforehand the enemy gunfire died down and the patrols which crossed met the fire of only a few isolated machine guns.

All along the Western Front the enemy were melting away. It was nearly over. Turkey had signed an armistice on 30 October; Austria-Hungary followed suit four days later. On 4 November the German Imperial Navy had mutinied when ordered to sea for a final and pointless battle, and the soldiers sent to suppress the trouble fraternized with the mutineers. There was street-fighting in Berlin and the Kaiser was about to abdicate. On 8 November the German envoys arrived at the railway-siding in the Forest of Compiègne to receive the terms of the Allies for an Armistice.

As Plumer's advanced guards skirmished on, horsed cavalry and cyclists in some places leading and covering seven miles or so each day, it was clear that the end of it all was close. But lives were still being lost among the men of the forward units as that famous signal percolated through to them that 'Hostilities will cease at 11.00 hours to-day, November 11th'. As a strange silence spread across the countryside on that misty morning, there were few scenes of wild rejoicing. Most men merely pondered upon their good fortune, or mourned the absence of their friends.

In one respect Haig remained true to form. At 11 am he had gathered his Army Commanders at Cambrai to discuss the future. Afterwards there was the need to satisfy the press:

General Plumer, whom I told to 'go and be cinemaed', went off most obediently and stood before the camera trying to look his best, while Byng and the others near him were chaffing the old man and trying to make him laugh.[87]

The most reliable and the most respected of his Army Commanders was still 'the old man'.

* * *

Plumer had fought his last battle. How then should he be rated among that much denigrated body of men, the general officers of the First World War? There were imcompetents among them, as in any calling, but those were usually rapidly removed. The calumny (to use Terraine's term)[88] of military bunglers was largely promoted by Lloyd George to absolve himself from blame for the terrible price paid for fighting and winning the war. Tilled by the able pens of military writers such as Liddell Hart and Fuller, and by their less able camp-followers, the myth was fertilized by the anguish of the war poets – Sassoon, Blunden, Owen and all the others who had suffered, and who mourned their friends and comrades.

In coping with war on a scale for which they had not been prepared and with weapons untried and hardly imagined beforehand, most of these British Generals had performed as well in battle as their French, Russian, German or Austro-Hungarian contemporaries who had been brought up to the handling of vast conscript armies.

Field-Marshal the Earl Wavell, a senior staff officer in that war and a famous commander in the next, poet and man of letters, thought deeply about his profession. Repeatedly over the years writers have described the qualities needed in a successful general. In 1938 Wavell gave the Lees Knowles lectures at Trinity College, Cambridge,[89] and in them he set out his views on the subject. For first principles he looked back to Socrates:

> The general must know how to get his men their rations and every other kind of stores needed for war. He must have imagination to originate plans, practical sense and energy to carry them through. He must be observant, untiring, shrewd; kindly and cruel; simple and crafty; a watchman and a robber; lavish and miserly; generous and stingy; rash and conservative. All these and many other qualities, natural and acquired, he must have. He should also, as a matter of course, know his tactics; for a disorderly mob is no more an army than a heap of building materials is a house.[90]

Administration, Wavell noted, came first on Socrates' list, tactics last. Logistics (although the term was then unborn) was the crux of generalship in Wavell's opinion,[91] although it was a subject rarely touched upon by most military scribblers.

We have seen how thorough Plumer's administrative preparations could be. It had been the hall-mark of his soldiering from the time he raised his irregular regiments so smoothly and rapidly in Southern Africa to his meticulous preparations for Messines and Passchendaele, the latter involving an army of three-quarters of a million men. But Plumer was not merely a brilliant administrator. His three consecutive steps at Passchendaele, starting on 20 September, the battles of the Menin Road bridge, Polygon Wood and Broodseinde, all but crushed the German Army which was saved only by the rain; they equalled Messines in their planning and able execution. The techniques of these 'step-by-step' advances, supported by overwhelming artillery fire, were first used by Pétain, but Plumer perfected them. The 'imagination to originate plans, practical sense and energy to carry them through' displayed by Plumer in these grim battles had first been revealed among the Matopos Hills, and then during the Boer War, where he was renowned as the most rapid moving of the column commanders.[92] 'Plodder rather than thruster' a journalist might describe him at the moment of his greatest victory, but it was hardly justified. In any case, the Western Front was to a great extent a plodder's war. Even there, when given the chance, Plumer could show great initiative; his disregard of Degoutte's instructions in the final push is just one example.

Wavell commented that Socrates failed to list the moral quality of robustness, the ability to withstand the inevitable shocks of war.[93] This Plumer had in plenty. Both in Africa and on the Western Front – even at Messines – he suffered his share of those reverses inseparable from war, and which commanders at every level all experience. But such setbacks he always surmounted. Only in 1916 did his confidence flag when the newly appointed Haig showed little confidence in him and kept him under threat of dismissal. After Messines Plumer again found his feet, and thereafter he stood his ground as need be against Haig, the Commander-in-Chief reputed to have been feared by all his subordinates. It was Plumer whom Haig claimed after Messines as his most reliable army commander; it was Plumer whom Haig was reluctant to lose to Italy, and Haig who warmly welcomed him back to the Western Front; when faced with near disaster in 1918, it was Plumer whom Haig was relieved to have with him at such a time of crisis. It was Plumer who was ready to relinquish his best divisions from Flanders to stem the German advance against the Third and Fifth Armies, and Plumer who always remained steadfastly loyal to Haig. This quality of robustness, insisted upon by Wavell, was yet again to be displayed by Plumer, as he had done at Second Ypres in 1915, when the Channel Ports were under threat in April, 1918, and when the line was being held by troops so young and raw that even he for a time queried their ability to fight.

It was Wavell's conviction that the less time a general spent in his office and the more with his troops the better. Plumer thought the same. The greater part of his days were spent travelling around his units and depots, judging their quality and discovering their needs. In the process he became a recognizable figure and in this he was undoubtedly helped by his unusual physical appearance, so unlike the stereotype of a general. Yet in some manner he conveyed his quality of robustness to those who saw him even though he did not look the part. At the same time he gained a reputation of being a commander who cared for his troops and who sent them into battle as well prepared and trained as could be. Again and again, those who served under him, private soldier or general, Etonian or Australian backwoodsman, have described the confidence he inspired. Even the intellectual young Osbert Sitwell could be moved by his clarity of thought and expression.

The very intelligent Wavell stressed the need for common sense in a general, *le sens du practicale*, the knowledge of what is possible and what is not.[94] Napoleon's views were similar: accuracy, simplicity and character were the qualities he sought in his marshals and generals rather than cleverness. They were also a summary of Plumer's virtues. So many highly intelligent men, of whom Lloyd George was the most prominent, have deplored the lack of intellect among the generals of the First World War – and other wars also for that matter. Yet the qualities needed to win battles are those specified by Wavell and Napoleon, especially the robustness to disregard the human cost if need be. Paradoxically, intellect can often be more valuable in peace than war. The analysis of future trends in weapon development twenty or more years ahead, together with the political and geographical factors involved in their use, calls for mental capacity of the very highest order. It could be argued that it is in this, rather than the command of armies in the field, that the British Army has been found wanting.

Wavell laid down two simple rules to govern a general's relationship with his staff: first, never try to do his own staff work; second, never to let his staff get between him and his troops.[95] These were Plumer's principles, and this at a time when the proper use of staff officers was still an evolving skill; so short a time ago as the Boer War commanders such as Kitchener and Roberts had almost no understanding of how they might best be used. As Harington has recorded, Plumer always kept his finger on the pulse and made his own decisions after listening carefully to his advisers. His wishes were then made quite clear to his staff, but the details were left to them.[96]

When the future Field-Marshall Montgomery laid the foundations of his reputation at Alamein in 1942, the methods he then adopted and later refined in Tunisia, Italy and Normandy were seen at the time as inspired innovations. They were, in fact, those Plumer had used so successfully twenty-five years earlier. Because Montgomery had served as GSO2 of IX Corps in Plumer's Army from 6 June, 1917, onwards, his task the writing of the detailed orders for the operations of his Corps, he had been well placed to observe and profit from Plumer's tactical and administrative skills. His choice of limited objectives, his deep and powerful predicted artillery fire, and his leap-frogging of fresh units and formations to capture successive objectives were merely the duplication of the methods used by Plumer for his three-step autumn attack on the Passchendaele Ridge; the same applied to Montgomery's sound logistics, together with his detailed preliminary training and thorough briefing of the troops taking part.

Again, Montgomery's methods of command were much the same as those he had observed at Plumer's headquarters: his use of his staff, especially his Chief-of-Staff, Major-General de Guingand, to whom he delegated responsibility as Plumer did to Harington, his forward liaison officers bypassing the normal channels and reporting direct to him, even his small and distraction-free mess. All these were tools first developed by Plumer. Like Plumer also, Montgomery made himself a familiar figure to his troops, although the deliberately flamboyant and eye-catching image he cultivated was of a rather different order. And, as with Plumer, Montgomery was very aware that a general gains the confidence of his troops by a thoroughness of method, a care for their well-being and an insistence that they should enter battle well prepared.

Needless to say there is no record of Montgomery ever even suggesting that he had profited from serving under Plumer. In his memoirs, after he had condemned the losses and deprecated the generalship and staff work of the First World War, he does go so far as to admit that 'There were of course exceptions and I suppose one such was Plumer', but he then added, 'I had only once seen him and had never spoken to him'[97]. Later in the war, as GSO1 of the 47th (London) Division, Montgomery developed a system of sending officers with wireless-sets forward to the leading battalions so as to provide rapid and reliable information: this, he claimed, was a new departure and the germ of his well-publicized use of liaison officers in the next war.[98] In IX Corps how familiar Plumer's system must have been to him.

Unlike Haig and Plumer, Montgomery possessed the fast-moving, mobile armour with which he could exploit the breakthrough and so produce decisive victories. The essential preliminary stages, the hard slogging by infantry and artillery to make the breach and so costly in casualties, was no more than the updating of the successful methods Plumer had originated at Messines and Passchendaele.

If Lloyd George had managed to sack Haig and if he had replaced him by

Plumer, would the latter have done any better or even as well in producing that final victory in 1918? As the Official Historian accurately maintained, the Army as a whole had great confidence in Haig, and there might have been a loss of morale in France even if he had been replaced by Plumer.[99] Plumer's common humanity might also have told against him. Resolute he was, but, since he had first seen friends killed in the Sudan, war's wastage had deeply saddened him: he was as careful of life as any commander on the Western Front could be. His thorough and deliberate planning, his so-called 'plodding' methods, had their roots in his determination to win battles without unnecessary losses; and, in any case, men were becoming much harder to replace as the war dragged on. Despite the calumnies, neither was Haig profligate in his men's lives, but he was probably prepared to drive them that much harder than Plumer, and hard driving was needed to end the war before the 1918 winter set it.

Plumer would surely have been a success as CIGS. He certainly possessed the diplomatic skills needed for the job, the ability to work well with the politicians, both his own and those of the Allies, as well as the Allied military commanders. This he had proved in Italy, and was to demonstrate further in his post-war career. Nearly everyone trusted Plumer, politicians and soldiers alike, and most of them liked him as well. Perhaps he lacked a finely tuned intellect, but his mental qualities were quite up to the task. He would have chosen capable men to serve him, and he already possessed a sound knowledge of the machinations of Whitehall and Government, gained during his time as Quartermaster-General.

But this is speculation. It is as an Army Commander that Plumer must be judged. In success and in adversity he did as well, if not far better, than any of his fellows, in general a capable body of men, the equal of their counterparts in other armies and arguably of their successors as well. Plumer certainly fulfilled the criteria demanded by Socrates and by Wavell. Let Liddell Hart have the last word in a remark that reflects that writer's disparagement of First World War generalship. Plumer had 'perhaps the nearest approach to military genius in a war singularly devoid of that inspired quality.'[100]

12 The Rhineland and Malta

By the terms of that historic Armistice, signed at 5 am on 11 November, 1918, the German Army was obliged to quit, within fifteen days, those parts of France, Belgium and Luxemburg which it had over-run, together with the whole of the Alsace-Lorraine; during the subsequent sixteen days German troops were to evacuate all of their country which lay on the west bank of the Rhine, together with three bridgeheads on the eastern bank of the river at Mayence, Coblenz and Cologne. French, American and British forces were to occupy this German territory. To command the British contingent Haig chose Plumer with his Second Army Headquarters, its role to garrison the District of Cologne of some 1000 square miles, in which lived some 1 million Rhinelanders.

Four infantry corps, each of four divisions (two of them Canadian) and with cavalry in addition, made up Plumer's command. Marching first through Belgium, where the liberators received on the whole a frenzied welcome, the first of the cavalry crossed into Germany on 24 November, watched by shaven-headed children and a few adults peering through the chinks of shuttered windows. During the long march it had rained for much of the time; after twenty miles or so daily over cobbled roads the infantry's boots were wearing out fast, and both men and officers were often still verminous. The already shattered railway system was fast collapsing under the strain, roads were choked with returning and hungry refugees and prisoners-of-war of all nationalities, food and supplies were scarce: it was hardly surprising that the advance was often delayed.

With the signing of the Armistice, Plumer scraped five days' leave, his first visit to the United Kingdom for over a year. He returned to the Continent in time to accompany King Albert on his triumphal entry into Brussels. Not until 12 December, however, was he able to take the salute as the main body of troops crossed the Hohenzollern Bridge over the Rhine into Cologne.

As Plumer had forecast with some accuracy in a letter to his wife dated a week before, the command of the Army of Occupation was 'not to be a bed of roses by any means', great honour though he saw it.[1] In him had been vested the supreme control of the civil government of a hungry population; riots that came close to civil war were spreading in every direction, while the troops with whom he was to enforce martial law among a proudly hostile people were quickly to lose their cutting edge as badly conceived demobilization plans damaged both efficiency and morale.

To remedy the shortage of food was the major challenge facing Plumer. Although Germany could grow nearly all of what she needed, by the closing weeks of 1918 famine and disease threatened to complete the devastation of the war, as it was to do in most countries of Eastern Europe. The scarcity was worsened by the near collapse of the civil government outside the occupied areas, by the rapacity of the disbanding German Army, and by widespread profiteering; at the same time the continued Allied blockade prevented food from being imported. Fighting both bureaucracy and the understandable malevolence aroused by the war, Plumer did manage to obtain something from British stores to feed the poorer inhabitants of his district, but a Treasury demand for cash before delivery stultified these early efforts.[2]

To lift the blockade became the concern of all the soldiers involved. It was not just humanitarianism. Haig was not alone in fearing that:

If we don't feed her, Bolshevism will spread. This will result in the devastation of Germany and probably in our having to intervene. And furthermore, Bolshevism is likely to to spread to France and England.[3]

After staying for the inside of a week with Plumer in February, Rawlinson described his visit in a letter to Wigram, presumably for the information of the King. After touching upon Plumer's 'splendiferous mansion with all the luxuries and comforts of a modern house', and the excellence of the opera 'in no way affected by the war', much of the rest of his letter was devoted to the civilian food shortage.[4] Then, a month later, as conditions continued to worsen and there was still no indication that anything was to be done for the starving Germans, Plumer despatched a telegram direct to the Prime Minister. It was opportune that it should have arrived as Lloyd George was attending a meeting of the Supreme Economic Council at Versailles. To its members, the Prime Minister read out Plumer's sombre words pleading that food should be provided in order to combat communism and pointing out also how the suffering of German women and children would affect the morale of the British Army. Lloyd George ended with the declaration 'Gentlemen, you cannot say that General Plumer is pro-German'.[5] The eloquence succeeded. Food was released, together with the shipping to carry it, first for the occupied zone but later for Germany as a whole.*

For what he had accomplished, Plumer was assailed from every side. A letter to the *Morning Post,* addressed from the Savile Club, reflected the attitude of many people in England and most in France, bitter after five years of slaughter, deprivation and occupation. After complaining of the 'harrowing tales' of starving Germany that filled the papers and what the writer had heard of the rich living like 'fighting cocks' in Hamburg and Westphalia, the writer ended his letter:

> Now General Plumer is a British officer and gentleman, and he would be hopelessly outmatched by the low cunning which is habitually practiced by the Hun. It would not occur to him that the spectacle of suffering German women and children had probably been specially prepared for his benefit.[6]

As for the reaction in Germany, soon after the decision was made to lift the blockade, a conspiracy to assassinate Plumer was revealed.[8]

For long afterwards, Plumer was remembered as the man responsible for saving Germany from starvation. And, as usually happens, time assuaged the rancour aroused in Britain. A decade later, at a Remembrance Day Service in Glasgow, General Sir Ian Hamilton in the course of a fighting speech, encouraging its citizens to tackle the evil of unemployment, declared:

> Then you shall save Glasgow in spite of herself, just as the Army of the Rhine and Field-Marshal Lord Plumer, better known in the Army as 'Old Plum', saved the Versailles Councillors from the eternal execration of humanity when, on the 8th March, 1919, Lord Plumer telegraphed to Mr Lloyd George 'a bad effect is being produced upon the discipline of the British soldiers by the spectacle of the sufferings of German women and children'. Then they got frightened, raised the blockade, and let the cornships through into Germany.[9]

In his letter to Wigram, Rawlinson had mentioned also that 'The people

---

*Dr Chaim Weizmann, later the first President of Israel, recounts an odd anecdote. Due to lunch with Lloyd George on Armistice Day, he found his host reading the Psalms and close to tears. The first thing the Prime Minister said was, 'We have just sent off seven trains full of bread and other essential food, to be distributed by Plumer in Cologne'. As Plumer had not then been picked for the post and was not to arrive in Cologne for another month, it is all a little strange.[7]

of Cologne are well content to have us there as it means security to life and property.[10] For most of the population this was certainly so. Germany was rent by near civil war. The young Weimar Republic was struggling for its survival against the twin forces of insurgent Marxist Spartacism and the reactionary military bodies, such as the *Frei-Korps*, which it was perforce employing to combat the revolutionary violence. Düsseldorf, just over Plumer's border, was the scene of constant fighting.

When strikes in the Occupied Zone began to threaten water and electricity supplies, Plumer acted. Using his powers of martial law, in early April he issued a proclamation forbidding all strikes but announcing that industrial disputes would be brought before Arbitration Courts of British officers sitting with industrial assessors. It was, as he emphasized on the posters, 'my firm intention to safeguard the rights of workers to the fullest degree'.[11] The good sense of the Rhinelanders prevailed, and Plumer's summary jurisdiction was accepted. In a strife-torn country, Cologne remained a peaceful enclave.

What is more, Plumer managed to hold in check the restlessness that beset both soldiers and officers, a compound of war weariness and impatience with the exasperatingly unfair arrangements that had been put in hand for their demobilization. At a time of widespread anxiety that the British Army might follow the example of the Russians and make for their homes of their own accord, Plumer enforced strict standards of discipline, but ensured that they were tempered by tact and consideration.[12]

* * *

Plumer's stay in Germany was short. On 21 April, 1919, he handed over the British Army of the Rhine, as his command had been named, to Robertson who had, since the previous June, been in charge of the Home Forces. Although Plumer had ruled in Cologne for only four months, he left his mark there. It had also been a valuable apprenticeship for the next two challenges of his career that awaited him, the first of which was Governor and Commander-in-Chief of Malta.

But first he was able to enjoy six weeks leave in England, a short enough period for a sixty-two-year-old to recuperate from almost six years of crushing responsibility. During those few weeks of relaxation, his countrymen took the opportunity of showing their appreciation in a number of ways. To receive their Freedoms, he visited Torquay, York and Tenby, the last little place the home of his sister, Beatrice, and brother, Frederick, now retired from the Royal Navy as a lieutenant-commander, after many years working in the Coastguard Service; there Plumer had often spent much of his leaves. The Worshipful Companies of Grocers and of Salters also granted him their Freedoms, and, together with seventeen other Old Etonian generals, his old school formally welcomed him back.

On 19 December, 1918, soon after the Armistice had been signed, Plumer and his fellow Army Commanders had accompanied Haig to London. Met at Charing Cross by the Duke of Connaught and the Prime Minister, they had driven through crowded streets to Buckingham Palace by way of Pall Mall, Piccadilly and Constitution Hill, there to receive the thanks of their King. At that time Lord Stamfordham, on the King's behalf, was trying to persuade Haig to accept the peerage that was his due, arguing that Admiral Beatty, the Commander-in-Chief of the Home Fleet, was to be made an earl and Plumer a viscount. Lloyd George increased the pressure, but Haig steadfastly refused to accept any further honours until he could be satisfied that the Government intended to make proper provision for the men disabled by the war.[13] Not until July, 1919, did he agree to take the title of Earl Haig of Bemersyde, the name of his family home overlooking the Tweed. The estate had passed elsewhere, but a grateful nation bought it back for him, and to maintain his position the Exchequer granted him £100,000, the sum to be held in trust for him and his heirs. At the same time Plumer was promoted to the rank of Field-Marshal and he was created a Baron with a grant of £30,000. Somehow the previous plans to make him a viscount had miscarried.

Plumer's choice of the title of Baron Plumer of Messines and Bilton in the County of York is puzzling. Already touched upon has been the ownership of Bilton House, between York and Harrogate, by Plumer's great-great-uncle, Hall Plumer. That pleasant Georgian dwelling had, however, passed elsewhere some years before Plumer was born, and his direct forebears had lived, not there, but at Lilling, north of York, and later at Canon's Park. There could have been confusion between the two Hall Plumers, one his father and one his great-great-uncle, but a little research could have established the facts. It is hard indeed to understand why Plumer should have chosen a place with which his family had had only a passing connection. On the other hand his wife, a socially ambitious woman, could just possibly have prevailed upon him to take a title that reflected a country background in Yorkshire, rather than, say, Canon's Park, then in the process of being swallowed by creeping suburbia.[14] Certainly, Plumer seems to have lacked an interest in his family history.

Some of Plumer's descendants appear to have been raised in the belief that their roots lay in Bilton: his eldest daughter, Eleanor, placed a memorial to her father in the village church, and the church history contains the inaccurate statement that the Field-Marshal's father and grandfather lived in the nearby big house.[15] However, Plumer's sister, Beatrice, who was to be killed by a V1 flying bomb in her London house, and his son

288

Thomas, the second Viscount, were both buried near earlier family graves at St. Lawrence Whitchurch, close to Canon's Park.

As for Plumer's inclusion of the village of Messines in his title, when its people returned to the pile of red rubble into which it had been pulverised to make a start on rebuilding their homes and their lives, they found it hard to comprehend why this English general should have added the name of their village to his.[16]

* * *

Near the end of his time on the active list, a senior and distinguished officer might hope for a pro-consulship to ease his path into retirement. The job of Governor of Malta had been seen as such a sinecure, but it was not to be so for Plumer. Beleaguered by German submarines during the war, the island was an unhappy place. There had never been enough work for its people, 2000 of them to a square mile of shallow soil, held in place by its white limestone walls, so reminiscent of the Cotswolds on a bright day. Now, at the end of the war, the large number of the island's men who had been working in labour units at Gallipoli, Salonika and elsewhere, had all lost their jobs. Unemployment was rife, trade had been slow to start recovering, and the price of bread had trebled since 1914 without any compensating wage rise. Hunger was widespread.

Plumer, delighted by his appointment, does not appear to have been told what awaited him. His predecessor, Lord Methuen, a Field-Marshal despite his demotion by Lord Roberts for incompetence in South Africa, had managed to fight off an attempt by the Royal Navy to capture the post as a prize for an admiral, a ploy condemned by Stamfordham as 'preposterous'.[17] In a barely legible handwritten letter (as so many were when penned by busy men), Methuen had assured Plumer that his work 'should prove most interesting'; that the compulsory education for which Methuen had pressed would be introduced; and that he doubted whether Plumer would 'have much to do with the "Constitution" question, which had bored us all to [illegible] extinction'. Quoting someone whose name is also indecipherable, Methuen added 'they don't know what they want and they won't be satisfied till they get it'. Methuen also mentioned that he had recommended that the annual salary of £3000 should be increased.[18]

Malta's upper and middle classes knew quite well what they wanted. They looked for control over their own affairs to satisfy a fast-growing national pride. They would then, they were sure, be able to cure their island's ills. An earlier measure of self-government had been abrogated in 1903, since when successive British Cabinets had been reluctant to pass control of their country's main Mediterranean base to a ruling class that was, at the time, Italian both in language and sympathy, Maltese being no more than a spoken tongue, only just starting to emerge as a written language. There existed an Advisory Council, it members elected on a franchise of only one-eighteenth of the male population, but these were outnumbered by the official members. In any case, power lay with the Executive Council appointed in London and headed by the Governor.

It was a recipe for trouble, and into it swept Plumer. As he was enjoying the summer sea voyage on his way to the island, he received a wireless message from the GOC troops, the acting Governor, advising him to delay landing because of serious riots. On 7 June militant crowds had been organized by local politicians to demonstrate in favour of a new constitution which was being drafted for consideration by the British Government. The mob, strengthened by university students, labouring under a number of genuine grievances, rapidly got out of hand. First shops were forcibly closed, then Union Jacks were hauled down from public buildings, soon the destruction of property began – an Anglophile newspaper office, the university laboratory and library, the houses of unpopular politicians and prominent millers, the latter held responsible for both the poor quality and the high price of bread. The police vanished from the streets and the badly paid locally enlisted troops, whose sympathies lay with their fellow countrymen, proved both ineffective and unreliable. With only about fifty British soldiers available, sailors and Royal Marines were landed from the Fleet. By the evening of 8 June order was almost restored, but four Maltese had been killed, one bayonetted in the stomach, and dozens had been injured. For two days the authorities had lost control of the situation.

When Plumer landed on 10 June the capital city of Valetta was paralysed, the atmosphere tense. After receiving the usual and formal address of welcome at the Customs House by the Grand Harbour, he drove with his wife by his side up the steep hill to the Palace, through the narrow, ancient streets packed with surly but inquisitive crowds. Disregarding the safety of both himself and his wife, he ordered his driver to move at walking pace. On arriving at the Palace, he found the square in front packed with thousands of people. Stopping the car, he emerged and coolly enquired the whereabouts of the ceremonial guard which was awaiting him but which was hidden from view by the packed throng. As he walked in the direction of the guard, the crowd parted, revealing two laurel wreaths on the ground, placed there to mark the spot where two victims of the rioting had been shot. After giving orders for the wreaths to be removed immediately, he inspected the guard and entered the courtyard of the Palace. There he discovered a large body of Bluejackets. 'What is this?' he asked the GOC. 'Your guard, sir', was the reply. 'How many are there?'

was the next query. 'Three hundred, sir', was the answer. 'March out all but twenty within ten minutes,' ordered Plumer.[19]

This public display of courage, coolness and decision had its effect. The Maltese saw that they had acquired a Governor who would stand no nonsense and who meant what he said. He quickly revealed other and quite different qualities. His Lieutenant Governor, a civil servant, his name by an odd coincidence also Sir William Robertson, had expected a caustic enquiry for the reason for the disturbed conditions. Instead he received a cheerful 'Hullo!' (not then the standard greeting that it was to become) and a cheerful grin. As Leo Amery, by then Under Secretary-of-State for the Colonies, described his arrival, 'his kindliness, sympathy and twinkling good humour' put everyone at ease.[20] Readily absorbing the rapid briefing he received, Plumer then sent for the island's political leaders and listened carefully to their grievances. Later that day, he confined the troops to barracks, imposed a severe censorship on the press, and ordered a number of arrests, and instructed Robertson to gather the students together and warn them to give no further trouble. Concessions came later.

Plumer then set about absorbing information about the island, its people and its problems, making himself a familiar figure as he did so and impressing the many he met with the speed with which he had mastered complicated problems and was producing solutions for them. Robertson was especially impressed by his skill as a public speaker. 'Without any flights of oratory, he made one feel that he had a message and this he gave with all the arresting simplicity of Lincoln.'[21] In a short time the Maltese discovered that Plumer could be sympathetic and helpful as well as firm.

Before he left London Plumer had been instructed to find out how the Maltese might be given a greater share in government without imperial interests being prejudiced; this Robertson had made known to their leaders before the new Governor arrived. Then, at the end of August, Amery, who at the time knew Plumer only from repute and a few chance meetings, visited Malta, his decision to do so having been taken after a meeting with Methuen at which the chronic state of the Colony's finances had been discussed, a subject about which Plumer had already been in touch with him.[22] Amery had his doubts about the welcome he might receive from such a distinguished soldier, so many years older than himself. He had no need for alarm. Plumer showed him everything and arranged for him to speak to everyone. Not only were the doubts he had entertained about the capacity of military governors to cope with complicated financial and political matters laid at rest, but he also established that within a few short weeks Plumer had already won the confidence and affection of large numbers of people.

Towards the end of his stay Amery concluded that the Maltese should be permitted to run their own affairs, provided that the security of the base were to be left in the Governor's charge. By this means the obstructive and negative criticism at which the educated classes excelled might disappear, and an ever-growing cause for dissatisfaction be removed. He did fear, as he put it, that 'such a conception of the situation might well be unfamiliar to a Military Governor', and he broached his ideas with no little hesitation, especially so as he was dealing with a man who had so expeditiously asserted his authority in the island. Plumer, he quickly discovered, was wholeheartedly in sympathy with his ideas.[23]

The machinery of government moved with such uncharacteristic speed that on 20 November it was announced in both Houses of Parliament at Westminster, and by Plumer to the Council of Government in Malta, that 'the time had come to entrust the people of Malta with full responsible control of their purely local affairs, the control of the naval and military services and functions of Government as are connected with the position of Malta as an Imperial Fortress remaining vested in the Imperial Authorities'. At the same time Plumer's request was agreed for a grant-in-aid of £250,000 to put straight the parlous finances of the island which in large measure were the outcome of the war. The constitution was to be based upon the draft already submitted by the Maltese to the Home Government, but the details had to be settled by endless correspondence between Malta and Whitehall and at meetings between Plumer, his principal advisers and Maltese politicians and other leaders. At last, on 12 June, 1920, Plumer was able to lay the Draft Letters Patent before the Council. Malta was to be ruled by a dyarchy: Imperial and military matters were to be the concern of the Malta Imperial Government, consisting of the Governor and his official advisers, while all else was to be dealt with by an elected Assembly and Senate, with executive authority in the hands of Ministers appointed from members of either house. As President of the two bodies, both composed of men inexperienced in the working of democratic government and concerned with justifying their actions to their House and to the electorate, Plumer carried a heavy burden.

Unfortunately this constitution was to be suspended in 1933 because of bitter feuds about the language question, these exaggerated by religious issues. The over-enthusiastic champions of Italian as one of the two official languages were to be encouraged by Mussolini's rise to power and his overseas ambitions, to counter which the colonial government paradoxically supported a greater use of the once-despised Maltese tongue, the oral patois of the lower classes, issuing schoolbooks of Maltese history in the Maltese language, and in due course 'elevating Maltese from the kitchen to the courts'.[24] The use of their own language was to be a major factor in consolidating Malta's national identity, but these are problems outside our scope.[25]

On 1 November, 1921, His Royal Highness the Prince of Wales – the future King Edward VIII – inaugurated the new Maltese Parliament in the Hall of St Michael and St George in the Palace of Valetta, built after the so-called Great Siege of 1565 against the Turks as the residence of the Grand Master of the Order of the Knights of Malta. With its walls decorated with scenes of the siege and its magnificent painted ceiling, it was a suitable setting for such a celebration of Imperial might and benevolent patronage. Trumpets sounded their fanfares; outside in the Palace Square the Guard of Honour was fringed by happy crowds, a contrast indeed to the sullen mob of 1919; overhead there reverberated the sound of the 21-gun salutes fired by the Royal Malta Artillery and the great ships of the Royal Navy which studded the Grand Harbour. It had been a break in the young and popular Prince's celebrated journey to India, his first Royal progress, and it was an occasion thoroughly enjoyed by the Plumers, especially Annie Constance who cherished her contacts with royalty.[26] The country's high hopes of the Prince are reflected in this letter from Stamfordham to Plumer:

The King and Queen have read your letter of the 6th. instant with the utmost pleasure and are so gratified that the Prince of Wales's visit to Malta gave such satisfaction and that, in your opinion, it will have lasting good effect. His Royal Highness's personality, tact and charm of manner are indeed remarkable and he is a very valuable possession to the country. He lands today, and one hopes and believes that his time in India will be as successful as it has been in other parts of the Empire.[27]

He was not the only heir to a throne to visit Malta. Before they left, the Plumers entertained the then Crown Prince of Japan on his first visit to Europe.

To escape the intense summer heat, the Plumers moved each June from the Valetta Palace, which Lady Plumer loved, to what has been described as the fairy-tale castle at San Antonio, the magnificent gardens of which kept eighteen gardeners busy, their wages fortunately paid by the Maltese Exchequer. With the Royal Navy present in strength, Malta was a pleasant place in which to live, the only snag being the social barriers which the British, as ever, had erected between themselves and the friendly local people; these barriers Plumer devoted much time and energy to weakening, even though he failed to gain them admittance to the island's main club.[28]

Sixty-five years afterwards, an officer who had served there on Plumer's staff remembered all this and also Plumer's drive and energy, the pleasure he found in the company of the young, and the frequent and pleasant parties given at the two palaces. Utterly straightforward and in no way pompous, Plumer was, for all that, conscious of his position as the King's representative.[29] Lady Plumer, on the other hand, was rather too aware of her husband's dignity. When Plumer's good-natured elder brother, Frederick, a mere lieutenant-commander, stayed with them, she took him to task for not rising to his feet when the Governor entered the room; to this rebuke he is said to have replied, 'I have not been in the habit of standing up when Herbert appears, and, what is more, I have no intention of starting to do so now', brave[30] words indeed to that formidable lady.

Despite the vigour and good humour that Plumer radiated, for much of his time in Malta he was far from fit. The summer before the visit by the Prince of Wales, he had been obliged to return to England for a prostate operation, the doctors having warned him that the consequences of delay might be serious.[31] At that time the operation was both painful and risky, especially for a man who was already suffering from the strain of the long years of war. Looking rather thinner and still weak in the legs, he called upon Sir Henry Wilson (still the CIGS) before he returned to Malta and confided to him that his doctors had told him that he could expect to be a great deal better and stronger than he had been for the past ten years.[32] It was a reflection of the burden he had been carrying. A short time after he arrived in Malta Wilson had suggested to him that he might move to be Commander-in-Chief in Ireland, then racked by the post-war rebellion that was soon to bring the country its independence. At sixty-three it was hardly to be wondered at that so sick a man was reluctant to undertake such a task, but Wilson, in his usual acerbic manner, had commented to Churchill that 'Plumer is a good judge of what to avoid'.[33]

Another burden Plumer had been carrying during the war years was his unhappiness about his only son, in whom had appeared some of the unfortunate characteristics of his father, Hall Plumer. For all that, Thomas Plumer had grown into a very pleasant man, whose good qualities outweighed his faults. When he left Eton, he had spent a spell at the Royal Agricultural College at Cirencester, after which he emigrated to Canada to work in forestry. Enlisting in British Columbia, he joined the Canadian Army Service Corps, his faulty eyesight having prevented him from entering one of the more combatant corps, but he was to serve as an Assistant Provost Marshal in different Canadian formations and be decorated with a Military Cross, a Croix de Guerre and Mentioned in Despatches.[34] In many ways he was a son of whom a father might be proud, but there was this wild streak in the Plumers. Herbert's other sister, Constance, had run off to America with a married man,[35] unusual and reprehensible behaviour indeed for a well-reared young lady of the Victorian middle classes.

When Harington saw his old chief off to Malta from Victoria Station in 1919, Plumer had said to him, 'Do what you can for the boy. He is engaged to a very nice girl'. Just before his departure, Plumer had met his son, but, according to Harington, that was the last time they ever saw one another.[36] It is hard to reconcile such behaviour in someone who was otherwise so kindly and generous hearted, one who had even contributed towards a small allowance paid to Constance when she fell on hard times.[37] Until some time after her husband's death, Lady Plumer was unrelenting in her disapproval of her son's conduct,[38] and there is small doubt that this rather intolerant woman influenced a too devoted husband, one who deferred to her in all matters concerning the upbringing of their family.

*　*　*

Plumer brought his influence to bear on nearly every facet of life in Malta. Education was his special interest, as it had been his predecessor's and, so far as money could be found, he did all he could to encourage its spread. Among several other measures, he gave strong support to the inclusion of Malta in the Rhodes Scholarship scheme for the entry of able colonials to Oxford, to the development of a distinguished School of Archaeology in the island, and to assisting and encouraging the University. But everything he set his hand to required a bedrock of secure government, and Plumer's first action after he arrived had been to reorganize the police. When investigating why they had failed so badly at the time of the riots, he had discovered that they were discontented, their discipline low and their efficiency poor. Plumer's appointment of a new Chief-of-Police, a man in whom he had every confidence, was all that was needed. In little over a year, Robertson noted, the island possessed an efficient and reliable force, a tribute to Plumer's capacity for finding the right man and leaving him to get on with the job.[39]

To improve the standard of the local military forces was rather more difficult. Money was needed to accomplish this and Plumer was faced with persuading a reluctant War Office to disgorge what was needed. However, new and improved pay scales had come into force soon after Plumer arrived and these helped him considerably. The regular local unit was the Royal Malta Artillery, its major task the defence of the naval base, but Plumer was intent upon obtaining a small contingent of Maltese infantry for internal security duties. His correspondence with the Secretary of State for War upon this subject did not mince words,[40] but his letters to Sir Henry Wilson on this and other matters were always most friendly, an indication of a close relationship between the two men. Negotiations continued until 1922 when Plumer at last obtained the £25,000 he needed to raise a cadre company of the King's Own Malta Regiment, and then only after he had been obliged to threaten to resign following a blank refusal to find the money.[41]

Plumer's letters to Wilson were always to the point, well expressed and in lucid English. They ranged well outside Maltese questions. In one of them he complained that the taxpayer was not getting a proper return from the Board of Education when young British soldiers, after five or six years in a Board School, were left 'knowing nothing'.[42] There was to be small improvement for another two decades. Wilson often confided his worries to the older man. One of his letters dwelt on politicians in general and Lloyd George, the Prime Minister, in particular, overcommitting the armed forces to tasks beyond their competence.[43] It elicited a reply startlingly Machiavellian and prescient also. Posing the rhetorical question, 'Who is to get us out of this mess?', Plumer answered, 'I think a Labour Government in the first instance, don't you, to bring all this domestic trouble to a head. A few good rows at home on a big scale to clear the air and then a reaction with sensible men closing their ranks.'[44] Three years later the country's first Labour Government took office, to struggle on for ten months before being defeated at a General Election, largely as a result of the so-called 'Zinoviev Letter', alleged to have been sent by that Russian leader to British Communists (then almost indistinguishable from the Labour Party in many people's eyes), urging them to promote revolution. The 'sensible men' then closed their ranks around Stanley Baldwin for several years.

The need Plumer had foreseen for adequate and efficient local forces was quickly demonstrated. In 1922 Harington was in command of the occupation forces in Istanbul. The post-war anarchy in Turkey which brought about Kemal Ataturk's resuscitation of his country and his bloody expulsion of the invading Greeks from Smyrna (now Izmir) led to Turkish troops confronting Harington's at Chanak on the Dardanelles. Reinforcements had to be scraped together from wherever they could be found, and Plumer cheerfully relinquished his two British infantry battalions to his old friend, leaving his local forces to look after the island. The Chanak incident was to bring Harington fame. Ordered by his government to present an ultimatum to the Turks to withdraw and to use force if need be to compel them to do so, Harington instead temporised and so avoided the start of yet another war for which the British had neither the taste nor the troops. Reproved officially for disobeying his instructions, the success of his diplomacy was acclaimed everywhere. The end result was to be the break-up of the Coalition Government and the political eclipse of Lloyd

George who, despite his mishandling of his generals, had done so very much to win the war.

The praise bestowed upon Plumer when his five-year tour ended in May 1924, went far beyond the usual formal tributes heard at such times. Acclaimed by those who had worked with him both in Malta and outside for his arresting simplicity, his single-minded honesty, his genuine and warm affection, the Maltese Parliament petitioned the King for his tour to be extended. Hardly surprisingly, the War Office refused on the grounds that it would block the expectations of others, a stand with which the King agreed.[45]

Plumer's governorship, as a distinguished Maltese had recently written, 'must be counted as one of the outstanding of Administrations which our Island has had during its long and difficult political evolution'.[46] A nationalist historian has described him as 'the man required at the moment, a great leader of men and a perfect English gentleman – kindly, resolute and fearless, placid in temperament, methodical in manner, and blindly trusted by those under him'.[47] Driving from San Antonio into Valetta on the day he left, Plumer passed through densely packed streets, hung with bunting and thick with laudatory placards. The air was full of flowers, flung down upon him from crowded balconies, and when he emerged upon the balcony of the Valetta Palace and saw the sea of faces below, all that ever-emotional man could find to say was the word 'Good-bye'. Swarms of launches and other small boats followed his ship out of the harbour and into the Mediterranean.

Soon after Plumer returned to England, the Australian Government asked for him to be appointed as their next Governor General, an offer that much appealed to Plumer himself and which would have been popular with many of the returned Australian ex-servicemen. Only the King had his doubts, confiding to Amery that he did not think 'Lady Plumer was up to it'.[48] But only a wealthy man could maintain the state demanded in the post, and Plumer, despite the £30,000 he had received at the end of the war, just could not afford it.[49] His decision much disappointed the Australians, who asked him to reconsider it. Among his papers is pencilled what is presumably a copy of his reply, sent through the Colonial Office:

Please inform Australian Government I am deeply sensible of their wish that I should reconsider my decision but financial considerations make it impossible. I consider other alternative definitely settled.[50]

The 'other alternative' was the post of High Commissioner to Palestine, offered to him by Amery.

13 Palestine

In retrospect, Leo Amery, who had moved up to be Colonial Secretary in Baldwin's Conservative Government, admitted that he had hesitated for some time before pressing 'a man in his sixty-eighth year to undertake one of the most difficult and thorny tasks in the field of Empire'.[1] These doubts were even more clearly expressed in the entry he made in his diary on 21 April, 1925: 'It is a difficult policy to carry out and I only hope that old Plumer will manage with Symes's* help to keep an even keel.'[2] At the time of his appointment as High Commissioner for Palestine Plumer was suffering from very painful shingles, and Amery well understood that his health might get worse under the strain of office. For this reason Plumer was not asked to commit himself to the usual five-year term of office, but was told that Amery would be happy if he were to stay for three. This was to prove more than enough.

This 'difficult and thorny' task was the dilemma which Lloyd George's coalition wartime Government had created for its successors, the impossibility of reconciling the conflicting interests of Jews and Arabs, the quandary from which the world still suffers.

On 2 November, 1917, when the fortunes of the Allies were at their nadir, Arthur Balfour, then Secretary of State for Foreign Affairs, had written this letter to Lord Rothschild:

> I have much pleasure in conveying to you, on behalf of his Majesty's Government, the following declaration of sympathy with Jewish Zionist aspirations which has been submitted to, and approved by, the Cabinet.
>
> His Majesty's Government view with favour the establishment in Palestine of a national home for the Jewish people, and will use their best endeavours to facilitate the achievement of this object, it being clearly understood that nothing shall be done which may prejudice the

---

*Colonel Stewart Symes was to be Plumer's Chief Secretary.

civil and religious rights of the non-Jewish communities in Palestine, or the rights and political status enjoyed by Jews in any other country.

I should be grateful if you would bring this declaration to the knowledge of the Zionist Federation.

This was the celebrated 'Balfour Declaration', the product of idealism wedded to self-interest. Although many historians have devoted their working lives to studying the background to this imprecise document,[3] the exact reasons for the Cabinet authorizing Balfour to pen it have still to emerge. The Foreign Secretary himself was among Zionism's many sincere supporters who ardently believed that the wrongs suffered by the Jews at Christian hands would be righted only by founding a 'National Home' for them in Palestine; there what he esteemed as the most gifted people since the classical Greeks could find their true role.[4] But, as Balfour conceded, material considerations also affected the issue. Earlier in 1917, before the United States entered the war, there had been the need to influence American-Jewish opinion on behalf of the Allies; later in the year there was still some hope that British encouragement of Zionist aspirations might persuade the many Jews among the Russian Bolshevik leaders to favour continuing the fight against Germany. Imperial strategy may also have influenced Balfour and the Cabinet, the need to keep a garrison in Palestine in the future so as to protect communications with India and forestall French ambitions in the Middle East.

Unfortunately the Balfour Declaration conflicted with imprecise pledges already given to the Arabs to encourage them to revolt against the Turks. These, and subsequent promises made to Arab leaders, were quite incompatible with the undertaking given to the Zionists. The consequence was that Plumer and his successors were to be faced by a conflict between newly emergent Arab nationalism and intractable Zionism, both American and European.

* * *

When General Allenby entered Jerusalem in December, 1917, on the heels of the retreating Turks, Palestine did not exist as such, its very name all but forgotten. A collection of sub-provinces of the Ottoman Empire, its total population numbered no more than 700,000, only about a tenth of whom were Jews, mostly 19th century refugees from Russian pogroms. With the country still under British military rule, the first racial violence occurred in March, 1921, when Arabs attacked a Jewish settlement; the following month both Arabs and Jews were to die in communal rioting in Jerusalem. It was in the immediate aftermath of these disturbances that the Supreme Allied Council created the Mandated Territory of Palestine; civil administration replaced the military, and Sir Herbert Samuel was appointed as the first High Commissioner. The first practising Jew to be a member of a British Cabinet, Samuel was a brilliant scholar who had been raised in the finest traditions of Victorian Liberalism. He was also an able administrator, one needed in a country that, to use his own words, 'had for centuries been almost derelict, politically and materially'.[5] On being asked by the Prime Minister to undertake the appointment, Samuel warned him of the danger of the non-Jewish majority resenting measures imposed upon them by a Jew, an objection that Lloyd George appreciated, but which did not cause him to change his mind.[6]

When Samuel arrived, much had been done to repair the ravages of war, and many of the inhabitants were appreciating the novelty of rulers who seemingly were both just and altruistic. The birth rate was growing, the death rate falling, and the immigration of both Jews and Arabs was rising. For the Zionists it was the fulfilment of a dream – a Jewish ruler, Hebrew adopted with English and Arabic as an official language, and an increasing number of Jews returning to their Promised Land, that could well, before too long, again become the state of Israel. As High Commissioner Samuel was both just and impartial, but impartiality was a quality appreciated by few Jews and even fewer Arabs. There was no way either he, or his successors, could satisfy the aspirations of both races: The Arabs would not budge from their demand that the Balfour Declaration should be revoked and further Jewish immigration halted, while the Zionists sought a national state rather than 'a national home', as Balfour had described it. A concession to either side was invariably seen by the other as appeasement. The choices were stark and irreconcilable.

Plumer's appointment to succeed Samuel at the end of the latter's five-year term of office met with little enthusiasm anywhere. Although Samuel had sacrificed much of his popularity with his co-religionists by what they believed were his unnecessary concessions to the Arabs, they hoped for a man of similar stamp to succeed him – a cultured intellectual, and one of their own race. Samuel's appointment had, they assumed, set a precedent. Plumer, with his monacle, flowing white moustache and military background, was a caricature of the elderly ultra-conservative governor they most feared, certainly a friend of the Arabs and probably an enemy of Zionism, probably anti-Semitic as well; nearing his dotage, he had clearly been sent out to enjoy two or three years of pleasant surroundings as a prelude to final retirement.[7] One Zionist newspaper complained:

The Holy Land or the Jewish Homeland, whichever you will, are both objects of deep study calling for the highest attributes, intellectual and spiritual. In this respect Lord Plumer is only an average resident of England, the type of law-abiding, God-fearing, church-going, perfect old gentleman. . . . We stressed some time ago the necessity of having an intellectual government.[8]

The early Jewish settlers, of whom the writer was probably one, had difficulty in appreciating qualities foreign from those of the Eastern European intelligentsia in whom they had their origins.

Unlike many of his associates, Dr Chaim Weizmann, later Israel's first President and, at the time, the leader of British Zionism, well understood the difficulties of establishing a Jewish state among a hostile Arab population. Perceptive and far-sighted, he favoured a gradual approach. Because he was in close touch with prominent people in London, including Lloyd George, he was especially well informed. Surprise, as well as a measure of doubt, can, therefore, be detected in a letter he wrote to Frederick Kisch, his representative in Jerusalem, on 4 June, 1925. Telling Kisch that he had not been consulted about Plumer's appointment, he added that it had been 'rather a bomb' and that Plumer suffered from 'shingles which is rather a serious disease in a man of his age'; because of Plumer's age and disposition, he feared that responsibility would fall upon Symes, the Chief Secretary.[9]

Kisch's reply must have expressed concern, for Weizmann, who had by then met Plumer, wrote again to reassure him that 'Plumer makes an excellent impression. He seems to be without prejudices and I am perfectly sure that, if he is properly handled in Palestine, you may get on with him very well. He made an excellent impression as a benign, quiet and well-disposed gentleman.'[10] Afterwards, in his autobiography, Weizmann was to describe Plumer as 'a staid and serious English aristocrat of the Victorian era'.[11] Kisch was the very man to get on well with Plumer, and so he did. A retired regular officer of the British Army, he had foregone what could have been a brilliant career to work with Weizmann for Zionism; in the Second World War he was to serve as Montgomery's able and popular Chief Engineer of the Eighth Army, and he was killed in action in Tunisia.

Weizmann wrote in similar terms to Morris Rothenberg, the Zionist leader in New York: Plumer was 'very straight and willing to learn. . . . After a very long conversation, he told me he would not have taken on the office – as he realized that it will be full of difficulties – were he not convinced that he can carry out the policy.'[12] The policy, of course, was to implement the Balfour Declaration. These first and favourable impressions of Plumer were to be confirmed. Weizmann, who had the knack of getting along well with members of the British upper classes, developed a sound and friendly relationship with Plumer.

It was paradoxical that, while many Jews were perturbed by Plumer's appointment, some of his British officials were apprehensive because they feared he might take too firm a line with the Arabs.[13] They had other doubts as well. Symes, who had been told by someone that Plumer 'looks silly, but isn't', wondered how the new High Commissioner would relish life in the Levant and cope with the alarms and excursions of Palestine.[14] Ronald Storrs, the prominent Arabist and then Governor of Jerusalem, was openly disloyal, if Weizmann's letter to his wife was soundly based: 'Storrs,' he wrote, 'isn't happy with Plumer, he thinks he won't be staying long.'[15] A letter from Samuel's Military Secretary to his mother says something about the atmosphere ruling in the High Commission prior to Plumer's arrival:

We have amusing accounts of my successor, Major Brooks [sic] who is Lord P's son-in-law (the other son-in-law incidentally is a Jew!!!). One is that he is 'very clever . . . but his wife treats him like a dog', which amuses me. I think Lord P is also bringing out his eldest daughter aged about 45, who is, I believe, a little trying, so it will be amusing to see how this menage settles in. We think they will be horrified by the furniture which we have here at present. I can't bear it myself, and I think it is odious. They have been accustomed to a glorious old palace at Malta. I hope the old man will survive it!!!![16]

The writer's prejudices were not uncommon at the time. Such he had admitted in an earlier letter, in which he wrote that British officers tended to be anti-Jewish partly because they thought that immigration of Jews was bad luck on the Arabs and particularly because they found the Jews in Palestine 'uncongenial to them'.[17]

After so many years of separation, Plumer loved having his daughters around him. Said to have been his favourite[18] that 'trying' daughter was Eleanor, in fact only forty years of age, ancient by the standards of the time, and suspect also for being a blue-stocking. Although educated by the customary governess, she had taken a good degree at King's College for Women at London University. After a distinguished academic career, she was to become President of St Anne's College at Oxford, where she displayed many of her father's attributes – a phenomenal memory for people, fine powers of organization, an attractive personality, kindness, a brisk manner and an infinite capacity for hard work.[19] As for Major Brooke, the other victim of this gossip, he is remembered in the Plumer family as one of the kindest and most lovable of people.

* * *

Plumer landed at Jaffa on 23 August, 1925, seven weeks after Samuel's departure, his arrival having been delayed by his illness. The official photographs show him looking tired, understandably so for a sick man of sixty-eight, and unsuitably dressed for a Palestinian summer in thick service-dress, but topped by a Wolseley helmet. Lady Plumer, by his side, wearing a silk dress and the immense hat that was her hallmark, is spry and upright, slim and handsome. Storrs was among the party of welcoming officials, and the speeches by the local mayors went on and on. Warmly, spontaneously and unexpectedly cheered, as his train drove through the Jewish city of Tel Aviv, he and his party reached the little bunting-covered railway station at Jerusalem to be received by yet more speeches. The formalities, that had started at 8.15 am, lasted until the evening.[20]

At the end of the speeches, the first glimpse of Plumer's character was noted. Two kavasses bearing silver staves, magnificent in gold-laced blue Turkish uniforms and girded with curving scimitars, were awaiting him, their function to precede the High Commissioner, thumping their staves in unison on the ground. To their chagrin, Plumer straightaway dismissed them with orders to see his baggage to his new house; thereafter their duties were to be limited to carrying messages between government offices.[21] Plumer disliked unnecessary pomp as much as he did security precautions he believed to be unnecessary. He not only gave orders that his driver and the motor-cycle outriders who accompanied him on official occasions should no longer be armed, but he abolished the 'Changing the Guard' ceremony outside Government House, despite its value as a tourist attraction; thereafter his guard was reduced to a Palestinian corporal and a few truncheon-bearing constables. In his leisure hours he would delight in exploring the crowded and bustling alleyways of the Old City, dressed as if for Pall Mall in regulation blue suit, bowler hat and rolled umbrella, and he would object strongly if he spotted one of the plain-clothes policemen whose task it was to keep some sort of eye on him. Altogether he gave the police much cause for concern – too much, if the truth be told. Assassination was already an ever-present threat in the Middle East, and Sir Lee Stack, the Governor General of the Sudan and Commander-in-Chief of the Egyptian Army, had been murdered only the previous November. If their High Commissioner had been gunned down, the police would have carried the blame. However, they worried in vain. After he had left Palestine it was said about him that 'No one ever raised a hand against Lord Plumer except in salutation.'[22]

As the outgoing Military Secretary had accurately forecast, the interior decorations of Government House were something else which did not find favour with Plumer. The Kaiserin Viktoria Augusta Hospice, adapted for

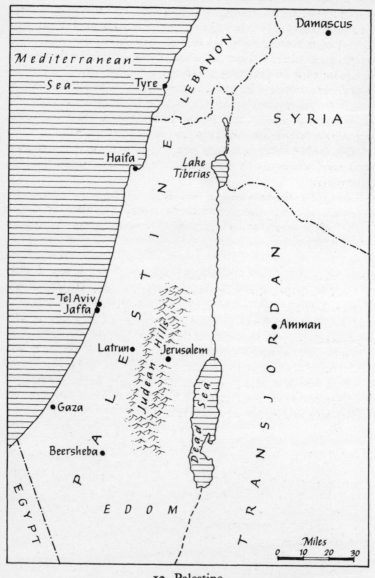

13. Palestine

that purpose, was a vast neo-Gothic pile, perched on Mount Scopus with magnificent views across the jagged Judean Hills to the Mountains of Edom far away across the Dead Sea. The hundred-roomed edifice had reminded Samuel of an uncomfortable Rhineland castle.[23] The day after taking up residence there, Plumer instructed the Public Works Department to remove what Harington described as the 'new art decoration' of his predecessors, and have the furniture scraped and restored to more sedate colours.[24] Lady Plumer's taste was extremely good. She was a lover of antiques and an accomplished needlewoman, but she was clearly out of sympathy with twentieth-century trends, probably influenced in Jerusalem by C.R. Ashbee, the notable designer and architect of the Arts and Crafts Movement, and employed in post-war Jerusalem to advise on the city's rehabilitation.

Among the admirers of the new High Commissioner was Helen Bentwich, wife of Norman Bentwich, the Attorney General and himself a Jew. In September, she wrote home with her first impressions of the new arrivals:

> He is a small man with a fierce moustache and twinkling blue eyes. Lady Plumer is tall and thin, and at first I though her rather formidable. But a few days later they invited us to Government House to tea with them alone. We found them both charming, and I'm sure we will get on with them very happily. She dresses in the old style, with long skirts reaching mostly to the ground. Our men-friends say how nice it is at last to see a woman with a waist where a waist should be★ . . . They have already refurnished their rooms, and laid out their trophies and her objets d'art, and made Government House look like an old-fashioned country house belonging to a retired public servant.[25]

It was at such intimate tea, lunch and dinner parties that the Plumers got to know his staff and their wives, and at which they gained a reputation of being delightful hosts with the knack of putting people at ease, however junior they might be. Disliking formal dinners and such-like, Plumer eschewed them whenever he could. At receptions and garden parties, lounge and even linen suits replaced the customary silk hats and morning coats. Around her husband Lady Plumer created a warm and cheerful atmosphere in which a 'great lady' of the old school presided. Nor was she a snob. A daughter remembered her saying that she cared nothing for

---

★The flappers had arrived by 1925, their waist lines girdling their hips and set just above the edges of their attentuated skirts.

a person's background provided that they were honest.[26] One who knew her at the time wrote that the Plumers were 'a pair of the happiest and brightest children utterly simple and direct; loving and beloved'. She was 'a wise and comprehending partner who would not hesitate to assert control when it became necessary, even to the expedient of hiding his clothes when he was not considered fit in health to go to church'.[27]

While on the subject of clothes, Plumer's reputation for being dapper (sometimes belied in his photographs) may have been due in part to Lady Plumer's supervision. Towards the end of the war, in October, 1918, William Orpen, as an official war artist, painted Plumer's portrait. His subject, he remembered, was 'A strange man with a small head, and a large, though not fat body, and a great brand of humour. He was also very calm, and made things easy for me, but his batman was not so easy to please. When I got the General the way I wanted him, the batman leant over my shoulder, and said: "Is the Governor right now?" "Perfectly", I replied. "No, he ain't," said he, "not by a long chalk." And he went over to the General and started pulling out creases in his tunic and said: "'Ere, you just sit up proper – not all 'unched up the way you are. What would Her Ladyship say if I let you be painted that way?"'[28]

* * *

Plumer had begun to explore his province as soon as he arrived, as he had done in Malta. During his first month he managed to visit nearly every town or village of any importance, inspecting schools and hospitals, and listening to the local notables. Storrs was to accuse him of being vague about education, relating how he would 'never forget the astonishment of Lord Plumer, that fine flower of the public school spirit, when he inspected the town of Gaza in Palestine and announced that in honour of his visit the schools should be given a half-holiday, at finding the news greeted by his studious Arab pupils with almost tearful dismay'.[29] The anecdote hardly accords with other evidence. Two months later he was discussing educational problems with deep understanding, and – incidentally – criticizing the lack of taste in the furniture and metal-work exhibits at a Tel Aviv exhibition. Kisch, who was present, reflected that 'The old Field Marshal is certainly a man of wide interests who has read and thought on many subjects, and I feel sure that his regime will be beneficial in a variety of ways'.[30] The reaction of Storrs to his new High Commissioner was, however, guarded, if not sour. 'The Plumers have made a good start,' he wrote, 'but I . . . am always irritated by the chorus of adoration projected upon the rising sun. Everything that either of them does is construed to the disadvantage of their predecessors.'[31]

During these visits Plumer made his first journey by air, travelling to Transjordan to meet that country's ruler, the Emir Abdullah, for the first time. It was no easy trip for an elderly man, still suffering from the after-effects of shingles, who found it difficult to squeeze himself in and out of the small machine.[32] Circumstances in Transjordan, also the subject of a British Mandate, were in every way different from those prevailing in Palestine, although as Plumer complained to Amery in 1926, those differences were often lost sight of.[33] The son of the Hashemite King Hussein of the Hejaz, leader of the Arab revolt against the Turks, Abdullah was the brother of the Emir Feisal, who with T.E. Lawrence's help had captured Damascus in 1918. Proclaimed King of Syria, Feisal had been thrown out by the French and had accepted the throne of Iraq instead. Abdullah, who had marched to his brother's aid, realized when he reached Amman that he could in no way challenge the French; instead he established himself in Transjordan, as the territory was to be named, by right of occupation but helped by British backing and British subsidies.

While Palestine was self-supporting, Transjordan depended for its existence upon the British taxpayer. Palestine was peaceful, but in Transjordan lives and property were safe neither from internal disorders nor external aggression: in both 1922 and 1924 the puritan Wahabi Bedouin had raided across the border. As a result, Plumer warned the Colonial Secretary vehemently against coupling the two countries together, as so often happened.[34] Any attempt to coerce the Palestinian taxpayer to assist Transjordan was certain to arouse resentment. As for Abdullah, that wise ruler was only too aware of the dangers of too close an association with a country in which Jewish influence was powerful, and would certainly be more so.

* * *

In the chapter of their memoirs headed 'And The Land Had Rest', the Bentwiches epitomized Plumer's time in Palestine. It was, they wrote, 'a period of almost unbroken tranquility and progress. So there is little to record'.[35] Only in Palestine, among all the Arab-speaking countries, had peace been maintained since the end of the war without any major act of suppression. This was all the more remarkable when the French in Syria were, during Plumer's time in office, fighting a ruthless war against the Druse tribesmen on Palestine's northern border in which thousands died.

Although much of the credit for Palestine's brief spell of tranquility was due to Plumer's firm but gentle control of the country, other factors played their part. Concessions to Arab nationalism made by Sir Herbert Samuel had done much good, as had Weizmann's temporary success in curbing his Zionist extremists. A further, and even more potent reason for this peaceful interlude was the economic collapse of Poland, the place from which the most recent wave of Jewish immigration into Palestine had originated. Thousands of these men and women, who had depended upon remittances from Poland to establish themselves, became penniless; business went bankrupt and unemployment spread. The consequence was that Jewish emigration from Palestine in 1927 well exceeded fresh immigration. An attractive alternative for the Polish Jews was Germany, the home of the most prosperous Jewish community in the world, outside the United States, and just regaining her industrial and commercial wealth and standing; by comparison, pioneering in a strange, possibly dangerous and partly barren land, where milk and honey were produced only by bitter toil, held out few attractions for even the most ardent Zionists.

One of Plumer's first tasks was to reorganize the security forces in order to save money and introduce a little logic into their structure. Some saw it as unusual, if not aberrant, that such a distinguished soldier, one who had some experience of the consequences of insurrection, should substantially reduce his peace-keeping forces, violence being so widespread in the Arab world. Impelled, however, by Treasury stringency – there were financial crises in the United Kingdom and unemployment there was hovering around the unacceptable million mark – Plumer cut his forces so as to use the money saved for economic development.

The Palestine Government had maintained three separate bodies. The first was the British Gendarmerie, 750 strong when first raised in 1922, but already reduced by one third, and recruited largely from ex-members of the Royal Irish Constabulary, some of them the notorious 'Black and Tan' auxiliaries, redundant since Ireland's partition. Plumer disbanded this unit, transferring 200 of its officers and constables to the Palestine Police, a force previously composed of Arabs and of Jews, with only a handful of British senior officers and specialists, so raising its strength to 2000. The third armed body was the Palestine Gendarmerie, also manned by both Arabs and Jews, and also 2000 strong. This force Plumer disbanded as well, but from its ashes rose the Transjordan Frontier Force, a splendidly uniformed and mounted regiment, its ranks representing every Middle Eastern race, Jews included, as well as Germans, Greeks and Jugo-Slavs, its tasks to guard the northern frontiers of both Palestine and Transjordan against Wahabi raids.

Yet another body that felt the edge of Plumer's axe was the colourful Arab Legion, Transjordan's own army, but funded largely from the British Treasury. To help set up the Transjordan Frontier Force, the Arab Legion was cut by some 600 men, so reducing it from an effective little military body to a 900-strong gendarmerie, lacking artillery, signals and machine guns. It was a mistaken decision. Plumer may have been putting his faith in a reliable mercenary force, British-officered, as opposed to the Bedouin Arab Legion, whose allegiance was to the Emir Abdullah, but this cut in his army displeased not only the Emir but most of his subjects as well.* What is more, like the Transjordan Frontier Force, horsed for the main part, never proved especially capable of intercepting the camel-riding raiders. Nevertheless, Abdullah became another of Plumer's admirers, describing him in his autobiography as 'a noble, frank and distinguished man; and very well liked in Palestine . . . and he assisted me within the compass of the policy laid down for his guidance'.[37] Plumer was to be largely responsible for the success of the protracted negotiations which culminated in 1928 with his setting his signature to a treaty with the Emir in which his position as High Commissioner was ratified, the United Kingdom recognizing the Emir's sovereignty provided that some progress was made towards democracy. With that bitter enemy of the Hashemites, Ibn Sa'ud of Hejaz and shortly the founder of Saudi Arabia, as a neighbour, it was a settlement that the independent Abdullah was very happy to accept.

In making these quite drastic cuts among the locally enlisted armed forces, Plumer had informed the British Government just what reinforcements would be needed from outside at the first sign of any serious internal trouble;[38] on his behalf Symes had also tentatively and informally sounded out both Jewish and Arab opinion in Palestine, pointing out that only by making such savings could the money be found for constructive development. Both sides were cooperative. The Arab leaders gave Symes their assurances that their intentions were peaceful, and the Jews expressed their willingness to support a programme of reforms which were designed to help the Arabs, rather than themselves.[39] During Plumer's time in office, the officials could even persuade the two sides to meet and discuss their differences, something that became increasingly rare after he had departed.†

This willingness to seek some sort of *modus vivendi* did not prevent the Jews from ensuring that they could look after themselves if the need arose. At the height of the French war against the Druse, the Jewish Agency proposed that a Jewish militia should be raised to protect their settlements, an idea that Plumer rejected out of hand, replying that it

---

*Glubb Pasha, who later commanded a much enlarged Arab Legion with such distinction for many years, decided that Plumer made his cut as a consequence of his inspection of an Arab Legion guard-of-honour during that first visit to the Emir – a guard that looked fine when standing to attention, but which collapsed in a shambles on being dismissed.[36] It is an unlikely explanation. Plumer, with his wide experience of units far more irregular than these exotically garbed Bedouin, was not the man to make snap decisions upon slender evidence.

†The last such meeting was held between Ben-Gurion and the Mufti of Jerusalem on the eve of the 1929 troubles.[41]

would do an infinite amount of harm.[40] Rifles and ammunition had been issued to some of the outlying *kibbutzim* after the 1922 troubles, to be kept in sealed containers and opened only on the authority of the head of the colony concerned, who was to be held responsible for the security of the weapons. During 1924, the Government had arranged for the return of many of them, a process that Plumer completed.[42] But, determined not to be left defenceless, thereafter the Jews resorted to illegal means to protect themselves, a process that culminated in the emergence of one of the world's most efficient armies.

The regular forces available to support these local units consisted of no more than a single squadron of the Royal Air Force and a couple of squadrons of its armoured cars, the last Army battalion having left the country at the time Plumer arrived. In the immediate post-war years exaggerated claims had been made about the ability of this new arm to keep the peace in colonial territories, the theory being that recalcitrant tribesmen could be bombed and machine-gunned into submission from the air, the airfields themselves being protected by locally raised levies, supported by a few armoured cars. As a consequence the responsibility for the security of the mandated and colonial territories of the Middle East had been handed over from the Army to the Air Ministry, and the Army units had been withdrawn. Between Egypt and India there was no longer a single infantry battalion; reinforcements for Palestine had to be summoned from Egypt, if the need were to arise, a three-day journey away. It says something of the parlous state to which the country's defences had been reduced that when Plumer required a gun to signal the two-minute silence on Armistice Day, the Mufti had to be asked for the loan of the antique weapon used for marking the start and end of the Ramadan fast. Plumer commented that the best indication of the peacefulness of Palestine was this borrowing of a cannon from an ecclesiastical dignitary.[43]

* * *

It was a little time before either the Jews or the Arabs quite appreciated the diplomatic skills of their new High Commissioner. Their subtly devious politicians were very ready to trap this seemingly simple soldier into unguarded statements. When Rothenberg, visiting Jerusalem from New York soon after Plumer arrived, tried to draw him out on the subject of his policy for Palestine, Plumer replied, 'I have no personal policy but am here to carry out the policy of his Majesty's Government. You know what that policy is. If I were not in sympathy with the policy, I would not have accepted the appointment. On the other hand, if I do not carry out the policy properly, I will expect H.M.G. to remove me from my appointment. That is all I have to say.'[44] His daughter, Eleanor, related another incident that occurred very shortly after this meeting. On attending a Jewish sports meeting in Tel Aviv, they were presented with Zionist badges. Asked by his daughter what should be done with them, Plumer muttered through his conveniently luxurious moustache, 'Put it on and take it off outside'. Then, when the meeting ended, everyone stood for 'God Save the King', but as the party relaxed after the final bars, the band broke into Hatikvah, the Zionist anthem. Straightaway Plumer again removed his hat and motioned his group to attention. 'What is being played?' whispered Eleanor. 'I don't know,' replied her father, 'but we'll find out later.' The following day an Arab delegation called upon him to protest that he should have paid tribute to their enemies in such a way. Plumer pointed out that for a guest to have done otherwise would have been a gross breach of good manners. 'What would you have done in the circumstances?' he enquired. Confused as much by the social conundrum as by the suggestion that they could have attended a Jewish function, the Arabs hedged. Plumer, however, pressed his advantage, insisting upon a reply, so reducing them to silence. It was fortunate that they knew nothing about the Zionist badges.[45] The Arab leaders did, however, seize the opportunity of condemning Samuel's regime in no uncertain terms, to which Plumer bluntly rejoindered that he expected to follow in his predecessor's footsteps and that his administration would concentrate upon economic improvements and agricultural developments.[46]

In treading his delicate path between the two races, Samuel had committed few errors, but one was his appointment of Haj Amin El Husseini to succeed his half-brother as Grand Mufti of Jerusalem. A dignified and outwardly sincere man of great personal charm, the new Mufti managed to convey the impression that he was moderate in his views despite his determination to keep Palestine as a Moslem country. It was several years before the British fully appreciated his hatred for them and his addiction to violence.* He was soon to be involved in another attempt to challenge Plumer's authority. It had been decided that, in December, 1925, the King's Colour of the 40th Battalion of the Royal Fusiliers, one of the three Jewish battalions of that regiment, raised for the defence of Palestine during the war, should be brought out from England and hung in the Churvah Synagogue in the Old City, after being escorted through the Jewish quarter to its last resting place. Thereupon the Mufti, at the

---

*Fleeing from Palestine during the disturbance just before the Second World War, the Mufti found refuge in Berlin, where he is said to have been 'a keen and effective coadjutor' of Hitler's 'Final Solution' for the Jews. When he fell into French hands at the end of the war, his captors were suspected of allowing him to escape and return to the Middle East.[48]

head of another delegation, waited upon the High Commissioner and demanded that the parade be cancelled because of the danger that it might excite the Arab population of the city. When Plumer refused, the Mufti made the error of disclaiming responsibility for any violence that might occur. Plumer's reply was to the point: he alone was responsible for law and order, and he would be liable for any violence that might occur. There was none.[47] Another time, when some Moslems threw stones as the foundation stone for a new Bible Society building was being laid, Plumer summoned the Mufti to Government House and reprimanded him for the 'insult that had been shown to the Christian faith. When the Mufti disclaimed responsibility, Plumer merely told him that he would be replaced if the same thing were to reoccur, brushing aside the Mufti's protests that it was impossible for him to do so.[49]

In what Arnold Toynbee describes in a preface as a 'non-polemical and factual book supporting the Arab cause', Plumer was depicted as a person of such formidable character that order was maintained almost by the force of his personality.[50] With memories of four centuries of Turkish sloth, oppression and neglect still very much alive, a soldier-ruler of Plumer's character and reputation appealed to many Arabs, while many of the less extreme Jewish leaders developed a personal liking for this outgoing man, who was seen to be both fair and impartial. Only at Government House would the leaders of the three religious communities meet on a social footing. Such an occasion was a reception, attended by both the Grand Mufti and the Patriarch, at which the Tel Aviv Opera Company sang in Hebrew. Helen Bentwich described this rather bizarre occasion, adding that 'Lord Plumer remains completely detached from local politics and national prejudices. Everyone respects him, and those who know him well soon love him.'[51] She also provided another glimpse of Plumer's sentiments in her description of a dinner party where one of the guests was an old warrior who had won the V.C. in the Sudan forty-four years earlier, who continually lamented 'the good old days'. 'Good old days,' Plumer protested, 'Not a bit of it. Slow old days, I call 'em. Give me these days any time.'[52]

Eleanor Plumer stated that it was some time before Weizmann dropped his suspicion that Plumer was an enemy of Zionism,[53] but neither Weizmann's published correspondence nor his autobiography reveal any such misgivings. What is certain is that Plumer developed and retained a sound and friendly relationship with the three members of the Palestine Executive of the Jewish Council, Harry Sacher, also a man of British birth and upbringing, Frederick Kisch and the American, Henrietta Szold.[54] Founder of *Hadassah*, the Zionist Health Organization, Miss Szold won his support for the social measures she was initiating in Palestine.

Her biographer, Joan Dash, was to comment that she and Plumer were exactly the same age, both were formed by the humane and high-minded liberalism of the nineteenth century, and both were religious but not given to religiosity. Her appeal for increased support for education, Arab as well as Jewish, produced from Plumer's administration a substantial sum of money. It was but one of the projects they worked on together with a sense of mutual appreciation.[55]

Another British Jew, the young Wellesley (or Pinchas, as he was known in Israel) Aron, a Cambridge graduate and a keen cricketer, had been despatched to Palestine by Weizmann in 1926 to work for the Jewish Agency. Sixty years later his memories of meeting Plumer were still vivid. At a Boy Scout Jamboree, to which Wellesley had escorted a party of boys, Plumer summoned him for a chat. 'If you can do anything to bring together the youth of the two peoples of this country,' Plumer confided to him, 'there is no greater challenge and no better purpose to which you could apply yourself. The peaceful evolution of this country depends on mutual understanding. Both you, the Jews, and they, the Arabs, have no greater need.' Aron found it hard to conceal his surprise. His friends had criticized the High Commissioner as a man in his dotage with the limitations to be expected in a soldier. Instead he had met an observant and sensitive individual (to use his own words) who possessed a deep understanding of the country's problems and needs.[56] After a lifetime of distinguished service to his country, Wellesley Aron became President of *Ne've Shalom* – the Oasis of Peace – , a community established in the grounds of the Trappist monastery at Latrun, where Jews and Arabs live together in friendship, and where teenagers of the two races meet on short courses to gain an inkling of that 'mutual understanding' deemed by Plumer to be vital. There a start had been made in trying to eradicate deep-rooted and apparently indestructible prejudice.

* * *

Within the limitations of the little money available, in a number of ways, some great and some small, Plumer did all he could to improve life for his people. His was paternalism of the highest order. Assisted by Symes, his very able Chief Secretary, who left to become Governor of Aden just before his tour ended, Plumer's legislative and administrative reforms were remembered as having been planned like a military campaign. Instructions to his staff had the hallmark of the methods he had used at Messines.[57] Symes recalled how his youthful zest inspired enthusiasm in others, and that, if he did make a mistake, he would acknowledge it with a grin. When asking a question, he listened attentively to the reply, not always the habit of men in such positions, as Symes shrewdly observed. Relating how Plumer thought long and hard before reaching a decision, his Colonial Secretary remembered how, before he attended a meeting of the Permanent Mandates Commission, he gave Plumer a memorandum to read as he wished to be clear on his master's general policy on the subject under discussion: two months later the papers were returned, merely with instructions to go ahead on the lines indicated.[58] Like Harington, Symes always knew just where he stood with Plumer.

One of the reforms concerned the local municipalities. Previously their members had been nominated by Government, but Plumer introduced elections with separate voting rolls for Moslems, Jews and Christians, the three communities being given the power to tax their members for common purposes, including education, a concession that was to be taken advantage of only by the Jews. So as to develop a Palestinian identity, a national currency and national postage stamps were introduced, as well as Palestinian citizenship, the holders of which obtained the status and benefits of British protected persons.

Mention has been made of the Polish economic crisis. The resultant decline both in remittances to established settlers and in the numbers of new immigrants hit especially hard the building of houses, then Palestine's main industry. With a programme of public works that included road improvements, land reclamation and a new harbour at Jaffa, Plumer did all he could to lessen the consequent unemployment; it was a successful Keynesian solution for the economic depression, and one that benefited Arab as well as Jew. An opportunity to help Arab agriculture was taken in 1927, when Plumer arranged to move thousands of animals from the drought-stricken areas around Gaza and Beersheba to the much less seriously affected north.[59]

Plumer tried and failed to deal with one serious cause of inter-racial bitterness. A family of absentee Arab landowners had, in 1920, sold an area of some 50,000 acres to a Zionist organization, and the Arab tenant farmers were evicted to make room for the Jews. The consequences were predictable. A government ordinance framed to avoid further and similar scandals failed to accomplish anything, largely because of the complexity of land-tenure and the guile of the individuals operating it. In a further attempt at simplification, Plumer put his officials to work to produce a basis for a fresh ordinance, but it too failed to produce a solution to the problem. Nor did a succession of similar measures which appeared in the years after his departure and which did little more than anger the Jews without helping the Arabs. It was yet another insoluble problem.

An even more serious catastrophe than the drought hit Palestine in 1927. On 11 July the country was shaken by an earthquake, the loss of life and damage being increased by a second and more serious shock which occurred two minutes after the first, just as people who had rushed out of their houses at the first were returning to ascertain their losses. Public buildings, as well as dwelling houses, were damaged, including the Basilica of the Holy Sepulchre, which was to remain shored up for the next two generations.

At the time of this disaster the Plumers were on leave at home, where, on 23 July, he had unveiled the Menin Gate Memorial, that monument to those who had died around Ypres and who had no known grave; at the same time he had laid the foundation stone for St George's Chapel, the English memorial church that had been planned for Ypres. Six days later Plumer cut short his leave and returned to Jerusalem. As he visited the stricken areas and the refugee camps set up to care for the homeless, he chivvied the officials to speed the relief work.[60] It was while he was touring the country, seeing for himself what damage had been done, that he ran into trouble, the only time his safety was at risk. The Arabs, who tended to live in the more flimsy houses, had suffered the worst, and the administration was blamed for doing too little for them and that too late. Demonstrations against the High Commissioner were planned for his visit to Nablus, and, as his unescorted Vauxhall approached the town, his unarmed driver spotted an old car ahead blocking the road. Swinging the steering wheel to avoid it, the driver ploughed along the bank, encouraged by the calm voice of his passenger telling him to keep going as fast as he could. On reaching Nablus, where the demonstration had begun, two policemen jumped on either side of the running board (younger readers may need an explanation of the term) to shield the High Commissioner. Fortunately, nothing happened. Plumer's habit of travelling unarmed and unescorted was, in the opinion of the police, bordering on the eccentric,[61] but he endeared himself to the members of the force.

So badly damaged by the earthquake was Government House that the Plumers were obliged to move into a wing of a small convent. Cold in winter and hot in summer, the discomforts of their temporary home were said to have contributed to the illnesses from which this elderly couple both suffered during their final year in Palestine.[62] The summer of 1928 was especially hot and the house completely airless, and all the while Plumer was ailing. When the time came for him to go home, his health was so precarious that his doctor insisted on accompanying him on the first stage of his journey as far as Port Said. Helen Bentwich remembered how old and tearful both Lord and Lady Plumer seemed as they shook hands with those who saw them off from Jerusalem.[63] The strain of three strenuous years had out-taxed the strength of a man already elderly when he went to Palestine;[64] by the end of his tour he was old for his years.

The customary tributes to a departing pro-consul had again rung sincere, but there was one unfortunate incident, at a farewell audience for a delegation of the Jewish National Council. An onlooker wrote:

> Unfortunately I had reckoned without the persistence through the ages of the feud between the Pharisees and Sadducees. Rabbi Kook acquitted himself quite honourably – if at excessive length – of the task of delivering the farewell benediction, but Rabbi Jacob Meir found it necessary to exploit the occasion for a demonstration against the Chukath-Hakilloth and the Kneseth Israel. He was personally aggressive and offensive to Lord Plumer in the matter, and when he observed that the official interpreter was tactfully toning down his words, he repeated them in French, adding in conclusion: '*Vous pouvez dire cela, si vous voulez, à sa Majesté*'. Poor Lord Plumer, who had prepared himself for an exchange of farewells, could not understand what it was all about, or how he had erred. It was indeed most painful.[65]

It may or may not have been a coincidence, but in September, 1928, just a month after Plumer's departure, a violent incident occurred at the Wailing Wall, the tall rampart of massive stone blocks, all that remains of Herod's Palace, the sacred spot where Jews throughout the ages had lamented its destruction. The trouble was contained, but the next year the tenuous peace collapsed with Arabs attacking Jewish settlements and twice massacring isolated communities. There was no way the small and largely partisan police force could cope with such widespread bloodshed: Arab constables refused to fire upon their co-religionists, and the authorities were reluctant to use Jewish members of the force for fear of exacerbating the situation. British troops had to be brought into the country to restore order, and Plumer was blamed for allowing the security forces to be so reduced that lives were lost in large numbers before reinforcements could arrive. In 1926 the Ninth Session of the Permanent Mandates Commission had expressed disquiet at the reductions to which Plumer had consented, and the Shaw Commmission which carried out the post-mortem on the affair criticized the administration directly for the rundown.[66]

Plumer erred on the side of optimism. Possibly he failed quite to comprehend the strength of the underlying racial bitterness and the emptiness of promises made by individuals such as the Grand Mufti. Christopher Sykes suggested that he was so modest a man that he may have underestimated his own personal influence on the two communities and the extent to which he had himself been responsible for the peaceful interregnum.[67] The Jews with whom he habitually dealt, men such as Weizmann and Kisch and women such as Szold, were in no way representative of the extreme face of Zionism, glimpsed at that final meeting with representatives of the Jewish National Council, while the Arabs, although unremitting in their demand for the revocation of the Balfour Declaration and an end to Jewish immigration, were outwardly peaceful and usually reasonable in manner. In such circumstances it was possible to believe that things were getting better, and that reasonable men could discover some peaceful solution to the country's problems. The chimera was not to disappear in the future.

Under the rule of this old soldier, Palestine had, however, enjoyed three years of steady consolidation and progress, especially in commerce, industry and agriculture. He was to be long remembered, in Transjordan as well as in Palestine, with affection and gratitude. He was always fair, but he could not always be even-handed. The policy of His Majesty's Government was to implement the Balfour Declaration within the terms of the Mandate, and Plumer was obliged to carry out his Governments's policy. The British soldier and diplomat, Richard Meinertzhagen, himself a Jew and not an impartial one, wrote, 'Opposition to Zionism has come from men of small calibre, the second-rates. Sympathy and encouragement has come from the big men, Roosevelt, Truman, Lloyd George, Churchill, Plumer.'[68] The insuperable problem for a just man such as Plumer was to reconcile Zionism with the rights of the Arabs whom the Jews were attempting to displace.

Just fifty years after Plumer's death, *The Spectator* carried an article, *Pilate's Prisoner*, the contributor John Hills. Some words from it bear repeating:

A little old man, he had once commanded an army; now he had only his unarmed soldier-servant and such policemen as he might see fit to summon. During his proconsulship nothing happened, nothing we find worth recording in our history books. We do not remember his name in our churches, and in a few years it will be quite forgotten. But if we prize peace more than war, and concord more than bloodshed, then let us praise God for that little man Plumer, Viscount of Messines and of Bilton in Yorkshire, during whose three years governorship Jews and Arabs performed in peace their lawful occupations. For it was he who gave them peace.[69]

His name is forgotten in his own country, but in Ypres, in Malta and in Jerusalem, streets or squares still bear his name.

317

14 The Last Years

Plumer's health gained some benefit from the sea voyage home, but when King George V received him upon relinquishing his appointment as High Commissioner, the now Sir Clive Wigram, who had succeeded Stamfordham as Private Secretary, remarked that he looked far from fit.[1] A fortnight of fresh Buxton air seemed to do him a lot of good, but he needed a much longer rest than that. However, his simple philosophy was that a man should work for his country so long as he was able to do so. Many bodies had awaited his patronage, or had already obtained it, among them Toc H, in which he had been a prime mover ever since its inception at Poperinghe, near his Second Army Headquarters; others which were to benefit from his leadership and advice were the Soldiers' Daughters' Home at Hampstead, the Ypres Society, the Friends of St George's Chapel at Ypres, the Society of Yorkshiremen in London and the Yorkshire Society, the Veteran's Association and Sir Frederick Milner's Fund for Village Settlement. The task that gave him the greatest satisfaction – and pleasure – was the Presidency of the M.C.C.; it also provided him with the excuse to spend most of the summer of 1929 at Lords.

His work in Palestine had been rewarded with a step in the peerage, gazetted in the 1929 Birthday Honours List, and it was as Viscount Plumer that he was first heard in the Upper House. His speeches were rare but pertinent; the first in April, 1930. Drawing upon his experiences in Malta and Palestine, Plumer protested forcibly against Lord Trenchard's proposals that internal security duties in certain parts of the Empire should be handed over to the Royal Air Force. He had learned through personal experience that this new service was unsuitable both in character and in nature for such a role; to bomb unruly subjects from the air, he made it clear, with the risk of casualties among women and children, real or manufactured for propaganda purposes, was hardly likely to contribute towards the pacification of troubled areas, but would instead intensify hatred and resentment.[2] The following week he spoke both lucidly and persuasively upon the need to retain the death penalty for offences committed in the face of the enemy, pointing out that the alternative of imprisonment could provide the safety for which a deserter often sought.[3] He spoke once more, in May of the following year, this time in support of Trenchard, who had moved that control should be unified over British policy in the Middle East, an area which both men recognized as being vitally important in the future, but which was handled by six different departments of the Home Government and the Government of India as well.[4]

By the time Plumer made this third speech his health had collapsed irretrievably. Photographs of him at Foch's funeral in 1929 show the face of a haggard old man, all the chubbiness gone, and in the following year he was obliged to spend much of the winter in Mallorca.[5] He had been Colonel of the York and Lancaster Regiment since 1917, and he had always attended, among the Regiment's other functions, the dinner of the London Branch of its Old Comrade's Association; now the task was beyond him, and his wife went in his place. On his return from Palestine he had also been appointed Honorary Colonel of the Inns of Court Regiment, in whose affairs he became deeply involved until illness ended it all.[6] So far had his condition deteriorated by the opening months of 1931 that he was obliged to dictate all his correspondence to his wife: one received by Kisch was signed with a shaky hand, but its recipient noted that it was still 'characteristically hopeful for the future'.[7]

Cheerful though he may have appeared to those of his old friends who visited or corresponded with him, he was deeply troubled about his children. To his unhappy relationship with his son, Thomas, was added anxiety about his daughter Marjorie Brooke (known as Madge in the family), whose mental condition was a matter for increasing concern.[8] So far as is known, Plumer never saw Thomas again after he sailed for Malta. His will reflects the various stages of his disillusionment with his heir. Written in March 1920, his son did not benefit from its provisions, what might have been his share in the estate being bequeathed to his son's wife. Only articles presented by public bodies and the treasured portrait of his great-grandfather by Sir Thomas Lawrence were left to Thomas and his heirs, although they were to be retained by his widow during her lifetime. However, codicils written in 1921 and 1929 passed the portrait to his eldest surviving daughter and his Field-Marshal's baton and his decorations to his Regiment.[9] For some years before he died, Plumer never mentioned Thomas's name to Harington, nor did his wife meet her only son again until her husband's funeral, and, even then, her family had to exercise great pressure upon her to agree to her attending. Members of the family also attempted to prevail upon her to arrange for Thomas to see his father just before he died, but to no avail. It was altogether a wretched business, made worse by her placing the blame for her attitude upon her dead husband, an accusation hard to accept.[10]

When, after Plumer's death, Eton decided to erect a memorial to him, Tom Plumer, himself an Old Etonian, was neither asked to subscribe to it nor to attend the unveiling ceremony. As a result, one of the Public Trustees responsible for administering the late Field-Marshal's government grant appealed personally to Sir Clive Wigram, to warn him what was happening and to ask for his help in countering what he described as 'the machinations' of Lady Plumer. Tom Plumer, he wrote to Wigram, was living quietly, doing his best to justify the position to which he had been called by his father's death, and devoting himself to working for the alleviation of distress among the unemployed in Barnet where he lived.[11] In turn Wigram approached Harington,[12] who told him how 'difficult to handle' the old lady was, but promised that he would see her.[13] The first appeal failed, but Harington kept up the pressure, and some little time later he was able to tell Wigram that the matter had been brought to a satisfactory conclusion; Lady Plumer had asked her son to tea on his birthday, an invitation described by Tom to Harington as 'the best birthday present' he had ever received. The King, Harington thought, might be interested.[14]

It is hard to reconcile this behaviour towards his son with a man who, in all else, was so kind and generous hearted. His stern and domineering wife, who could when she wished turn such a pleasantly friendly face to the outside world, in family matters would seem to have exercised a quite extraordinary influence upon a husband who may have been just too devoted to her.

* * *

The last time Plumer's close friend Bishop Gwynne, who had been his senior Chaplain in France, saw his old commander to speak to was during the summer of 1931, when he was just capable of rising from his chair and moving to the luncheon table. He had been as cheerful and full of fun as ever. 'The doctor tells me,' he apprised the Bishop, 'that I am eighty-six, although I am only seventy-six. That comes, he says, from not resting after the War. How could I?' His condition was to worsen after an operation in February, 1932, but his brain remained active until the end.[15] During his last weeks 'Tubby' Clayton, the founder of Toc H, was to visit him regularly for a short chat and to say a simple prayer.[16] As then happened, *The Times* charted almost daily on its centre page his sad and slow deterioration in terms such as 'not quite so well' or 'weakening'.

The end came on 16 July, 1932, at 22 Ennismore Gardens. The many fine provincial newspapers then existing, as well as the national dailies and the Sundays, filled their columns with tributes to him, in the main accurate, but all balanced and thoughtful. It was almost fourteen years since the war had ended. Although historians, novelists, poets and politicians had by then done much to destroy the reputations of those who had directed their country's armies during those cruel and bloody years, a keen interest in and affection for this elderly Field-Marshal still permeated the country. Not all his obituaries were mere panegyrics. Mentioned often were his quiet resolution, his sympathetic understanding and consideration for others, the depth of his religious feeling, his placid and methodical methods, his loyalty to others and his popularity. But there was little attempt to saddle him with virtues he did not possess. 'Sound rather than brilliant,' was the verdict of The Times, 'essentially a safe commander,' one whose career, both as soldier and administrator, had been marked by quiet, regular progress, rather than spasmodic and brilliant actions.[17]

Five days later, Plumer was buried in Westminster Abbey. There he had worshipped regularly and he knew all the vergers by their names. It was a signal honour, the first military internment in the Abbey for fifty years. His resting place was the Warrior's Chapel, just a few yards from the simple tomb of the Unknown Warrior; it had been inaugurated by the Prince of Wales only the month before, and it was to be completed as a memorial to Plumer. The ceremonial was the finest the country could stage. The previous night he had lain in state at the Guards Chapel, next to Wellington Barracks, his coffin guarded by Territorials of the Inns of Court and covered with the faded Union Jack that had been used at Haig's funeral four years earlier, an occasion that had evoked the same manifestations of genuine sorrow that were now being experienced. Under a leaden sky, presaging the intensely hot and humid day that was to follow, the coffin was placed on a gun carriage which was drawn by six horses along Birdcage Walk and around Parliament Square to its final resting place. Behind was led a charger, his empty boots reversed in the stirrups, and this was followed by Harington and three other of his officers carrying on velvet cushions his vast display of British and foreign orders and decorations. Among the pall-bearers marching on either side were Baden Powell and Cavan, Trenchard and Robertson, Allenby and Jacob, elderly men wilting in the heat in plumed hats and full dress uniforms. Behind walked a long and glittering procession of British and foreign service chiefs, drably dressed politicians from many countries, military attachés and bemedalled veterans from the British legion, scarlet-coated Chelsea pensioners and khaki-clad officers who had served under him, and the Boy Scouts in whom he had taken such a close interest. Either lining the route or part of the procession were the Life Guards, the

King's Dragoon Guards, the Inns of Court Regiment, six battalions of Foot Guards and their massed bands together with detachments from his beloved York and Lancasters, whose two regular battalions were absent from England, one in Delhi and the other in Londonderry. Outside the Abbey's gate waited the King's representative, his friend, the eighty-two year old Duke of Connaught, Queen Victoria's son, under whom Plumer had served at Aldershot and first met in Aden fifty years before.

Observers commented that men outnumbered women by ten to one in the great multitude that came to pay their respects to their departed war leader. Few wore medals, some were smartly dressed, some pathetically shabbily. They came from all classes. Most were near middle-age. They were ex-servicemen in their countless numbers who had turned out to say goodbye to a man whom few had met and many never even seen, a general of the First World War, supposedly one of those who had so carelessly squandered the lives of their friends and comrades fourteen years and more before.

THE END

Notes

Glossary (pp xiii-xiv)

1. When merely the author and title, or the author alone, appears in the source notes, full details can be found in the bibliography.
2. 'OH' refers to the British Official History unless otherwise stated.
3. 'Harington' alone in the source notes refers to that writer's *Plumer of Messines*.

Preface (pp 1-5)

1. Edmonds Papers, II/1/63A, Harington to Edmonds, 21 November, 34.
2. ibid.
3. Blake, 13; Travers, 25-6, quoting letters from Lady Haig to Edmonds, 10 February and 3 November, 28.
4. Dr David French, *'Official but not History' Sir James Edmonds and the Official History of the Great War*, RUSI Journal, March, 1986.
5. Edmonds Papers, I/2B35a, Edmonds to Brigadier Barclay, 7 April, 50.

Chapter 1, Regimental Officer (pp 7-28)

1. As Emery, *Marching over Africa*, 142, points out, the use of the term 'fuzzy-wuzzy' in writing had not been traced back earlier than 1890. They were the Beja, the hill tribesmen of the Suakin area, whose frizzed hair stuck up in every direction, made famous in Kipling's lines
   An' 'ere's to you, Fuzzy-Wuzzy, with your 'ayrick 'ead of 'air –
   You big black bounding beggar – for you broke a British square!
2. Broughton, 87.
3. Harington 5.
4. D.N.B. entries for Sir Thomas Plumer and the first Viscount Plumer; memorials in St. Helen's Church, Sheriff Hutton, North Yorkshire; memorials in St. Lawrence Whitchurch, Little Stanmore, Middlesex; Plaques in St. Helen's Church, Bilton-in-Ainsty, North Yorkshire; *Some Historical Notes on the Parish and Parish Church of St. Helen's Church, Bilton-in-Ainsty and Bickerton*, 1973; family information; Yorkshire directories. The D.N.B. entry for Sir Thomas incorrectly describes him as the eldest son.

323

5. Winnie Myers, *Canons*, 1956. Unpublished ms.
6. 1881 census.
7. D.N.B.
8. Repington, *Vestigia*, 22-32.
9. Harington, 308.
10. *Eton College Chronicle*.
11. Repington, *First World War*, ii, 525.
12. Harington, 2-3.
13. ibid, 3.
14. WO 76, Record of Service.
15. Harington, 3.
16. *Sheffield Daily Telegraph*, 18 March, 84. Emery, 135, was my source for this quotation.
17. Harington, 4.
18. The 65th were part of the 2nd Brigade square. The 1st Brigade was commanded by that controversial soldier, the then Brigadier General Sir Redvers Buller, VC.
19. Harington, 5.
20. Bond 138-9; 151.
21. Repington, *Vestigia*. 77.
22. Harington, 6.
23. *Roll of the Staff College, 1858-1887*.
24. op. cit.
25. op. cit. xxxv, 1891, 1077.
26. Harington, 7.
27. The story of Parkes's courtship at Canons of the beautiful Fanny Plumer and his subsequent adventures with Loch in China is contained in Stanley Lane-Poole, *The Life of Sir Harry Parkes*, i, Macmillan, 1894.
28. Harington, 8.
29. ibid, 9.
30. ibid, 9-10.
31. Index to War Office personal file.
32. Harington, 12.
33. ibid.
34. ibid.
35. ibid, 13.
36. ibid, 13.
37. ibid, 13-15.
38. Hillcourt and Baden-Powell, 122.
39. Harington, 15.
40. ibid, 15-16.
41. ibid, 19-20.
42. ibid, 18.

Chapter 2, The Matabele Rebellion (pp 29-45)

1. F.W. Sykes, 58.

2. ibid, 72.
3. Ranger, 53, quoting Milner to Selbourne 2 June, 97. *The Milner Papers* ed. C. Headlam, i, 105-8.
4. Baden-Powell, 25.
5. F.W. Sykes, 90.
6. Plumer, 97.
7. F.W. Sykes, 97-8.
8. ibid, 117-8.
9. ibid, 98-9.
10. Major Arthur Glyn Leonard, *How We made Rhodesia*, Kegan Paul 1896, 272.
11. Plumer, 249.
12. ibid, 128.
13. F.W. Sykes, 175.
14. ibid, 173.
15. Ranger, 237, quoting Carrington to Rosemead, 11 September, 96, CO CP 520, 543.
16. ibid, 244-5.
17. Harington, 24.
18. Plumer, 194.
19. McDonald, 253-7.
20. Plumer, 203-4.
21. Harington, 26-7. Plumer reproduced neither this letter nor the following one in his book.
22. Ibid, 25.
23. Plumer, 195-6.
24. WO 32/7840. Report by Carrington, *Operations in Rhodesia*, 1897.
25. ibid, Earl Grey to High Commissioner, 28 July, 97.

Chapter 3, The Boer War (pp 55-85)

1. WO 32/7852, Memo of 17 July, 89.
2. Harington, 32-3.
3. Creswicke, iii, 129.
4. Plumer Papers. Letter from Buller.
5. Harington, 33.
6. *Cambridge History of Africa*, vi, 681.
7. OH, iii, 141.
8. WO 32/7950, Report by Plumer of 17 January, 00.
9. WO 108/185, 1.
10. WO 6411/1,/6.
11. WO 32/7852, Memo of 1 July 99.
12. ibid.
13. *Royal Commission on the South African War*, ii, 420.
14. ibid, 423-4; *Milner Papers*, ed. C. Headlam i, 521.
15. *Times History*, iv, 199.
16. WO 32/7862, Telegram Base Commandant Frontier Force to C-in-C, SA, 30 October, 89.

17. Creswicke, iii, 27-9.
18. ibid.
19. ibid.
20. OH, iii, 393.
21. Hickman, 167.
22. OH, iii, 143.
23. ibid, 145 and Appx 5.
24. WO 108/185, 5.
25. ibid, 15.
26. In his book de Montmorency condemns himself out of his own mouth.
27. WO 108/185/24.
28. ibid, 15.
29. ibid.
30. WO 105/7.
31. OH, iii, 202.
32. Harington, 35.
33. Harington, 35-6.
34. *Times History*, iv, 183-4.
35. ibid, 208.
36. WO 106/16 T15.
37. WO 108/185 39.
38. ibid, 48.
39. In time both Botha and Smuts were to become honoured and loyal soldier-statesmen of the British Empire. De Wet, supported by de la Rey, led a rebellion against the British in 1914 which Botha and Smuts crushed.
40. Arnold-Forster, 148.
41. *Royal Commission on the South African War*, ii, Q.8033-9.
42. op cit, v, 69.
43. OH, iv, Appx 17.
44. Harington, 47.
45. Green, 62.
46. Harington, 45; various newspaper obituaries.
47. Harington, 45-6.
48. T.E. Lawrence, *Seven Pillars of Wisdom*, Cape, 1935, 157.
49. Smuts, 68.
50. OH, iii, 473.
51. WO 108/185, 52.
52. De Wet, 491-2.
53. 'Bushmen' distinguished those units that were raised for service in South Africa, as opposed to Colonial Regular or Volunteer units of the permanent cadre.
54. OH, iii, 448-54; *Times History*, v, 61-4.
55. Harington, 48-9.
56. Creswicke, iv, 211.
57. De Wet, 270.
58. ibid, 275.

59. Green, 62.
60. *Tiger and Rose*, November, 01. A note states that the editor believed that the lines were originally published in the *Morning Post*.
61. Abbott, 220.
62. op cit, v, 265.
63. PRO 30/57/22.
64. ibid.
65. PRO 30/57/29.
66. op cit, v, 293-4.
67. Harington, 49-50.

Chapter 4, General Officer (pp 86-105)

1. Harington, 50-1.
2. Plumer Papers.
3. ibid.
4. Harington, 53.
5. op. cit, 15 November, 02.
6. Kitchener Papers, PRO 37/57/20/61.
7. Harington, 52.
8. ibid, 51.
9. Robertson, *From Private to Field Marshal*, 95.
10. *Royal Commission on the War in South Africa*, iii, 334-342.
11. RA W38/83.
12. Harington, 55.
13. Roberts Papers, NAM 7101. 23. 46. 121.
14. Harington, 55-6.
15. Repington, *Vestigia*, 358.
16. Admiral of the Fleet Lord Fisher, *Memories*, Hodder & Stoughton, 1919, 172.
17. *Spectator*, 13 February, 04, 293.
18. WO 163/9 and 10.
19. RA W18/17 and 30/37; W19/16 and 33,
20. Bond, 200-01.
21. *Spectator*, 24 December, 04.
22. Harington, 61.
23. ibid, 60.
24. op cit.
25. Sommer, 167.
26. Harington, 268.
27. ibid, 57-62.
28. A reference in *The Times* of 18 July, '32 to a difference of opinion between Plumer and Arnold-Forster produced an indignant rebuttal from the latter's widow five days later. At the time of his death, there were several references to his having 'resigned' as QMG.
29. Arnold-Forster Papers. BL Add Ms 50343, Diary 17 December, 05.

30. Marker Papers. BL Add Ms 52277, Repington to Markham, 15 December, 05.
31. Arnold-Forster Papers. BL Ass Ms 50343, Diary 15 December, 05.
32. ibid, 16 December, 05.
33. Haldane Papers, Ms 5874, Letter to mother, 15 December, 05.
34. Edmonds Papers, H/1/163A, Harington to Edmonds, 21 November, 34.
35. Harington, 29.
36. Gooch, 126.
37. Arnold-Forster Papers. BL Add Ms 50343, Knowles to Arnold-Forster, 1 December, 05.
38. Amery, *My Political Life*, i, 209.
39. Arnold-Forster Papers. BL Add Ms, 50343, Knowles to Arnold-Forster, 1 December, 05.
40. Harington, 62.
41. ibid, 189-90.
42. Family information.
43. op cit., All Saints, Ennismore Gardens, June, 1941.
44. Family information.
45. Robertson, *From Private to Field Marshal,* 169.
46. Harington, 66.
47. ibid, 66-7.
48. Osbert Sitwell, *Great Morning,* Macmillan, 1949, 143-4.
49. French, 146.
50. Kitchener Papers, PRO 30/57/49.
51. French, 146.
52. ibid.
53. Kitchener Papers, PRO 30/57/49.
54. Ballard, 152.
55. ibid, 127-8.
56. Roberts Papers. NAM 7101.23.188.

Chapter 5, Second Ypres (pp 106-129)

1. Ballard, 478.
2. Terraine, *General Jack's Diary,* 155, makes this point.
3. WO 158/200, Robertson to Smith-Dorrien, 27 February 15.
4. OH, 1915, i, 5.
5. Harington, 71.
6. OH, 1915, i, 5.
7. ibid, 31.
8. ibid, 37-50; 57.
9. ibid, 373.
10. ibid, 163-4.
11. ibid.
12. ibid, 165.
13. ibid, 166.

14. ibid, 177.
15. ibid, 271
16. French, 178.
17. Harington 72. In those unsophisticated days, information on operational matters was often confided in this way to wives – and sometimes to others.
18. OH, 1915, i, 217. Divisions had already set about manufacturing respirators in their rear areas. By 26 April, an experimental laboratory had been set up at GHQ, and over the next three days three academics arrived from the UK to help staff it.
19. Harington, 72.
20. OH, 1915, i, 394.
21. Smith-Dorrien Papers. Smith-Dorrien to Robertson, 23 April, 1915.
22. OH, 1915, i, 233.
23. ibid.
24. ibid, 394.
25. ibid, 234.
26. ibid, 357.
27. ibid, 258.
28. ibid, 400-2.
29. ibid, 402.
30. ibid, 403.
31. ibid.
32. ibid, 405-6.
33. Harington, 72.
34. OH, 1915, i, 278.
35. ibid, 404-5.
36. ibid, 299.
37. ibid.
38. ibid, 288.
39. Binding, 65.
40. Bonham-Carter, 117. For many years this anecdote was thought to be apocryphal, but the author discovered an eye-witness who verified its accuracy.
41. OH, 1915, i, 304.
42. ibid, 321.
43. ibid, 336.
44. French, 205-6.
45. ibid, 206.
46. ibid.
47. OH, 1915, i, 353.
48. Liddell Hart, *History of the World War*, 254.
49. Bond, 307, quoting Edmonds who described Douglas as 'a man with the talents of an orderly-room clerk'.

Chapter 6, Army Commander (pp 130-152)
1. OH, 1915, ii, 393.

2. ibid, 51-2.
3. Beckett and Simpson, 21.
4. OH, 1915, ii, 394.
5. ibid, ix.
6. ibid, 86.
7. ibid, 85.
8. ibid, 98-100.
9. ibid, 102-3.
10. ibid, 104-5.
11. ibid, 4, 106-8.
12. ibid, 108-9.
13. French, 216.
14. Robertson Papers, 1/21/4b.
15. Bridges, 163.
16. Eden, 71.
17. ibid, 75-6.
18. ibid, 124.
19. Ironside, 82.
20. Eden, 125.
21. Harington, ix.
22. ibid, 191, 300; *Tim Harington*, 217.
23. Aylmer Haldane Papers, BL 20246 – 314, 20249 – 51-2.
24. Lt. McK Hughes Diary, 14 December, 16.
25. ibid, 2 February, 17.
26. ibid, 24 April, 16.
27. ibid, 8 August, 16.
28. Terraine, *General Jack's Diary*, 294.
29. ibid, 265.
30. ibid, 280.
31. Cassar, 261-2, quoting letters to Mrs Bennett, 18 and 21 April, 15.
32. Blake, 36-7.
33. Haig Diary, 5 August, 14.
34. ibid, 11 August, 14.
35. ibid, 17 October, 14.
36. ibid, 9 October, 15.
37. Bridges, 138.
38. Haig Diary, Haldane to Haig 4 January, 17.
39. OH, 1916, i, 155-6.
40. ibid, 162-74.
41. Haig Diary, 18 February, 16.
42. Haig Letters, Haig to Lady Haig 17, 18 and 20 February 16.
43. Robertson Papers, I/22/23a and 24a Haig to Robertson, 17 and 18 February 16.
44. ibid, Robertson to Haig, I/22/26 20 February 16.
45. RA GV Q832/116, Haig to King, 9 January 16.
46. Duff Cooper, i, 39-40.
47. Terraine, *Douglas Haig*, 35.

48. ibid, 133.
49. Haig Letters, Haig to Lady Haig 3 March, 16.
50. Haig Diary, 14 January, 16.
51. Liddell Hart Papers, II/1935/58. Note of talk with Edmonds 10 January 35; Charteris, *Earl Haig* 13.
52. OH 1916, i, 177-93.
53. Nicholson, 26-8; Haig Diary, 17 and 28 April 16.
54. Haig Diary, 21 April 16.
55. ibid, 17 March 17.
56. Aylmer Haldane Papers, BL 20249. Diary 20 April and 24 June 16.
57. ibid, 6 April 16.
58. A reading of Aylmer Haldane's diaries will confirm this.
59. Aylmer Haldane Papers, BL 20248. Diary 17 and 18 June 15.
60. OH 1916, i, 231.
61. ibid, 243.
62. ibid, 31.
63. ibid, 32.
64. ibid.
65. ibid, 490-1.
66. ibid, ii, xv.
67. Ludendorff, i, 304.
68. RA GV Q2521/iv/119, Godley to Wigram 1 May 16.
69. Bean, iii, 114.
70. Harington, 234.
71. A.H. Farrar-Hockley, *The Somme*, Pan, 1966, 221.
72. Parrington War Diary, II, 181-2.
73. Repington, *First World War*, i, 271.
74. Bridges, 164.

Chapter 7, Messines, The Preparations (pp 153-176)

1. Harington 76-7; Tim Harington, 41-52; DNB. Like Robertson, Harington was to reach high rank without ever commanding more than a company or squadron.
2. The expression 'chief-of-staff' had no official recognition in the British Army during the First World War, or for the earlier part of its successor. Unofficially the senior operations officer at brigade headquarters and above assumed the role.
3. Gibbs, 46.
4. ibid, 389.
5. Terraine, *Smoke and Fire*, Ch. XIX, provides a different and more objective view of the staff.
6. Gibbs, 47-9; 389-90.
7. Charteris, *At GHQ*, 228.
8. Harington, 79.
9. ibid, 166.

10. ibid, 82.
11. Eden, 137.
12. Gibbs, 390.
13. Pedersen, 157.
14. Interview Rathbone; Harington 165; interview Miss Coombs, who was told by Plumer's factotum, Sergeant Back, that Plumer did not suffer fools gladly.
15. Liddell Hart, *History of the World War*, 418.
16. Terraine, *Smoke and Fire*, 177.
17. Blunden, 225.
18. Parington War Diary II, 177-88.
19. Storey Papers.
20. Maurice Baring, *Flying Corps Headquarters 1914-18*, Buchan & Enright, 1985, 90.
21. W.W. Wadsworth, *War Diary of the 1st West Lancashire Brigade*, Daily Post Printers, Liverpool, 1923, 56.
22. Blunden, 158.
23. OH 1917, i, 534.
24. OH 1917, ii, 64.
25. Terraine, *Road to Passchendaele*, 24-5; *Statistics of the Military Effort of the British Empire*.
26. Haig Diary, 20 December 16.
27. ibid, Haig to Nivelle 6 January 17.
28. Binding 150.
29. Haig Diary, 15 January 17.
30. Ludendorff, ii, 421.
31. OH 1917, ii, 273.
32. ibid, 557-8.
33. ibid, 28.
34. ibid, 12.
35. Haig Diary, Robertson to Haig, 26 April 17.
36. OH 1917, ii, 102.
37. ibid, 3-4.
38. ibid, 7-10.
39. ibid, 406-7.
40. ibid, 13.
41. ibid, 15.
42. ibid, 15-16.
43. Bean, iv, 559.
44. Haig Diary, 1 May 17.
45. Lloyd George, iv, 2121-3.
46. ibid, 2120.
47. ibid, 2150.
48. OH 1917, ii, 22.
49. ibid.
50. ibid, 23.
51. ibid, 24-5.
52. Harington, 84.

53. Haig Diary, 22 May 17.
54. Terraine, *Douglas Haig*, 212.
55. Harington, 99-100.
56. OH 1917, ii, 34-45; Grieve and Newman provide a detailed account of mining operations on the Western Front.
57. OH 1917, ii, 41-2.
58. General Sir Martin Farndale, *History of the Royal Regiment of Artillery: Western Front 1914-18*, Royal Artillery Institute, 1986, 332. I am indebted to this book for much of the information contained in this paragraph.
59. OH 1917, ii, 42-23.
60. ibid, 40.
61. Harington, 79.
62. OH 1917, ii, 35.
63. Blunden, 206-7.
64. Eden, 184-5.

Chapter 8, Messines, The Battle (pp 177-196)

1. Eden, 141.
2. Gladden, 59-61.
3. OH 1917, ii, 54.
4. ibid, 416-7.
5. ibid, 418.
6. ibid, 44-5.
7. ibid, 41-6.
8. ibid, 62.
9. ibid, 66.
10. Coombs, 11.
11. Harington, 103. Like his commander, Harington was deeply devout.
12. ibid, 311.
13. OH 1917, ii, 418.
14. Macdonald, 30.
15. OH 1917, ii, 47.
16. Terraine, *Douglas Haig*, 315-7.
17. Haig Diary, 22 May 17.
18. ibid, 24 May 17.
19. Pedersen, 164-5.
20. ibid, 163, quoting Monash Papers, National Library of Australia.
21. Cutlack, 78-9.
22. Lloyd George, VI, 3382.
23. Haig Diary, 6 June, 17,
24. ibid, 7 June, 17.
25. Charteris, *At GHQ*, 228.
26. Edmonds Papers, II/I/63a. Harington to Edmonds, 21 November, 34.
27. Lloyd George, ii, 1689.
28. OH 1917, ii 75-7.

29. ibid, 71.
30. ibid, 72-5.
31. Bean, iv, 609-11.
32. ibid, 624.
33. Guinness, 158.
34. OH 1917, ii, 81.
35. ibid, 93.
36. ibid, 85.
37. ibid, 82; Bean, iv, 638-40.
38. OH 1917, ii, 85; Bean, iv, 644.
39. Haig Diary, 7 June 17.
40. Gladden, 72.
41. OH 1917, ii, 87-8.
42. Bean, iv, 679, quoting *Schlacten des Weltkrieges*, xxvii, Flanderen 2, 1917, and General von Kuhl, *Der Weltkrieg 1914-18*, ii, 1924, 114.
43. Terraine, *Douglas Haig*, 318.
44. Harington, 97-8.
45. Liddell Hart, *History of the World War*, 417.
46. Robertson, *From Private to Field Marshal*, 311.
47. Bean, iv, 679.
48. Gibbs, 48.
49. Either Lady Plumer, or his eldest daughter, the Hon. Eleanor Plumer, kept scrapbooks of newspaper cuttings of Plumer's military successes and his death and funeral. Unfortunately few of them bear a note of their newspaper of origin or their date.
50. Lloyd George, iv, 2111.
51. OH 1917, ii, 88.
52. Haig Diary, 8 June 17.
53. OH 1917, ii, 89-90.
54. ibid, 51.
55. ibid, 90-5.

Chapter 9, Third Ypres, (pp 197-230)

1. Repington, *First World War*, ii, 58.
2. Haig Diary, 2 June, 17.
3. ibid, 9 June, 17.
4. ibid, 2 Jun, 17; 13 and 14 Sept, 17.
5. OH 1917, ii, 96; Lloyd George, iv, 2149-2204.
6. op. cit.
7. Terraine, *Road to Passchendaele*, 185-8, quoting Haig to Army Commanders, OAD 538.
8. OH 1917. ii, 115.
9. Bean, iv, 716.
10. OH 1917, ii, 116.
11. Binding, 173.
12. Terraine, *Douglas Haig*, 337.
13. OH 1917, ii, 131.

14. Repington, *First World War*, i, 605.
15. OH, 1917, ii, 127.
16. Haig Diary, 14 December, 17.
17. Guinness, 162.
18. Gough, 193.
19. OH 1917, ii, 127-8.
20. ibid, Appx. XV.
21. op. cit.
22. OH, 1917. ii, 129.
23. Bean, iv, 697.
24. Gough, 198.
25. Haig Diary, 28, 29, 30 June, 17.
26. Ian F.W. Beckett, *The Army and the Curragh Incident*, Bodley Head, 1986, 372.
27. Carrington, 189.
28. OH 1917, ii, 136.
29. Haig Diary, 21 July, 17.
30. Guinness, 162.
31. Terraine, *Road to Passchendaele*, 213, quoting reminiscences of Col. R. Macleod.
32. Bean, iv, 720.
33. OH 1917, ii, 177.
34. Blunden, 135.
35. Haig Diary, 17 August, 17.
36. Gough, 205.
37. ibid, 206-7.
38. Charteris, *At GHQ*, 248.
39. Haig Diary, 24 and 25 August, 1917.
40. Liddell Hart, *Memoirs*, i, 366.
41. OH 1917, ii, 207.
42. ibid, Appx. XX.
43. ibid, 244.
44. Bean, iv, 679.
45. ibid, 748.
46. OH 1917, ii, 209.
47. ibid, 209.
48. Lloyd George, iv, 2292.
49. OH 1917, ii, 234.
50. Ludendorff, ii, 479.
51. Haig Diary, 17 September, 17.
52. ibid, 18 September, 17.
53. ibid.
54. Gladden, 114.
55. Binding, 172.
56. Gladden, 120.
57. ibid, 125-7.
58. Blunden, 229.
59. OH 1917, ii, 250-1; Bean, iv, 754; Haig Diary 21 September, 17.

60. RA GV Q2521/X/77. Birdwood to Wigram, 24 September, 17.
61. Repington, *First World War*, i, 99.
62. OH 1917, ii, 251.
63. ibid, 250.
64. Gladden, 134 and 139.
65. Colonel H.C. Wylly, *The Green Howards in the Great War*, Privately printed, 306.
66. Ludendorff, ii, 488.
67. OH 1917, ii, 249. 278-9.
68. Blunden, 234.
69. Carrington, 198.
70. OH 1917, ii, 292-3.
71. Harington, 125.
72. OH 1917, ii, 315-6.
73. Bean, iv, 877.
74. Ludendorff, ii, 490.
75. Lloyd George, ii, 1319.
76. Carington, 191.
77. Haig's proposed use of cavalry afterwards produced much mockery. His critics forgot that with tanks confined to the pace of the infantry, there was nothing else available for rapid movement. Unlike the German and French cavalry, the British were trained as mounted infantry.
78. OH 1917, ii, 296-7; Gough 212-3.
79. op. cit.
80. OH 1917, ii, 316-7.
81. Haig Diary, 4 October, 17.
82. OH 1917, ii, 328.
83. Harington, 110.
84. OH 1917, ii, 325.
85. Haig Diary, 3 October, 17.
86. ibid, 9 October, 17.
87. Bean, iv, 885.
88. ibid, 884.
89. OH 1917, ii, 327.
90. ibid, 330-1.
91. ibid, 338.
92. Bean, iv, 912.
93. Pedersen, 204.
94. Cutlack, 202.
95. Haig Diary, 12 October, 17.
96. ibid, 13 October 17; OH 1917, ii, 345.
97. Haig Diary, 5 October, 17.
98. OH 1917, ii, 320.
99. ibid, 351.
100. Lloyd George, iv, 2110.
101. OH 1917, ii, 366.
102. ibid, 361.

103. For the best analysis of the subject, see Terraine, *Road to Passchendaele*. 343-7.
104. Terraine, *Smoke and Fire*, 46.
105. Terraine, *Road to Passchendaele*, 129-30, quoting CAB 27/6.
106. L.F. Ellis, *Victory in the West*, i, Normandy, HMSO, 1961, 307.
107. OH 1917, ii, 209.
108. Gibbs, 398.
109. OH, 1917, ii, 362.
110. Lloyd George, iv, 2215.
111. ibid, 2120.
112. ibid, 2215.
113. Harington, 111; OH 1917, ii, 296-7; Gough 212-3.
114. Liddell Hart Papers, II/163a Harington to Edmonds. 21 November, 34.
115. ibid.

Chapter 10, Italy: The Reluctant Commander-in-Chief
(pp 231-253)

1. OH, Italy, 36.
2. Trevelyan, 167.
3. OH, Italy, 90.
4. ibid, 58-60.
5. ibid, 93.
6. Haig Diary, 7 November, 17.
7. Charteris, *At GHQ*, 266.
8. Harington, 134.
9. ibid.
10. ibid.
11. Haig Diary, 9 November, 17.
12. Harington, 133.
13. Harington, 135.
14. Lloyd George, v, 2332.
15. OH, Italy, 94 and Appx X.
16. Villari, 170.
17. *Tim Harington*, 66.
18. OH, Italy, 95.
19. Harington, 137-8.
20. OH, Italy, 96.
21. ibid, 95-6.
22. Robertson Papers, I/34/37/3.
23. OH, Italy, 109; Harington, 137.
24. Robertson Papers, I/34/37/2.
25. ibid, 1/34/38.
26. ibid, I/34/40.
27. Harington, 111.
28. Robertson Papers, I/34/36.
29. OH, Italy, 107, Villari, 100.

30. OH, Italy, 107.
31. ibid, 111-2; Falls, 91.
32. OH, Italy, 135-6.
33. Robertson Papers I/34/43.
34. ibid, I/34/46.
35. Trevelyan, 296.
36. Robertson Papers I/34/39.
37. OH, Italy, 16; Harington, 140.
38. OH, Italy; 99.
39. ibid, 100.
40. Repington, *First World War*, ii, 99.
41. OH, Italy, 163.
42. ibid, 132-3; Falls, 140.
43. Repington, *First World War*, ii, 99.
44. Lloyd George, v, 2790.
45. ibid.
46. Charteris, *At GHQ*, 273.
47. Calwell, i, 283.
48. Lloyd George, iv, 2266.
49. Roskill, i, 297.
50. Haig Diary 11 October, 17. Robertson to Haig, 9 October, 17.
51. ibid, 19 February 18.
52. Lloyd George, v, 2820-1.
53. Haig Diary, 9 February, 18.
54. Haig Diary, Robertson to Haig, 15 February, 18.
55. Calwell, ii,58.
56. Amery, *My Political Life*, ii, 145.
57. RA GV F1259/4.
58. OH, 1918, i, 88.
59. RA GV F1259/26.
60. *Tim Harington*, 67.
61. Roskill, i, 493.
62. *Tim Harington*, 68.
63. Roskill, i, 496.
64. Edmonds Papers, VI/9, Robertson to Edmonds, 31 August, 45.
65. OH, Italy, 152.
66. Harington, 144-5.
67. OH, Italy, 155.

Chapter 11, Victory (pp 254-283)

1. Haig Diary, 7 November, 17.
2. ibid. 5 March, 18.
3. Harington, 147.
4. RA GV Q2521/II/81.
5. Haig Diary, 18 March, 18.
6. OH 1918, i, 47; ii, 472.
7. OH 1918, i, 1223.

8. ibid, ii, 476.
9. ibid, i, 393.
10. Haig Diary, 23 March, 18.
11. Bean, v, 251.
12. Charteris, *At GHQ*, 294.
13. Harington, 148.
14. Haig Diary, 24 March, 18.
15. OH 1918, i, 539-40.
16. Binding, 208.
17. ibid, 209-10.
18. OH 1918, ii, 488-90.
19. ibid, 149-53.
20. Bean, v, 419.
21. OH 1918, ii, 146 and 150.
22. ibid, 160.
23. Haig Diary, 19 September, 17.
24. OH 1918, ii, 187.
25. ibid, 215.
26. ibid, 512.
27. Godley, 236.
28. Bean, v, 437.
29. ibid, vi, 440.
30. OH 1918, i, 44 and 100.
31. ibid, ii, 299-300.
32. Harington, 161.
33. ibid, 162.
34. OH 1918, ii, 354-6.
35. Calwell, ii, 92.
36. ibid.
37. OH 1918, ii, 328.
38. ibid, 437; Haig Diary 17 April, 18.
39. OH 1918, ii, 33-6.
40. ibid.
41. ibid, 353-4.
42. ibid, 416.
43. Wilson Papers, Haig to Secretary of State, 1 May, 18.
44. OH 1918, 484.
45. ibid, 454.
46. RA GV Q2521/V, 155.
47. RA GV Q832/19. Letter of 27 April, 18.
48. ibid.
49. OH 1918, ii, 427.
50. Repington, *First World War*, ii, 297.
51. ibid, 341.
52. Blake, 301, quoting letter Haig to Derby.
53. Calwell, ii, 100.
54. ed A.J.P. Taylor, Lloyd George: *A Diary by Frances Stevenson*, 307.

55. Lloyd George, vi, 3380.
56. OH 1918, ii, 470.
57. ibid, 455.
58. Haig Diary, 3 June, 18.
59. ibid, 20 July, 17.
60. Terraine, *To Win a War*, 104.
61. OH 1918, iv, 88.
62. ibid, 427-9.
63. ibid, 434.
64. Maj-Gen John F. O'Ryan, *The Story of the 27th Division*, NY, 1920, 196.
65. Plumer Papers. Extract from *Ypres Times* quoted by the Rev. 'Tubby' Clayton in an unnamed Toc H publication.
66. Haig Diary, 29 August, 18; OH 1918, iv, 383.
67. OH 1918, iv, 508.
68. Esher, iv, 120.
69. Haig Diary, 29 August, 18.
70. Roskill, i, 495 and 497.
71. Haig Diary, 6 September, 18.
72. *Army Quarterly*, xxxvii, January, 39, 204.
73. OH 1918, iv, 463.
74. ibid, v, 58.
75. ibid, 73.
76. ibid, 75-6.
77. ibid, 83-4.
78. ibid, 89.
79. Marshal of the Royal Air Force Sir John Slessor, *The Great Deterrent*, Constable, 1957, 51-2.
80. Haig Diary, 12 October, 18.
81. OH, 1918, v, 281.
82. ibid, 287.
83. Haig Diary, 15 and 16 October, 18.
84. OH 1918, v, 561-2.
85. Haig Diary, 24 November, 18.
86. OH 1918, v, 445.
87. Haig Diary, 11 November, 18.
88. Terraine, *Smoke and Fire*, 171.
89. Wavell, 13.
90. ibid, 14.
91. ibid, 21-2.
92. OH 1917, ii, 131.
93. Wavell, 15.
94. ibid, 21.
95. ibid, 25.
96. Harington, 166.
97. Field-Marshal Viscount Montgomery, *Memoirs*, Collins, 1958, 35.
98. ibid, 36.
99. OH 1918, ii, 358.

100. *Daily Telegraph*, 18 July, 32.

Chapter 12, The Rhineland and Malta (pp 284-297)

1. Harington, 186.
2. OH, Occupation of the Rhineland, 126-32.
3. Haig Diary, 19 February, 19.
4. RA GV Q2522/2, Rawlinson to Wigram, 17 February, 19.
5. OH, Occupation of the Rhineland, 128-9.
6. *Morning Post*, 11 March, 19.
7. Weizmann, *Trial and Error*, 208.
8. OH, Occupation of the Rhineland, 128.
9. Hamilton Papers, 29/13/328.
10. See Note 4.
11. OH, Occupation of the Rhineland, 139.
12. Harington, 193.
13. Haig Diary, 23 February, 19.
14. Neither members of the family nor the College of Heralds have been able to throw any light on the matter.
15. W.V. Crapp, *Some Historical Notes on the Parish and Parish Church of St. Helen's, Bilton-in-Ainsty*, 1973, 6.
16. Interview, M. Albert Ghekiere.
17. RA GV L1455/8 Stamfordham to Methuen, 24 March, 19.
18. Plumer Papers, Undated letter Methuen to Plumer.
19. Frendo, 151; 171-2; Harington, 206-7; Laferla, 221-5; Samut-Tagliofero, 374-5.
20. Amery, *My Political Life*, ii, 193.
21. Harington, 211.
22. ibid, 268.
23. ibid, 271; Amery, *My Political Life*, ii, 195.
24. Frendo, xi.
25. Frendo, x-xi, 172-3; Harington, 208-217; 268-72; Laverla, Ch.13.
26. Among the few surviving Plumer papers are letters from the Private Secretary to Queen Alexandra thanking the Plumers for a present of oranges, and one from the Princess Mary thanking Lady Plumer for a wedding present.
27. Plumer Papers, Stamfordham to Plumer, 17 November, 21.
28. Amery, *My Political Life*, ii, 191.
29. Interview. Late Brigadier Rathbone.
30. Family information.
31. Wilson Papers, Plumer to Wilson, 31 March, 21.
32. ibid, Wilson to Rawlinson, 21 July, 21.
33. ibid, Wilson to Churchill, 4 April, 20.
34. Record of Service, National Archives of Canada.
35. Family information.
36. RA GV 02377/4, Harington to Wigram, 5 May, 33.
37. Family information.

38. See Note 33.
39. Harington, 221-2.
40. Interview. Late Brigadier Rathbone.
41. Wilson Papers. Wilson to Plumer, 7 January, 22 and 14 February, 22. When writing to Wilson, Plumer addressed him as 'Dear Henry' or 'Dear Harry'. In none of his other surviving letters to contemporaries does he use a christian name.
42. ibid, Plumer to Wilson, 2 March, 20.
43. ibid, Wilson to Plumer, 26 July, 20.
44. ibid, Plumer to Wilson, 7 August, 20.
45. RA GV Ll904/8, 9 and 15.
46. Samut-Tagliofero, 390.
47. Laferla, 233-4.
48. Amery, *Diaries*, 409.
49. Harington, 273.
50. Plumer Papers, Colonial Office to Plumer, 17 April, 25 and attached note.

Chapter 13, Palestine (pp 298-317)

1. Harington, 274.
2. Amery, *Diaries*, i, 408.
3. C. Sykes, 16.
4. ibid, 18.
5. Samuel, 161.
6. ibid, 150-1.
7. C. Sykes, 105; Dash, 188-9; Aron, 1.
8. C. Sykes, 105.
9. Weizmann, *Letters and Papers*, xii, 378.
10. ibid, 368.
11. Weizmann, *Trial and Error*, 451.
12. Weizmann, *Letters and Papers*, xii, 378.
13. Kisch. 182.
14. Symes, 51.
15. Weizmann, *Letters and Papers*, xii, 385.
16. Monckton Papers, III, Letter of 5 July, 25.
17. ibid, DS. 154: 52.
18. Family information.
19. Eleanor Plumer is described in Butler, R.F. and Others, *St. Anne's College, Oxford*, Privately Printed, 1957, and Reeves, Marjorie, *St. Anne's College, Oxford: An Informal History*, Privately Printed, 1970.
20. Harington, 279; Kisch, 198.
21. Harington, 261; Sykes, 106; Bowle, 199.
22. Horne, 100-7.
23. Samuel, 105.
24. Harington, 261; Bowle, 43.
25. Bentwich, N. and H. 106.

26. Family information.
27. Obituary in *Biblelands*, the Quarterly Journal of the Anglican Bishopric in Jerusalem, July, 41.
28. Orpen, Sir William, *An Onlooker in France*, Williams and Norgate, 1921, 93-4.
29. Storrs, 11.
30. Kisch, 212.
31. Storrs, 437.
32. Harington, 279-80.
33. CO 733/116, Plumer to Amery, 24 August, 26.
34. ibid.
35. Bentwich, N. and H. 106.
36. Lunt, 66.
37. Abdullah, 227.
38. Symes, 57.
39. ibid, 56.
40. Weizmann, *Letters and Papers*, xii, 18.
41. Monroe, 79-80.
42. Esco Foundation, 294.
43. Harington, 250-2; Horne, 76, 102-3; Bentwich, N. and H. 109, 120.
44. Kisch, 205.
45. C. Sykes, 107-8, quoting a communication from Eleanor Plumer.
46. Esco Foundation, 293.
47. Harington 263; Bentwich, N. and H., 117-8; Kisch, 217, 223, 225.
48. C. Sykes, 316.
49. Harington, 241.
50. Abu-Lughod, 286 (essay by Richard N. Verdery).
51. Bentwich, N. and H., 108.
52. ibid, 110.
53. C. Sykes, 109, quoting Eleanor Plumer.
54. Bentwich, N. and H., 108.
55. ibid, 107; Dash, 200-1.
56. Aron; correspondence between Aron and author.
57. Bentwich, N. and H., 118.
58. Symes, 51, 59.
59. Harington, 256.
60. ibid, 256-7, 282.
61. Horne, 113-4, 347.
62. Harington, 257, 282.
63. Bentwich, N. and H., 117.
64. Harington, 267.
65. C. Sykes, 124.
66. Esco Foundation, 294.
67. C. Sykes, 125.
68. Meinertzhagen, diary entry 4 July, 49.
69. *Spectator*, 3 April, 53.

Chapter 14, The Last Years (pp 318-322)

1. RA GV N2559/4. Wigram to Harington, 18 August, 28; Harington, 284.
2. Hansard, Vol. 77, 36-9.
3. ibid, 131-5.
4. ibid, Vol. 80. 1301-2.
5. Harington, 286.
6. ibid, 327-8.
7. Kisch, 379.
8. Family information.
9. Will of the First Viscount Plumer, Somerset House.
10. RA GV 02377/4, Harington to Wigram, 5 May, 33.
11. RA GV 02377/1, Public Trustee to Wigram, 3 May, 33.
12. RA GV 02377/2, Wigram to Harington, 4 May, 33.
13. RA GV 02377/4, Harington to Wigram, 5 May, 33.
14. RA GV 02377/10, Harington to Wigram, 26 June, 33.
15. Harington, 242-3; 337.
16. Plumer Papers, Article by Clayton in an unmarked cutting from a Toc H publication.
17. *The Times*, 18 July, 33.

Bibliography

Manuscript Collections

Arnold-Forster Papers, British Library
Baden-Powell Papers, National Army Museum
Colonial Office Papers, Public Record Office
De Montmorency Papers, Public Record Office
Edmonds Papers, King's College, London
French Papers, Imperial War Museum
Haig Papers, National Library of Scotland
Aylmer Haldane Papers, British Library
J.B. Haldane Papers, National Library of Scotland
Hamilton Papers, King's College, London
Lt. T. McK Hughes Diary, Imperial War Museum
Kitchener Papers, Public Record Office
Marker Papers, British Library
Monckton Papers, Middle East Centre, St. Antony's College, Oxford
Parrington Papers, Imperial War Museum
Plumer Papers, privately held
Roberts Papers, National Army Museum
Robertson Papers, King's College, London
Royal Archives, Windsor Castle
Saunders Papers, Middle East Centre, St. Antony's College, Oxford
Smith-Dorrien Papers, Imperial War Museum
Staff College, Camberley, Records
Wilson Papers, Imperial War Museum
War Office Papers, Public Record Office
War Office Records, Ministry of Defence

Other Official Papers

Army Lists
Hansard
Malta Blue Books

Unpublished Manuscripts

Aron, Wellesley, *The High Commissioner.*
Myers, Winnie, *Canons*, 1956.

Printed Books and Articles:

General

Amery, L.S., *My Political Life*, Vols 1-2: Hutchinson, 1953-5.

Leo Amery Diaries, ed. John Burns and David Nicholson, Vol. 1: Hutchinson, 1980.

Barnett, Correlli, *Britain and her Army, 1509-1970*: Allen Lane, 1970.

Bridges, General Sir Tom, *Alarms and Excursions*: Longmans, Green, 1938.

Broughton, Lieutenant-Colonel E.C., *Memoirs of the 65th Regiment and 1st. Battn. The Yorks and Lancaster Regt. 1756 to 1913*: William Clowes, 1914.

Creighton-Williamson, Donald, *The York and Lancaster Regiment*: Leo Cooper, 1968.

Esher, Viscount, *Journals and Letters, 1915-30*, Vol. 4: Ivor Nicholson and Watson, 1938.

Fisher, Admiral of the Fleet Lord, *Memories*: Hodder & Stoughton, 1919.

Godley, General Sir Alexander, *Life of an Irish Soldier*: Murray, 1939.

Harington, General Sir Charles, *Plumer of Messines*: John Murray, 1935.
        Tim Harington Looks Back: John Murray, 1940.

Jeal, Tim, *Baden-Powell*: Hutchinson, 1989.

Maurice, Major General Sir Frederick, *Life of Viscount Haldane of Cloan*: Faber, 1937.

Repington, Charles à Court, *Vestigia*: Constable, 1919.

Roskill, Stephen, *Hankey: Man of Secrets*, Vol. 1, 1877-1918: Collins, 1970.

The Military Correspondence of Field Marshal Sir Henry Wilson, 1918-1922, ed. Keith Jeffery: Bodley Head for Army Records Society, 1985.

Wylly, Colonel H.C., *The York and Lancaster Regiment 1758-1919, Vol. 1*. Privately printed. 1930.

CHAPTER 1. (Regimental Officer less South Africa)

Colville, Colonel H.E., *History of the Sudan Campaign*, Part I: H.M.S.O. 1889.

Emery, Frank, *Marching over Africa: Letters from Victorian Soldiers*: Hodder and Stoughton, 1986.

Godwin-Austen, Brevet Major A.R., *The Staff and the Staff College*: Constable, 1927.

Graham, Lieutenant General Sir G. *Report on Operations at Tamai*: HMSO, 1885.

Plumer, Captain H.C.O., *The Military Resources of the Island of Jersey*: *R.U.S.I. Journal*, October, 1891.

Royle, Charles, *The Egyptian Campaigns 1882 to 1885*: Hurst & Blackett, 1900.

Warner, Philip, *Dervish: The Rise and Fall of an African Empire*: Macdonald, 1973.

CHAPTERS 1, 2 and 3. (South Africa).

Abbott, J.H.M. *Tommy Cornstalk*: Longmans, Green, 1900.

Amery, L.S. (ed), *Times History of the War in South Africa, 1899-1902*: Vols. 1-5: Sampson, Low & Marston, 1902-7.

Baden-Powell, Colonel R.S.S., *The Matabele Campaign, 1896*: Methuen, 1897.

Belfield, Eversley, *The Boer War*: Leo Cooper, 1974.

Colonial Office. *Instructions issued to Colonel R.E.R. Martin relative to the control of the Armed Forces in the territories of the British South Africa Company. Instructions issued to Maj.-Gen. Sir F. Carrington relative to military operations against the Matabele. (c 8060)*: 1896.

Creswicke, Louis, *South Africa and the Transvaal War*, Vols 3-4: T.C. and E.C. Jack and Blackwood, Edinburgh, no date.

De Montmorency, Harvey, *Sword and Stirrup: Memoirs of an Adventurous Life*: G. Bell & Sons, 1936.

De Wet, Christiaan, *Three Years War*: Constable, 1902.

Doyle, A. Conan, *The Great Boer War, 1899-1901*: Smith Elder, 1903.

J.D. Fage and Roland Oliver (ed), *The Cambridge History of Africa*, Vol 6: 1870-1905: Cambridge University Press, 1985.

Gardner, Brian, *Mafeking: A Victorian Legend*: Cassell, 1966.

Godley, Lieutenant-Colonel R.S., *Khaki and Blue*: Lovat Dickens & Thompson, 1935.

Green, Rev. J., *The Story of the Australian Bushmen*: 1903.

Hall, D.O.W., *The New Zealanders in South Africa, 1899-1902*: War History Branch, Department of Internal Affairs, Wellington, N.2., 1949.

Hensman, Howard, *History of Rhodesia*: Blackwood, Edinburgh, 1900.

Hillcourt, William and Baden-Powell, Lady Olave, *Two Lives of a Hero*: Heinemann, 1964.

Laing, Major D. Tyrie, *The Matabele Rebellion 1896*: Dean & Son, 1897.

McDonald, J.G., *Rhodes: A Life*: Philip Allen, 1927.

Macready, General Sir Nevil, *Annals of an Active Life*, Vol. 1: Hutchinson, 1924.

Maurice, Major General Sir Frederick, *History of the War in South Africa 1899-1902*, Vols. 1-4: Hurst & Blackett, 1906-10.

Nutting, Anthony, *Scramble for Africa*: Constable, 1970.

Pakenham, Elizabeth, *Jameson's Raid*: Weidenfeld & Nicolson, 1960.

Pakenham, Thomas, *The Boer War*, Weidenfeld & Nicolson; 1979.

Plumer, Lieutenant-Colonel Herbert, *An Irregular Corps in Matabeleland*: Kegan Paul, Trench, Trubner & Co., 1897.

Ranger, T.O., *Revolt in Southern Rhodesia*: Heinemann, 1967.

Selous, F.C., *Sunshine and Storm in Rhodesia*: Rowland Ward, 1896.

Smuts, J.C., *Jan Christian Smuts*: Cassell, 1952.

Sykes, Frank W., *With Plumer in Matabeleland*: Books of Rhodesia, Bulawayo, 1972 (facsimile of 1897 edition).

Vindex, Cecil Rhodes: *His Political Life and Speeches, 1881-1900*: Chapman & Hall, 1903.

Walker, Major H.S., *Operations in Southern Rhodesia, 1896*: HMSO, 1897.

CHAPTER 4 (General Officer).

Arnold-Forster, M, *The Right Honourable Hugh Oakeley Arnold-Forster*: Edward Arnold, 1910.

Bond, Brian, *The Victorian Army and the Staff College, 1854-1914*: Eyre Metheun, 1972.

Gooch, John, *The Plans of War: The General Staff and British Military, c 1900-1916*: Routledge and Kegan Paul, 1974.

Report of the Royal Commission on the War in South Africa, Vols 2 and 3: Comd. 1790-1791.

Sommer, Dudley, *Haldane of Cloan: His Life and Times 1856-1928*: George Allen & Unwin, 1950.

Spiers, Edward M., *Haldane: An Army Reformer*: Edinburgh University Press, 1980.

CHAPTERS 5-11 (First World War).

Ballard, Brigadier General C., *Smith-Dorrien*: Constable, 1931.

Bean, C.E.W., *The Australian Imperial Forces in France*, Vols 3-6: Angus & Robertson, Sydney, 1929-42.

Beckett, Ian F.W. and Keith Simpson (ed), *A Nation in Arms*: Manchester University Press, 1985.

Bidwell, Shelford and Graham, Dominick, *Fire Power: British Army Weapons and Theories of War, 1904-45*: Allen & Unwin, 1982.

Binding, Rudolph, *A Fatalist at War*: George Allen & Unwin, 1929.

Birdwood, Field-Marshal Lord, *Khaki and Gown*: Hodder & Stoughton, 1920.

Blake, Robert, *The Private Papers of Douglas Haig, 1914-19*: Eyre & Spottiswoode, 1952.

Blunden, Edmund, *Undertones of War*: Cobden-Sanderson, 1928.

Bonham-Carter, Victor, *Soldier True: The Life of Field-Marshal Sir William Robertson*: Muller, 1963.

Buchan, John, *A History of the Great War*, Vols. 5-6: Nelson, 1921.

Calwell, Major General Sir C.E., *Field-Marshal Sir Henry Wilson*, Vols. 1-2: Cassell, 1927.

Carrington, Charles, *Soldier from the Wars Returning*: Hutchinson, 1965.

Cassar, George H., *The Tragedy of Sir John French*: University of Delaware Press, 1985.

Cavan, Field-Marshal the Earl of, *Some Tactical and Strategic Considerations of the Italian Campaign: Army Quarterly*, October 1920.

Charteris, Brigadier General John, *At G.H.Q.*: Cassell, 1931.

—*Field-Marshal Earl Haig*; Cassel, 1929.

Churchill, Winston, *The World Crisis, 1916-18*: Butterworth, 1927.

Clark, Alan, *The Donkeys*: Hutchinson, 1961.

Coombs, Rose E.B., *Before Endeavours Fade: A Guide to the Battlefields of the First World War*: Battle of Britain Prints, 1983.

Cooper, A. Duff, *Haig*, Vols 1-2: Faber, 1935.

Cutlack, F.M. (ed), *War Letters of General Monash*: Angus & Robertson, Sydney, 1935.

Dalton, Hugh, *With British Guns in Italy*: 1919.

Eden, Anthony, *Another World 1897-1917*: Allen Lane, 1976.

Edmonds, Brigadier General Sir James, and others, *Military Operations France and Belgium*; 1915, Vols. 1-4; 1916, Vol. 1; 1917, Vols 13; 1918, Vols. 1, 2, 4 and 5: Macmillan and HMSO, 1922-47.

Edmonds, Brigadier General Sir James, and Major General H.R. Davies, *Military Operations, Italy, 1915-1919*: HMSO 1949.

Falls, Captain Cyril *Caporetto, 1917*: Weidenfeld & Nicolson, 1966.

Farrar-Hockley, Anthony, *Goughie: The Life of General Sir Hubert Gough*: Hart Davis MacGibbon, 1975.

French, Major the Hon. Gerald, *Some War Diaries: Addresses and Correspondence of Field-Marshal the Earl of Ypres*: Herbert Jenkins, 1937.

French, Dr David, *"Official but not History"? Sir James Edmonds and the Official History of the Great War*: R.U.S.I. Journal, March, 1986.

Gathorne-Hardy, Major General J.F., *A Summary of the Campaign in Italy and an Account of the Battle of Vittorio Veneto: Army Quarterly*, October, 1921.

Gibbs, Philip, *Realities of War*: Heinemann, 1920.

Gladden, E. Norman, *Ypres 1917*: Kimber, 1969.

Gough, General Sir Hubert, *Soldiering On*: Arthur Barker, 1954.

Grieve, W. Grant, and Newman, Bernard, *The Tunnellers*: Herbert Jenkins, 1936.

The Diaries of Walter Guinness (First Lord Moyne) 1914-1918, ed. Bond, Brian, and Robbins, Simon: Leo Cooper, 1987.

Hamilton, Nigel, *Monty: The Making of a General*: Hamish Hamilton, 1981.

Hart, B.H. Liddell, *Foch: The Man of Orleans*: Eyre and Spottiswoode, 1931.

—*A History of the World War, 1914-1918*: Faber, 1930.

—*Memoirs*, Vol. 1: Cassell, 1965.

—*Through the Fog of War*: Faber, 1938.

Haldane, General Sir Aylmer: *A Soldier's Saga*: Blackwood, Edinburgh, 1948.

Holmes, Richard, *The Little Field Marshal: Sir John French*: Cape, 1981.

Ironside, Lord (ed), *High Road to Command: The Diaries of Major-General Sir Edmund Ironside*: Leo Cooper, 1972.

Ludendorff, General, *My War Memories, 1914-1918*, Vols 1-2: Hutchinson, no date.

Lloyd George, David, *War Memoirs*, Vols. 2, 4, 5 and 6: Ivor Nicholson & Watson, 1933-36.

Macdonald, Lyn, *They Called it Passchendaele*: Michael Joseph, 1978.

Maurice, Major-General Sir Frederick, *Life of General Lord Rawlinson of Trent*: Cassell, 1928.

Nicholson, Colonel G.W.L., *Official History of the Canadian Army in the First World War*: Queen's Printers, Ottawa, 1962.

O'Ryan, Major-General John F., *The Story of the 27th Division*, Vol. 1: Wynkoop Hallenbeck, New York, 1920.

Pedersen, P.A., *Monash as a Military Commander*: Melbourne University Press, 1985.

Pulteney, Sir William and Brice-Miller, B., *The Immortal Salient*: Murray, 1925.

Repington, Charles à Court, *The First World War*, Vols 1-2: Constable, 1920.

Robertson, Field-Marshal Sir William, *From Private to Field-Marshal*; Constable, 1921.

—*Soldiers and Statesmen*, Vols 1-2: Constable, 1926.

Sixsmith, Major General E.K.G., *British Generalship in the Twentieth Century*: Arms and Armour Press, 1970.

—*Douglas Haig*: Weidenfeld & Nicolson, 1976.

Smith-Dorrien, General Sir Horace, *Memoirs of Fifty-Eight Years Service*: John Murray, 1925.

Smithers, A.J., *The Man Who Disobeyed: Sir Horace Smith-Dorrien and his Enemies*: Leo Cooper, 1970.

Statistics of the Military Effort of the British Empire, 1914-1920: HMSO 1920.

Stewart, Colonel H., *The New Zealand Division 1916-1919*: Whitcombe & Tombs, 1921.

Terraine, John, *Douglas Haig: The Educated Soldier*: Hutchinson, 1963.

—*The First World War: 1914-1918*: Hutchinson, 1965.

—(ed). *General Jack's Diary, 1914-1918*: Eyre & Spottiswoode, 1964.

—*The Road to Passchendaele*: Leo Cooper, 1977.

—*The Smoke and the Fire*: Sidgwick & Jackson, 1980.

—*The Western Front*: Hutchinson, 1964.

—*To Win a War: 1918, The Year of Victory*: Sidgwick & Jackson, 1978.

Travers, Tim, *The Killing Ground*: Allen & Unwin, 1987.

Trevelyan, G.M., *Scenes from Italy's War*: T.C. & E.C. Jack, 1919.

Villari, L. *The War on the Italian Front*: Cobden & Sanderson, 1932.

Warner, Philip, *Passchendaele*: Sidgwick & Jackson, 1987.

Wavell, Field Marshal Earl, *Soldiers and Soldiering*: Cape, 1953.

CHAPTER 12 (The Rhineland and Malta).

Cambridge History of the British Empire, Vol. 2: Cambridge University Press, 1940.

Edmonds, Brigadier General Sir James, *The Occupation of the Rhineland, 1918-1929*: HMSO, 1944.

Frendo, Henry, *Party Politics in Fortress Malta*: Midsea Books, Malta, 1979.

Laferla, Captain A.V., *British Malta, 1800-1921*, Vol. 2: Aquilina, Malta, 1947.

Samut-Tagliofero, Brigadier A., *History of the Royal Malta Artillery*, Vol. 1: Lux Press, Malta, 1976.

CHAPTER 13 (Palestine)

King Abdullah of Jordan, *Memoirs,* ed. Philip P. Graves): Cape, 1950.

Abu-Lughod, Ibrahim (ed), *The Transformation of Palestine*: Northwestern University Press, Evanston, USA, 1971.

Bentwich, Norman, *Palestine*: Ernest Benn, 1934.

Bentwich, Norman and Helen, *Mandate Memories, 1918-1948*: Hogarth Press, 1965.

Bowle, John, *Viscount Samuel*: Gollancz, 1957.

Dash, Joan, *Summoned to Jerusalem: The Life of Henrietta Szold*: Harper & Row, New York, 1979.

Duff, Douglas V., *May the Winds Blow*: Hollis & Carter, 1948.

Esco Foundation (published for), *A Study of Jewish, Arab and British Politicians*: Yale University Press, USA, 1947.

Horne, Edward, *A Job Well Done: A History of the Palestine Police Force, 1920-1948*: Privately printed, 1982.

Kisch, Lieutenant-Colonel F.H., *Palestine Diary*: Gollancz, 1938.

Lunt, James, *Glubb Pasha*: Harvill Press, 1984.

Meinertzhagen, Colonel R., *Middle East Diary, 1917-1956*: Cresset Press, 1959.

Monroe, Elizabeth, *Britain's Moments in the Middle East, 1914-1956*: Chatto & Windus, 1963.

Samuel, Viscount, *Memoirs*: Cresset Press, 1945.

Storrs, Ronald, *Orientations*: Nicholson & Watson, 1963.

Sykes, Christopher, *Cross Roads to Israel*: Collins, 1965.

Symes, Sir Stewart, *Tour of Duty*: Collins, 1946.

Weizmann, Chaim, *Trial and Error*: Hamish Hamilton, 1949.

Weizmann, Chaim, A Biography by Several Hands, ed. Meyer W. Weisgal and Joel Carmichael: Weidenfeld & Nicolson, 1963.

The Letters and Papers of Chaim Weizmann, Vol. 12, ed. Basnet Litvinoff; Vol. 13, ed. Pinhas Ofer: Transaction Books, Jerusalem, 1977-78.

Newspapers and Journals

The Army Quarterly
Daily Malta Chronicle
The Daily Telegraph
Eton College Chronicle
The Illustrated London News
The Morning Post
The Journal of the Royal United Services Institute for Defence Studies
The Sheffield Daily Telegraph
The Spectator
The Tiger and the Rose (The Journal of the York & Lancaster Regiment)
The Times
Vanity Fair

INDEX

Abdullah, Emir (King of Jordan), 307, 309

Aborigines Protection Society, 32

Albert, King of the Belgians, 267, 272, 284; commands Group of Armies of the North 273, 276, 277

Aldershot, 53, 55, 88, 90, 97

Allenby, FIeld-Marshal Lord, 125, 133, 134, 248, 299, 321

Amery, Leo, 297, 307; opinion of Plumer, 95, 291; visits Malta, 291-2; persuades Plumer to go to Palestine, 298

Anthoine. General, 201

Aosta, Duke of, 234

Arab Legion, 308-9

Arabi Pasha, 16

Army Council, 90-2

Arnold-Forster, H.O., 70, 92; plans for Army, 93-4; admiration for Plumer, 94-7

Aron, Major Wellesley (Pinchas), 313

Arras, Battle of, 160, 163, 170, 175, 215, 227

Ashbee, C.R., 305

Asquith, Herbert (Earl of Oxford and Asquith), 101, 141, 145, 161, 248

Athlone, Major-General the Earl of, 267

Aubers Ridge, Battle of, 125, 131

Australian Military Forces, 72, 73, 77-84, 136, 147, 149, 152, 212, 259, 263

  1 ANZAC Corps, 151, 211, 212, 214ff,

  2 ANZAC Corps, 151, 160, 179ff, 191, 192, 208, 211-2, 219ff, 228.

1 Australian Div, 151, 211, 214, 219, 262-3

2 Australian Div, 151, 211, 214, 216, 219

3 Australian Div, 157, 179, 182, 212, 229, 220, 224, 225

4 Australian Div, 151, 179, 189, 190-1, 211, 218-9

5 Australian Div, 151, 211, 218-9

3 Queensland Mounted Infantry, 68

Queen's Imperial Bushmen, 76

1st, 2nd and 3rd Australian Bushmen, 76

Back, Sergeant, 1

Baden-Powell, Lieutenant-General Lord, 13, 27, 54, 321; in Matabeleland, 39ff; his character, 42; writes *Matabele Campaign*, 42; compliments Plumer, 45-9; in Rhodesia 1899, 57-9; Siege of Mafeking, 59-70; relinquishes command, 72; and Boy Scouts, 98-99

Badoglio, Marshal, 237

Baker Pasha, Colonel Valentine, 16,18

Baldwin, Stanley (Earl Baldwin), 296, 298

Balfour, Arthur (Earl of), 92, 249

Balfour Declaration, 298-9, 317

Baring, Maurice, 159

Barthélemy, Father M, 52

Bean, Dr, 168, 205, 208, 256

Beatty, Admiral of the Fleet Earl, 288.

PEN & SWORD MILITARY CLASSICS

We hope you have enjoyed your Pen and Sword Military Classic. The series is designed to give readers quality military history at affordable prices. Pen and Sword Classics are available from all good bookshops. If you would like to keep in touch with further developments in the series, including information on the **Classics Club**, then please contact Pen and Sword at the address below.

Published Classics Titles

PEN AND SWORD BOOKS LTD

47 Church Street • Barnsley • South Yorkshire • S70 2AS

Tel: 01226 734555 • 734222

E-mail: enquiries@pen-and-sword.co.uk • **Website:** www.pen-and-sword.co.uk